Frederick Perry Noble

The Redemption of Africa

A Story of Civilization, with Maps, Statistical Tables and Select Bibliography

Frederick Perry Noble

The Redemption of Africa
A Story of Civilization, with Maps, Statistical Tables and Select Bibliography

ISBN/EAN: 9783744760492

Printed in Europe, USA, Canada, Australia, Japan

Cover: Foto ©ninafisch / pixelio.de

More available books at **www.hansebooks.com**

THE
REDEMPTION OF AFRICA

A STORY OF CIVILIZATION

WITH MAPS, STATISTICAL TABLES AND SELECT BIBLIOGRAPHY OF
THE LITERATURE OF AFRICAN MISSIONS

BY

FREDERIC PERRY NOBLE

SECRETARY OF THE CHICAGO CONGRESS ON AFRICA, COLUMBIAN
EXPOSITION, 1893

The lesson of the missionary is the enchanter's wand. — DARWIN.
The religious idea at the bottom of our civilization is the missionary idea. — W. T. HARRIS.
The first duty of a historian is never to venture a false statement; next, never to shrink from telling truth; so that his writings may be free from all suspicions of favor or malice. — LEO XIII.

VOLUME TWO

CHICAGO   NEW YORK   TORONTO
FLEMING H. REVELL COMPANY
MDCCCXCIX

CONTENTS

VOLUME TWO: BOOK III

THE EXPANSION OF MISSIONS

CHAPTER		PAGE
14	AFRICA IN AMERICA	477
15	UNDENOMINATIONAL AFRICAN MISSIONS	513
16	THE NEW MISSIONARY	551
17	OLD FRIENDS AND MODERN METHODS	579
18	FOUNDING A MISSION	625
19	REPRESENTATIVE MEN	646
20	LOOKING BACKWARD — AND FORWARD	683

APPENDIXES

STATISTICAL SURVEY OF MISSIONS IN AFRICA, THE ANTILLES AND MADAGASCAR - - - - - - 767
   EDUCATIONAL STATISTICS, PP. 769–777.— LITERARY STATISTICS, PP. 778–787.— MEDICAL STATISTICS, PP. 788–790. — PHILANTHROPIC STATISTICS, PP. 791–793.—CULTURAL STATISTICS, PP. 794–796.

DIRECTORY OF AGENCIES FOR THE CHRISTIANIZATION OF AFRICAN PEOPLES - - - - - - 798
   CLASS A: ALPHABETIC LIST OF SOCIETIES, PP. 799–811. — CLASS B: CLASSIFIED CATALOG OF CHURCH=BODIES, PP. 812–813. — NUMERICAL RECAPITULATIONS, PP. 814–816. — TENTATIVE ESTIMATES, P. 817.

BIBLIOGRAPHY: PRINCIPAL AUTHORITIES - - 821

INDEXES

INDEX OF PERSONS	835
INDEX OF PLACES	840
INDEX OF PRINCIPAL SOCIETIES	843
INDEX OF SUBJECTS	845

ILLUSTRATIONS

	FACING PAGE
JOSEPH E. ROY, D.D.	491
THE REVEREND ANDREW MURRAY	534
ROBERT W. FELKIN, M.D.	554
LOVEDALE INSTITUTION: CLASSES IN AGRICULTURE AND PRINTING	568
LOVEDALE INSTITUTION: CLASSES IN CARPENTRY AND WAGON=MAKING	570
JAMES STEWART, D.D., M.D.	576
MISS MARY LOUISA WHATELY	594
SPECIMEN PAGES OF A CARAVAN=DIARY	634
ALEXANDER M. MACKAY	642
ROBERT MOFFAT, D.D.	654
CARDINAL LAVIGERIE	674
DAVID LIVINGSTONE, D.C.L., F.R.G.S., LL.D., M.D.	698
LOOKING BACKWARD — AND FORWARD } TWO NATIVE CHRISTIANS	752

BOOK III

THE EXPANSION OF AFRICAN MISSIONS: EMANCIPATION AND
INDUSTRY

FROM WILLIAM WILBERFORCE TO STEWART OF LOVEDALE

1833 = 1898

CHAPTER 14

1502 = 1898

AFRICA IN AMERICA: MISSIONS TO BLACK AMERICANS

Tell them we are rising!
                                    Wright to Howard

O black boy of Atlanta, but half was spoken!
The slave's chains and his master's alike are broken.
The one curse of the races held both in tether.
They are rising, all rising, the black and white together.
                                    Whittier

RESPONSIBILITY FOR THE BLACK AMERICAN. AFRICAN MISSIONS IN AMERICA. (I) ANGLICAN AND EPISCOPAL MISSIONS. ANGLICAN MISSIONS. EPISCOPAL MISSIONS. REFORMED=EPISCOPALIAN MISSIONS. (II) BAPTIST MISSIONS. THE BAPTIST AND THE BLACK. REGULAR BAPTISTS (WHITE) OF THE SOUTH. REGULAR BAPTISTS (BLACK) OF THE SOUTH. REGULAR BAPTISTS (WHITE) OF THE NORTH. (III) CONGREGATIONAL MISSIONS. WORK BEFORE 1861. ORIGINS OF THE AMERICAN MISSIONARY ASSOCIATION. THE ASSOCIATION: ITS ACHIEVEMENT. AUXILIARIES. (IV) FRIENDS' MISSIONS. "QUAKER" ABOLITIONISM. FRIENDS AND FREEDMEN. (V) METHODIST MISSIONS. NEGRO METHODISM. SOUTHERN WHITE METHODISM. NORTHERN WHITE METHODISM. (VI) PRESBYTERIAN MISSIONS. PRESBYTERIANISM AND THE SLAVE. NORTHERN PRESBYTERIANS AND THE FREEDMAN. (VII) ROMAN MISSIONS. CATHOLICISM AND THE AMERICAN NEGRO. A SLAVE OF SLAVES. ROME IN LATIN AMERICA. ROME IN THE SOUTH OF THE UNITED STATES. REPRESENTATIVE ROMANISM? ROME AND THE FREEDMAN. (VIII) RESULTS OF FREEDMEN'S MISSIONS. REVELATIONS FROM THE NATIONAL CENSUS OF 1890. NEGRO DENOMINATIONS. NEGROES IN OTHER CHURCHES. TWO LARGE FACTS. THE AFRICAN INFLUENCE OF MISSIONS AMONG FREEDMEN.

The Negro problem came to America in the wake of Columbus. Papal and Protestant Christianity, men of

Roman descent and their brothers of Teutonic blood, are alike accountable. The commencement of the career of the two Americas was all but coeval with the beginning of the slave-trade from Africa to America. The wealth of the Latin and Teutonic continents, of the south and the north in the United States was mainly created by the blood and sweat of the black bondman. The persistence of Britain in thrusting the slave-trade upon the colonies, despite their persevering attempts to end it, and the fear that the Anglican state-church would be established were among the causes of American independence. The American nation, even before declaring all men equal, barred out the slave-traffic and branded it as piracy. This was the first time such a stigma had ever been set on the crime against humanity; and Hopkins the Congregational clergyman was the first to suggest that Negroes be emancipated and transferred to Africa (1776). But until 1863 the Almighty was less potent with the federal congress than was the almighty dollar. Only when God said from out the whirlwind, thunder and smoke of war: Let this people forth from the house of bondage, — was the Negro loosed from the hand of the slave-holder.

Americans are often reproached by Europeans for the lateness of American abolition and for lack of interest and success in African missions; yet history can not tolerate these assertions. Facts refute assumptions and outweigh hypotheses. Emancipation occurred in the remaining British colonies, in Portuguese and in Spanish America after slavery had existed there for centuries; but the United States required only eighty years of independence to rid themselves of the inheritance of iniquity bequeathed by Europe. Again, missions among American Negroes are as ancient as those of modern Europe, are prosecuted with equal energy, and present results that pale the splendor of all other mission=fields. American Negroes constitute the greatest numerical success of missions since 1520, for in the Antilles, Latin America and the United States ten millions of them have been won for Christianity. Many are but nominal Christians; yet as Satan and sin are agents of God, so slavery was made an instrument in bringing ten times as many Africans into the church as societies working in Africa have gained. Missions among American Negroes are as really African missions as if they operated in the pagan continent, for the importation of African bondmen was the transplantation of Negro heathenism. The Americas, especially the United States whose black population of over eight millions comprises more than half of all American Negroes, have personal interests in Africa that Europe can not know. Africa is not at the gates but within. The African without Christ would have proved a Hannibal for the new civilizations. Under Christianity, however, he has already contributed more toward the evangelization of the Negro in Africa and America than the world dreams of, and may ultimately become the leader in this spiritual conquest. Mission=work among black Americans was an inseparable and integral portion of African missions before the arrival of the Jesuit or the "Moravian", and has its peculiar and specific function in the preparation of Africa for Christianity. In America as in Africa the Anglican, Baptist, Congregational, Friends, Methodist, "Moravian", Presbyterian and Roman communions have wrought for the Negro. In fact, this branch of their African work began so soon after the arrival of each church in America that consideration of it should be put in the forefront of the religious partition of Africa, were it not that after 1860 work among the freedmen of the United States accompanied an enormous expansion of African missions.

"Moravian" efforts for the slaves have already been handled in the discussion of the Unity of Brethren*. Lutherans report none such. Episcopal endeavors form the sequel to those of the Anglican. Hence the omission of the first two churches from this sketch, and the union of American and British Episcopacy†.

I

Anglican and Episcopal Missions

In 1520 a Spanish slaver visited South Carolina; in 1526 another Spaniard brought Negro slaves into Virginia; and forty years later Florida received the bane of two races. In 1619 a Dutch slave-trader imported a cargo of Negroes into the Old Dominion, selling them at reluctant Jamestown. Next year the Pilgrims landed at Plymouth, and an irrepressible conflict of ideas began. It was not until about 1670 that Negro slavery gained firm footing in our social system. Though black freedmen and white advocates of abolition were never unknown in the south; though Negro slaves and Saxon defenders of slavery existed in the north; the south was chained to slavery, the north allied with freedom. From 1620 to 1865 the principles of two opposing civilizations wrestled for the possession of a virgin continent. In this contest the Anglican or Episcopal church, according to the testimony of its adherents, studiously avoided the

---

*In Florida a planter once supported a "Moravian" missionary detailed for labor among his slaves.

†Commissioner Harris' *Report* for 1893 and the Slater *Occasional Papers*, reached the present writer after composition was completed. The *Report*, v. 2. chap. 4, pp. 1551-73 contains the best statement as to the education of the Negro This and the monographs of Messrs Curry, Gannet and Weeks constitute an ideal apparatus for the specialist.

question of slavery and all religious problems with political bearings. No historic church has done so little for the black American.

English bishops, indeed, in charge of Anglican missions, showed warm interest in the religious instruction of the Negro. The Gospel=Propagation Society soon after 1701 founded missions in the Carolinas, Connecticut, Massachusetts, New Jersey, New York, Pennsylvania and Rhode Island. Among its missionaries was Wesley; and his efforts in Georgia were rendered nugatory through his high=churchmanship (1736= 37). Yet Wesley embodied the best elements in the spiritual life of the Anglican communion, and men of his piety and purity formed the exception in the Episcopal clergy of America. This absence of educated, self=denying and upright men from the mass of Anglican ministers and missionaries before 1783 and the failure of their worthy members to influence the Negro made black Episcopalians as few as white blackbirds. In Virginia about 1725 the masters with some exceptions favored instruction for slaves, and the missionaries embraced the opportunity to instruct them. But the introduction of the cotton=gin (1793) and the rise of the slave=power to supremacy (1820=60) condemned the bondman to ignorance and provoked general jealousy of Christian influence.

The best showing for Anglican missions among black Americans appears in the Antilles. The Propagation= Society until 1782 gave occasional assistance in books and money to Antigua, Jamaica and other islands. In 1818 it began operations in Barbados, afterward pushing into Bahama, Bermuda, British Guiana, Grenada and Tobago. Codrington College, an institution of the society, has since 1829 supplied the church of England in the British West Indies with several hundreds of clergymen. The Church Missionary Society entered in 1815, working with the sister=society in the same fields but adding Trinidad as an independent sphere. Episcopacy in 1850 enumerated only six hundred and ninety=six Negro communicants throughout the West Indies, but in 1880 Bainbridge reported twenty [?] thousand adherents. The Church Society withdrew from Jamaica in 1852, from Guiana in 1858.

In 1865 the Episcopal church of the United States organized a freedmen's commission. Next year it opened three schools, and in 1895 these numbered but eighty. The Episcopal effort for the evangelization and education of the Negro has long been in charge of the general mission=society; but in 1893 Bishop Dudley of Kentucky publicly confessed the outlook dark and discouraging. This he chiefly ascribed to "the Episcopal church not having realized her duty and having allowed other religious bodies to take the lead" and to "want of interest and sympathy". The society is responsible for the salaries of bishops and the stipends of missionaries in the following jurisdictions possessing Negro populations: Oklahoma; northern Texas; western Texas and southern Florida. It also assists in the dioceses, among others, of Alabama; Arkansas; eastern Carolina; Florida; Georgia; Kansas; Kentucky; Louisiana; Maryland (where it merely assists the work among Negroes); Mississippi; Missouri; North Carolina; South Carolina; southern Virginia; Springfield, Ill.; Tennessee; Texas; Virginia (again aiding only work among Negroes); western Missouri and West Virginia. Two hundred and fifty men and women in round numbers then worked in the south among the Negroes at a cost of $54,000 (1893). Maryland and the Old Dominion also performed a measure of Negro mission-work through the voluntary activity of Episcopalian parishes and St Andrew's Brotherhood. Twenty-seven colored clergymen were deacons; thirty-five, priests. The general agent is himself a Negro, formerly bishop of Liberia.

The Reformed Episcopal church has, absolutely, done little, relatively, much, for the American Negro. In 1875 Bishop Cummins granted canonical recognition to four hundred colored Episcopalians in South Carolina. Stevens, his evangelist, afterward bishop, opened a training-school for the ministry. Since 1882 the work has received aid from the general council. In 1892 these Reformed Episcopal Negroes numbered twenty lay-preachers, thirty-eight congregations and eighteen hundred and twenty-four communicants; maintained a parochial school at Charleston; and supported a girl in India. The women also send annual aid to Africa. Bishop Stevens before 1861 trained the boys who as Stevens Battery fired the first shot at Fort Sumter; in 1893 he participated in the Chicago Congress on Africa. So swift are the changes of life and especially in America*! When Turner, a Negro bishop of a Methodist denomination, spoke of the wrongs of his race, the southern white man solemnly affirmed that the southern black man was right. The Episcopalian and the Methodist alike advocated governmental aid for the Negro emigrant.

II

Baptist Missions to Black Americans

Baptist churches influence more Negroes than does any other denomination. Northern Baptists number

*Since this sentence was penned the Americo-Spanish war of 1898 has afforded fresh proof of the reunion of the republic and of the south's love and loyalty to the nation.

eight hundred thousand, and have since 1863 spent over $2,775,000 for the Negro. Southern black Baptists number one and one-half millions, and despite the Negro being the pauper of America have achieved marvels for education and evangelization. Southern white Baptists number one and one-third millions, but spend only $88,640 a year in home-missions against an expenditure of about $175,000 annually for the Negro by the northern Baptists. By actual church-membership or by domestic and social ties four million black citizens of the United States possess Baptist affiliations. The Baptists therefore acknowledge that the peculiar claims of the Negro upon them have not been met; that some of their best black schools already enjoy the reputation of third-rate institutions; and that the Congregationalists and Methodists, though the colored membership of the latter is smaller and that of the former far smaller, have outstripped them.

Negro Baptists to some extent are a monument of the religious activity of southern white Baptists. In 1801 the Charleston association petitioned the legislature of South Carolina to remove restrictions on the religious meetings of slaves. Pastors, some of them the most eminent, labored faithfully among them. Planters frequently paid liberally toward the support of home-missionaries to the Negroes. As a rule black and white Baptists, bond and free, worshiped together, though the increase of Negro converts in the cities sometimes rendered separate churches necessary. These were independent in spiritual matters, but the colored members of mixed churches had a voice only in cases relating to their race. Between 1845 and 1861 the white southern Baptists did much for Negro evangelization, but from 1865 till recently they showed only slight interest. They looked at the education of their black fellow=Christians with indifference, with lukewarm interest, even with positive disfavor. They formed no Negro schools, contributed sparsely to those founded by northern Baptists and regarded them unfavorably. The notable exceptions afforded by individuals or communities merely accentuate the fact that hitherto the white Baptists of the south have played no part in uplifting the free Negro. Happily, however, their sentiment is changing. They appeal to their northern brothers for help in re=establishing educational institutions, and co=operation in behalf of the Negro is now afoot*.

The attitude of southern white Baptists toward black Baptists tended to develop independence and self=reliance in the latter. What they lack in knowledge and sanctified intelligence they make up in zeal. Negro Christianity has always been open to criticism for its divorce of morality from religion and for excess of emotion; but these defects are not so much due to the Negro nature as to the imperfect Christianity of slave=holding Protestants and Romanists. Negro Baptists now build their own churches, meet current expenses, support their pastors, contribute to missions, and spend increasing amounts in establishing, equipping and maintaining schools.

American Baptists have scarcely worked among the Negroes of the Antilles, but a Baptist society, organized at Utica, New York, in protest against slavery, for years sustained a successful mission in Haiti. Boyer, while president of this black republic, brought six thousand Negroes, chiefly Baptists and Methodists, from the United States (1824=35), and protected them in their religion. The Haitien Baptists in 1893 had four ordained

* Freewill Baptists are reported to be considering the advisability of opening an African mission.

pastors — two of them Jamaicans, two natives — and the mission=society of the Baptist Negroes in Jamaica works here. The southern white Baptists have a mission in Cuba, which, probably, included the Negro as well as the Spaniard before the present war. It may be assumed that it will certainly do so when Cuba shall have become the home, not of a free state only, but of a free church.

The home=mission and publication societies of the northern Baptists have done practically all that this denomination has contributed toward the salvation of the American Negro. The Home=Mission Society, though debarred from missions in the south during 1845=62, has accomplished ninety=nine hundredths of the white Baptist achievement among the freedmen and their sons. The Publication Society, through its Bible=distributing colporters and Sunday=school missionaries, and the women's auxiliaries render invaluable assistance. But, as a Baptist answer toward solving the Negro problem, the organization whose specific object is the promotion of domestic missions towers above other Baptist agencies. Its work forms a historic sequel to the action of Baptist Rhode Island (1652) in forbidding the slave=trade and in prohibiting Negroes from being retained more than ten years in bondage.

This society began work in three channels. (1) For many years it devoted special attention to sending northern ministers and to supporting colored missionaries or pastors. (2) Ministerial institutes formed a constant and important feature. (3) But the chief stress was thrown on education. Common schools to teach the masses to read were pushed for ten years, though since 1872 the society has more and more restricted itself to fostering schools for Negro teachers, preachers and leaders. The Women's Home Mission=Society is an efficient assistant in the maintenance of these institutions, whose existence was demanded and justified by the unfitness of the white race to meet the racial needs of the Negro genius. In 1895 there were fourteen institutions for higher education; fifteen secondary schools; about seventy=five colored teachers; nearly six thousand pupils, fifteen hundred of them preparing to teach; and over four hundred students of theology. The educational policy consists in establishing in each southern state at least one college for Negroes and a system of secondary schools and in developing self=help. The situation has radically changed since 1863. Higher education must for many years be controlled by the white Baptists, but the secondary schools devolve chiefly on the black people. Separateness between the black and white Baptists of the south promises, alas! to become permanent.

III

Congregational Missions to Black Americans

Congregationalism brought democracy and the spirit of freedom to America. Peter Brown the carpenter came to Plymouth in *The Mayflower*, and his children's children for ten generations, though always prosperous, never owned a slave. This instance is representative and typical of American Congregationalists as a body. Though individuals and local churches disabled them between 1820 and 1860 from discharging their whole duty toward the slave, the genius of emancipation gave birth to English Independency, nurtured New England Congregationalism, and supplied the leading liberators with anti=slavery sentiments from Congregational sources. Given Congregationalism and Peter Brown the English Pilgrim, — the inevitable, logical outcome must be John Brown of Harper's Ferry and the marching soul of freedom.

Congregationalists before 1861 were a northern denomination. Lacking organizations in the south, they remained free from ecclesiastical entanglements. The true picture of Congregationalism and slavery, though not without dark shades, is luminous and winning. New England, the Puritan and the sons of the Pilgrim and the Puritan were always in advance of all other Christians in their attitude toward the Negro. The exceptions and the guilt of a few communities and personages can not away with this fact. In 1645=6 the Massachusetts legislature restored two Negroes to their African home whom a member of the Boston church had imported and sold. Eliot became an apostle to the Negro as truly as to the Indian. As early as 1701 Boston besought her representatives to abolish slavery. Sewall wrote an anti=slavery pamphlet (1700), and "essayed to prevent Negroes and Indians being rated with cattle" (1716). The great revivals renewed the sensitiveness of the New England conscience as to slavery. Bellamy, Edwards, Emmons and Hopkins, Calvinists more Calvinistic than Calvin, preached against the hydra=headed evil. Hopkins and Stiles (1773) appealed for missionaries to Africa, a suggestion by Hopkins, before Englishmen mentioned Sierra Leone, furnishing the germ of Liberia and inspiring Mills; and the Presbyterians would have entered Africa but for the outbreak of the war for independence (1776=83). Massachusetts in 1770 through the Lechmere case anticipated Britain by two years in pronouncing that when the slave touched British soil he became free. In 1777 Vermont emancipated the Negro, and in 1784 all New England had followed her lead. The Puritan abolition of slavery was due to love of justice.

It is needless to demonstrate in detail the antagonism of Congregationalists to human bondage between 1784 and 1840. It was only necessary to present the preceding proofs of the forces that caused them even more than the Friends to remain comparatively free from the guilt of slavery and to receive special training for service to the Negro. The Amistad Committee of 1839, the Union Mission=Society and the West India Commission were Congregational protests against the slave=power. The American Missionary Association — not the American Board of Commissioners for Foreign Missions — was formed (1846) in equally, if not more, emphatic disapproval of slavery; and the preceding societies with the Western Missionary Association merged themselves and their missions with it. Hence the African missions of the new Congregational society among the Kopts (1854 [?] =59), the freedmen of Jamaica (1837), the Mindi of Sierra Leone (1841=83)* and the Negro refugees in Canada. The Association also explored Egyptian Sûdan between Khartum and Sobat in 1881 for the purpose of founding a new African mission, but the Muslim Messiah estopped further endeavor. American Negroes constituted the chief field of the Association from its birth.

Work for the southern Negro began in efforts for the white man. The Association inaugurated the first decided endeavors during the existence of slavery that avowedly based themselves on opposition to slavery. Fee of Kentucky organized non=slaveholding churches, educated and evangelized Negroes no less than white men, and paved the way for the foundation of Berea Col-

*The Amistad slaves were successively freed, educated and sent here as missionaries.

lege (1848-60). Adair (a brother-in-law of John Brown), Jones, Vestal and Worth stood beside him. But in 1861 the Association opened the first day-school in America for slaves. This was at Hampton, Virginia, where the Dutch slave-ship of 1619, more fatal than the Trojan horse, had disgorged its horrible cargo. Congregationalists entered earlier than other Christians among the freedmen of the United States; and the mansion of Tyler the Virginian slave-president sheltered their Negro Sunday-school. Mrs Peake, the daughter of an Englishman and a free quadroon, was the first teacher. The whole affair is fraught with the symbolism of Providence.

During the war the missionary, preacher and teacher followed the soldier. Parochial and primary schools sprang up in swarms. The Negro's eagerness to read was universal. After 1867 the enlargement of opportunity through the establishment of schools by the nation and in increasing degree by the states enabled the Association to turn more and more toward supplying higher education. Only fifty-three primary schools are retained, and these mainly in connection with churches. The progress of the pupils called for instruction in the superior studies. Graded and normal schools, colleges and seminaries were required to prepare the students to preach and teach. The response to this need is Atlanta, Fisk, Howard, Straight and Tougaloo Universities; Berea and Talladega Colleges; and Avery, Hampton and Tillotson Institutes. Atlanta, Berea and Hampton have already grown through self-support into independence. The Negro jubilee-singers made Fisk famous the world around, thrilled millions to tears and laughter, and won hundreds of thousands of dollars for their university. Armstrong at Hampton set the pace for indus-

JOSEPH E. ROY, D.D.
Originator of the Chicago Congress on Africa

trial education. Booker T. Washington his pupil follows the master, and leads a race. The Association controls twenty=eight of the thirty=nine normal and training= schools in the south, and in all its institutions educates nearly fifteen thousand students annually. It has founded nearly one hundred and fifty churches of southern Congregationalists in eight associations, without regard to color, and stands in unyielding opposition to caste. It had in 1895 invested over thirteen millions of dollars, contributed by Congregationalists*. Though these number but six hundred thousand communicants and are not a wealthy people, they have given more than twice as much as any other body of American Christians But even more significant and valuable than such material benefactions is the mental, social and spiritual stimulus bestowed by them upon African evangelization and the American Negro. It was Joseph E. Roy, a secretary of the Association, who originated the idea of an African congress at the Columbian exposition; and this, according to Stewart of Lovedale, has already aided Africa. It was another Congregationalist who made the congress.

The Bureau of Woman's Work (1883) and the Sunday= school Society also operate with the Association. Woman, however, had entered in 1846 and in 1861, and it is impossible to exaggerate the worth of her services, especially among the Negresses. The Association also crowns its southern work by missions among the white highlanders. This mountain=folk numbers two and a half millions, opposed the slave=holders' rebellion, and with the Negro will make the new south.

* British Congregationalism must be credited with a share in the work, 1861= 71. British Freewill Baptists, Friends and Wesleyans also aided. All Britain contributed one million dollars in clothing and money.

IV

Friends' Missions to Black Americans

In 1688 German Friends in Pennsylvania protested against slavery. In 1787 no American Friend held a slave. No other body can quite equal this record. The Congregationalists, indeed, anticipated it through the Massachusetts legislature of 1641 restricting slavery and through New England abolishing bondage as early as 1784; but it is not absolutely certain that every Congregationalist elsewhere was a non=slave-holder. This was the case with every acknowledged Friend. Moreover, during the eighteenth century the Friends did more than other American Christians for the Negro. The Unity of Brethren in the Antilles excelled them in Christian service to the slave; but American Friends, beside accomplishing something for his Christian culture and education, toiled unitedly and not merely as individuals for universal emancipation. Fox, who in Barbados rendered missionary services to Negro slaves; Penn; Burling, Coleman and Standifred; Lay; Woolman (1746=67); Benezet of Huguenot ancestry and the inspirer of Clarkson; Rush, who shared in leading the congresses of 1774 and 1776 to ban the slave=trade; and Lundy, who aroused Garrison — these represent the true spirit of Friends toward the Negro. If after 1820 they felt disinclined to attack slavery, the unfaithfulness was transient.

New occasions, Lowell sang, teach new duties. As soon as Negro refugees fringed the northern edge of the war, Friends recognized the duty. At first (1863) they were obliged to devote themselves to the relief of physical suffering; but they quickly added education and missions to their activities. Their schools sprang up by scores, and stood among the main agencies in teaching the black man before the reconstruction of the southern states. When local authorities became able to take good care of these institutions, nearly all were relinquished. Since 1889 the mission=board of the Friends in New York continues the school=work. Friends have spent over one million dollars for the freedmen; sustained more than one hundred schools, four of which remain in their charge; and have remembered the exhortation of Fox: When the Negroes are free, let them not go empty= handed.

V

Methodist Missions to Black Americans

Wesley while in Georgia protested against slavery. Whitefield denounced the system and its barbarities (1739). Wesley wrote from England to Davies of Virginia as to slavery, and gave books for his Negro parishioners (1755=57). In 1758 he baptized the first black Methodist, and in 1766 the first congregation of American Methodists included a Negress*. Methodism began with faithfulness to the Negro.

Five families of American Methodists present themselves for consideration in connection with missions to black Americans. These comprise the African, Colored, Methodist, Southern Methodist, Union and Zion Churches. The African, Colored, Union and Zion Churches consist solely of Negro Methodists; the Methodist Church, of black and white Christians together; and the Methodist Church *South*, of white members exclusively.

*Gilbert of Antigua inaugurated Methodist missions among the Negroes of the British Antilles, but these were a British achievement. Cf. chap. 10.

Negro Methodism expresses the conviction that separation enlarges the opportunity for racial abilities and self-help and that it lessens the liability to friction from prejudice. The Union Church, though originating in 1813, has accomplished little, as its membership is but twenty-five hundred. The African Church (1816) has achieved great success, having grown to five hundred thousand members and founded thirty-eight schools. Among these are ten colleges or universities, schools in Bermuda, Haiti and Sierra Leone and a theological seminary. The Colored Church (1876), though born with eighty thousand communicants and now numbering nearly one hundred and fifty thousand, is still too poor and young to have accomplished much. Four schools and five hundred students are all it has to show. The Zion Church (1820) possesses almost four hundred thousand communicants but only one college and a few small schools. Before 1861 the chief strength of Negro Methodism lay in the eastern states, extending westward with emigration. It could have no churches at the south outside of Delaware and Maryland*. The Zion Church opposed slavery, though slaves were among its communicants, and advanced the cause of abolition. While white applicants for membership would not be rejected, its officers and pastors are exclusively Negroes. After 1861 the African and the Zion Church became factors in the evangelization of the southern freedmen. The African Church at first enjoyed its chief southern gains along the sea-board, especially in Florida and South Carolina. Seventy-five thousand Negro members of the Methodist Church South swarmed into the African Church. The Zion Church experienced its chief southern expansion in Alabama and North Caro-

* A lone church at Charleston; at Louisville; at New Orleans constituted no exception.

lina, and acquired twenty=five thousand Negro members
from the southern Methodists. The grand total of all
Negro Methodists of the United States is one million,
two hundred thousand. Three millions more, exclusive
of these communicants, complete the number of Negroes
under Methodist influences*.

Slavery embarrassed American Methodism even before organization (1784=85), but the northern Methodists
always opposed it. The development of the west so
increased the power of this anti=slavery element that in
1844 it disciplined a slave=holding bishop. Consequently the southern Methodists, after dominating the
church for more than half a century, organized separately. But Methodists of whatever opinion or section
agreed in Christianizing the slave. Down to 1844 the
organization of independent Negro denominations and
the successful founding of plantation=missions constituted the epochal events in the dealings of Methodism
with the black American. The former was more the
work of the north, the latter that of the south. In 1816
thirty thousand of the forty=two thousand Negro members of the *Methodist* Church were southern slaves. Itin-
erants had preached faithfully, in connection with permanent pastorates, but the converts came mainly from
the home=servants. Paganism reigned among one and
one half million field=serfs. There must be a movement
in addition to ordinary church=work, if Christian civilization were to acquire any hold on this Africa in America.
Southern Methodism stepped into the breach. Capers
of South Carolina established missions to the plantation=
slaves (1829), and southern Methodists sustained them.
As a rule black and white Methodists in the south worshiped together, separate churches and services being

*The Negro Methodists of Canada organized in 1864 as the British Church, and sustain a prosperous mission in Bermuda.

provided only when it was desired or where, especially in cities and large towns, the colored membership was a considerable one. Successful Negro preachers, whose ministrations were acceptable to white people, were not unknown; but from 1766 to 1816 all Negro organizations remained under the charge of the white man. The plantation=mission attained its greatest success in South Carolina, though in 1844 it had no less than twenty=two thousand converts in nine of the southern states. After the separation southern Methodists prosecuted the work with heightened earnestness and increased success. From 1829 to 1844 they had given $200,000; between 1844 and 1864, when this mission ended, they spent $1,800,000 in addition. Their Negro membership rose from one hundred and eighteen thousand, nine hundred and four to two hundred and nine thousand, eight hundred and thirty=six. It should, however, be remembered that they were the sole Methodists enjoying access to nine tenths of the slaves. In this light the fact that but sixty=six thousand, five hundred and fifty=nine of the southern Negro Methodists in 1861 were converts from the plantation=missions qualifies our satisfaction. In 1866 the Methodist Church South organized its Negro communicants separately, and provided that, if they should desire it and should form two or more conferences, self=government should be granted. Ten years later this resulted in the formation of another Negro denomination among Methodists, composed exclusively of Negroes and officered wholly by black men. The Methodist Church South, whose one and one half millions of communicants make it the second Methodist denomination in America, thus became a southern church and a white man's church, sectarian and sectional. In 1883 it took a forward step in the education of the Negro. It appointed a board to work beside the Colored Church, and founded Paine Institute. To this it has contributed about $75,000.

The Methodist Church before division had one hundred and fifty thousand Negro members (1845). Northern Methodism retained thirty thousand. Only ten thousand were free. Only eighteen thousand remained in 1865. The aggressions of independent Negro Methodism and the inability to reach the southern Negro cost northern white Methodists this loss of twelve thousand black communicants. Nevertheless, northern Methodism accomplished something. It remained faithful to the principle that its black and white adherents must be one body. It founded the first Methodist institution for the higher education of the Negro. Wilberforce University, now the intellectual capital of the African Church, originated in 1857, and remained until after 1863 in the care of its founders. At the outbreak of war the northern Methodists worked through undenominational societies in relieving the physical suffering of the fugitives from the south and in giving primary education, but in 1866 they formed a Methodist Freedmen's Aid and Education Society. This in 1898=99 appropriated $55,400 for schools among black people; $7,875 for schools among the whites; and $43,725 for other purposes. The Missionary Society, in addition, assigned $44,005 to colored work, mostly in the south, during 1898. More than any other denomination Methodists devote themselves to organizing churches and to primary education. The outcome consists of two hundred and fifty thousand Negro communicants* (one tenth of the total membership), and twenty=two Negro schools. These

*The Methodist Church during the early years of its missions among the freedmen received twenty=nine thousand Negroes from the Methodist Church South.

comprise a theological seminary, ten colleges and eleven academies. The teachers, not including one hundred and fourteen "practice=teachers", number three hundred and thirty=three; the pupils, five thousand. Three hundred and thirty=five are in manual or training= schools, two hundred and ninety=two preparing to become doctors, two hundred and fifty=six for the ministry and only one for the law. Such figures possess special significance. Separation of the races is opposed, being permitted only at the mutual preference of black and white Methodists alike. The work has cost over six and one= fourth million dollars, but Dr Hartzell, formerly secretary of the Freedmen's Society, writes that American "Methodism need not boast, for with her resources and opportunities far more ought to have been accomplished".

VI

Presbyterian Missions to Black Americans

The Presbyterian Church between 1786 and 1837 six times officially advocated the abolition of slavery. It had previously attempted to serve the Negro, Davies of Virginia, afterward president of Princeton College, receiving between forty and fifty black Christians into communion and teaching them on Sundays (1756). In 1774 and 1780 it had moved in behalf of the slave. In 1787 it advised such education as would fit him for freedom. Though between 1805 and 1830 it suffered from the prevalent spinal weakness of anti=slavery sentiment, while its official action after 1832 exposed it to criticism from the foes and the friends of slavery, it did not abandon its missions among American Negroes. Presbyterians believed that "no more honored name could be conferred on a minister than that of apostle to American slaves".

The southern members of the undivided church so promoted Negro evangelization that in 1861 the black Presbyterians numbered fifteen thousand, and Ashmun Institute was educating Negro ministers and missionaries. The southern Presbyterians organized separately in 1861=62, and until recently attempted little for home=missions among black Americans. As Negro Presbyterians were supposed to desire church independence, this formed the goal and has been attained. Its advocates believe that black Presbyterianism will grow faster and take firmer hold on the Negro than white Presbyterianism. As this goes to press, it is learned that the Presbyterian Church South has failed to support freedmen's missions in earnest while Negroes remained within it. Now that it has persuaded five Negro presbyteries to form "The Separate and Self=Governing Synod of the United States and Canada" [!] it will aid work among black Presbyterians less than ever.

The northern Presbyterians deem educated ministers and refined womanhood the supreme forces in elevating and saving the Negro. The home is the center of their work, the creation of home=makers the central object. The educational policy makes Negro religion less emotional and irrational; pays the closest attention to industry, manners and morals; and separates the sexes. Needy students are aided, but self=support is required. The organization of churches and schools began in 1866. In 1893 these included two universities, four female seminaries, ten secondary boarding=schools, seventy=one parochial schools, twelve thousand pupils, two Negro synods, one hundred and fifty colored ministers and seventeen thousand black Presbyterians in full fellowship with the northern church. This has nine hundred thousand communicants, and has spent eighteen hundred thousand dollars for the freedman, but "does not claim that it has done all it should*".

VII

Roman Missions to Black Americans

The Roman Church claims that in Latin America it attended from the first to the spiritual wants of the slave and that in Teutonic America it is responsible for slavery only in Kentucky, Louisiana, Maryland and part of Missouri. It can not claim that it has in either America done what it ought to have done. Such individuals as Claver form singular exceptions to the practice if not also to the principles of the papal communion in America since 1520. When such Christians as Beecher and Garrison were striving for emancipation, Marshall sneered at them as professional abolitionists, and announced that the Roman church tolerated slavery. Protestant ministers led the American anti=slavery crusade, but no papal prelate then lifted hand or voice to acquire freedom for the black man. Latin Christianity remains responsible for the existence of slavery and the prosecution of the slave=trade in Arkansas, Florida and Texas, for these territories belonged to papal powers before they came under Protestant control; and Maryland, while Roman in religion, established the slave=traffic. In Carolina (1520), Virginia (1526) and Florida (1565) the first slave=owners and slave=traders were Catholics. The Roman Church disclaimed all sympathy with such advocates of Negro emancipation as Phelps the Congre-

* The Reformed Presbyterians have freedmen's missions.

gationalist or Scott the Methodist. Chief=Justice Taney (1836=64) was a Catholic of Maryland. *A priori* there seemed double reason for assuming that he would prove predisposed in behalf of the enslaved Negro. In spite of the two=fold fact, he pronounced the Negro slave to be not a person but a chattel. Brazil, Cuba and Haiti fairly represent Latin America. Rome has had the fields to itself. Religion has as much to do with the outcome as race, climate or civilization. Yet Brazil did not abolish slavery until 1888, and Haiti remains an Alsatia*.

Claver the Jesuit affords an instance of self=sacrifice for the Negro, which, although rare, is represented as common among Romanists and unknown to Protestants. The son of a noble Catalan family in Spain, he entered the Company of Jesus at the age of twenty. He celebrated the close of his noviciate by a pilgrimage to Montserrat where Loyola had nearly a century before hung up his sword in renunciation of the world. To the day of death Claver never spoke without emotion of this visit to a sanctuary hallowed by the prayers and vigils of his spiritual father. He came to Cartagena, Colombia, then New Granada, in 1610. The misery of the slave so shocked him that he vowed to be until death the slave of the Negro. If slavery under Portuguese or Spanish masters were the blessing that it has been asserted to be, why did this Christian take so special a vow†?

*The Reverend Emmanuel Van Orden, a Presbyterian missionary in Brazil, has publicly stated that it was through missionaries from the United States, aided by British Bible=Societies, that the Brazilian people abolished Negro slavery. *Cf. Report of the Centenary Conference on Missions*, London, 1888, pp. 356-357.

The population of Cuba is over 1,500,000, about one third being of Negro blood. The Philadelphia Manufacturer, March 16, 1889, is quoted by Mr Moret as saying among other things: "The most degraded and ignorant Negro of Georgia has more fitness for the presidency of the United States than the average Cuban Negro for the rights of citizenship. They have not yet risen above barbarism".

†Dr Slattery, the devoted chief of a papal institution for missions among black Americans, publicly characterizes the treatment of slaves by the Spaniards as "atrocious".

When the appearance of a slave-ship was announced, Claver's face, usually emaciated and livid, assumed the hue of health. On its arrival he descended, attended by interpreters, into the hold where the human cattle were herded together; embraced them; distributed the refreshments he had begged from wealthy townsmen; told the blacks he loved them; and to the utmost of his power assisted and comforted them. While the outcasts gazed in wonder at the friend, he spoke of God and endeavored to enlighten their spiritual darkness. He was also in the habit of visiting the plantations, when his first care again was for the sick. For these he brought fruit and wine, accompanying them by a few simple exhortations. Assembling other slaves, he explained the principal truths of Christianity through pictures and, when the Negroes were sufficiently instructed, baptized those who desired it. Such baptisms, it is affirmed, numbered three hundred thousand. Muhammadan Negroes from Guinea and multitudes of Moors and Turks are asserted to have been among these proselytes. Perseverance at last established morality and piety; and, when Claver died (1654), Cartagena, in acknowledgment of his services, buried him publicly and at the cost of the city. A century later Benedict IV declared him venerable (1747), and in 1850 Pius IX beatified him as St Peter Claver.

Claver's achievement almost exhausts the list of papal efforts in behalf of the Negro slave in America, for "there is little allusion to efforts in behalf of the Negro", "few notices in her [the Roman Church's] history of Catholic Negroes", and "such details as we have been able to gather of the work of the church in behalf of the colored race " prove to be scanty and unsatisfying*. The language of Roman writers as to the results attained

* *The Catholic Church and the Negro Race in America:* Address at the Chicago Congress on Africa; by Dr Slattery.

by their church among the Negro populations of Latin America is not that of men who believe it to have achieved a large measure of accomplishment. The papal clergy did not wholly neglect the interests of the black victims, and in South America and the West Indies the Roman Church sometimes proved a friend and protector to the unfortunates; but the spiritual condition of the Negro to=day in the Catholic lands of the new world, when viewed in the large light and perspective of four centuries of papal occupancy and power, demonstrates that this denomination effected practically nothing for him in the Antilles, Central America and South America. The Dominicans claim unexampled success among the Negroes of Surinam about 1826, the Jesuits boast of their experience with those of Cayenne in 1763=66, but these instances, even if valid, form exceptions. Catholic authors bewail the state of their sect in the Greater Antilles, consoling themselves with its more prosperous condition in the lesser islands. But the untrustworthiness of Roman statistics renders it impracticable to make an estimate of the numbers and social standing of the Negro Catholics in Latin America.

The record of Rome for the Negro of the northern continent is quite as cheerless. While Louisiana remained under French rule there was much neglect of the slave. The masters were traders and regarded the Negro as barter=goods. The Jesuits toiled for the field=hands, but the government denied them access to those within municipal limits. The Ursuline nuns from 1700 to 1824 devoted themselves in a modest way to the blacks, and during the Spanish sway, when the government exerted itself to improve the morals and religion of the slave, had a school for Negro children. The Sisters (colored) of the Holy Family originated in 1842, and carry on the Ursuline work. These, however, numbered only fifty half a century later, though the Roman Church claimed a Negro "population" of one hundred thousand in the state. Kentucky is credited with six thousand Negro Catholics, and Maryland, where from the day of settlement till now papal missionaries have labored for the black man, with six times as many. But of Kentucky, Louisiana, Maryland and Missouri, all in great measure colonized by Catholics, Slattery writes: "Slavery was as strongly encouraged as in the other [*i.e.*, Protestant] slave=holding states".

Florida is an occasion of pride to the Catholic communion. Colonists came from Spain in 1565 with five hundred Negro slaves, murdered the French settlers and founded the oldest papal congregation within the present United States. To=day, if we draw inferences from the following utterance, the spirit of Menendez dominates Floridian Romanism. "Northern fanatics well=salaried [?] by their societies have in many places put up meeting=houses for them [the Negroes]. These simple, misguided people are drawn by political excitement; inflamed harangues in the name of liberty; singing; shouting; clapping hands; dancing; confused vociferations; and other indecorous exhibitions which they fancifully call religious worship"*. The Negro members of the Roman Church in the diocese of eastern Florida number only twelve hundred, yet she "believes that the population has received due attention". It is confessed that outside of St Augustine she has made no gain among Floridian Negroes. As excuses for this sterility of papal missions are put forward the very limited number of clergy and their still more limited pecuniary resources.

* Sadlier's Directory, 1893, p. 420.

The Americo=Roman church can hardly be said to have recognized its duty and opportunity in regard to the southern black until after he became a freedman. Twenty=one white sisterhoods are working among black as well as white people, and teaching over eight thousand pupils. Four more communities of white sisters and three of Negresses also devote themselves exclusively to the Negro. But it was not until 1866 that the hierarchy appealed for priests to evangelize the black American; and it was as late as 1871 before the response came. Nor was it made by American but by British Catholics. In 1884 the council advanced another step. It authorized an annual and general collection from the papal churches of the United States, the sole universal collection ever levied by the Roman bishops in America on their own authority. An episcopal commission distributes this fund among missions for the Indians also and not merely among those for the Negro, but makes no statement as to the absolute amount or the relative percentage assigned to each. The contribution amounts to less than $60,000. In 1888 St Joseph Seminary, in 1889 Epiphany Apostolic College, both at Baltimore, began to train men for work among the former slave and his children. The two institutions have between one and two hundred students, and the field=force consists of over thirty priests laboring exclusively for the colored people in about thirty=five churches and of one hundred and fifteen schools. The church claims one hundred and fifty thousand Negro Catholics in the south, but the federal census of 1890 credits it with less than one tenth of that number of Negro communicants in the whole country*.

* *Report on Statistics of Churches*, p. 49.

VIII

Results of Freedmen's Missions

Thirty=five years ago, even thirty years ago, the Negro lay under every disadvantage involved in slavery. American Negro Christians, judging from the fact that in 1860 the Baptists and Methodists together numbered about five hundred and twenty=five thousand black communicants and in 1895 comprised ninety=seven and three hundredths *per cent.* of all Negro church=members, could not have exceeded five hundred and forty thousand communicants. In 1890 the churches reported two million, six hundred and seventy=three thousand, nine hundred and seventy=seven Negro members. In 1860 the Negro population amounted (in round numbers) to four millions, but only one in every seven of these was a Christian, for the Baptist, Episcopal, Methodist, Presbyterian and Roman communions had fallen far short of fulfilling their measure of duty to the slave. In 1890 our black fellow=citizens numbered seven million, four hundred and seventy thousand and forty, and one in every two and seventy=nine hundredths communed with a Christian church. While America's Negro population doubled, her Negro Christians quintupled. Then the American church had fourteen *per cent.* of our brethren in black within its pale; now it controls thirty=six *per cent.*, having increased this percentage and consequent ratio of gain two and one half times in a single generation. Not only do Negro church=members to=day outnumber those of 1860=65, bulk for bulk, but their proportion to the Negro population is far greater. This stupendous achievement is one of the spiritual wonders of history. It is the work as a whole of the black American himself, though helped by churches and individuals of the white race, for the Negro Baptists and Methodists of the south and the white Baptists, Congregationalists, Methodists and Presbyterians of the North have borne the heat and burden of the day. The Negro of the United States multiplied marvelously, but the Negro Christian grew miraculously. No group of millions of people has ever advanced as has the man who through the furnace of war came naked from the house of bondage.

A result, too little known, of missions among black Americans is the existence of ten colored denominations as well as of Negro organizations in nineteen other churches. These denominations and organizations are in addition to the Negro communicants, by no means few, belonging to white churches and rated without regard to color. The Negro bodies consist of the African Methodist Episcopal Church; the African Methodist Episcopal Zion Church; the African Union Methodist Protestant Church; the (colored) Baptists; the Colored Methodist Episcopal Church; the (colored) Congregational Methodists; the (colored) Cumberland Presbyterians; the Evangelist Missionary Church; the Union American Methodist Episcopal Church; and the Zion Union Apostolic Church. These boast two million, three hundred and three thousand, one hundred and fifty-one communicants, the Baptists (Regular) being not only the largest of Negro churches but the largest Baptist body in America. Next in adherents comes the African Church with four hundred and fifty-two thousand, seven hundred and twenty-five communicants; and third the Zion Church whose members number only three hundred and forty-nine thousand, seven hundred and eighty-eight. From the Colored Methodist Church of one hundred and twenty-nine thousand, three hundred and eighty=three communicants the six remaining Negro denominations rapidly dwindle through the Cumberland Presbyterians (twelve thousand, nine hundred and fifty=six), the African Union Methodist Protestant Church (three thousand, four hundred and fifteen), the Zion Union Apostolic Church (two thousand, three hundred and forty=six), the Union American Methodist Episcopal Church (two thousand, two hundred and seventy=nine) and the Evangelist Missionary (nine hundred and fifty=one) to the pitiful corporal's guard of Congregational Methodists (three hundred and nineteen). Of the ten Negro denominations six are Methodist bodies, a fact provoking inquiry whether the sects are the result of a stand for principle or are mere schisms.

The nineteen churches having Negro organizations include the Baptists (Regular) of the north and of the south; the Christian Connection; the Congregationalists; the Disciples; the Episcopalians; the Freewill Baptists; the Independent Methodists; the Lutheran Synodical Conference; the Lutheran United Synod in the South; the Methodist Church [north]; the Methodist Protestant Church; the Old Two=Seed=in=the=Spirit Predestinarian Baptists; the Presbyterians of the north and of the south; the Primitive Baptists; the Reformed=Episcopalians; the Reformed=Presbyterian Synod; and the Roman Church. Here it is not the Baptists but the Methodists who lead in numbers, the Methodist Episcopal Church [north] boasting two hundred and forty=six thousand, two hundred and forty=nine Negro communicants, the northern Baptists thirty=five thousand, two hundred and twenty=one and the Primitive Baptists eighteen thousand one hundred and sixty=two. The Disciples, however, not the Primitive Baptists, rank third, the former exceeding the latter in Negro members by four hundred and twelve. The northern Presbyterians (fourteen thousand, nine hundred and sixty=one) snatch fifth place from the Roman Church (fourteen thousand, five hundred and seventeen) by almost as slight an excess. The Congregationalists (six thousand, nine hundred and eight), "Christians" (four thousand, nine hundred and eighty=nine), the Methodist Protestant Church (three thousand, one hundred and eighty=three), the Episcopalians (two thousand, nine hundred and seventy=seven), the Reformed=Episcopalians (one thousand, seven hundred and twenty=three) and the Presbyterian Church South (one thousand, five hundred and sixty=eight) follow in order from the seventh to the twelfth place. The southern Baptists, the Freewill Baptists, the Predestinarian Baptists, the Lutheran Synodical Conference and the Independent Methodists present a pitiful appearance as they fill the thirteenth to the seventeenth position with less than one thousand black communicants each. Only the southern Baptists have over five hundred. But the Lutheran United Synod and the Reformed=Presbyterians occupy the eighteenth and nineteenth places with ninety=four and seventy=six Negro members apiece.

Between the black members of such churches as that of the northern Methodists and those of the northern Baptists and the Congregationalists exists a difference. The Methodist Church [north] has white as well as colored members in the south, and the separation between the black and white fellow=churchmen expresses the caste spirit and the color=line; but the Congregational churches and the northern Baptists enjoy next to no membership among the southern whites. The Negro organizations of the denominations that withstand racial prejudice represent nothing more serious than the absence of white southerners. Another noteworthy fact brought out by the statistics is the failure of the Roman Church. This vast body of six million, two hundred and thirty=one thousand, four hundred and seventeen communicants has, on the basis of the census, one one=hundred=and=eightieth of the Negro Christians and one five=hundred=and=thirty=third of the Negro population. According to its own returns of Catholic population only one in every forty=five Negroes is within this influence, and only one in every fifty=six and one half Catholics is a black American. Rome is strong in such northerly, border=state cities as Baltimore, Cincinnati=Covington, Louisville and St Louis and in the Franco=Spanish southwest; but why could she not before 1860 have evangelized the Negro of Alabama, Arkansas, the Carolinas, Delaware, the District of Columbia, Georgia, Mississippi, Tennessee and Virginia instead of confining herself to Florida, Kentucky, Louisiana, Maryland, Missouri and Texas; and to=day where are her Hands, Peabodys and Slaters to match the philanthropists of Protestantism? The Honorable Charles H. Butler of Washington City agrees with Dr Slattery that the Roman Church has been remiss in discharging its duty toward the Negro. The good priest justly acknowledges that Romanism may in part be held responsible for the present irreligiousness and immorality of the vast majority of black Americans, and that race=prejudice is shared by Catholics; but he unjustly characterizes this prejudice as a Protestant instinct.

It is hoped that if facts be demonstration, this chapter has shown the bearing of missions among American Negroes upon the evangelization of Africa. Should the argument from evidence fail to convey this conclusion convincingly, it is believed that credence will be given to testimony uttered long after the present writer's views were formulated. On July 8th, 1897, at Cape Town, William Hay of Cape Colony publicly addressed The South Africa Political Association thus: "The natives are attracted to the colored people of the United States. The coming of minstrels was not important, but the performances gave intelligent natives new ideas. They saw Europeans crowd to hear colored people sing. They began to give entertainments, which made natives feel they might become more than hewers of wood and drawers of water. They found these minstrels able to travel without passes and enjoy liberty because they are American citizens who, if interfered with, can appeal to their own consul and claim protection of the government. When Stewart of Lovedale visited America [1893], he found a Sutu in a college where all the professors and pupils are black. Having heard he could get a good education in America, the young Sutu traveled there, and was pursuing his course at his own expense. More recently a deputation went from this colony to invite the Colored Methodist Episcopal Church [?] to take the people the deputation represented under its care, and branches of this church are established all over our country. Christian natives look to their countrymen in America to guide them in religion and provide them with education. The movement is carefully watched; because important political and ecclesiastical results may flow from the visit and the present labors. In discussing this venture with Mr Davanie I pointed out many difficulties in the way of success and dwelt on the mental and moral qualities of our natives. His reply was interesting and significant. He said responsibility had never been carried by colonial natives, but after seeing the people in the southern states, remembering how lately they were slaves, and noting how they have their own doctors, ministers, politicians, professors and teachers — he thought the people [colored] in this country would in a reasonable time show that they could make as satisfactory progress. If the new church=movement induce natives [Negroes] from America to become teachers and ministers here, there is no doubt the race as a race will become attached to its American brethren and look to America to give what we are not willing to bestow. An American Negro will never be required to submit to colonial native legislation. The moment you ask him for a pass or haul him to prison under the infamous Transkei act, he will appeal to his government, and . . . the English and colonial governments will wish at least one prominent parliamentarian had in South Africa adopted the political principles he lauds the United States for possessing in greatest realization".

Mr Bryce in *The American Commonwealth* and in *Impressions of South Africa* confirms the view that America's determination of her Negro problem will help shape that of Africa. Right-minded Americans themselves realize that their Negro problem is chiefly this: Will the white man be loyal to the national constitution and render justice to his black fellow=citizen?

CHAPTER 15
1661 = 1898

UNDENOMINATIONAL AFRICAN MISSIONS

The Church of Christ has from the beginning been one. The one indivisible church is the soul that animates the divided visible churches. Denominationalism is a blessing. Philip Schaff

BIRD'S=EYE VIEW. (I) MISSIONS FOR EVANGELIZATION. THE SOCIETY OF FRIENDS. THE EVANGELICAL MISSION=SOCIETY AT BASEL. YOUNG MEN'S FOREIGN MISSIONARY SOCIETY OF BIRMINGHAM. LIVINGSTONE INLAND MISSION. EAST LONDON INSTITUTE AND ITS KONGO=LOLO MISSION. THE NORTH AFRICA MISSION. THE CHRISTIAN AND MISSIONARY ALLIANCE. THE SHILOH MISSION. ARNOT'S MISSION. THE SALVATION ARMY. MISSIONS OF THE YOUNG MEN'S AND THE YOUNG WOMEN'S CHRISTIAN ASSOCIATION. THE EAST AFRICA SCOTTISH MISSION. THE SOUTH AFRICA GENERAL MISSION. THE SÛDAN PIONEER MISSION. THE ZAMBEZI MISSION. (II) LITERARY AUXILIARIES. THE RELIGIOUS TRACT SOCIETY. THE BRITISH AND FOREIGN BIBLE=SOCIETY. MEN AND METHODS IN BIBLE=DISTRIBUTION. THE TRINITARIAN BIBLE=SOCIETY. THE AMERICAN BIBLE=SOCIETY. THE PURE LITERATURE SOCIETY. THE NATIONAL BIBLE=SOCIETY OF SCOTLAND. THE ASSOCIATION FOR THE FREE DISTRIBUTION OF THE SCRIPTURES. (III) MEDICAL MISSIONARY SOCIETIES. THE EDINBURGH MEDICAL MISSIONARY SOCIETY. THE CHILDREN'S MEDICAL MISSIONARY SOCIETY AND THE MEDICAL MISSIONARY ASSOCIATION OF ENGLAND. THE INTERNATIONAL MEDICAL MISSIONARY SOCIETY. THE INTERNATIONAL MEDICAL MISSIONARY AND BENEVOLENT ASSOCIATION. (IV) ORGANIZATIONS LESS DIRECTLY PROMOTIVE OF MISSIONS. THE SOUL=WINNING AND PRAYER UNION. THE FOREIGN SUNDAY=SCHOOL ASSOCIATION. THE STUDENT VOLUNTEERS. THE BIBLE=READING ASSOCIATION. THE INTERNATIONAL MISSIONARY UNION. ANGLO=AMERICAN INTERDENOMINATIONALISM. THE YOUNG PEOPLE'S SOCIETIES OF CHRISTIAN ENDEAVOR.

Interdenominational and undenominational agencies for Africa's evangelization number fewer or more as we draw the line of churchood hard or loose. Perhaps thirteen devote themselves to evangelism proper. The rest either are general auxiliaries, aiding evangelization through literature or publication; or medical societies; or organizations of philanthropic rather than religious character. For historical and logical reasons evangelizing missions claim precedence. It seems best to present these, not alphabetically, but in the order of time, as they arose or entered Africa. With the exception of the Basel Society and the Friends, they come on the scene after 1875. Second in importance and, as a whole, second also in time, stand the literary and unclassifiable auxiliaries, only eight of which were at work for Africa before 1876. Third come medical missions and societies for such missions, all but one of these being less than eighteen years old. Livingstone's death and Stanley's descent of the Kongo aroused individuals not in sympathy with denominationalism to participate in the African effort that the churches had been carrying on, some for scores, others for hundreds, of years. Finally, as freedom and self=government characterize Protestantism, non=denominational agencies represent only Teutonic Christianity.

I

Missions for Evangelization

America filled Fox with fellow=feeling for the Negro, and set his soul on fire with hatred for slavery (1671). Stitch away, cried Carlyle to the peasant missionary and shoemaking saint; every prick of that little instrument is pricking into the heart of slavery! Fox wrote: All

Friends everywhere that have Indians or blacks are to preach the gospel to them; nor have Friends ever forgotten his injunctions. Three "Quakers" felt themselves moved by the Spirit to go to China and Ethiopia (1661), two actually reaching Alexandria and delivering His message to Kopt and Muhammadan. In 1819, 1823, 1827 and 1830 Mrs Hannah Kilham visited West Africa, Senegambia, Sierra Leone and Liberia successively; planned largely for the use of the languages and of native agency; taught two Yolofs in England and learned their speech; and made a first beginning in Gambia. She died on her home=journey in 1832 while bringing back several philological works, but not before she had wakened renewed interest among Friends in African missions. Backhouse and Walker examined missions in Mauritius and South Africa (1838). Friends, like "Moravians", have always been remarkable for the devotion of almost every member to missions as well as other philanthropies, assisting all evangelical missions, but they could not enter Madagascar before 1868*. They came to the kingdom at exactly the time. The queen's adoption of Christianity had given an immense impulse to missions. Two Americans and one Englishman were the first "Quaker" missionaries in Madagascar, and the Friends' Foreign Missionary Association in England is almost the only agency of the Society engaged in evangelizing African natives. It began by aiding the educational department of the Congregationalists, whose missionaries were straining every nerve to meet the swiftly spreading demand for Christian teaching. As the work grew, Imerina was divided into districts, and one al-

---

*King Radama I, who made entrance easy for the London Society, had a "Quaker" friend, named Hastie, and as this Friend gained influence he used his power in behalf of the Congregational missionaries. Friends, long before entering, gave large pecuniary support to schools, and for twenty years Sewell looked forward to actual mission=work.

lotted to Friends. At Tananarivo they established a boys' school and, later, a training=college under the care of a young Malagasi, which supplies almost all teachers employed in rural schools. At a printing=office boys are taught printing, lithography, map=making and kindred arts. The Friends have also locked hands with the Congregationalists in supporting a hospital and medical mission. Native students are trained for medical work, native nurses taught and a medical school founded for Malagasi physicians. The Madagascar "Quakers" numbered thousands of adherents before the French came, and maintained and managed a local missionary society and an orphanage. Merely nominal Christians have now mostly left the mission=churches, a loss that is gain, and the situation as a whole is considered encouraging.

In Natal is the sole African mission of Friends. This independent work originated in 1878 among unevangelized Zulu. The mission is a pioneer, but is partly self= supporting through the sale of produce from a farm surrounding the homestead and mission=buildings. Preaching and teaching, industrial and medical work are carried on.

The Basel Society entered Africa in 1827=28. It attempted to open a mission in Liberia, but the break= down or the death of every man necessitated retreat. Until 1887 the Gold Coast remained the one African field. Its history for the first twelve years is a record of the decease of as many missioners, who saw no result from their toil. Removal from the deadly sea=side to the supposedly healthy inland hills proved of no advantage, until (1843) Negroes from Jamaica founded a mission=colony for the society among the savages. During the first half=century thirty=nine out of one hundred and twenty-seven missionaries died after terms of service averaging only two years, and fifty returned as invalids. The more graves, however, the more sheaves. Between 1840 and 1843 the opposition of the Danish governor, who had in 1828 invited the mission to settle at the Danish possessions but had afterwards misrepresented the missionaries, was overcome. Denmark promised to protect them in the unhampered discharge of their task and to allow full liberty to Negroes connected with the mission. Akropong in the Aquipim hills and Ussu on the sea began to thrive. Schools for boys and girls were opened. The Akra or Ga and the Otshi or Twi, the languages of the Gold Coast, were reduced to writing, the Scriptures translated into both, and a dictionary and grammar compiled for the latter. Many text-books and tracts have also been published. The Ashanti war of 1869 broke up the mission, and two missionaries were held prisoners at Kumasi until 1874. A British invasion released them, and resulted ultimately in the expansion of the Basel sphere from the coast to Kumasi and across the Volta into Togo. The Basel men are everywhere most successful in making a native ministry. According to the latest statistics available the foreign missionaries numbered ninety-seven and the native workers three hundred and nine. There were sixteen thousand, three hundred and seventy-eight adherents; six thousand pupils in one hundred and seventy-one daily and weekly schools; and $7,500 in native contributions. The mission now has sixteen chief stations and eight thousand communicants.

This German and Swiss, this interdenominational and undenominational society has several unique features. It affiliates with many Protestant churches. Its missionaries are ordained by Free, Lutheran or

Presbyterian churches. Its mission=churches are Presbyterian in principle, but use a simple liturgy. Its candidates for mission=service between 1816 and 1882, mainly from southern Germany and Switzerland and numbering eleven hundred and twelve, consisted, with the exception of one hundred and six teachers or theologues, of artizans, farmers and petty traders. The Basel training=school instructs such burghers and peasants, if they possess intellectual capacity, in studies extending over six years. The course includes the elementary branches, the studies of a divinity=school and special training for missions. But Basel uses every talent and never rejects an earnest man. If a candidate prove dull at books but reveal sense and zeal, he is after a year or two at the mission=house sent to a foreign field to teach his trade to the natives, to do colporterage and to exert Christian activity in every relation. Throughout the course, whether long or short, every student works at a selected trade. Like Paul, the Basel missionaries take their tools into missions, and consecrate industry and skill to the Son of the Nazarene carpenter*.

To Africa is due the most remarkable, perhaps the most significant development of the Basel missions. The Guinea stations were directly dependent for all necessities upon commerce with Europe. Their Negro converts had no means for earning a livelihood. On so inhospitable a coast missions must result in the establishment of a supply=depot and the instruction of the Negro in farm-

---

*For the sake of avoiding confusion the following figures, illustrating the growth of Basel in Africa, are put in this footnote. In 1886 it had forty=eight men and twenty=five women there; in 1896, ninety=one men and forty=nine women; nineteen ordained native pastors, twenty=four native women=workers and one hundred and ninety=eight native male assistants of the pastors; three thousand, one hundred and fifty=five "Christians" (including one thousand Ewe church=members); and two thousand, seven hundred and ninety=four males, eleven hundred and fifty=nine females, in the schools. From 1886 to 1897 the Basel community grew from seven thousand, three hundred and ten people to fourteen thousand, nine hundred and fourteen souls.

ing and the handcrafts. Accordingly the society purchased ships and opened trading=posts (1850). From the start the commercial and industrial department has been a paying investment. To=day it furnishes seventeen *per cent.* of the annual income of about $275,000. Of the industrial results Johnston, the British proconsul of Nyasaland and Zambezia, writes: "That wholly satisfactory results may follow this inculcation of industry is seen on the west coast, where the Basel missions have created a valuable class of skilled artisans, — carpenters, clerks, cooks and telegraphers — and obviated the necessity of the introduction of any save the higher classes of European workers or superintendents". This testimony bears only on the secular side, but experience appears to prove that this enterprise in business has not brought detriment to the spiritual interests*. There would seem, then, to be warrant for the hope that in Kamerun, where the Basel Society has since 1886 cultivated the former field of the English Baptists at their request, equal success is attained. Strong church=discipline was introduced — rightly — and, though some of the former adherents withdrew, the mission has grown into the interior, especially up the Abo and Wuri Rivers. A native chief opened the way by preaching the gospel, and native Christians calling themselves "God's Men" have leagued themselves against impurity and paganism.

The Young Men's Missionary Society of Birmingham, England, entered Africa in 1877, choosing Natal as its field. The scale of work is of the most modest, but evangelism, industry and teaching are all employed for the Grikwa, and results appear to be as satisfactory as could be reasonably expected.

*Yet Schott, Inspector from 1879 to 1884, withdrew, largely because conscientiously opposed to what he considered the secular influence of the mercantile establishments.

Before Stanley completed his first descent of the Kongo, Tilly, a director of the mission=society of the English Calvinist Baptists, had invited East London Institute for Missions to join in sending missionaries upon the water=road to regions beyond. Before Stanley reached Europe, messengers of Christ were on the road (1878). This was the origin of Livingstone Mission. The intention was to form a chain of stations reaching far beyond the coast into the interior. Self=support was also aimed at; but it was found that the climate precludes this for Europeans, that agriculture is out of question and that trade causes the heathen to regard the missionaries as self=seekers. Between 1880 and 1884 the Institute directed and supported Livingstone Mission. Since then this has been a denominational mission of the northern Baptists of the United States, though the Institute aided it until 1888. During the years 1877=79 the universal ignorance of white men as to circumstances and conditions in the new worlds of tropical Africa nullified almost every effort of this pioneer mission. It was realized that the resources of the stations were meager to niggardliness, and that if ever the upper river was to be occupied the force must be far more fully equipped. But for four years more the records of Livingstone remained chiefly a story of disaster and death. By 1885 eleven of the forty=five missionaries since 1877 had died*. Not till 1883 was the heroic struggle for Stanley Pool crowned with success. Meanwhile, however, the Fyot language was reduced to writing; Bible stories and readers written in it for the mission=schools; two Kongo lads trained in England for service; and an elementary grammar of their language prepared with their assistance. In

---

*Warneck: "The mission showed courage and self=denial, but was not altogether reasonably and healthily founded." (*Outline of Prot. Missions*, 1884).

1883 Sims planted a station at Leopoldville on the upper river. This gave a key to the interior, since the water= way between Stanley Pool and Stanley Falls is navigable, with its tributaries, for thousands of miles; renders missions independent of porters; and greatly reduces expenses. When the Americans received Livingstone Mission, six stations had been founded around the cataracts; various tribes favorably influenced; twenty=five missionaries acclimatized; a few converts made; and a base secured for inland operations. This success had cost $125,000.

The establishment of Equator station extended the line of Livingstone to the enormous distance of eight hundred miles. The Baptists rightly felt that this would make it unwise for them to pass the equator for years to come. The Institute, especially when British Christians failed to contribute for an American enterprise, asked itself: What of the peoples beyond? Hence the resolve in 1888 to enter Africa again. The new field consists of the horse=shoe of the Kongo, an area nearly five times larger than England and inhabited by the Lolo. It is therefore called the Kongo=Balolo Mission. The Lolo are more civilized than the Fyot, and it was expected that this inland plateau would be healthier than the districts down=stream. But twelve of the thirty=six missionaries despatched thither by 1893 were disabled. Dr Guinness holds that this "proves the old idea about the healthfulness of the inland plateau to be without foundation". The sphere of these Lolo missions comprises the six southern tributaries of the Kongo beyond Equatorville. The support of them belongs to the Institute, but Young Men's and Young Women's Christian Associations defray the expenses of individual missionaries. So do local churches and personal friends. Literary work has been accomplished, one strong industrial station formed at which building, carpentry, engineering and farming are taught, and four churches organized with eighty members (1893).

Before Pearce and his wife founded a mission (1881) among the Kabyles of Algeria, there was not a Protestant missionary to Islam between the Atlantic and Egypt or from the Mediterranean to Sûdan and Equatoria. Glenny changed that. The North Africa Mission has established stations for a thousand miles east and west, and has sent nearly one hundred missionaries. It initiated others who work independently. It stirred other societies to despatch still other missionaries to these spheres. Though it is still the day of small things, much seed=sowing has been accomplished. Excluding the agents and colporters of the Bible Society, the North Africa Mission seems to have eighty=six foreign missionaries, thirteen stations and seven native workers. It mentions no communicants. The Gospel of John has been translated into Kabyle, Matthew into Riff and other portions into Kabyle. Large tracts in North Africa must for many years remain unevangelized, and Sahara and Sûdan are fastnesses of intolerant Islam, "yet when we [Glenny] compare our experience with a few years ago, how thankful we ought to be that the country is as open as now".

It is instructive to contrast the views of Cust and Glenny upon the results of Islam. Cust writes: "Pagan and Mahometan Africans are described for the benefit of the untraveled home=public as sunk in every kind of debauchery, disgusting sin and degradation. I have visited the northern region of Africa, and did not find it so". Glenny avers that "we find, especially in countries under Muhammadan government, the grossest oppression, the most terrible unrighteousness, the vilest immorality . . . The impression formed on my mind by traversing four hundred miles of country was to deepen my feeling of the utter hopelessness in which the followers of the Prophet are sunk; a hopelessness that enters into every department of life, religious, political, social". This view is that of the majority; but Cust's opinion as a modifying factor is not lightly to be set aside.

In 1860 Maltzahn wrote: "Islam has long been undermined. Now it appears to be on the eve of general collapse. All that formerly constituted its glory has long left it. Political power has become a laughing=stock. One thing only seems to stay the collapse — fanaticism. A remarkable instance of this decline is shown by the decrease of the population. Thus the population of Katsena, in the seventeenth century the first city of Central Sûdan, has been reduced from one hundred thousand to eight thousand".

Though all that has been accomplished toward the evangelization of the peoples of North Africa is nothing to what remains, the Kabyles are so heterodox Musulmans that no little success ought to be won among them*. Sharp (1894) confessed himself "convinced that one of the greatest works of contemporary Christianity is being fulfilled there in divers ways and through divers agencies. . . . Indubitably it is a great wrong to insinuate, as is done in so many ways, that Christian missions have failed in Africa, and that Muhammadanism is everywhere militant and triumphant. The opposite is the truth. Throughout Algeria, Kabylia and Tunisia, the Christian church and school are supplanting the mosque and mdrasa.

*The French (? Swiss ?) Methodists in 1887 inaugurated a Kabyle mission.

The Christian and Missionary Alliance, better known as Simpson's Mission, and Taylor's missions introduced a new variety of self=supporting missions. The Alliance made a beginning on the Kongo in 1884, and in 1890 had a small place near Vivi. It now claims nine stations and fifty=eight missionaries. The missionaries then lived by hunting, smoking the flesh of game and selling it to the natives. This left little if any time to learn the difficult languages, to preach or to translate.

Shiloh Mission near Bassa, Liberia, has been independently conducted since 1885, but the deeding of the property in 1889 to American Episcopalians ensures the work becoming an Episcopal mission at the death or the disablement of the present promoters. It is mainly self=supporting, and defrays its additional expenses by the sale of cassava, coffee and other products cultivated on its farm. A boarding=school is maintained; services held, chiefly for children; and work done among the neighboring heathen as circumstances permit.

Garenganze or Katanga Mission originated in 1886 with Arnot. Moffat regarded him as in spirit a martyr, and his undertaking as a noble one. Like Livingstone a Scot, Arnot is in some respects a second Livingstone. In fact, his work is one of the many results of Livingstone's last visit home. The words of Livingstone, though Arnot was very young when he heard them, awakened a strong desire to go to Africa. This never changed nor ceased, but grew into a master purpose. After preparing himself in the carpenter=shop, at the forge and in the medical school he reached Natal in 1881 and the Rutsi of the upper Zambezi exactly a year later. Here he spent nearly two years in such Christian endeavors as lay in his power, and Coillard (1885) derived advantage from them. Then he completed his transcontinental journeyings by visiting Benguela. While near Bailundu, Msidi, chief of Katanga, sent an earnest appeal that white men come to Garenganze. Arnot had been debating whether to return to Zambezia or to push out to the southwestern source-streams of the Kongo. This coincidence closed the debate. After eight and a half months of travel, for Msidi lived nine hundred and fifty statute miles in an air-line from Benguela and eight hundred and fifty from Zanzibar, Arnot arrived in February, 1886. It will be seen that the immense distance from the coasts and the peculiar inaccessibility of Katanga from the Atlantic, the Kongo, the lakes and the Zambezi involve this mission in greater difficulties of communication and consequently in larger relative expenses than any other in Africa. It is hoped that the Zambezi-Shire-Nyasa route may yet be made practicable, for this portion of the journey is done by steam-boat and the remainder of the route, although by land, is less than five hundred miles. Msidi was then independent and powerful, and though cruel from necessity and policy impresses us more favorably than any other pagan monarch in Africa. Arnot gained his esteem and respect and those of the natives to a remarkable degree, accomplished much pioneer mission-work in two years, and planted evangelization on a lasting basis. The decay of Msidi's power (1889-91) and his death on Dec. 20, 1891, brought dangers and discouragements; and the exercise of authority by the Belgians, for Katanga lies within Belgian Kongo, adds new difficulties; but the position is improving. The advantages of a comparatively healthy climate and of a naturally superior people are in favor of the missionaries. Their future depends largely on their appreciation of the just requirements of their friendly critics.

The Salvation Army is the Jesuit order of Protestantism. It enjoys the military advantages of the papal militia *plus* the personal and social reinforcements derived from the family and from marriage. It has regained the compulsion of souls, a forgotten factor in Teutonic Christianity, and has in largest possible degree availed itself of the service of woman. But its missions among Muhammadan or pagan peoples stand on substantially the same level as those of the Jesuit. The Army entered Zululand in 1888, and for the Zulu its officers became Zulus. The Salvation movement in the orient, so lauded as the sole model for missions, employs mere asceticism as its main means to master barbaric or semi=civilized men. The Salvationist must leave English dress and habits behind. Male officers evangelizing Zulu villages wear red jackets bearing the words, Salvation Army, on the breast in Zulu; but the remainder of the costume conforms as closely to native fashion as decency permits. Officers even discard English names and assume native titles. They live in Zulu huts. They beg food from door to door. So nearly are all Salvation missions self=supporting that on the average these missionaries do not cost the London headquarters more than $24 a year. They go, in fifties or sixties at a time, on the understanding that they are to receive no salary and never to return home. They are regarded as fakirs by the heathen. Half their "converts" apostatize. In December, 1887, the Army had sixty=five stations and one hundred and eighty=five officers in South Africa (including St Helena); in December 1894 it numbered only sixty=three corps and one hundred and ninety=four officers. This does not look like growth and success. Mr Rhodes, however, discerns a possibility of their work proving advantageous, and promises large tracts of land. The Army is now among the Chwana and has a corps at Bulawayo, Rhodesia. Though converts are everywhere used as missionaries, it seems as if native agency in Africa, if employed, avails the Army little. It appeals to the emotions rather than the intellect, and is a vast organization for revivals. Hence backsliding and desertion occur far more frequently than in any other religious body. Commissioner Railton "does not question that a great deal of what at first appears to be genuine is only an appearance. Many a score of true penitents turn out in a few months as bad as ever". General Booth states that "great numbers fall away". Non=Salvation missionaries complain of the proselyting tactics of the Army. In India all the native officers with whom Dr Ashmore talked had been trained in mission=schools outside the Army, or connected with mission=churches. As like lines are followed in all Army missions, it must be that in Africa also burnt districts of the worst sort remain*.

In America the college and the student have from the first been foremost in missions. Mills at Williams, Judson at Andover and other students at other colleges or seminaries awakened the American churches of this century to their interest in missions. During the seventy years between the haystack=meeting and the organization of Young Men's and Young Women's Christian Associations in the colleges the students formed and supported scores of societies for missions. Under the influence of the revival of missions between 1805 and 1810 a student published an appeal that led Scudder to India as a medical missionary (1819). His example caused James Brainerd Taylor to devote his life to

*Cf. *Captain Great Heart and . . . the Salvation Army*, in *The Missionary Review of the World*, vol. V, no. 3, March, 1892. The Army also works among the Negroes of Jamaica and the United States.

Christian service, and to found the Philadelphia Society at Princeton. This took the lead in establishing intercollegiate associations of Christian men and women. They are thus the child of missions and born to an inheritance in missions. They took up the work of the collegiate mission=societies, and became permeated with the spirit of missions. In 1886, at the first conference of students at Northfield, Massachusetts, one hundred of the two hundred and fifty collegians present devoted themselves to missions. Their act proved to be the germ of the voluntary enlistment of thousands of collegiate students throughout the world. The Student Volunteer Movement, a branch of the Young Men's Christian Association and its affiliated organizations, has already sent nearly twelve hundred missionaries into the foreign field and under the control of churches or societies. In 1888=92 Wishard visited the missions of twenty countries, including Egypt. Missionaries everywhere performed the principal part in the extension of the Association among Christian natives. The Tung=Chu' Association of Chinese students became so interested in missions that, in addition to meeting monthly to study the progress of Christianity throughout the world, they assumed the support of a student in a Natalese school who was preparing himself for missions among the Zulu. Nothing could so forcibly accentuate and illumine the brotherhood of Christendom and the growing smallness of the globe, daily dwarfing more and more into an Arthurian Table Round — that image of the mighty world —, than this locking of hands in Christian service on the part of Africa and China. Had the Association accomplished nothing else, this would have justified its existence. But in 1889 it resolved, not to send general missionaries, but to establish itself in fit foreign fields.

As the Association had already existed in Africa for many years among men of European blood, this advance, though naturally affiliated, should not be confused with the older work. This numbers twenty=four African and two Malagasi Associations, excluding Dutch Reformed Associations in Cape Colony*. The new movement organizes and trains the natives whom the missions have brought into Christianity. It is of course not meant that the church fails to do this; but only that the Association, strictly subordinating itself to the church as an auxiliary to its missions, promotes special work for young men in non=Christian lands. The British associations have a representative of this interest in Egypt; South Africa has a Student Volunteer Movement or Union; and wherever an association exists to=day missions receive systematic study†.

On April 1st, 1891, the late William Mackinnon, then president of the Imperial British East Africa Company, Peter Mackinnon, T. Fowell Buxton and others resolved to establish a religious, educational, medical and industrial mission in Ibea. They chose Dr Stewart of Lovedale, a fellow=worker with Livingstone and in every way exceptionally qualified by Nyasan pioneering, as its founder. President Mackinnon gave $10,000 from his private purse. His eleven comrades contributed $40,000. The plant thus represented a capital of $50,-000. On August 1st Stewart was collecting the nucleus of a caravan at Zanzibar; and though labor=troubles —

---

*See *Fifty Years' Work*, a review of the Associations in 1894. The Antillean Associations number eight. Africa also has six Young Women's Christian Associations.

†Mr Douglas M. Thornton, author of *Africa Waiting*, educational secretary of the British Student Volunteer Missionary Union and fraternal delegate to the Cleveland convention in February, 1898, intended to enter Al=Azhar, the fanatical Muslim university at Cairo, in September as the representative of the Church Society among its ten thousand students. All who met him bid him God=speed.

For details as to the Student=Volunteer Movement among American Negro students consult *The Student Missionary Appeal*, pp. 159=167.

for Africa has so far progressed in civilization as to "enjoy" conflicts between wealth and wages — delayed preparations, a force of two hundred and seventy=three carriers marched on September 21st. At Kibwezi, two hundred miles northwest of Mombaz, the natives, longing for protection against the Masai, their dreaded enemies, invited Stewart to remain. As they offered land for building and cultivation and proved to be perfectly friendly, he decided, after examining two other sites, to do so. His reasons for accepting their invitation show what a backwoodsman a mission=founder needs to be. Kibwezi is but ten days' journey from the coast for mail=men. In the sixteen days' travel for laden caravans this means a saving of thirty=three *per cent.* in the cost of transportation. The situation is one of beauty and rich vegetation. On clear mornings the snowy crest of Kilima=Njaro is visible fifty miles south. Its vast snow=mass influences the climate beneficially, but wherever there exist a constantly high temperature and a powerful sun, there must always be more or less likelihood of fever. This liability can be very largely lessened by good food, regularity in diet and work and the avoidance of needless exposure to the sun. For equatorial Africa the climate is remarkably healthy. If ordinary precautions be taken, it is healthier than we could expect from that latitude. Stewart sees no reason why women should not enjoy fair health at Kibwezi. Though 1891 was a year of exceptional rain, only one of six Europeans died, only three of the carriers. The station has already become useful as a sanitarium for disabled men from passing caravans. Though the day= temperature rises to ninety in the shade, the altitude, three thousand feet above sea=level, causes nights so cool that mosquitoes are unknown and one must sleep under blankets. The soil is good, easily worked, free and with any quantity of accessible lime; the supply of excellent timber almost limitless, while the lack of it would render carpentry — the most needful part of industrial work — nearly impossible; and excellent water abounds, the best between Mombaz and Uganda. On December 7th, accordingly, Stewart bought five hundred acres of arable land, forest and jungle for one hundred and sixty yards of calico and certain fathoms of brass wire.

To expect the accomplishment of much actual mission-work yet would be unreasonable. Until a language be acquired and reduced, little preaching or teaching can be directly done. Twice each Sunday, by translation from English into Swahili and often from this into Kibwezi, a few of the most elementary truths of Christianity are conveyed to the dark souls. Though there was not a single convert in June, 1892, the mission had won the confidence of the people. Perfect mutual confidence exists. Some of the natives thought that the missionaries came for reasons utterly different from those professed; but this simply shows how vast an interval separates the thought of the African from that of the European, and how alien to his experience have been the ideas of honesty, industry and kindness. In all missions the first stages of progress are invariably slow. Long patience is required for the highest results in spiritual fruit. The gospel of kindness and honest work is opening these hearts and minds to the reception of the chief message. If Sabbath-preaching, school-teaching and trade-teaching move steadily forward, no prophet is needed to foretell showers of blessing.

There is no reason why Kibwezi should not grow into more than a mere station. It lies on the main caravan route, which is also the shortest and healthiest road to Uganda. When the Mombaz and Lake Victoria railway becomes a fact, the line should pass quite close to the mission. For several years the chief effort will be concentrated on Kibwezi, but 1905 may see missionaries settled at Machako, one of the rejected sites, eight days further inland and five thousand feet above tide=water. The district was foreordained as a sanitarium and a site for a European colony. Another natural and probable extension is a northward movement among the Galla beyond Tana River. We may discern the finger of God pointing thither. From the north Krapf in 1838, the Hermannsburg Society in 1858 and the American Missionary Association in 1881 attempted to reach the Galla. Providence perhaps intends to bring this to pass from the south. In 1888 an Arab slave=dhow containing many Galla, most of them mere children, was captured off the eastern coast. In August 1890 forty=two boys and twenty=two girls were sent to Lovedale. The Free Presbyterians of Scotland have spent over $15,000 on their education, for the divinely appointed field of these waifs lies among their countrymen. If but thirty of the young men and women turn out fairly useful agents, they should be equivalent to sixty white workers. This would prove no small force with which to push into a region almost untouched by missions. Kibwezi should be both a strategic center and a source of spiritual statesmanship.

The East Africa Mission, despite its newness, rewards study of its methods and their results. It offers the best example of commercial enterprise and scientific system afforded by any African mission. It is worth while to know how so great success was attained in a single year. The open secrets are these: No time was lost in Africa in considering how to proceed. Mackinnon and the committee supplied men and means in abundance. While they made it feasible to push the general, preliminary work, Stewart devoted three months to choosing his staff and procuring his equipment. Since the mission is not evangelistic alone, but educational, industrial and medical, it required a fourfold larger and more varied outfit as well as a larger force. Its backers, though expecting to spend $20,000 the first year, expended $25,000. To quote only one item, native food and labor at Kibwezi, on account of the large number of caravans, cost four times as much as at Nyasa. But the committee with acumen and generosity held the financial cable firm, and freed the strength, time and thought of the missionaries for their true task.

New Year's Day, 1894, brought a glad new year to missions in Cape Colony. The Cape General Mission, founded in London on March 12th, 1889, amalgamated with the Southeast Africa Evangelistic Mission. The consolidated societies took the name of the South Africa General Mission, and united the fields and the function of each of the parent bodies. The new organization, strictly speaking, is a society of domestic rather than foreign missions. It operates not only among the colored populations but upon the colonists and other European residents. But the missionaries and their home=supporters are so predominantly British that the work is virtually one of the foreign missions of Britain as well as a home=mission of the Christians of Cape Colony. Since September 5th, 1889, the force has grown from six to eighty=six, two thirds of whom are women, and the annual income has risen to $25,000. Fourteen of the workers are at the Cape Town Nurses' Home, sixteen at Johannesburg, in not a few respects the most difficult of African fields. Better, however, than any augmentation of funds, expansion in spheres of missions or multiplication of workers is the increase in spirituality. The threefold aim of evangelizing the heathen, rousing the church to holier life and aiding missions already in existence seems to be receiving realization. The publications accentuate the spiritual side of mission=work. The society has missions in almost every state of South Africa. Coillard, no incompetent judge, regards "the rapid extension in so short a time [six years] as truly wonderful". Basutuland, Cape Colony, Grikwaland, Natal, Pondoland, Swaziland, Transkei, Transvaal and Zululand have been invaded. Aggressive religious activity is directed to the Muhammadan Malays of Cape Town; at sailors and soldiers, police, post=men and railroaders; city slums and country infernos; Africans and Europeans; blacks and whites; Jews, Kafirs, nominal Christians and Zulus; in short, toward all classes and conditions of Christless men between the Cape and the Zambezi. Nor is industrial and medical work neglected, for a model farm near Pretoria is mentioned, and nursing the sick and visiting the lepers are parts of the regular routine. Under the wise and magnetic leadership of Andrew Murray, author of religious works possessing spiritual unction and vital Christliness, pastor of a Dutch Reformed church in Wellington, Cape Colony and president of the mission, this Anglo=African enterprise employs about every means for saving men that the church and secularism have ever devised. The stress laid on preaching the gospel, on the presence of the Holy Spirit and on simple, scriptural Christianity arouses hope as to the future of the colonial church.

Zambezi Industrial Mission is another English endeavor. Only five years old, for the missionaries

THE REVEREND ANDREW MURRAY

did not set out before April of 1893, it must be distinguished from the Evangelical Zambezi Mission. The latter is the work of the French Presbyterians among the Rutsi of the upper Zambezi; the former, that of Britons representing no church and settling among the southern Ngoni on the Shire uplands between Lake Nyasa and Zambezi River. Two of the three men were accompanied by their wives, a fact indicative of belief in the coolness and healthiness of the climate. The mission, it is claimed, will be conducted on the most practical lines, whatever these unknown quantities may be; and each station is to support itself by means of coffee=plantations as early as the end of the third year after the date of opening. Such assertions give ground for anxiety as to the permanence of the work*.

Sûdan Pioneer Mission, though now partly controlled by the Church Society, originated in the American branch of the Christian Association. Its non=denominational history is a sad story of zeal without knowledge. In 1889 the spiritual destitution of Sûdan, where there is a population of possibly sixty millions without one Christian missionary, was presented by an English promoter of missions to American Christians and especially to the Young Men's Association in Kansas and Nebraska. In each state twenty men volunteered as Sûdanese pioneers; and in every town where a meeting was held a branch of the mission was founded. The larger colleges and cities of Kansas were afterwards visited, and some of the large towns in Arkansas, Illinois, Indiana, Minnesota and Wisconsin. Several young men from the Association at St Paul, Minnesota, and thirty Negroes from the south offered themselves. In 1890 Kingman accompanied Wilmot=Brooke and his party from

* Zambezi Industrial Mission Paper, October 1896.

England as far toward Sûdan as Liberia; and a corps of eight Americans, including two men and two women from the St Paul Association who went with the van of an "Upper Kongo Mission=Colony", sailed separately from America to Africa. The entire force went in faith without other support than that which it supposed the Scriptures to pledge. The mission is sustained by voluntary contributions, and the missionaries receive no stipulated salary. When the inevitable illnesses of tropical Africa occurred, the lack of means and medicine involved needless loss of life. Self=sacrifice may be magnificent, like the charge of the British brigade at Balaklava, but, unless it justify itself to men who are as wise as zealous, it is not war. The world wonders, yet it knows that some one blundered. The church marvels at the heroism of these Sûdanese pioneers, whom it would gladly crown as martyrs did not justice forbid; but it mourns over this fanatical man=slaughter for which someone stands morally responsible. Africa can not be conquered for Christ through such measures or methods. The survivors are attempting from regions behind Freetown, Sierra Leone, to reach West Sûdan, nominally a Muhammadan region, where, it is said, the missionaries are to adopt the costume of Islam. But it will be many years, if ever, before they can plant a station in the dark forest=tract between the Kongo and Welle Rivers. This is the *Ultima Thule* of the Sûdan mission; but the only part of the venture that looks at all hopeful is that under the ægis of the Anglican church.

The World's Gospel=Union, as this society is now called, has entered Marocco. Here also are a Central and a South Marocco Mission. The Open Plymouth Brethren and other non=denominational workers are in

Algeria. Still other small societies work in Tunis. The Bundes Conference of American Mennonites in the Dakotas, Kansas, Minnesota and a few other western states has missionaries somewhere in Africa, but no information can be obtained. The Mennonites ought, perhaps, to have been mentioned among Baptist denominations.

II

Literary Auxiliaries

Second only to the spoken preaching of the gospel stands the silent preaching of the Scriptures. The book can go where the man may not enter. Hence the hundred agencies for the publication and distribution of religious literature. The Religious Tract Society ranks first in age (1799) and foremost in activity among such auxiliaries of African missions. From it sprang the first society for universal distribution of the Scriptures. The older organization affords advantages, otherwise unattainable, to almost every missionary and society for missions throughout the world. The publications that it either fosters or renders possible speak two hundred and fifteen languages. Thirty=four of these are African, one is Malagasi. As its work is typical of that of all publication or tract societies, a description of its methods may represent those of its associates.

The professed object of this society is to publish and scatter Christian literature. It accomplishes this end through colporters, grants to societies for religious literature or for missions, and special agents. Wherever practicable, it works through scholars and translators on the field. It gives about $100,000 annually to missions. It employs its grants to stimulate liberality. It generally meets only from one to three fourths of the expense. This Pearson method obliges others to give, and sends such books as *More about Jesus* to the Kongoans in their own language. The great mission=societies acknowledge the advantage and need of Christian literature in their fields; but it is not always feasible to gain the ablest and worthiest men for it. For the society to share directly in the literary preparation of the periodicals that preach Christianity is rare; but if it withdrew aid, the bulk of this activity would cease or suffer permanent crippling. The society develops this department through gifts of money; grants of electrotypes or the sale of them at nominal prices; above all, through grants of enormous quantities of printing=paper. It sends Christianity to many through its ability to endow missionary editors and mission=publications with blank=paper! In so doing it fires no blank=cartridges, for by this instrumentality it aids in creating the extensive Christian literature of Madagascar. Among the literary gifts bestowed by this society on African missions may be specified the New Testament in Arabic, with annotations and paragraphs; *Pilgrim's Progress* (which has done more than any other book except the Bible for the evangelization of men), in Amharic, Fanti, Kafir and Malagasi; a hymn=book in Chwana; an Arabic edition of *The Silent Comforter*, published at Cairo; an Arabic series of four=page tracts, consisting of Scriptural passages on the basic truths of Christianity and intended for circulation among Muhammadans; a dictionary of the Bible, a hymn=book with the tonic *sol=fa* notation and a new edition of *Pilgrim's Progress* for the Sutu; *Line upon Line* and *Peep of Day* for the Kongo; and a catechism, a life of Luther and a volume of sermons for Madagascar.

The British Bible=Society circulates the Scriptures,

minus the apocryphal books, without comments or notes. It entered Africa in 1806 when it made a grant for British settlers at Cape Colony, and attempted to reach the Khoi=Khoin as well as the Dutch, English and French. The succeeding ninety years tell one story of constant enlargement and almost uniform success. To commemorate the abolition of slavery in the empire, the society gave one hundred thousand New Testaments to Negro freedmen who could read or were heads of families (1836). The jubilee of the society was celebrated in Africa as well as in other countries (1853). It has published the Scriptures in whole or part in sixty=eight of the languages spoken in Africa; planted auxiliaries in Cape Colony, Gambia, Lagos, Malta, Mauritius, Natal, Orange Free State, Sierra Leone, St Helena and Transvaal; and employs colporters in the Azores, Egypt, Madeira, Mauritius and North Africa, with Bible=women in the Seychelles. In 1896 its Bible=women for Egypt numbered twenty, for Mauritius and the Seychelles five, while in Africa at large it had sixty=three zenana=visitors, in Madagascar only twenty. Malta long remained the base of operations for Egypt and North Africa. Arabic, Berber, Koptic and Ethiopic versions were distributed thence; and though efforts in North Africa were circumscribed, they did not fall resultless. To=day, however, Alexandria forms the head=quarters for an Egyptian agency whose sphere includes Arabia, Egypt and Syria. Aden, Cairo, Massawah and Port Said are among its depots. In South Africa the colonial auxiliaries of the British Society numbered one hundred and fifty in 1890. In West Africa the English organization itself has depots in Angola, the Azores, Christiansborg, Lagos, Madeira and Sierra Leone.

The preparation and sowing of Christian literature

have ever held a foremost place as evangelizing agencies. The object is so to present spiritual truth as to attract notice, kindle thought and spur conscience in men not personally accessible; and to guide inquirers. Construction, not destruction, is the aim. The evangelistic publications include tracts in simple style, stating a single Scriptural truth with personal emphasis; books explaining the Bible or Christian truths; and periodicals. Publications for the use of the missionary as a pastor in distinction from his functions as an evangelist comprise general literature and text=books in theology and others of the higher branches. As the distribution of the Bible and literature plays so great a part in Protestant missions, a rôle long envied by the missioners of Rome and henceforth to be more and more followed by them, it is imperative upon the student of African missions to understand the detail, method and routine.

The agents of Bible=distribution consist of individuals, miscellaneous organizations, mission=societies and societies formed specifically to edit, distribute, translate and publish the Scriptures. Couriers or dragomen along the Mediterranean or on the shores of the Nile will gratefully show the Testament that the Christian merchant or traveler has quietly put into their hands. The Christian Association and the tract=societies often make Bible=distribution a special feature, and accomplish not a little. The mission=societies, especially in the earlier period of Bible=distribution, often hold a place more prominent than that of the Bible=societies themselves. The native evangelist, pastor and teacher are distributors perforce. These are sometimes quite the only agents, the superintendent of a Bible=society finding that he can work through them at less expense yet with larger effectiveness. But the great Bible=distributor is the Bible=society.

The leading organizations hold that their purpose is not merely to bring the Scriptures within reach of every accessible Muhammadan and pagan in Africa but to ensure proper use of them. Since men value property in proportion to its cost, to sow Bibles broadcast was to provoke contempt for Christian literature as the sacred pages were defiled and disfigured. The better to exercise a beneficial influence the societies generally sell rather than give; but their prices are so low that many sales are little more than grants. In missionary lands the day=wage of a laborer often sets the gauge for the price. The societies confine themselves to circulating the Bible either in integral portions or as a whole. They hold to independence, but their catholicity renders them an international force, a pan=denominational factor in promoting the federation of Christendom in Christian activities. They choose fields according to a previous occupancy of them by a mission=society or according to special circumstances. American mission=societies usually look to an American Bible=society, English associations to a British organization, Scotch bodies to a national society in Scotland, and so on. When a mission=society of one nationality occupies a territory that is or becomes the natural sphere of a Bible=society representing a second nationality, the society for missions generally turns toward its native land for such assistance as it may need from a society for the Scriptures. The United Presbyterian missionaries in Egypt being Americans and Egypt having virtually become a British province, the Presbyterian mission=society would not unnaturally prefer to deal with an American Bible=society.

The first foreign efforts of Bible=societies transpired

through mission-societies. The former at first simply distributed through the latter, but gradually assumed the publication of missionary versions. If a society sustaining missions in Sûdan desires a version, it arranges with a Bible-society that the former shall set a missionary or several missionaries at translation, while the latter generally takes their expenses. The version is printed in Africa, if good binderies and presses be accessible, or at home. The British Bible-Society, *e. g.*, printed its Malagasi version in Madagascar (1831, 1834 and 1861). The translation becomes the property of the society incurring the expense, and each regards the rights of others. In the case of the Turkish version, which circulates in Osmanli-speaking populations of Africa, several Bible-societies divide the expenses and privileges. As a rule each Bible-society assists all others.

Distribution is accomplished through colporters, depots and readers. Organization and system are carried to a remarkable degree of efficiency. Comity is practiced to the fullest extent that the present circumstances and provisional conditions of missions render feasible. An agent is stationed at such commanding capitals as Cairo, Cape Town, Tananarivo or Zanzibar. He informs himself upon the needs of his assigned sphere of interest; arranges affairs; clasps hands with Christian workers; watches for openings; and stands ready to seize opportunities for increasing the circulation of the Scriptures and universalizing knowledge of them. He establishes Bible-depots in all considerable towns, and these sale-rooms and storage-stations serve as centers of influence. Since Bible-work inevitably merges into missions, one of the great Bible-societies has surrendered the position that mere distribution comprises all its functions. Multitudes of people unable or unwilling to read, especially in Egypt where eye=diseases prevail, were aroused by Bible=readers to interest in the Scriptures and to a wish to own them. Mission=societies found it impracticable to provide such workers. Hence the acceptance of professional Bible=readers as legitimate agents of Bible=societies; hence their preaching and teaching as virtual lay=missionaries. But the colporter makes the mainstay of the Bible=society.

There is scarcely a country where the hamlet as well as the town remains outside the allotted field of an individual colporter. He is generally a plain man, chosen for his ability in Christian diplomacy and his capacity to rub shoulders with men. He must be harmless as the dove, yet wiser than the serpent. He gains access to places none other can enter. More than the preacher or the teacher he reaches bitter opponents of Christianity. His attempt to put the Bible into the hands of every person who will read or study it compels him, though not expected to preach or teach and though discouraged from discussing doctrines or rites, to explain the Book. Some of his arguments with infidels, Jews and Muslims would not discredit theological professors. His activity is necessarily restricted to lands enjoying settled government or tolerating Christianity; but even here he meets with experiences as thrilling as any in the history of missions. North and South Africa have so far afforded the chief scope for his enterprise; but as social conditions improve in tropical Africa, he will move from north and south upon the equator. He is accomplishing an achievement unsurpassed in importance by that of any other African missionary.

The Trinitarian Bible=Society works chiefly in papal lands or among Christians using the Roman or Vulgate version. Thus the French, Portuguese and Spanish possessions in Africa fall within its domain. It has prepared Portuguese and Spanish versions from the original texts, and printed Salkinson's Hebrew translation of the New Testament. Of this it circulated one hundred thousand copies within three years among Jews throughout the world, including those of Africa. So far as feasible the society avoids colportage, distributing mainly through the agents of other organizations.

The American Bible=Society opened its African campaign in 1836. Few agencies reach such a multitude of languages and races as does its Levantine post. It works both through colporters or special agents and through Bible=societies or mission=societies. It has prepared special versions of the whole Bible in Arabic and Turkish; printed the entire Scriptures in Zulu; and published parts of them in Benga, Dikele, Grebo and Pongwe. It also circulates a Hebrew=Spanish version in the Levant, whose inhabitants include the Jews of Egypt. Alexandria is a subagency, Assiut its most southern outpost. The subordinates devote themselves not only to Bible=work but to education and missions. In this they follow Isaac G. Bliss, their grand exemplar, chief=agent for the society in the Levant from 1857 to 1889. It was his desire to push Bible=work into Africa's very heart.

The National Bible=Society of Scotland distributes and publishes for Africa among other fields. It has published an Efik version of the whole Bible for Old Calabar and the New Testament in Nyanja. Though it does not chiefly act through special agents, its colporters have been mainly instrumental in the formation of not a few churches. Its preferred method is that of co-operation with mission=societies.

The Association for Free Distribution of the Scriptures puts forth special effort for Muhammadans. It claims that to give to them instead of selling is an absolute necessity. It also includes the Zulu in its operations. The annual income is about $2,000; but as no agent receives pay, a large circulation has been attained.

The Pure Literature Society, though giving libraries to the British in Egypt as well as to colonists elsewhere, makes no accessible statement that would justify classing it among missionaries to African natives, whether black or white.

III

Medical Mission=Societies

In medical as in other missions among Africans the British lead; yet it was Peter Parker, the American medical missionary who "opened China at the point of a lancet", that also inspired Abercrombie of Edinburgh to found the first British society for medical missions; and America remains the foremost nation of the world in this cause. Its history is its justification. The Edinburgh and other societies educate and encourage Christian physicians to settle among Christless peoples, and aid as many professional agents at mission=stations as their funds permit. Livingstone was a member of the Edinburgh Society; and as a memorial to this medical missionary it erected (1877) a training=school for missionary=physicians. It thus gave no small impulse to medical missions. It has spent thousands upon thousands of dollars in grants to medical missions or missionaries for instruments, medicines and similar objects. It now has several hundreds of representatives in foreign fields,

The Medical Missionary Association of England promotes medical missions in Africa, if not directly, yet indirectly through an auxiliary of children. This supports cots in Egyptian hospitals, and arouses interest among English boys and girls.

The International Medical Missionary Society sends medical missionaries independently, as mission=societies find themselves unable to engage more than half of its graduates. It thus aids and reinforces boards of missions, the more so that the men and women representing it are, it is claimed, to stand on an undenominational basis and to support themselves. Its three years' course costs but six hundred or seven hundred and fifty dollars, and it grants considerable financial assistance to needy students. Between 1892 and 1895 it received four hundred applications.

The American Medical Missionary Society at Chicago had representatives in Africa, but seems for several years to have been in a state of suspended animation. Its standard was so high, its procedure so sound, that it is desirable that it revive. The International Medical Missionary and Benevolent Association, superintended by Dr Kellogg of Battle Creek, Michigan, conducts The American Medical Missionary College, a separately incorporated institution in Chicago which prepares only those who have consecrated their lives to medical missions and are recommended by a properly constituted mission= board. The Association has for years had a sanitarium at Cape Town, and is putting two self=supporting mis= sionary=physicians into the district between Sierra Leone and the Niger sources. At least this is the information furnished. The Chicago Medical Mission, it is interesting to note in this connection, is Africa's gift to Darkest Chicago. Messrs Francis and Henry Wessels of Cape

Town founded it in 1893 by a gift of $40,000 to the Association. This has Seventh=Day Baptist affiliations.

IV

Organizations Less Directly Promotive of Missions

The Bible and Prayer Union, formed in Scotland in 1880 and with a membership of about five thousand, supports Bible=women and missionaries in Belgian Kongo, Marocco and Old Calabar. It observes the tenth of each month as a time of united prayer for missions.

The International Missionary Union is an organization of returned missionaries whose international and pandenominational affiliations render their annual meeting almost an ecumenical council. The society promotes coöperation and sympathy on the foreign field, and discusses in America the principles and problems of missions. As African missionaries are among the members, the results of the sessions make for the advantage of African missions.

The Sunday=school as a missionary differs from ordinary Sunday=schools. It becomes the parent of a church. It is often the only available evangelist. By approaching children first it reaches parents who would otherwise remain beyond Christian influence. The Foreign Sunday=School Association enumerates Africa as one of its fields, but supplies no information as to any African activity.

The Bible Lands Missions' Aid Society, formerly the Turkish Missions' Aid Society, originated in 1854 under the Earl of Shaftesbury's auspices. C. G. Young, a clergyman in northern England, had been greatly impressed by the American Congregational missionaries of

Constantinople. He urged British Christians of every church to unite in aiding evangelical missions in all Bible=lands. Accordingly the new and undenominational organization based itself on the resolution that opportunity, success and circumstance "called for special effort to furnish pecuniary aid for the wider extension of missionary operations" and on the rule that its "object is not to originate a new mission but to aid . . . especially that carried on by the Americans". This large aim has been largely realized. Missionaries in Egypt, no less than in other Bible=lands, have borne grateful witness to the importance and value of this British interdenominational auxiliary as a factor in the evangelization of the orient. During the civil war (1861=65) in the United States, which so seriously crippled the financial resources of their mission=societies, the assistance afforded was especially helpful and was so acknowledged. The annual income now averages about $7,500, but the ethical worth of this instance of Anglo=American fellowship and Protestant union is not to be measured in money.

The Bible=Reading Association, an English society, specifies British Guiana (Demerara), South Africa and the West Indies among its spheres, but does not state whether it works among the black populations.

The Inter=Seminary Missionary Alliance consisted mainly of American students of theology, and did substantially the work of the International Missionary Union and the Christian Associations.

General councils on missions, though not permanent organizations but temporary reunions, can not be left out of account as forces in the evangelization of Africa. The conferences at New York on May 4th, 1854 — perhaps the first ever held — ; at London in October of the same year; at Liverpool in 1860; at Mildmay Hall, London, in 1878; at London again in 1888; and at Chicago in 1893 brought reinforcements to African as to other missions, and proved themselves to be sources of power. This is especially true of the Centenary conference and the Columbian congresses. African missionary societies ought to hold ecumenical conferences every five years.

The Christian Endeavor movement, though the youngest, is perhaps destined to become the greatest child of the church. It boasts fifty=two thousand societies throughout the world and a membership of three million young men and young women*. If divinity= schools and universities are to furnish the future leaders and shepherds of the church, these churches within the church may enlist the lay workers and drill the recruits through whom the mighty army of the church militant can march to the grandest conquests for the cross that Christendom has yet known. The interest of these societies in missions was born with the first society (1881); and the initial letters, Y. P. S. C. E., of their full name have been interpreted as meaning: your privilege — spreading Christianity everywhere. Secretary Baer states in reply to an inquiry: "We employ no missionaries ourselves, but work through existing societies". But during 1893= 94 they gave over $350,000 to missions through the boards of their respective churches, and inaugurated a movement for missionary extension by means of lectures from authorities and specialists as to missions. It was expected in 1895 that they would contribute $1,000,000. In Africa itself the societies number thirty=nine, in Madagascar ninety=three. Boers and Huguenots, Kongoans, Liberians and Zulu constitute but a few of the African Endeavorers whose enlistment amazes and whose

*On March 10, 1898 the societies numbered 52,717, the members 3,163,020.

endeavors delight. The Antilles and their black no less than their white inhabitants know the Young People's Society of Christian Endeavor, which is here represented in sixty=nine organizations; and it flourishes in the African Methodist Episcopal Church of America. The adoption of the movement by representatives of the prominent boards of missions has been enthusiastically characterized as second to no event of missions since Mills of Williams College, Massachusetts, held the haystack missionary meeting.

CHAPTER 16

THE NEW MISSIONARY: PHYSICIAN, FARMER, ARTIZAN

Laborare est orare.
A medical missionary is a missionary and a half; or, rather, a double missionary. Robert Moffat

(I) MEDICAL MISSIONS. THE MISSIONARY=PHYSICIAN IN BAPTIST, CONGREGATIONAL, EPISCOPAL, LUTHERAN, PRESBYTERIAN, ROMAN AND UNDENOMINATIONAL MISSION=SOCIETIES. SCENES AT A MEDICAL MISSION. A FEW CONSEQUENCES. GROUNDS FOR MEDICAL MISSIONS. OPPORTUNITIES AND SUCCESSES OF THE MISSION=PHYSICIAN (II) INDUSTRIAL MISSIONS. NEED AND SCOPE OF INDUSTRIAL MISSIONS. SOME EMPLOYERS OF THE INDUSTRIAL MISSIONARY. EX UNO DISCE OMNES. ORIGIN AND GROWTH OF INDUSTRIAL LOVEDALE. ITS OBJECTS AND OUTREACH. METHODS AND SCOPE. ORGANIZATION. DEFECTS AND DRAWBACKS. EDUCATED VS. UNEDUCATED KAFIRS. A DIFFERENCE BETWEEN THEM. EFFECTS OF LOVEDALE ON INDIVIDUALS. RANK OF LOVEDALE IN COLONIAL EDUCATION. IS LOVEDALE'S WORK GENUINE AND PERMANENT? EXPERIMENTAL SCIENCE AND THE WORKING HYPOTHESIS. WHAT RESULTS FOR CHRISTIANITY AND CIVILIZATION HAS LOVEDALE ACCOMPLISHED?

I

Medical Missions

In 1834 the American Board sent Parker, a Massachusetts Congregationalist, to China as a medical missionary; and shortly after the London Society followed suit by dispatching Hobson to Macao. Congregationalism in America and Britain was the first Protestant communion if not the first Christian church to make medicine a feature in missions. To this extent the physician is one of the new missionaries of the last sixty years. For Africa 1840 may, perhaps, be indicated as an approximate date for the modern beginning of industrial and medical missions. But medical missions originated in the practice of Jesus the great Physician; the twelve and the seventy were commissioned no less to heal than to preach; and Luke the beloved physician was also a missionary. At bottom, therefore, the medical missionary is an old rather than a new missionary, and the modernness of medical missions consists in the applications of an ancient art and science, especially of its highest and most recent developments, to evangelization. Yet it would seem as if the church did not realize the potency of this tree of life whose leaves are for the healing of the nations, for in 1893 the unevangelized world had only three hundred and fifty=nine fully qualified medical missionaries or about one physician for every three million patients. The American Congregationalists, Methodists and Presbyterians; the Anglicans; the British Congregationalists; the Canadian Presbyterians and the Established, Free and United Presbyterians of Scotland appear to be the Protestant churches devoting earnest attention to medical missions. America led with one hundred and seventy=three missionary physicians; Britain followed with one hundred and sixty=nine more; Canada had seven; and Germany claimed three. China received one hundred and twenty=six, India seventy=six and Africa forty=six medical missionaries*. In attempting to obtain information as to the medical missions of Africa, letters to seventy=five of the societies working there received but thirty=four replies, and only one of these came from

* *The Medical Missionary Record*, New York, 1893. But Nassau reported sixty for Africa in 1893.

THE NEW MISSIONARY 553

a papal source. Twelve of the societies answering had neither medical mission nor medical worker. Of the remaining twenty-two organizations one was distinctively a society for medical missions. In most of the societies, however, and among their pioneers are and have been men who added medical training to their theological education.

As special societies for educating or sending medical missionaries have been already considered, we need to note their work in the African field as agents of the ordinary organizations for missions. These are best handled in the alphabetical arrangement.

The American Baptist Missionary Union has two or three medical missionaries, among them Sims of Leopoldville, who has not only proved exceedingly useful in medical work but has distinguished himself by his labors in several of the languages of the middle Kongo. At Banza-Manteke after a thousand conversions the missionary was immediately thronged with patients. For weeks from three to four hundred sick received medical aid. It was not medicine but conversion that brought these patients. As the natives gave up fetiches and belief in the Satanic origin of disease, they came for medical assistance in great numbers, thousands of cases being treated by a single practitioner.

The American Board in Zululand long considered medical training needless on account of the accessibility of British and Dutch physicians.

The Baptist Missionary Society of England states that though very few of its missionaries are fully qualified medical men, nearly all have some knowledge of medicine and minor surgery.

The Basel Society had two medical missionaries on the Gold Coast, both almost exclusively occupied with medical mission-work and with giving medical aid to sick missionaries.

The Berlin Society had not sent out any medical men as such, but its missionaries receive a brief course in medicine.

The Church Missionary Society finds East Africa a field where doctors are specially needed but the difficulty of supplying them the greatest. Nine medical missionaries had been sent there since 1875, but only three were at work.

East London Institute sends no medical missionaries, but all its agents have to do medical work, and several have received special education for that purpose.

The Episcopal Society has had eight medical missionaries in Liberia from 1836 to 1886. Doctor Savage became widely known as a scientist of recognized ability. He was a corresponding member of several scientific societies, and gave critical attention to the fauna and flora of the Grain Coast.

The Finland Society requires its missionaries to take a medical course before it sends them. They are instructed in the treatment of ordinary diseases and the use of the less dangerous remedies.

The Hermannsburg Society's medical missions are in their incipiency, but a brief medical course is always given to its probationers. In its African field no special necessity for medical work appears. [?]

The London Society sustains two medical missionaries. In Madagascar this society opened medical missions as early as 1862. In 1873 came the Royal Medical College with forty-one students, a hospital for eighty patients, three dispensaries, fourteen native Christian women in training as nurses and ten thousand treatments annually. The Tananarivo hospital renewed

DR FELKIN
Medical Missionary, Uganda, 1879

operations in 1881, and the year 1886 saw the birth of a medical missionary academy. At Analekely a hospital was opened in 1864, Doctor Davidson hoping that he could educate young Malagasi to practice medicine as well as to preach the gospel.

The Norse Society has since 1876 had two doctors in Madagascar almost continuously, a hospital with a dispensary at the capital and a small dispensary at every station. The number of cases at the Antananarivo hospital has reached fifteen thousand a year. The effect of the operations for eye-diseases is marvelous. An aged heathen loaded with protecting charms came to the oculist. After the operation, when he perceived that he again had sight, he exclaimed: "Henceforth the doctor shall be my God". The physician advised him to go to church. When he came thence, he cried: "Now I know my God is in heaven". The society has also a home for lepers with nearly two hundred inmates living in model houses inside the same inclosure. These and a small hospital are under the care of two ladies with medical training. In 1893 a medical man was to be sent there, and a large hospital built. At the same place the society has built a bath over the remarkable hot springs with medicinal mineral waters. In connection with this bath is a sanitarium where the missionaries of all societies may recuperate.

The North Africa Mission has medical missionaries and stations at Tetuan, Tangier, Fez and Casablanca.

The Presbyterians of America have contributed six medical missionaries for Corisco since 1857, though this did not become a mission of the mission-board of the northern church before 1870. One of these medical men is Doctor Nassau of Gabun who has been in Africa since 1861, is still in service and ranks as the oldest living medical missionary in Africa.

The Presbyterian Free Church of French Switzerland has an African medical missionary who studied at the universities of Berne, Edinburgh and Geneva. This church intends to make his work permanent by founding dispensary and hospital service. All its missionaries after completing their theological studies are given six months or more of a partial course in medicine and surgery and in hospital work at the schools of Edinburgh, Glasgow or London.

The Presbyterian Free Church of Scotland has been prominent for its use of medical missionaries, having Doctors Cross, Elmslie, Henry, Laws and Revie in Nyasaland, Dalzell in Natal and Stewart in Cape Colony. It has encouraged the rapid extension of medical missions. Doctors Laws and Stewart have long been famous for efficiency and for great influence over the natives through their medical services, Stewart standing second only to Nassau in length of service. Livingstonia Mission sustains competent physicians at Bandawe, Blantyre and Mweniwanda, administering medical treatment to twenty-five thousand patients annually. At Livlezi valley, above the entrance to Nyasa lake, there are three physicians in attendance, with overwhelming numbers of cases. On the north shore Cross in 1886 founded a medical mission and, during a war (ending 1889) waged by slave-stealers on the missionaries and the mercantile company, performed heroic and valuable services. To the wounded of both parties he rendered medical aid, meanwhile caring for the sick and needy among the Africans.

The Roman Church refused any reply to requests for information as to its medical missions. During the sixteenth and seventeeth centuries papal missionaries largely used medicine as an aid to mission-work, and put the world largely in their debt for quinine, which in fever-smitten lands has accomplished so much toward enabling Europeans to live and toil; ipecac; and other remedies. Perhaps we should not so soon have acquired these new drugs, had it not been for the Dominican, Franciscan or Jesuit. Protestant medical missionaries also frequently add fresh medicines to our pharmacopœia.

Taylor Mission sent Doctors Harrison, Mary Myers, Reed, Smith and Summers. Doctor Summers did good service at Malanji, Angola, over three hundred miles inland, during 1885-86. The natives bestowed a wonderful reception on him. When he proposed to establish a station further inland, they as if their lives depended on his remaining begged him to stay and offered large pay. As he insisted on removal, the grateful people overwhelmed him with gifts. Through these he was enabled to load thirty-six carriers and to reach Lualuaburg in the Shalanji country on the further side of the Kongo and six hundred miles inland. His society could not give him a dollar. After several years of service there, founding a mission and ministering to the sick, he died in 1888.

The United Brethren in Christ have never sent missionaries exclusively medical, but a number of their men have combined knowledge of medicine with preparation for ministerial work.

Universities' Mission maintains medical men in Zanzibar, Sambara and Nyasaland.

Whately Hospital, Cairo, annually relieves more than seven thousand sick and suffering poor, exclusive of twenty-two thousand and ninety-seven patients in 1894 from outside districts and villages. The Church Missionary Society has granted money for the site of a new dispensary and hospital and for houses for the doctor and the nurses, but needs $12,500 for the hospital and dispensary themselves.

Zanzibar possesses Tophan Hospital, and medical missions exist in Madeira; but it is uncertain whether the former adds evangelization to philanthropy, and data as to the latter are unattainable. Special medical missions for African Jews are carried on at London and at Rabat and Safed in Marocco.

The information vouchsafed by the societies, though leaving much to be desired, enables us to define the medical mission. It is the systematic combination of the healing art with the preaching of the gospel. Having seen how the society trains the missionary=physician, we have to see how he works and to judge whether the history of medical missions be their justification. The daily routine at a station of the Universities' Mission substantially represents all African medical missions.

Every morning a motley group gathers round the steps of the Zanzibar dispensary, waiting for the 9 o'clock bell that summons the Mkunazini boys to school and the nurses to their patients. The look of suffering on some and the terrible wounds of others remove wonder at the constant appeals for help or drugs. First may come a finely=dressed, grand=looking Arab suffering from dyspepsia or consulting for a wife not allowed to come out in day=time. The doctor must either visit her that afternoon or have her come at night. Next may be a group of chattering women with the most miserable looking babies on earth. Meanwhile the native helper works at the chronic leg=ulcers of all degrees of badness. Then some one will come straight from prison with wounds from the irons on ankle and wrist that have eaten almost to the bone; or another with back frightfully lacerated by his master; still others with every form of ophthalmia. In the room adjoining the dispensary are poor people so ill as to be obliged to remain constantly under a doctor's eye. To nurse them in their dark homes with their scant ventilation and without conveniences of any kind would be impracticable. If there be need to wash them, basin=water, soap and towel must be taken. In the cottages around, mostly occupied by married Christians, there are generally two or three ill and wanting medicine and nursing. The Arabs and native traders and well=to=do natives pay for their medicines. Even the poorest like to feel that they are paying their share, and though none is ever sent away for lack of money, these try to bring their gift. Consequently the dispensary pays its way; not, of course, for drugs from Europe but for what is bought in Zanzibar, consisting of rice for the very poor, eggs and milk for the very ill.

Sometimes it might seem as if little were done to teach or to Christianize, yet it is something to know that under the cross is help for suffering bodies and that through this knowledge men may be won to the divine Physician of souls. Near or far each and all turn with a pressing cry for help to the mission's drug=fund. Perhaps it is at Magila that the natives have most highly appreciated the medical mission. Vaccination demonstrates the indispensability of this. Only those who have lived where vaccination is unknown can realize how horrible a scourge is smallpox. From seeing that the vaccinated boys in the mission=schools escape it the Magila folk awoke suddenly to the importance of vaccination. One morning a whole village requested it immediately. Morning after morning people kept coming in seventies or eighties until the whole neighborhood had been vaccinated. Not an instant too soon! An epidemic devastated the district. Hundreds perished. Villages were unpeopled. Yet the Magila region was untouched, or suffered so slightly that none died. After such lessons it is not surprising that the natives have exalted ideas of medical skill, and believe implicitly in those who thus minister. A blind man inquired if his eyes could be cured by next day, as he was starting on a journey. He was deeply disappointed on learning that to make the absolutely blind see is beyond human power.

"All genuine missionary work", said Mackay of Uganda, "must in the highest sense be a healing work". The Christ's earthly ministry of healing affords divine sanction for medical missions, and would be their justification were justification needed. The story of the murdered millions is the justification of medical missions. The union of medical and spiritual work in a single missionary is confirmed by the ideas of the heathen. Among the natives one and the same man is both doctor and priest. Hence African pagans who otherwise would not bring themselves under spiritual influences seek relief from Christians for physical ills. The double cross of cure for body and spirit is the conquering cross. Faith=healing and mind=cure and "Christian science" must, however, be withstood, as Negro superstition would claim to have found endorsement in the mystery surrounding this "miraculous" treatment of disease. The heathen are better impressed by a tangible drug or by the use of visible means; and their self=respect should be developed by requiring them to pay for the medicines.

Medical missions are self=supporting and unsectarian.

They pioneer for denominational missions and supplement their efforts. They reach far in material, mental, moral, social and spiritual effects. They sap caste and weaken anti=foreign feeling. They secure protection and provision. Finally, they seem less liable to failure than are intellectual agencies. Chatelain has been quoted as claiming that at Malanji a trader offered him a home in his house and $1,200 a year to look after his family, assuring the missionary that others would increase the sum to $5,000 if he would remain. Churches have been quickly formed where dispensaries have been located, and missionaries' lives have been spared by mobs because they were recognized as fellow=workers of mission=doctors. Medical missions open a new and vast field for Christian laymen. The opportunity of unordained or medical missionaries is as open for women as for men, and more so in countries where only women may prescribe for women. For these reasons and in order to avoid detriment to the regular mission=societies every mission should have a medical agency as a supplement to its spiritual work. This agency may act through the hospital, the dispensary or private practice. The dispensary reaches more patients but not the greatest suffering, and its opening for evangelistic work is ephemeral. The physician must be perfectly the master of his profession, in order to gain ready entrance for Christianity; to train native medical students as missionary physicians; to preserve or restore the health of all around him; and, least important of considerations, to lessen expenses, though self=support is of course the ultimate goal for all missions. Each society should require every missionary to have a measure of medical knowledge.

II

Industrial Missions

Another new missionary in Africa, who after all is not so new, is the artizan or the farmer. Commissioner Johnston of British Central Africa asserts that the inculcation of industry has not always formed part of missionary teaching; but Doctor Taylor, formerly the Methodist missionary=bishop for Africa, claims that for more than fifty years the majority of the greatest mission=societies have made industrial education a feature of their African missions; and the historic fact is that the "Moravian" and the Roman missionaries have always emphasized industry, the mastery of useful arts and self=support as factors in Christianizing Africans and as constituent elements in native Christianity. Some of the ancient missioners, notably those in Abyssinia and among the more southerly settlements in North Africa, and many of the medieval monks were industrial missionaries.

The absence of the arts and industries from Africa in comparison with China or India and their inadequacy to the requirements of Christian civilization compel insistence on the dignity of labor. These reasons render it necessary to reinforce the native industries in order to add another to the instrumentalities for securing self= supporting and self=propagating churches among all Africans. Industrial missions, therefore, are not an end in themselves but merely a means toward a far higher end. If this truth were more firmly held or more frequently remembered, there would be less of ill=judged laudation of mere industry as a missionary and more appreciation of the spiritual work as the first and final force in the civilization of the Negro. It is wise to teach Africans the use and value of the buzz=saw; but experience has proved it still wiser to teach them that the secret of America's greatness and Britain's prosperity springs from the open Bible.

The American Board, the Basel Society, the Catholic missions, the Lutherans in Liberia, Lovedale Institution, the former Taylor Mission and the Wesleyans may be cited as instances among others of organizations that inculcate industry in their African adherents. The Congregational missionaries have taught agricultural and mechanical arts to the Zulu. Their introduction of new modes of agriculture created an immediate demand for American plows. The papal missioners are famous and praiseworthy for educating the African as artizan, farmer, manual laborer or tradesman. The American Lutherans have accomplished good secular as well as spiritual work at Muhlenberg. The British Wesleyans in South Africa, though not incorporating any system of industries into their missions, received appropriations from Grey, when governor of Cape Colony, for supplementing three of their schools with industrial departments, and encourage the natives to learn and use the industries of civilized life. About 1825 Shaw induced Khama of Kafraria to buy a Dutch wagon and to break sixteen of his bullocks to the yoke. Hundreds of natives imitated the example set by the chief, and for seventy years Christian Kafirs have been the principal carriers of inland commerce in Austral Africa. The Natalese government makes appropriations for industrial schools connected with the missions in that colony. The Basel missions of Guinea supply boat=builders, boiler=makers, coopers, masons in brick and stone, riveters and still other workers. The educator in the business=house or work=shop enjoys the same standing as the ministerial missionary. Boys in the school are not taught mechanical industries, and those in the shop do not receive mental training. Both omissions are defects. School and shop together are needed for educating the *whole* man.

Taylor's missions made industry as well as self=support an essential. The industrial education that the ex=bishop claimed to give to the natives consists, not of the higher mechanics of civilized people, but of the agricultural and simpler mechanical arts that will enable Negro converts to support themselves and to work as missionaries. Doctor Taylor's chief aim was the development and utilization of indigenous resources, for he holds that in Africa literary education and religious teaching alone are not sufficient. Book=taught pupils, he asserts, abandon their native industries. "I know", he adds, "a mission [Methodist?] on the west coast which has for more than half a century been worked on this plan. Besides ordinary schools they had large seminaries, and planted nearly a dozen missions among wild heathen. Much good was done. A few of the pupils became ministers; the mass of them, not knowing how to dig, very dependent non=producers. The society in charge became discouraged and cut appropriations, down, down, down. Nearly all the seminaries were abandoned, nearly all the stations among the raw heathen closed. The English=speaking work is growing, but the purely missionary work among native tribes has demonstrated [?] the ineffective narrowness of the missionaries' plan of work".

Doctor Taylor thought that he had found the panacea for the defects and failures of what he termed the orthodox method. Instead of gathering one or two hundred children, bordering on their teens and ripe in paganism, and educating them in the common school, he established at each station a nursery of ten or twenty boys and girls, five or six years old, adopted them from heathen families before the children had been made heathens themselves, and put them under the management of a missionary matron. This feature may, perhaps, have been unique, though it seems to be merely a Protestant variation on the Roman practice of buying children, but it would require the test of twenty=five years' experience to prove its actual value*. The children as soon as able to handle a small hoe were to till the mission=farm three hours daily, study as many more and devote several hours to evangelistic or other religious work.

If the most of the societies, large or small, engaged in African missions do not yet push industrial missions as they ought to do, the shortcoming can not be ascribed to lack of leadership. Basel appears to have been in this century the Protestant pioneer on this African path (1850), but circumstances as well as inherent worth have raised Lovedale to a peculiarly influential, prominent and representative position. Since it is a fair type, almost an ideal type, of the industrial mission, it repays special study.

Lovedale lies about six hundred and fifty miles north=east of Cape Town, and draws its name from Love, an eminent member of the Glasgow Missionary Society, one of its Congregational founders (1821) and the first secretary of the London Society. The Kafrarian mission was attempted in 1824, but not till after three changes was the present site occupied. Presently the question of means and place for educating the missionaries' children and training native teachers called for

*For results compare chapters ten and fifteen.

consideration. The sanction of the home=directors and a grant having been obtained, Govan began work with eleven natives and nine Europeans (1841).
There was much to discourage. With the Kafir, education was a new thing. The natives believed themselves conferring a favor in allowing their young barbarians to attend school, and also believed that the parents should be paid!

Slowly and through many difficulties the institution made way. In 1855 Governor Grey visited it. He acquiesced cordially in the desire to fit the natives to teach, but suggested the addition of industrial departments, pledging the government to meet this expense. Hence industrial education at Lovedale originated with the layman and man of the world. In 1857 the additions were made in the shape of work=shops, but for years the apprentices were few, grants being allowed only for fifteen. For twenty years no allowance except for a year or two was made for trade=teachers. The risks, of so little value was the help of the state, had to be undertaken entirely by individual missionaries. Even the idea of learning trades was entirely new. It was long before one person could be induced to become a printer, Kafir experience not showing how a man could live and be useful by arranging bits of lead in a row. Development has been comparatively recent. During the first years all efforts were of a restricted kind. The wonder is that Govan was able to effect so much; but he built solidly and his results were excellent.

The considerable expansion in industrial work and teaching dates no further back than 1874. The highest point was reached in 1876, over four hundred and ninety receiving instruction. Twenty years later, owing to the diminution of grants and to the natives being long unable to pay fees, the pupils numbered but three hundred and sixty=seven. The revenue in bulk does not come from the colony. Governmental support has varied from a third to a fifth of the annual expenditure. The remaining two thirds or four fifths are drawn from native fees, from the Free Presbyterians and the missionary public in Britain and, when these pay, from the farm and industrial departments. None of the thirty buildings except those erected under Grey's auspices received any governmental grant. The amount given in his time was less than $15,000, one tenth of the amount expended. The sums given by the Scotch Free Church and generous friends, leaving the annual working=expenses out of account, have been over $150,000. The most satisfactory means for showing the amount of government aid consists in averaging the totals for every five years since 1860, as specifying the sum for a single year would produce fallacious impressions. These grants for school=allowances, industrial teaching, the board of apprentices, assistant=teachers, the elementary school and the girls' school from 1860 to 1864 averaged $1,200 a year, but from 1880 to 1887 over $12,000 *per annum*. Though the farm produced one thousand bags of maize and five hundred of barley and wheat in 1886, the proceeds did not pay the expense of production. The list of native payments since regular fees were introduced affords the best evidence of Kafir anxiety to secure education and of Kafir willingness to pay for it. From 1870 to 1886 these amounted to $85,000, an average of $5,000 a year.

Lovedale purposes to educate young men of intellectual and spiritual qualifications to become preachers; to train young men and women as teachers for native mission=schools; to educate native Africans in useful arts and industries; and to bestow general education on those who have not yet definitely determined their course in life. Its ultimate goal is growth into a native university, but at present the objects aimed at comprise godliness, cleanliness, industry and discipline. The first is the foundation of permanent change of habit, little being accomplished without it that is likely to abide. The absence of the second is a characteristic of barbarian life. Industry is also a new power requiring cultivation, — and its growth is slow. The educational means of course include books, *i. e.*, school=education, but more than books. Education and industry are carried on in separate buildings for men and women, the chief educational building costing $60,000. Each department has its specific aim, but the grand purpose of both is to Christianize. Conversion of individuals is the desire and object of the entire work. To Christianize successfully, however, it has proved of great service to civilize at the same time. Theological training, normal training, general education, field=work, carpentry, wagon= making, black=smithing, printing, book=binding, telegraphy, sewing and laundry=work have long been taught. The critic who thinks these too many contradicts the man who asserts that nothing practical is attempted.

The principles of administration comprise freedom from denominational connections; instruction in the Bible and applied Christianity as the first work of the day for every class; self=support, especially in the industrial departments; and suppression of sectarianism. Though Free Presbyterians sustain Lovedale, all denominations have at one time or another been represented. All colors and nearly every tribe in South Africa are found at Lovedale, a few coming even from the Shire and Zambezi Rivers. No influence is exerted toward

Class in Agriculture—Industrial Department
Class in Printing—Industrial Department

LOVEDALE INSTITUTION, SOUTH AFRICA (F.C.S.)

having students leave their denomination or join the Free Church. Students of theology training as workers for other bodies are not weakened in denominational loyalty. Self=support is an ideal, and in 1890 only twenty=five *per cent.* of the annual expenditure was drawn from Scotland. Lovedale, though not endowed, owns a farm of twenty=eight hundred acres, four hundred of which are under cultivation, and is attaining self=support. Nothing, however, except Doctor Stewart's ability as a practical farmer and his rare talent for administration kept it moving during his headship.

The educational department comprises three courses, each three years long, consisting respectively of elementary, literary or theological study. In the theological course there is a drift toward dropping Greek and Latin as unessential in the equipment of native pastors. Second in importance comes the training of native teachers for elementary schools. Teachers holding certificates from the educational department stand higher than others and secure good salaries. In the industrial department the native 'prentices, if satisfactory after six months' trial, are indentured for six years. In the evening they are given a part of the general education. They receive board and lodging and from two to five dollars a month. A small part of their wages is retained monthly in trust for them and repaid at the end of the apprenticeship. None is allowed to be idle, those not apprentices or not busy with other work engaging in manual labor about the fields and gardens. Many whites avail themselves of the advantages of education at Lovedale, and mingle freely with the Negroes. The number of students averages about seven hundred a year, nearly all of them boarders or residents, and spontaneous evangelistic and intellectual activity prevails. The teachers number two ordained missionaries, one of these being a physician; a Congregational minister at the head of the theological department; six foreign masters in the educational department; and six superintendents in the industrial division. They have trained over sixteen ordained native pastors; forty=nine interpreters and clerks; four hundred and twelve teachers; five hundred and eighty=five artizans; and hundreds of whom they afterwards received no information. The Institution has its own church, but there is a Kafir church with a native pastor.

The quality of native work is not high, except in a few who have enjoyed long training, *though not longer than that usually required for making a European a good artizan or clerk.* Close supervision and constant direction are necessary. If these and considerable time be given, fair work is produced. If the whole process be left to natives, the general result is absence of taste, roughness and want of exactness or thoroughness in measurements. People emerging from barbarism, to many of whom drawing a simple straight line is a difficulty and parallel lines or a rectangle a work of art, can not be expected to turn out remarkably efficient and intelligent mechanics after only five years' training.

Do the natives use their education? The Lovedale register of native students, as significant and valuable a publication as African missions have produced, answers the query. Here appear over four hundred teachers, male and female. Many receive good allowances. Many have advanced to better positions, others supplying their places. The variety of occupations accounts for the small number in each. Passing over natives in clerical, intellectual or religious occupations, notice the results of industrial or technical education. Not every

Class in Carpentry—Industrial Department
Class in Wagon-making—Industrial Department

LOVEDALE INSTITUTION, SOUTH AFRICA (F.C.S.)

one taught a trade follows it persistently after leaving and works at nothing else, but a reasonable number do. Many causes affect continuance at trades. For years before 1887 black=smiths and wagon=makers were hardly able to find employment. Printers are always in demand, but the number taught is so small as to be hardly noticeable when scattered through South Africa. When trade is depressed, the white man, because the better artizan, gains the preference. It is often discovered after trial, though sometimes too late, that applicants for a trade make poor craftsmen. In time these drop out, and take to such callings as that of day=laborer at much smaller wages. Ordinarily those who continue at trades easily earn from $5 to $7.25 a week. Of itself this is sufficient to keep them from sinking into day= labor at thirty=five cents a day. The frequent statement that "industrial grants are simply money wasted on the Kafir, who never takes to trade but prefers to lead an idle life" is erroneous in its application to the majority. It is the outcome of embittered prejudice or of ignorance too inactive to inform itself. It pretends that all who have for three years been subject to the discipline of school and for five years afterward to that of daily toil are as likely as the raw native in red clay and a blanket to lead a barbarian life the rest of their days. The majority, even when not following and wholly occupying themselves with handicrafts, are more industrious and progressive than those receiving no training. Their slight taste of civilized life has taught them that barbarism as well as civilization possesses discomforts and that the *ne plus ultra* of comfort in dress does not consist of one blanket and a smearing of grease and red clay.

For certain tasks the raw Kafir is superior to the educated native. The man in whom has been waked no desire for another and better-paid occupation will attend more carefully to herding cattle and sheep than one who has received education. His barbaric thought is of cattle and sheep, their markings and ways. If he make the master's interests his, he will notice more quickly when any stray or are sick. He uses a dozen words for kine with daplings of skin that would not strike a white man, our faculties being less perceptive in such matters. For farm-laborers and herders not much instruction is needed. But serious argument as to educating Africans does not stop with such points. The raw native is *not* better than one whose faculties have been awakened and sharpened by manual work and school instruction. Among the native population is growing up a small but steadily increasing class possessing acquirements of which the fathers did not dream. A number enjoy an amount of mechanical skill which in former times only one or two in a tribe had. In almost every tribe there are now workmen capable of instructing their fellows. The educated class through having received such training takes to higher grades of craftsmanship. On the average the work is neither very high nor very satisfactory, for if the mind be confused or feeble or its method defective, such must be the product at every stage and in its completed form. But graduates and pupils are improving. These classes are of greater economic value in what they consume and produce than are the untaught. The greater their wants, the larger their purchasing power. This means that they must work more and are a less danger than if left in ignorance and barbarism. Cattle-lifting and joining in rebellions have not been traceable to Christian and educated natives as a class.

Over two thousand have received industrial or school

training. Part of these have enjoyed both. One thousand more may be mentioned here, but not taken into account in this enumeration, which also excludes religious influences and results from the present reckoning. At least eighty *per cent.* of the two thousand have led industrious and useful lives. Many hold positions of responsibility, and receive salaries or wages far beyond what they could earn if untaught, the remuneration of some varying from $400 to $500 a year. They have been raised above herders with $2.50 a month and a half=bag of maize. But for their education and the previous labors of missionaries they would have remained unable to distinguish the top of a printed page from its bottom, unable to use even that complicated tool, the spade, as any one may satisfy himself if he send a raw native to dig his garden. They have been dragged from an abyss of ignorance and lack of manual skill. Yet the beneficial effects do not stop with individuals. A very large proportion of those now receiving instruction are the sons and daughters of Christian Negroes whom Lovedale taught a generation ago. Heathen parents desiring education for their children are comparatively few.

The educational bureau of Cape Colony publishes statistics comparing Lovedale with seven hundred other institutions and schools. The comparison shows that in the three grades forming the foundation of practical and useful knowledge Lovedale stands first. No greater mistake could be entertained than to believe that Lovedale wastes time and public money in giving to a few exotic specimens an education unfitted to native positions in after life. It is by attention, not to higher and special subjects, but to the fundamental elements that Lovedale won its rank. Even to friends, for they hear objections and unfair criticisms that do not reach the faculty, the latter constantly find themselves obliged to state that the Lovedale studies run chiefly along primary lines and mainly devote themselves to fundamental objects. In the secondary and the higher grades Lovedale occupies only the second place. The examinations for elementary teachers' certificates independently evince the same fact. When *all* grades of merit or success are grouped together, Lovedale stands first; but in "honors" and "competency", second; and in "honors" alone, merely third. These are great achievements; in academic and collegiate studies it is no small thing to rank even third among seven hundred schools; and though Lovedale has shared the beneficial changes introduced into colonial education between 1866 and 1887 by Dale, the superintendent of schools, the success of the representatives of Lovedale has sprung from conscientious and thorough work by the teachers.

Travelers have created a myth about Lovedale pupils returning in considerable numbers to heathenism and again donning the red blanket. This going back to the former life, this reversion to type, its last state worse than its first, is supposed to be the opprobrium of missions and the standing proof of their work wanting genuineness and solidity. Books of travel, whose authors have picked up a few current and untested opinions and transferred them to their journals, constantly refer to this error. In Huebner's *Through the British Empire* occurs the following instance: "It is no rare thing to see pupils who have scarcely left the excellent Protestant institution at Lovedale relapse into savagery; from want of practice forget all they have been taught; and scoff at missionaries". A work of fiction has also been based on the idea that in many the change produced by the acceptance of Christianity is but skin=deep, lasting only till the older and stronger instincts of barbarism overcome it. Both these beliefs are mistakes. They are due to the supposition, first, that all back=sliders have been professed Christians; and, second, that the numbers reverting to heathenism are much greater than investigation proves them to be. Not every native who for a time wears clothes or, as a pleasant variation in spending his days, comes to church, becomes actually a convert or even pretends to be a member of the congregation to which he adhered. It is true that many natives of Christian connections, including a few of the genuine Negro Christians, fall again into some heathen ways or pagan sins; but relapse into one or other of these habits and vices is one thing, relapse into open or utter paganism another affair. The frequent criticism that this occurs is shown upon examination to be as ill=grounded as common. Returns to barbarism and heathendom on the part of Lovedale graduates are extremely rare. Among sixteen hundred young men the number of actual and permanent relapses in thirty years and more appeared on most careful inquiry to be fifteen, less than one *per cent.* of the whole!

Not a little advice has been bestowed on missionaries, urging them to civilize the barbarian before attempting to Christianize him. The well=meaning profferers of such suggestions will appreciate the following incident. Bishop Colenso, an Anglican churchman of ability and knowledge, believed it necessary to civilize men before they could be converted. In order to demonstrate the truth of his scientific hypothesis by the experimental method, he obtained a dozen Zulu boys, pledged himself to their families that no effort should be put forth toward biasing them as to religious matters, and had them indentured to him for a number of years. He ministered to their needs and had them properly taught. They made decided progress. On the last day he told the youths the terms of the engagement under which they had come, reminded them of his fidelity, and appealed to them to receive the instruction which he considered of far greater importance than all they had yet acquired. Next morning every man had gone, back to native costume, back to native life. Their only gratitude was to leave behind the European clothes with which they had been furnished. Colenso went the third day to American Congregational missionaries, put $250 at their disposal, and said: "You are right. I was wrong".

Lovedale has never made this mistake. Govan, Stewart and the other wise men working with them have agreed with Plutarch that religion contains and holds society together and is the foundation, stay and prop of all. They believe with Carlyle that "no nation that did not feel that there is a great, unknown, omnipotent, all=wise, all=virtuous being superintending all men and interests — ever came to much, nor any man, who forgot that". They have seen that among the reasons for the slow progress of the Negro must be reckoned the practical absence of religious convictions with power over conduct, and that this involves lack of high moral forces. Among Africans natural religion is seldom sufficient to make for righteousness and to mold character. The mental vacuity and aimless, indefinite life characterizing barbarism are corollaries of this serious want. Heredity, too, has to do with the slowness of the African's advance. Those whom the influences of thousands of years are retarding can not progress at the rate of other and more favored races. Human nature is too steadfast to allow the African simply on our recommendation to fall at

DR STEWART OF LOVEDALE
Si monumentum requiris, circumspice

once into European ways and to adopt the white man's Christianity and civilization. The record of Lovedale in black and white shows that Christian endeavors to benefit African barbarians and pagans are more resultful than they have been often acknowledged to be. Doctor Colenso's experience demonstrates the Bible to be the missionary's chief text=book; the awakening of the strongest influence for future guidance through planting Scriptural beliefs to be his primary object; and spiritual effects his most important result. What Lovedale has by such means achieved for the native hand and heart and head and spirit in the regions between the Cape and Lake Tanganika is too vast for computation. Anthony Trollope and Sir Bartle Frere testified that "nothing would do more to prevent future Kafir wars than a multiplication of such institutions". Superintendent Dale, judging Lovedale with twenty or more years' knowledge of it, regarded it as undoubtedly one of the noblest and most successful missionary agencies. In 1890 Governors Grey and Loch, the former for New Zealand, the latter for Cape Colony, expressed their views of Lovedale. Grey wrote: "My heart is filled with gratitude to the missionaries who worked out so great and noble a success. I earnestly pray that heaven may still prosper the labors of such true friends of mankind. The success that has crowned your labors will secure great advantages to the Christian cause in this part of the world". Loch wrote: "The results of industrial education have by the blessing of God transformed Kafir tribes then war=like into industrious, progressive, peaceful citizens". Governor Grey was wiser than he knew. "How far that little candle throws his beam!" The influence of Lovedale radiates through Africa and to America and Australia. When Govan determined that Europeans and

Negroes must fellowship each other, he struck a first blow in the struggle to decide whether blacks the world around shall rank as men or sink to serfage. To say nothing of Blythswood and other industrial institutions in South Africa that owe their origin to Lovedale; to say nothing of the immeasurable impulse given to the industrial work of every church promoting missions there — from Lovedale sprang the more immediate inspiration for the industrial missions of the Anglicans and Scotch Presbyterians at Lake Nyasa. "Through these alone," according to H. H. Johnston, a witness whom we have already subpœnaed, "is growing up such civilization as exists in Nyasaland".

CHAPTER 17
1547 = 1898

OLD FRIENDS AND MODERN METHODS: WOMAN'S WORK FOR AFRICAN WOMEN

Wisdom hath sent forth her maidens.
Proverbs ix: 3
The women that publish the tidings are a great host.
Psalm lxviii: 11

THE BIBLE, CHRISTIANITY AND WOMAN. MODERN NEEDS AND METHODS. CHRISTIAN, MUHAMMADAN AND PAGAN WOMEN. WOMAN UNDER ISLAM. WOMEN UNDER PAGANISM. THE CHRISTIAN NEGRESS. WOMAN IN THE CHURCH. THE KAISERSWERTH DEACONESS. METHODS AND ORGANIZATION. KAISERSWERTH IN AFRICA. ANGLICAN SISTERHOODS. ONE ANGLICAN WOMAN=MISSIONARY. ANOTHER FEMININE TRIUMPH. SOME ANGLICAN FEMALE MISSIONARIES. "BISHOP" MARY WHATELY. BAPTIST WOMEN AND THE AFRICAN. FREEDMEN'S WORK OF AMERICAN BAPTIST WOMEN. BEFORE AND AFTER: AN INSTANCE. OTHER RESULTS. CONGREGATIONAL WOMEN: A PROPHECY. A SCOTCH HEROINE. FIRST YEARS OF MARRIED LIFE. THE ROUTINE OF THE MISSIONARY'S WIFE. "THEY ALSO SERVE WHO ONLY STAND AND WAIT". REUNION AND PUBLIC RECOGNITION. A SECOND PARTING. TILL DEATH US DO PART. WELL DONE, GOOD AND FAITHFUL SERVANT: ENTER INTO THE JOY OF THY LORD. CONGREGATIONAL WOMEN FROM AMERICA IN ZULULAND. LUTHERAN WOMEN. METHODIST WOMEN. "MORAVIAN", "QUAKER" AND UNDENOMINATIONAL WOMEN. SOCIETY FOR PROMOTION OF FEMALE EDUCATION. MISS HOLLIDAY. WOMAN IN METHODIST, NORTH AFRICA, SALVATIONIST AND UNITED BRETHREN MISSIONS. PRESBYTERIAN WOMEN. THE ROMAN SPOUSE OF CHRIST. WOMAN'S WORK THE NEW CRUSADE: "GOD WILLS IT, GOD WILLS IT!"

God in His primal revelation of the divine purpose for the redemption of man declared that He would put enmity between sin and woman. It should bruise the heel of her child, but he should bruise its head. God's creation of woman as the meet help for man had furnished the divine sanction for her sharing in the world's work; His placing hatred between evil and her originated her opposition to wickedness and her participation in missions when the fulness of time made these a part of human life; and the religiousness of woman as compared to man and her superior susceptibility to spiritual impressions and influences render her more loyal to God. It was not the father of Cain but the mother that said: *I have gained a man with Yahweh,* thus recognizing her child, however erroneously, as a fulfillment of God's pledge for man's redemption; and it was Eve again who regarded Seth as the appointed one substituted by God.

As it was in this divinely constituted marriage, home and family, so it has been at every crisis in spiritual history, at every development and turning-point in the kingdom of God on earth. With Abraham Sara entered Africa. Woman has shown herself more prompt than man in her response to divine leadings and providential unfoldings. Miriam and Deborah, Hannah and Esther under the old dispensation, despite the oriental status of woman in the Hebrew theocracy; Mary, Elizabeth and Anna in the twilight between the old and the new; Priscilla, who with Aquila taught the way of God more perfectly to Apollos the eloquent Alexandrine; the elect lady to whom John the Divine wrote his second epistle; Dorcas, Eunice, Lois, Lydia, Persis, Phebe and the prophet-daughters of Philip in the new dispensation, — these and the host of noble though nameless women reveal God's purpose as to woman's place and power in working out the progress and salvation of the world.

In the ancient church Monica the North African won

Augustine for Christianity. In medieval Christianity British women formed the first female missionaries; Clara, the spiritual sister of Francis of Assisi, had her Little Clares to match his Lesser Brethren; and the nuns and sisterhoods accomplished little less for Christian missions than did the brotherhoods, monks and orders. In modern times the spiritual daughters of Vincent Paul, with other bodies of missionary women, have prolonged the Roman tradition of Christian womanhood consecrated to service for the Christ in heathen lands; and Protestant wives, sisters and other female kin have from the first accompanied Protestant missionaries.

Pious women were among the first Lutheran, "Moravian" and Methodist missions, devout nuns amid papal missions since 1520 to Africa and to American Negroes. Mrs Marshman, wife of Carey's colleague, proved herself the truest of meet helps for the missionary; and the first ship to bear American missionaries to the pagan world carried Ann Judson and Harriet Newell. It was a woman, Harriet Beecher Stowe, that dealt the deadliest blow to American slavery; a black woman, Sojourner Truth, who revived the dying faith and courage of Douglass by the awful and solemn question: "Frederic, is God dead?"

But though woman had accomplished much for Christian missions through eighteen centuries, — more than men dream of — and did still more during the first half of the nineteenth century, its third quarter had nearly expired (in America if not in Europe) before this old friend began *en masse* to adopt modern methods. American women had as early as 1800 formed feminine mission= societies, and in 1834 Abeel, the Dutch Reformed missionary of the American Board, had persuaded British women of every Protestant church to found the interdenominational Society for Female Education; but as a class these societies were ephemeral, inadequate, lacking in knowledge and social power, local and wasteful; and it required the bitter cry of heathen women to reach Christian women's tenderness, to pierce and seize their hearts and to rouse them to concentrated, systematic, united action. The Christian womanhood of America and Europe saw that, under God, only it can save the woman of the orient. The freedman of the southern United States, the Negro and other races of Africa can not be raised or rescued unless the mothers, sisters and wives are Christianized and elevated. This the man=missionary can not do; this the woman must do.

Several classes of African women call for consideration. These consist of the American Negress, the Muslim woman of Africa and the pagan African. Probably the female Muhammadan is the most unfortunate of the three, for Negro Africa in not a few districts and in not a few respects is a land of woman's rights and America, n spite of the wrongs it inflicts on the Negro, gives Negro women their largest opportunity. What does Islam say and do for woman?

The idea that woman could or should be man's companion and counsellor never occurred to Muhammad. Sensuality lay at the root of the matter. Islam misunderstood the relation of the sexes. Its degradation of woman is one of its fatal weaknesses, concubinage its black stain. In no country where Islam prevails is woman not in a degraded position; and her degradation has degraded every after generation until, in the judgment of Lane=Poole, "it seems almost impossible to reach a lower level of vice". The Quran's most hopeful word for women is this: "Whoso doth good works and is a believer, whether male or female, shall be admitted to paradise"; but woman's good works consist in obedience to the husband. The disobedient wife can not enter paradise. Again, "men shall have pre=eminence over women . . . God preserveth them [women] by committing them to the care and protection of men". The Quran sanctions the beating and scourging of wives; allows four wives to every Muslim and as many concubines as he can support, promising to the faithful seventy=two houris in paradise; and permits the husband to divorce or kill the wife without reason or warning. Under Islam woman is a chattel and slave, and the orthodox view of womanhood is unutterable. The monument that the dead hand of Muhammadanism raises to woman is the magnificent mausoleum of the Taj Mahal. The Hindi Muslim pictures woman as the tablet to be written on, man as the stylus to grave whatever character fate wills. Since the position of woman measures the rank and value of a civilization, her place in Islam furnishes another criterion as to the effect of this faith on forty million Africans.

While we must guard against making hasty generalizations from insufficient data as to the standing of the pagan Negress, since social customs vary greatly among the many tribes, it is obvious that she must suffer from the disadvantages involved in barbarism. Illness affords a special instance of her suffering. Sickness is through the greater part of the non=Christian world regarded as a form of demoniacal possession or at least as the work of demons. The sick are objects of fear and loathing, their presence a pollution. If a cure be sought, drums and gongs are beaten, fires lighted as centers for diabolical dances and frenzied chants, exorcisms and incantations employed, the stomach of the patient clubbed to expel the demon and untellable tortures inflicted. The witch-doctor not only inflicts infinite wrongs on the innocent but horrible barbarities on the ill, and those to which women are subjected can not be uttered. Though there are efficacious remedies in the hands of native doctors, though their methods are not always intentionally barbarous, much of the barbarity resulting from crass ignorance and superstition, native midwifery abounds in practices that in thousands of cases cause permanent injury and in many produce fatal effects.

Slavery left the American Negress, despite some glorious and noble exceptions, only less animal than the American Negro. Virtue and knowledge were rendered unattainable for the black woman. The effects of inherited ignorance and immorality through eight generations of bondage can not be eliminated in thirty-three years nor even in a century; and in spite of the amazing advance made since 1861 by the Negro of the United States, learning and purity do not characterize the masses of our four million Negro women. So long as the one-room cabin forms the habitual and representative "home" of the Negro family, or so long as certain white men regard the Negress as having no rights against them, so long will the character and intelligence of Negro womanhood as a whole leave much to be desired.

First in importance, because an order of the church, stands the Rhenish Westphalia organization commonly called the Kaiserswerth deaconesses. These are no imitation of conventual life, of nuns, of sisterhoods, but an evangelical revival of the apostolic institution of deaconesses.

The word itself means helper, ministrant or servitor; and the apostles, especially Paul, emphatically recognized woman's fitness. Paul refers to women laboring in the churches. Help these women, he said. He commended Deaconess Phebe of the church of Cenchrea, directing the Roman congregation to assist her in every respect and to receive her as a saint deserved to be treated. Probably Persis, Tryphena and Tryphosa were also deaconesses, for the apostolic church utilized woman to a large degree and its quickspreading missions owed much to her ability and zeal. Chrysostom actually went so far as to maintain that Junias, to whom Paul sent greeting from Rome, was a woman, an apostle and a noted apostle. The centuries between Jerusalem and Nicea bear witness to the use of woman's winsomely aggressive power. The feminine diaconate was and is especially needed in countries where oriental seclusion of women prevails, but with the development of the hierarchy and its jealousy of lay influence woman lost her rightful place as a recognized force in church=work. In the eastern church deaconesses continued into the middle ages, and it is uncertain when they became extinct (1100?). The British — not English — church had female deacons as early as 400. In the Latin communion they did not become finally extinct before the tenth century. Among the Unity of Brethren and the Waldenses women from the first occupied the deaconship. Luther recommended the revival of the institution, saying: "The readiness to feel compassion is more natural to women than men; they have a gift for comforting and soothing sorrow. . . . But we dare not begin till God make better Christians". The first general synod of the Rhenish and Dutch Presbyterians reestablished the order (1568), the church at Wesel enjoying its services from 1575 to 1610. The Mennonites, a Protestant body originating about 1525, had deaconesses — were they derived from the Waldensians? — and possibly the

English Puritans and Separatists at Amsterdam (1593) borrowed the order from Dutch Mennonites. It is, however, more likely that Congregationalism revived the feminine diaconate independently. In Amsterdam a widow of sixty served as deaconess for many years and, Bradford tells us, "honored her place and was an ornament to the congregation. . . . She did frequently visit the sick and weak, especially women, and as there was need called out maids and young women to watch and do them other helps as their necessity did require; if they were poor she would gather relief for them from those that were able, or acquaint the deacons; and she was obeyed as a mother in Israel and an officer in Christ". But the deaconess did not influence the Christian church at large, though Gooch and Southey advocated organizations of Protestant women similar to the Beguines, until after the modern movement of missions was well under way.

Fliedner, a Luthero=Presbyterian clergyman, while in Holland saw the work of the Mennonite deaconess and while in England was impressed by the labors of Elizabeth Fry the Friend. These women convinced him of the value of such helpers, and in 1836 he founded the deaconess=society of Rhenish Westphalia. Amalia Sieveking of Hamburg had in 1831 attempted to draw German women into active participation in church=ministry, but none came. Now, however, the time was ripe. Though the papal populace of Kaiserswerth opposed Fliedner, he chose a Catholic as the first hospital=physician, and the first patient was a Catholic. Fliedner's wives successively advanced his life=work, perhaps even making it possible, and became the first deaconess=mothers. The order grew so steadily that in 1857 it entered Alexandria, and now has hospitals at Cairo (1884),

Kamerun and Port Said and nurses at Madeira. To=day the order numbers at least seventy houses and eighty= five hundred sisters in the four quarters of the globe. Moreover, it has caused the formation of deaconesses in several branches of the Protestant communion, and has graduated such nurses as Florence Nightingale. Mrs Fry in 1839 founded an order of deaconesses in England; Marie Gederschoeld another in Sweden; Vermail, a Huguenot minister and philanthropist, a third in Paris; and still others followed the precedent in Denmark and Switzerland. The Anglican and Episcopal sisterhoods, though younger than the Kaiserswerth order, are to some extent independent in origin and practice.

The Kaiserswerth deaconess differs from the Roman sister in retaining life=long freedom and full control of property. She takes no vows, promising only that she "will endeavor to do her duty in the fear of God according to His holy teachings"; and at death her property reverts to her family or to whomsoever she wills it. The candidate must be between eighteen and forty years old, and the probationer, if she stand steadfast to the end of her course of hard work, enjoys three years of training. Every woman begins with house=work and receives instruction in simple book=keeping, reading aloud and letter=writing. Then the future nurse goes to the medical and surgical wards, the future teacher to the normal school. A cheerful, modest, sanitary costume is worn as a uniform, and proves helpful as a protection against the rabble. The Kaiserswerth mother=house consecrates the deaconess; chooses and changes her station; clothes and feeds her; provides money for working=expenses; and supplies a home for the retired sister. She may at any time withdraw without disgrace, being, however, requested to signify her intention every five years; and service in epidemics or in foreign lands is not obligatory. Probationers frequently fall off, but few "ordained" deaconesses. Proselyting as a duty of the diaconate is discountenanced, Kaiserswerth sisters never obtruding their religion; but very many nurses and teachers are serving the church, and others in Africa, China and the East Indies are active as missionaries.

The Alexandria hospital has about twelve deaconesses, who on the average nurse about a hundred patients daily. Out of eleven hundred and sixty-three persons in 1892 the natives of Africa numbered six hundred and forty-one; the Muslims, five hundred and forty-eight. There were also an infant-school and a polyclinic with thirty thousand treatments annually. When the majority of the Europeans, in consequence of the Muhammadans massacring Christians (1882), fled from Alexandria, the Kaiserswerth hospital was as quiet as a peaceful haven and the sisters stood to their post. Among the Germans who took refuge with them was Schweinfurth the explorer. He wrote: "When I entered one of those crypts in which the Christians of the first century secured themselves from their persecutors, ancient Alexandria made itself real before my eyes. Loving and prudent sister N., constant in evil as in good days, set all an example of true Christian character as the religion of the first century in its blinding purity brings it before us. There was no wailing, no anxious disquiet; all were shining exemplars of manly resoluteness and tranquillity". This testimony justifies Kaiserswerth in teaching its women that when brought in touch with persons antagonistic or indifferent to Christianity, their best resource for spreading the gospel-life of love does not rest in words. Mrs Kinnicut rightly recognizes "The

One Source whence such a life day by day draws its own strength and sweetness".*

The Anglican bishop of London in 1850 emphatically commended the Kaiserswerth deaconess, and the Episcopal communions have since formed many sisterhoods. But the Mercy sisterhood has so strong a leaning toward the Roman idea of the nun that Howson in his work entitled *Deaconesses* passes them by, and expresses himself in favor not of a strictly organized, conventual system but of a free, flexible, parochial diaconate. Among Anglican sisterhoods active in Africa are those of All Saints, the Resurrection and St Raphael. The first works at Cape Town; the second at Grahamston; and deaconesses in Kafraria. Cape Town fifty years ago was a terrible place. Its evils as a garrison and harbor city were aggravated by the extraordinary medley of races and religions. There were heathen Kafir and Khoi=Khoin, Muhammadan Malays and nominally Christian Britons and Boers. Unsuccessful colonists frequently abandoned their children, whose only orphanage was the prison. Mary Arthur at last befriended them, and maintained those whom she adopted by giving music=lessons. Dean Douglas, in order to meet the many needs, formed a sisterhood in England, and this after arriving in Africa worked in many parochial missions till the death of Bishop Gray. It became so difficult then to keep the ranks of the order filled that it affiliated with All Saints Sisterhood in London. This now supplies laborers for the multifarious needs of Cape Town. Such are homes

---

*See *The Kaiserswerth Deaconesses*, an article by the present writer, in *The Standard* during 1897, for fuller details. The Kaiserswertherin in her toilsome activities finds the St John Sister most helpful. This is a lay "unordained" graduate of Kaiserswerth, a woman of any age and social rank, who has studied six months in its hospital. The Knights of St John pay her tuition and traveling expenses. She and her fellow Sisters in effect form a reserve.

for penitents, hospital work, orphanages and schools for the Kafir, the gentry and the poorer English.

Crowther's experience as a school=boy (1823) affords perhaps the earliest and surely a most valuable illustration of the success of woman as a missionary teacher. The men had so much to do that it was impossible to attend to the schools. The youngsters liberated from the slave=ships at Sierra Leone were sent to be educated, but the town=born boys bolted like rabbits before a dog. The teacher went after them with a whip. This only sent them further. What was to be done? A woman said: "I will fetch them. . . . Just get everything ready". She had brought lesson=sheets and pictures. She used no effort, no threat, no whip. She simply requested the boys to come. When Crowther and his school=mates appeared, she said: "Shall I teach you to sing?" They answered: "Yes, ma'am, we'll learn". So she began:

> This is the way we wash our hands
> Every night and morning.

All the boys began merrily enough to dance and sing. The children who used to run away heard the fun. They came; peeped; listened. Next morning they joined. Then all were daily dancing, and clapping and washing hands and faces. Before the week was out every runaway child was in school.

This woman made the compulsory school=system of Sierra Leone succeed.

The freedmen hesitated, however, to educate their daughters, "because girls could not be clerks or hawkers and could not be used in the office". But as soon as a woman opened a separate school for girls, they thronged to be taught. Though the Church Missionary Society supported some of them, a system of fees for education was enforced. When the people saw the superiority of the girls' education and how useful it made them, they grew willing to pay. The school is now a large institution, The Annie Walsh Memorial School, and was recently superintended by three ladies of Lagos.

When Crowther went to Bonny (1866), the chief and he agreed that the natives should pay for their children's education. About ten dollars a year were to be paid for every pupil, whether boy or girl. After a twelvemonth, when payment fell due, the chiefs objected to wasting money on the education of girls. "Our boys", they said, "can trade for us, write for us and do everything; but the girls can be of no use. We won't pay for them". "Very well", Crowther replied, having generously agreed previously to pay half the preliminary expenses of the mission; "it must be half=pay. If you will pay for the boys, I will pay for the girls". They very gladly said yes, and paid nearly five hundred dollars in cash for their fifty boys at school. Then Crowther's own son said to his wife: "Take care of the girls, and mind them well; they're your share". She taught them to sew, to knit, to bake beautiful bread. At an examination afterwards the fathers were present, and were entertained at dinner. "This bread", said Oko Jumbo as he ate, "is very fine and good; who made it?" "Your daughter Susan", was the reply. The chief was delighted; and all the black aristocrats thenceforth sent their children to school to learn household business. From that time native scruples as to the utility of investing money in the education of girls, because they unlike boys could not afterwards earn their living, disappeared in that mission. The entire population followed the example of the head=men.

This pioneering is but a part of what Anglican missions in West Africa have received from women as educators and evangelists. In Crowther's judgment female missionaries are most helpful to this day.

Another of these Anglican missionary=women was Mrs Gray, wife of the great bishop. She was "the truest help=meet that ever lived; one of those rare people who pointed out the up=hill way, if the right one, and encouraged her husband to take it instead of the easier path round. Her love never made her shrink from suffering for him; she would have encouraged him to go to the stake". She was the architect of most of the churches in Cape Colony. She accompanied the bishop on his visitations and acted as his secretary. She gave her life for the work, since these missionary journeys brought on her fatal illness.

With the Grays went Katharine Barter, who, though she succeeded only in isolated instances in working among the natives, gave curious pictures of the Kafirs and of herself among them in *Adventures of a Plain Woman* and in *Home=Life in Africa*.

Mrs Colenso and her daughter as well as the bishop of Natal had a deep affection for the Zulu. Such was the wife's devotion that, in the impossibility of trusting any one else to do so, she every night washed the feet of the native lads living and studying in the missionaries' home. Catholics are fond of asserting that Protestantism has no heroes and martyrs and of holding up Claver and his cleansing of Negroes as an instance of self=sacrifice; but every one acquainted with the stenchful person of the Zulu will appreciate the noisomeness of the office to which this delicate, refined woman subjected herself for the sake of Christ.

When the diocese of Natal was formed (1853), Mrs Woodrow volunteered for Durban. While learning Zulu she so spoke that "the hearers went away with tears in their hearts". She and her second husband settled at Umlazi River, and gathered Zulu boys and girls (bestowed by the parents), older converts and orphans. Their attempts to Christianize and civilize the girls were sorely hindered by the native custom of buying wives with cows. The Robertsons afterward moved back into the country behind, and formed the considerable settlement of Kwamagwaza or Place=of=Preaching. Mrs Robertson, though in the feeblest of health, was the soul of the mission, educating, influencing and winning souls. Of wild girls and women she made gentle, helpful Christians. She died in 1863, protecting a tiny Zulu boy to her last breath.

When Mackenzie, the youngest son of one of Walter Scott's friends, was chosen archdeacon of Natal (1855), Mrs Dundas his oldest sister wrote that his undertaking would raise the tone of the whole family; Anne, another older sister, went with him; and Alice, the younger sister, soon joined them. Their first Natalese home was built of mud, though graced with straight walls and a veranda, and boasted two apartments. One served as chapel, the other as living=room. Bee=hive Zulu huts did duty as sleeping=chambers. The sisters took the deepest interest in the mission, and on week=days kept school with their brother for the colonists' children (who would ride up on ox=back) and for the natives old or young. Anne, a woman of the frailest health, at first chiefly taught white boys and girls, but Alice "the black sister" devoted herself to the Zulu. The Mackenzies were often visited by the Robertsons, who also brought their adopted natives. When Charles and Anne returned to England on church affairs, Alice helped the Colensos in their Zulu home=school. When the brother was chosen bishop of Unversities' Mission, the sisters were ready to cast in their lot with him. When Mackenzie went ahead, Anne and Mrs Burrup, the young wife of one of the missionary=bishop's clergy, followed. Themselves almost dead with fever, they found the brother and the husband already slain by the same fell disease. Anne returned home, broken down and constantly suffering but unconquerable. In her sick=room she became a mother of missions. Until her death (1877) she surrendered herself to founding a Zulu bishopric that, in memory of her brother, should perpetuate his earlier work. This was the origin of Mackenzie Memorial Mission. This is the primary object of *The Net Cast into Many Waters*. Both the magazine and the mission commemorate a wonderful woman as well as a marvelous missionary. The concentrated enthusiasm and the charming sweetness of Anne Mackenzie promoted missions to no little degree, and she laid down a work far advanced and well organized.

Mary Whately, the gifted daughter of Dublin's grand archbishop, inherited extraordinary activity, energy and intelligence; received the finest training, mental, moral and religious, from her parents; and early surrendered herself to Christly service. Her Egyptian mission, beginning in 1860 and ending only with her death in 1889, originated the present activity of the Church Missionary Society in Cairo*. Labor in the ragged schools of Dublin, with teaching and visiting the Irish town's numerous Italian inhabitants, assisted her in training, however unknowingly, for work among Egyptian boys and girls, Greeks, Jews, Kopts, Muslims and Syrians. Escorted by a Syriac Protestant matron, she went out into the highways and byways of her Cairene home, persuaded

*Chapter 6.

MARY LOUISA WHATELY

mothers to let their girls come to learn to read and sew, and gathered nine into school. *Ragged Life in Egypt* forms the literary outcome of these earlier years. In 1869, at the suggestion of Albert Edward, Prince of Wales, Ismail the khedive gave her a site outside of the walls; British friends aided her to erect a spacious building; and the school grew to six hundred pupils. Half the boys and two thirds of the girls were Muhammadans. All were taught to read and write Arabic. All learned the Bible and Christian teaching. The boys also received secular education, and the girls became mistresses of the needle. To=day through Egypt these boys, now men, hold positions of trust under the government, in mercantile houses and in railroad and telegraph offices. After Miss Whately added the medical mission to her schools (1879) she daily read and explained the Scriptures to such patients as wished to hear. As if these multifarious activities were not enough, this masterful, versatile, vigorous woman must yearly spend a few days in a hired *dahabiyeh* distributing the Scriptures among the villagers along the Nile. Of course the bigoted or ignorant at first opposed this, but soon her arrival was welcomed, and crowds would gather to greet the woman of the Book. Women thronged around to hear her preach. For years she longed to purchase a barge for a mission=boat, but could not obtain the means. Though she supported herself from her private property, giving a sugar=mill to Livingstone's industrial mission near the Zambezi (1858), she was not well=enough=to=do for the purchase of a Nile=boat in addition to other demands on her purse. Had it not been for this, her life might have been prolonged. But her works follow her. Her reputation is world=wide. She still lives and serves. The larger part of the progress of the Anglican mission in Egypt to-day is derived from the moral force and propulsion of Mary Louisa Whately*.

The women's societies of the American Baptists in the north sent their first female missionaries to the Kongo in 1887. They enjoyed the experiences of pioneers. "One morning", so a lady wrote home, "the men took the tent down before I had my hair combed. When I turned round, all the carriers of one caravan were drawn up in a circle, watching me with awe-struck faces. I believe they were afraid of my hair. I am the only woman up-country with long hair". The ladies at Lukungu are teaching many children in three classes, and some of their boy-pupils have been already received into the church. At Palabala the hill on which their house was erected had borne a name meaning Death's Hill, because condemned witches had here been put to death; but after the coming of the women-missionaries the chief requested to have the hill's name changed, as it had become a hill of life. One of these missionaries, from whom, when first in a new place, the people ran away, stayed a few days. They flocked to her tent to hear more. When she first read the Bible to the villagers in their own speech, some ran screaming away, greatly alarmed that their language could be talked from a book. They had never dreamed such a thing. In the end, however, the natives pleaded to have the Christian lady stay and teach.

Among the southern Negresses of America Baptist women from the north are performing remarkable work. For thirty years or more Joanna P. Moore gave herself

---

*See *The Life of Mary Whately* (by E. Jane Whately) and Miss Whately's own *Letters from Egypt, Lost in Egypt, Peasant Life on the Nile* and *The Story of a Diamond* for information, unavoidably omitted here, as to her momentous work. "Miss Whately's mission", it is claimed, "stands first. It has reached the heart of Islam. The Scriptures are now read in Mecca and Medina; the authorities can not prevent it; and this is well known throughout the East". Miss Whately at least once received proof that a Bible given by her reached Jiddah the Meccan port.

to the emancipation of the Negro woman, and laid stress on special training for native workers. Her principles and procedure as well as those of other women find expression in the following words of their commission as missionaries: *Your work shall have special reference to the Christianization and elevation of the homes of the [colored] people.* Though the Christian schools of the Baptist and Congregationalist, the Episcopalian and the Methodist, the Presbyterian and the Roman are accomplishing much, they are comparatively few and can not reach the submerged nine=tenths. Among these neglected masses are one million children and youth outside of school. These can be touched only through the home; and Baptist women have struck out some original paths toward the seizure of this citadel.

The first of their methods consists of house=to=house visitation. In this the missionaries teach everything that the need demands, everything that opportunity renders practicable. These Christian ladies teach their black sisters godliness and then cleanliness and home= making. A feature of this is the fire=side school. Fathers and mothers are encouraged and helped in educational fellowship with their children, and expected to pursue a regular course of reading, which includes the Bible. A third agency is the industrial school; not the large, rare, well=equipped school, but the inexpensive, small school that may be organized wherever there is a properly qualified woman to take charge. Each week the children are gathered in church or home or school for several hours, and taught not so much the simpler industries as the nobility of labor. The kindergarten, the kitchen=garden, manual labor and sewing are employed, and instruction in ethics and social culture is given. Out of these schools have already come excellent artizans, house-servants, ministers, missionaries and teachers. A system of industrial and model homes has also been inaugurated. Not only has this made a successful beginning but the spiritual side is encouraging. The importance of Scriptural study receives recognition in the formation of scores of Bible-bands. From these are recruited the majority of workers in industrial, mission, Sunday and temperance schools and most of the elect for local training-classes. A sixth agency for helping the southern Negress is the mothers' meeting. This explains itself. Seventh comes the training-class for Christian workers. This consists of women able to spend time outside of the home in personal mission-work for the vicinage. The teachings of the Bible and the means of applying them are taught, and they are then sent to give what they have received. Such normal training for Negro women is growing into great proportions. In addition to The Moore Training-School and to an increasing number of classes the Baptist women sustain departments at Spelman Seminary and Shaw University for training Negro women as missionaries in Africa no less than in America.

A single instance of the application of several of the above principles will illustrate their practical effect.

In Indian Territory a Christian woman visited the Negro settlement of Sodom. Ignorance, immorality and pauperism held carnival. The missionary began quietly. Week after week she entered loathsome cabins in order to make friends with their inmates. After an interval she could question them. "Do your children go to school?" "No, honey". "Why not?" "Isn't no school". "Why not?" "We's too poor". "Do you use snuff?" "Yes, honey". "Do you use tobacco?" "Yes". "Do you drink beer?" "Yes, honey". "What does your snuff cost, your tobacco, your beer? Don't you see that you pay more for these than to pay your share of a teacher's salary and educate your children? Which do you love best: tobacco, snuff and beer or your little ones? Can you give up these harmful things for your children?" Some could and did. The town set an old cabin apart for a school and secured a colored teacher from a Christian boarding=school. In less than a year the men hauled lumber and erected a new school. This also served as meeting=house. The women cleaned the cabins, and some of the Negresses actually put in small windows. Finally all became ashamed of the name of the town, and Sodom became Pleasant Grove, with church and school, progressive homes and people.

Testimony as to the beneficent results of such endeavors is emphatic if not unanimous. In one southern city a white man said to the leader of an industrial school: "I can always tell the children who go to you; they have cleaner and brighter faces, their clothing is neater, their tones gentler, their conversation purer and their conduct better than that of children not under such influence". Of the effect of the Bible=bands on Memphis a Negro editor and pastor wrote: "The quietude that prevails is remarkable. Many minds that had gone wild over Baal= worship have settled, and the people are living and thinking better". A worker "sees steady progress all along the line. In the country there is a wonderful uprising of women". Another notices a much deeper interest among the older people in children and youth. A Tennessee Negress, educated, refined and successful, speaks of white southern women recognizing their black sisters more and more. She "believes the key=note struck that will eventually harmonize the terrible disturbance in our land. . . As she goes among her people she teaches *Romans* xii with application to the race=question, emphasizing verse 14: Bless them which persecute you; bless, and curse not". In many districts of the south Baptist women note a slowly widening but hopeful break in the Chinese wall of racial prejudice. In some localities white southern ladies of good standing in church and society are not only participating in Negro education and evangelization but asking assistance of the missionaries whom formerly they ostracized.

In 1713 Ann Bradstreet, widow of the late governor of Massachusetts, freed Hannah her Negro slave. This act of an American Congregationalist forms one of the earliest emancipations of black men and women, and was a prophecy of the participation of Congregational women in the evangelization of African peoples. Madams Ellis, Kennedy, Livingstone, Moffat, Moult, Mullens, Smith and Wardlaw from the United Kingdom; Madams Abraham, Lindley, Lloyd, Mellen, Robbins, Rood, Tyler and Wilder from the United States; and many unnamed and unmarried women have redeemed this pledge of Congregationalism.

Livingstone in 1843 entered his mission=station of Mabotsa or Marriage=Feast. The name inspired a prayer that "many might thence be admitted to the marriage=feast of the Lamb". It also became the omen of an earthly marriage. Till 1844 Livingstone had thought it better to remain independent. Then he met Mary, the daughter of the Moffats, and she revolutionized his ideas. My life=work, he argued, — so little can men dream of God's plan and their place in His purpose — will duplicate Moffat's. Mabotsa will be substantially another Kuruman. For influencing its women and children a Christian lady is indispensable. Who so likely to do this well as the child of missionaries, herself born in

Africa, educated in England, familiar with mission=life and gifted with the helpful, ready hand and winning manner essential to woman?

So thought, so done. The lady to whom Livingstone wrote: "Let your affection be toward Him [God] much more than towards me. . . . Whatever friendship we feel toward each other, let us always look to Jesus as our common friend and guide", was one in heart and mind and soul with her lover. Soon the maid and the man solemnized marriage and made a Christian home in the mission=hamlet of the marriage=feast.

Livingstone had erected a house of which he was both architect and builder, and declared it "pretty hard work, almost enough to drive love out of his head; but it was not situated there. It was in his heart, and wouldn't come out unless she so behaved as to quench it! . . . She must get a maid to come with her; she couldn't go without one, and a Khatla [native] couldn't be had for love or money". The last statement gives an idea of the difficulties of house=keeping and of the hardships the two had to endure. For a long while they used a wretched infusion of Kafir corn for coffee, but the exhaustion of this obliged them to go to Kuruman for supplies. When they arrived, to hear the old women (who had seen the wife depart two years before) exclaiming: "Bless me, how lean she is! Has he starved her? Is there no food in the country to which she has been?" was more than Livingstone could bear. What home meant to the lonely, toiling missionary may be inferred from a letter to his mother after a brief experience of married life. "I often think of you", he wrote; "perhaps more frequently since I married. Only yesterday I said to my wife when I thought of the nice, clean bed I enjoy *now:* You put me in mind of my mother; she was always particular about beds and linen. I had had rough times before".

At Kolobeñ, the third and ultimate station of the Livingstones and the sole permanent home that they ever had, the better half employed all the morning in culinary or other work. The family rose as early as possible, generally with the sun in summer, and had worship, breakfast and school. Then came incessant manual labor. At the same time it was endeavored to carry systematic instruction so far as practicable; but the pressure on the energies was so severe that little time was left for more missionary work. This was a sorrow; and likewise the fact that Livingstone "generally was so exhausted that in the evening there was no fun left. He did not play with his little ones while he had them; and they soon sprang up in his absences and left him conscious that he had none to play with". Well tired by dinner=time, the mother sometimes took two hours' rest but more frequently went without respite to teach the native children. School was popular with the youngsters, and their attendance averaged sixty but might rise to eighty. She managed all household affairs through servants of her own training; made bread, butter and clothing; educated her children most carefully; and kept an infant and sewing=school that had the largest attendance of any which the husband and wife opened. "It was a fine sight", Livingstone wrote after the death of his help=meet, "to see her day by day walking a quarter of a mile to town, no matter how broiling the sun, to impart instruction to the heathen Ba=Kwain. Ma=Robert's name is known through all that country and eighteen hundred miles beyond. . . . A brave, good woman was she". Nor did these labors exhaust the sum of her tasks. Every visitor enjoyed boundless hospitality and kindness in the humble mission=home. The wife accompanied the husband on his missionary travels, being with him and their squad of infantry at the discovery of Lake Ngami. On such journeys she was the queen of the wagon and the life of the party, sustaining all hearts and directing all arrangements. Her presence and that of the children were of no little advantage to the missionary; they inspired the natives with confidence and promoted kind relations and tender feeling. Mrs Livingstone must also have had rare self=control; for in 1851, while on the way to Sibituani, the party was without water for four days. The idea of the children perishing before the very eyes of the parents was terrible; and it would have been almost a relief to the father had the mother reproached him; but not a single syllable of upbraiding was uttered, though her tearful eye told of agony.

The year 1852 brought a long and painful parting. Providence sent Livingstone to the Zambezi on behalf of missions and Mrs Livingstone with the four children to England. To the directors of his society the father wrote in reference to the vile speech and ways of the pagan: "Missionaries expose their children to a contamination they had no hand in producing. . . . None of those who complain about sending children home ever descends to this. . . . Again, . . . no greater misfortune can befall a youth than to be cast into the world without a home. In regard to even the vestige of a home my children are vagabonds". To his wife he confessed among utterances too sacred for repetition that she had been a great blessing and that the longer he lived with her the better he loved her. Much of the honor for the lowly, self=sacrificing missionary's marvelous march to mid=continent, to the Atlantic and thence to the Indian Ocean ought to be awarded to Mrs Livingstone. The wife, poor soul!—Livingstone pitied her—proposed in 1850 to let her husband go while she remained at Kolobeñ; and he wrote that the directors of the society "were accustomed to look on a project as half=finished when they had received the co= operation of the ladies". For the wife the years of separation were years of deep anxiety, often of terrible anguish. Letters were repeatedly lost, none so frequently going astray as his to her. She was a stranger; homeless, invalided, poor, with the burden of wee bairns on hand and heart, yet through great stretches of time without tidings from the wanderer. The strain was so strenuous that sometimes her harassing apprehensions proved too strong for faith. Those who knew her in Africa could hardly have recognized her in England. She never knew an easy day nor passed a dreamless night. When her husband was longest unheard of, her soul sank utterly; but before announcements of his safety arrived, prayer restored tranquillity. She actually put the matter of his lengthy detention playfully, pretending a "source of attraction".

Livingstone reached home in 1856, but a final peril on the Mediterranean obliged him to write beforehand in explanation, saying: "I'm only sorry for your sake, but patience is a great virtue. Captain Tregear has been away from his family six years, I but four and a half"! Mrs Livingstone in the fond hope that she need never again part from her husband wrote verses of welcome in which were lines athrob with feeling. The following one proved prophetic: "I may tend you while I'm living, you will watch me when I die". Mrs Moffat in congratulating her daughter on Livingstone's return did not forget the shadow that falls over the missionary's wife when she must forsake her children and renew her foreign work. Mrs Livingstone, the mother wrote, had had a hard life in inner Africa and endured many trials; but if she spent her remaining years in the wilds that Livingstone had penetrated, she would suffer manifold privations. Nothing daunted the wife. She justified the faith of the husband in writing from the Zambezi in 1855 that whoever stayed behind she as well as he would go there as a missionary. At present, however, she enjoyed a richly deserved public recognition. The Royal Geographical Society received Dr Livingstone, and scientists and travelers hasted to express heart-felt gratitude to the wife, who was present. The London Society gave a reception for its missionaries, and Shaftesbury the philanthropist thus acknowledged Mrs Livingstone's worth: "She endured all with resignation, patience and joy, because she surrendered her best feelings and sacrificed private interests to the advancement of civilization and the great interests of Christianity". When it became known at a public dinner to Livingstone in 1858 that Mrs Livingstone was to accompany him to Lake Nyasa and the Zambezi, no announcement received more enthusiastic applause. It is, Livingstone declared to the guests, hardly fair to ask a man to praise his wife; but she "had always been the main spoke in his wheel and in this expedition would be most useful. She was familiar with the languages. She was able to work. She was willing to endure. She knew that one must put one's hand to everything. The wife must be the maid of all work, the husband the jack of all trades. Glad was he indeed that he was to be accompanied by his guardian angel".

Alas! Man proposes, God disposes.

On the voyage Mrs Livingstone's health declined toward fever. Obliged to stop at Cape Town and to go with her parents to Kuruman, she was unable to advance to the Zambezi before 1862. This was a great trial both to husband and to wife, and could she have gone, she would have rendered invaluable service. From Kuruman she returned to Scotland that she might be near the children. Though many friends were kind, the time was not a happy one. The lonely woman longed deeply to be with her strong Captain Great=Heart. She felt that in the shadow of his stalwart faith her fluttering heart and shrinking spirit would regain steadiness of tone. The letters to the husband reveal spiritual darkness; the replies to the wife are replete with earnestness and tenderness.

In January, 1862, escorted by the Reverend James Stewart, now of Lovedale, whom the Free Presbyterian Church of Scotland had sent to ascertain the possibility of founding a mission, even then, on Lake Nyasa, Mrs Livingstone arrived off the Zambezi. When the *Gorgon* encountered Livingstone's *Pioneer* it signalled: "Wife aboard". Livingstone signalled back: "Accept my best thanks", thus concluding what he called his most interesting conversation for many a day. The wife was still more thankful for this happy end to three and a half years of separation. She had been sadly disappointed when the *Pioneer* failed to appear, and speculated anxiously as to the cause of absence. When Stewart perceived Livingstone and said: "There he is at last", Mrs Livingstone brightened at the news more than the good doctor had seen her do any day for seven months before. But a long detention on the deadly coast ensued — at the deadliest season, too, when fever was at its height — and sowed the seed of catastrophe. On April 21st Mrs Livingstone became ill, and on the 27th her spirit returned to God. The husband who had faced a hundred deaths and braved a thousand dangers wept like a child.

From Griqua=town to Shupanga was but a brief life=journey of forty years (1821=62). Yet through what wildernesses! The careers of Mary Moffat and Mary Livingstone, *pulchra filia, pulchrior mater*, probably afford as adequate illustrations of the trials of a woman=missionary as do the lives of any women. The mother had one work to do, the daughter another; the former was more active, the latter more passive through the compulsion of circumstance; but who shall say which suffered or wrought the more? "They also serve who only stand and wait"; and the soldierly mother strung by strife to glorious endeavor deserves hardly more of praise and reverence than the heroic daughter who endured cruel inaction and suspense. Mrs Livingstone was more a Martha than a Mary, her mother writing that "though Mary could not be called *eminently* pious, she had the root of the matter". In this she was the child of her father, an idea confirmed by the fact that Livingstone and Stewart were struck with the identity of her face after death with the father's expression and features. "A right straitforward woman was she, no crooked way ever hers, and she could act with decision and energy". She experienced clouds of religious gloom, followed by great elevations of faith and reactions of confiding love, and among her papers was found this prayer: "Accept me, Lord, as I am and make me such as Thou wouldst have me". To a friend she wrote: "Let others plead for pensions, I can be rich without money; I would give my services from uninterested motives; I have motives for conduct I would not exchange for a hundred pensions". It is fit that the mortal frame of her whom

England gave to Ethiopia should rest in Afric soil, for as really a missionary as her father and as truly as her husband a martyr was Mary Moffat Livingstone.

The first Zulu convert of the American Congregationalists was a woman. She was an African Hannah and her son a Samuel, for he was afterwards ordained pastor of the church she thus founded. The devoted wives of the missionaries established kraal=schools for the lowest, station=schools for the children of Christians and the boarding=and=industrial school. The Zulu whether Christian or pagan loved and trusted these women implicitly. Several of them spent between thirty=five and forty years in Zululand. Mrs Lloyd, daughter of Doctor Willard Parker who defined medical missions as clinical Christianity, after the husband's death carried his work single=handed for several years. Thoroughly educated and wealthy, she gave herself gladly for the redemption of lost souls.

The Congregational women of America have two female seminaries in Natal, one at Inanda and the other at Umzumbe. Nearly a hundred girls attend Inanda, some having walked seventy miles to reach it. Frequently maids have run away from the kraal in their anxiety to enjoy teaching. As the Zulu father values his daughters highly, on account of the dowry in cattle that they bring when marriageable, a stern chase ensues. It would remind some Americans of their attempts to enforce the fugitive=slave law — and other Americans of their success in resisting it. The majority of the scholars come from heathenism, without preparation. Sewing, home=making and gardening are the industrial specialties. The Inanda gardens are solely cultivated by the girls, who, if denied outdoor life, could not be happy or healthy. At one planting=season an epidemic occurred. The pupils were sent home. It seemed as if there could be no harvest. But so firm is the hold of the school on the neighborhood that the natives came fifty strong, with twelve plows and seventy oxen, and broke and planted nearly seventeen acres. Later, the women weeded the crops. A few years ago a shirt made by the Umzumbe girls won the first prize at an intercolonial exposition in London. Graduates of this school are exerting salutary influence on heathen homes. From both seminaries come Christian motherhood, female church=membership, many invaluable assistants in higher grades of the mission=schools, Sunday=school workers, teachers of elementary schools and wives for helpers and pastors. Some students each year become Christian communicants. Revivals have been enjoyed, and graduates who are not confessing Christians are rare. Not every stone proves a gem, but the drift and tenor of the schools are toward elevation and spirituality. They are aiding in the formation of a new sentiment among the Zulu as to woman. Without suggestion the native church legislates in her behalf. One congregation ordained that "no polygamist should be allowed to become a member" and that "any who sell daughter or sister, treating them like horse or cow, can not be received into the church".

To handle the freedmen's work of American Congregational women would exceed limitations; but they anticipated those of other churches, employ substantially the same methods and surpass all in the gift of themselves and their means. Since 1846 over three thousand, five hundred Congregational ladies have educated and evangelized the southern Negro*. The Woman's Board

* *The Annual Report of the Bureau of Woman's Work* (1897); *A Plea for Colored Girls; A Plea for Woman's Work; Fifty Years of Woman's Work; I Didn't Have No Chance; A Negro Seaside School; Our Work in the Black*

of Missions of the Disciples, a Congregational communion independent of the Congregational churches, revived the men's Jamaican mission, which had fallen into decay. The ladies sustain five male missionaries, own property worth $20,000 in churches, day=schools and Sunday= schools, and claim thirteen [?] thousand communicants.

British Congregational women in 1891 identified their work with the general work more closely than ever before. The directors of the London Society consist of ladies as well as men. Though the selection and training of female candidates remain with a women's committee, all other details of woman's work run along the same lines and proceed under the same control as the whole work. The outcome will be awaited with interest. The work among Malagasi women follows the general course of that among Africans.

American Lutheranism, thanks to the inspiration of great=brained, great=hearted, great=souled Gustavus Adolphus, began grandly as to the Negro. Delaware, while a colony of Danes and Swedes (1638), disallowed Negro servitude and declared it "not lawful to buy and keep slaves*". But it was left for European Lutheranism and for its female missionaries to wear the laurels of victory in the struggle against African bondage and paganism. Mrs Albrecht, the Lutheran= born wife of a German missionary in the service of British Congregationalism, and Mrs Krapf, whose Lutheran husband was the glory of Anglican missions in Zanguebar down to 1855, stand out among the gifts of the Lutheran communion to Africa. Mrs Albrecht married for love of missions as well as for love of love, and died

Belt; Sister Clara; The African in America; Training Colored Girls; Two Girls' Work and *Work Among the Colored People* contain interesting and valuable details, but were sent too late for use.
    *Stevens, *History of Georgia*, vol. i, p. 288.

in the field for their sake. Rosina Krapf in heroism equalled the zeal of Xavier. With her husband she penetrated Abyssinia. When compelled to flee she shared his every exposure and privation. When their child was born (1844) on the Zanzibar coast, it was under the shade of a tree in the wilderness. As the father baptized the dying babe of sorrow, the mother gave it the Amharic name for a tear and despite her anguish sought to comfort. Through peril of land and sea she had been the husband's valiant comrade; with her last breath she bade him bear her body to the African shore that her grave might remind the Muhammadan and the pagan of what had power to bring her to this land, and that it might inspire other missionaries to bear the fiery cross through the Galla country into Abyssinia.

The missions in Ethiopia, Gallaland, Ibea and Uganda make one answer to that yearning; the rising of Norse womanhood offers another. When Dahle in 1888, after spending nearly fifty [?] years as a missionary in Madagascar, returned to Norway, he found a new factor in missions. Almost half the Christian young women were ready to become missionaries! Until then Norwegian ladies had been chiefly collectors of money. They formed hundreds of associations. They have a paper, edited by a woman, for missions among women. They have female teachers on the foreign staff. From Sweden, however, came the impulse in 1874 that led the Lutheran women of America to organize in behalf of non=Christian women.

Muhlenberg Mission has since 1860 had a school whose first girls came from a captured slaver. Many of the pupils marry and settle on land around the mission reserved for Christian families. Each couple receives five acres. In the thrift, comfort and habits of this Christian community its pagan neighbors see applied Christianity.

British Wesleyan women have missions at Lagos and in Austral Africa. At three stations here they have large schools, from one of which nearly twenty day=schools are worked. Recently one of the women=missionaries had a catechumens' class comprising thirty=five of the one hundred and six pupils. An unmarried American Methodist woman went to Liberia as a missionary in 1834, and when her comrades died or returned home ill, she stood stanchly to her post until the mission was reinforced. Meanwhile she underwent terrible experiences. Ann Wilkins, the successor of this unknown heroine, devoted herself for many years to the women of Liberia, establishing at White Plains a seminary that for a few years was quite successful, and leaving a name still fragrant with loving memories. But the work of America's Methodist women for Africa's dusky daughters is another of the African failures of American Methodism. The gracious lady who in 1893 presented woman's work for African women to the Columbian Congress on Africa at Chicago found herself constrained to pass in silence over the attempt of American Methodist womanhood in this field. She did not mention even the fact of such an endeavor. It is from other sources that we learn that the Women's Missionary=Society of the northern Methodists, whose communicants in 1875 numbered one and one=half million, made a beginning in Africa the year before, only to abandon African women afterwards. In 1898 it re=entered Africa, in Angola. The Women's Mite=Society of the African Methodist Episcopal Church aids especially in the evangelization of Haiti; but, though the annual income of their society is only about $1,000, these poor women founded it when they were still but a decade away from slavery, and have missionaries in Sierra Leone, San Domingo, St Thomas and Trinidad.

The Bohemian Unity of Brethren, the United Brethren in Christ and various undenominational organizations may be grouped here, since it is all but out of question to obtain *data* as to the African work of the women of these numerous and scattered bodies.

Among the Khoi=Khoin baptized by Schmid two were women. One of them, named Magdalena, kept the faith through all the dark and weary years between Schmid's expulsion and the renewal of the mission (1742=92). In 1828 Wilhelmina Stompjes, a Kafir convert of Gnadenthal, accompanied the "Moravian" missionaries and their Hottentot proselytes who founded Shiloh in Kafraria. Here she approved herself a good and faithful workman, providentially bestowed upon the mission. "The strong and admirable features of her Christian character", said a missionary not given to exaggeration, "her intense love for her countrymen and her mastery of their language gave her a great advantage over the missionaries, who could only hold intercourse with them by an interpreter. She faithfully used it in all humility for the furtherance of the Lord's work. With warm heart and overflowing lips she would tell of the love of God in Christ. Her word had such weight even with proud chiefs, that they were oft swayed, and did not deem it beneath their dignity to send special messengers to the lowly maiden". She cooked, tilled the garden, taught Kafir girls and translated freely for the preachers, interspersing frequent comments and remarks of her own. With the daily dole of bread to the beggars she also gave the Bread of Life. At her kitchen=door she received the emissaries of the chieftains. While toiling in her garden one day in 1829 Wilhelmina saw Bowana and Mapasa appear in war=costume with fifty warriors. To her native sagacity their array instantly revealed the red= handed purpose. But her instant and only thought was to rescue the missionaries. She faced the two chiefs. She upbraided them with the guilt of treachery and unwarrantable wickedness. She drove them off, and a few days later they actually sent an apology.

Though Mapasa's hatred continued, Wilhelmina remained a frequent channel for divine blessing and protection.

The Friends, from their entrance on African missions, have had women among their representatives. In fact, Mrs Kilham might be regarded as a pathbreaker for modern "Quaker" missions in Africa, for she traveled and worked during more than ten years along the Guinea coast. She left no means untried for the conversion of the Negro, devoting special attention to the languages, opening schools and becoming widely known through her philanthropic if somewhat eccentric efforts. The British Friends' first missionary to India was a woman (1866), and among their earliest missionaries in Madagascar was an American "Quakeress". The British Friends' Missionary Association in 1895 had about a dozen female missionaries, representing the faith of Fox, in the great African island. The "Quaker" women of America in 1890 consummated a missionary=union of ten societies, the oldest of which originated nine years before, and work, among other fields, in Jamaica. The Union is represented abroad by many more women than men, and at several points coöperates with English Friends.

Before Agamemnon there were also kings of men. Even Mary Whately had a predecessor in Egypt. This was Miss Holliday; and for a time she represented the great and undenominational society for the education of oriental women. This was instituted in 1834 by Abeel, is sustained by the women of the established and free churches of Britain, and has no masculine officer except a treasurer. The income averages about $35,000 annually; the organization publishes a monthly journal; and the missionaries number nearly fifty with twenty thousand pupils in two hundred and seventy=five or more schools. The society became the mother of more recent ones, and now includes half the globe in its beneficence. Its African fields comprise Egypt, the Levant, Mauritius, North Africa and South Africa; and its present work after sixty years of unremitting labor consists of house=to=house visitation, with Bible and sewing classes; medical missions; mothers' meetings, with branches of the Bible=and=Prayer Union and of the Young Women's Christian Association; schools — boarding=school, day=school and Sabbath=school; and the training of native women. This, the most important part of the mission, is diligently carried on, and has raised up a large number of African assistants who serve the society as Bible=women, district=visitors and teachers. Many schools not directly under its control constantly receive aid. In South Africa Kafir and Zulu girls have been rescued from degradation and misery by its excellent boarding=schools; and in West Africa it has long done good work in more than one locality, aiding many schools from its funds and by the sale of productions. From the first the society, in addition to aiding agents and stations directly under its own control, has everywhere assisted and coöperated with many independent workers who started on their own charges but found need of help from home. Miss Whately herself (1861=89) was among those who grasped the sisterly hand of this society. In early days the society could put forth educational effort only among the humblest classes, but now all are open. Everywhere, however, conversion forms the foremost aim; though great pains are taken to insure good and practical education of every sort, Christian training is the highest object. This is never lost from sight.

Miss Holliday, an English lady of superior education, becoming deeply interested in Egypt, became the Amelia Edwards of her time and devoted herself to Arabic, Koptic and Egyptology. But her great desire was to consecrate herself to the elevation of Egyptian women. Accordingly The Society for the Promotion of Female Education in the East put her in charge of a school of eighty-five girls in Cairo (1836). She had occupied the position but a little while when a new sphere of influence opened most unexpectedly. Mehemet Ali, the Albanian founder of the present dynasty and the maker of modern Egypt, formally requested her to educate the hundred women of his harem! The wazir wrote that "in introducing enlightened female education they would be striking at the root of the evils which afflicted them. He had been able to trace their debasement to no other cause than the want of efficient, moral, useful education for their women". When we recollect that this confession was uttered sixty years ago, and in the most Muhammadan city of Islamry, we may gain some appreciation of the momentousness and vital significance of the new forward movement*. After much prayer, after consultation with friends, Miss Holliday accepted the providential opportunity, especially as the pasha assured her that the education of his harem was but the beginning of education for all Egyptian women.

*Lane states that Egyptian Muslim women then were regarded by the Musulman world as the most libidinous of its women.

For ten years the English lady worked in the palace and organized schools in the city. When she entered, scarcely one woman could read; when she departed, hundreds were reading.

Berber Africa affords a wide field for female missionaries, since only they as a rule can enter the home and reach the woman. North Africa Mission recognizes this. In 1892 thirty=nine of its fifty=four missionaries were women. Though the sultan of Marocco forbade intercourse between these missionaries and Moorish women, believing that such "communication threatened innovations in the law and corrupted religion", women are generally regarded with less suspicion than men. The populace thinks them less able to pervert the faithful of Islam, but the rulers of the Muslim church and state rightly hold otherwise. French opposition, however, in Algeria and Tunis makes a more formidable barrier. French law prohibits the practice of medicine without a French diploma, French rulers prevented British and Swedish missionaries from preaching, and the French republic notified the North Africa mission to quit.

The Salvation Army owes its success under God to women; and the Taylor Mission was predominantly occupied by feminine missionaries. At one of its posts a woman who was a superior linguist and teacher was once the sole occupant. At another, so it was said, the missionary, who worked largely at her own charges, established a boarding=school for girls, made a coffee=farm and fruit=garden, and taught among the villages. Miss Kildare, single=handed, manned a station for ten years near Banana at the mouth of the Kongo. Miss Taylor, if report speak true, is also making a remarkable record among African missionaries for endurance and efficiency.

The Woman's Missionary Association of the United Brethren in Christ entered Sierra Leone in 1877. A single lady broke ground in a new district. Within five years the women's mission slew the slave=trade at Rotufunk. The Sowers Home for girls inhabited an attractive and substantial house, had over a hundred pupils, and instructed them in book=lore and also in all the arts of home=making. The Bompeh School enjoyed the services of no less a woman than Mrs Thompson, Crowther's daughter. The converts itinerated two=by=two through the country under the auspices of the missionaries. They reached many hamlets every day, and held preaching and song services.

Though the Huguenot College at Wellington, Cape Colony, and its three daughter=schools in Cape Colony, Natal and the Orange State are not agencies for missions among African aborigines but are institutions for the daughters of white people, the Huguenot Missionary Society, the women's mission=society, is affiliated with twenty=five colonial organizations, supports eight female missionaries, and during the past ten years has sent more than fifty women as missionaries to Kimberley diamond= mines, Johannesburg gold=fields, Lake Nyasa, the Nyai and the Shuna. The school was founded in 1874 by the Reverend Andrew Murray and by Misses Bliss and Ferguson, graduates of Mary Lyons' Mount Holyoke Seminary. The colonial government has granted $25,000; the four institutions have fifty teachers (from America, Cape Colony, England, Germany, Holland and Scotland) and nine hundred pupils; and the Wellington branch alone has prepared over six hundred teachers. The Mount Holyoke College of Africa is the light of the Cape and the great lakes, a maker of Austral Africa.

The Corisco=Gabun mission of the Presbyterian

Church (north) in America has ever enjoyed the services of sagacious, strong=souled women whose names will live among the workers for African womanhood. Such were Mrs Walker, Mrs Preston and Mrs Bushnell, connected with the school for girls at Baraka; Mrs Nassau, who left a deep impress on the hearts of the native women and composed hymns that are ever on the lips of the black Christians; Mrs Reutlinger and Mrs Heer who for years held posts and single=handed encountered responsibility; and Miss Nassau who for nearly thirty years prepared books for her schools, printed them on her own press, translating them when not originally written in the vernacular, and voyaged the rivers in the *Evangeline*, her own boat, with herself as crew and skipper.

The mission of Presbyterian women in Africa links itself so integrally with the general work of the Presbyterian churches; and so few of their missionary heroines in comparison with those of other communions stand out in picturesque personality, that it is more natural to consider both together. This course was adopted in the presentation of the African missions of the entire Presbyterian communion. But Mrs Coillard the Huguenot, Mrs Lansing the American United Presbyterian and Dr Jane Waterson the Scotch Presbyterian were characters of striking and unique interest, whose careers would reward study.

The Woman's Executive Committee of Home Missions of the Presbyterian Church (north) can show trophies won from American heathenism as remarkable as those gained by their sisters from African paganism. A Pennsylvania woman went in 1867 into Virginia, and under an oak opened a school for freedmen. In 1893 she was yet tilling the field, and her county had six

Presbyterian churches, six schools and a boarding=academy with one hundred and seventy=two pupils. Three of its teachers had learned the A B C *in the widespreading shade of that tree; and one tiny student of the oak= tree school graduated from Howard University with the highest honors. From a Texan school for Negro girls came this statement: "Were I able to visit every church, I could at once pick out the seminary girls by their modest, quiet, dignified manner. So far as we have been able to follow these girls after they leave, they have for the most part been faithful. They seem to have passed into a new world. Their religion instead of manifesting itself in noisy shouting finds expression in Christian activity".

Ex uno disce omnes! These solitary instances represent hundreds of equally successful efforts on the part of Presbyterian womanhood for the American Negro.

Scotch Presbyterians have at least two noteworthy women in Africa, one a medical missionary in South Africa, the other an industrial and self=supporting missionary in Nyasaland. The former appears to represent the Free Church, the latter belongs to the state=church. This lady learned book=binding and shoe=mending in order to teach these arts, and for the purpose of binding the school=books took the proper tools and two presses. She sailed in June, 1893, at her own charges and was to receive no salary. It would seem that she is not the sole self=supporting representative of the Established Church, for at the London conference on missions in 1888 Mr McMurtrie reported the following instance of feminine heroism and self-sacrifice. "I knew", he said, "three sisters who had a great desire to go to Africa. But they knew we were in difficulties in regard to money. They would not ask a penny. They were not rich. One was teaching. Another was in millinery. The other was doing something else. They simply said: 'We will make a bargain; two will stay at home and keep the third; she shall be a missionary'. She is now out in that mission".

The African activities of the women of the Roman Church, even if we regard these as running no further back than the council at Trent (1545-63), are too long-continued, too multifarious, too vast to be discussed in any less compass than a volume. In fact, the literature of the subject would form a library. Africa, America and the Antilles; the Abyssinian and the Arab, the Berber and the Egyptian, the Malagasi and the Negro, with all the racial varieties of the latter; the free man, the slave and the freedman; the African Christian, the Muslim and the pagan — have all known the ministrations of heroic and saintly woman-missioners from the papal fold. Four black and four white sisterhoods are working exclusively for the Negroes of America, while twenty-one additional communities of white sisters work among black as well as white populations. Nor, it is believed, do these exhaust the number. Mother Katharine Drexel, a wealthy Philadelphian, founded one of these organizations for the freedmen, and devotes herself and her vast fortune in their behalf. The Antilles enjoy the charitable, educational and evangelistic services of at least four sisterhoods whose devout women have consecrated themselves to the cause of the black Catholic and of Negro womanhood. The number of feminine organizations laboring in Africa and Madagascar for the Roman church is not ascertainable, but the number can not be few. Probably the most remarkable and successful of them consists of the Sisters of Our Lady of Africa, *les sœurs blanches* of Lavigerie's Algerian white fathers.

When Lavigerie proposed that women be the executors of domestic, social and spiritual regeneration for the Muslim, society protested against Christian ladies being sent into regions where their chastity could not be safe for a day; soldiers and statesmen predicted that the Arab would view their efforts with disdain and resentment; and even great churchmen regarded the project with doubt. But when Lavigerie publicly pointed out that Christian women alone could reach Muhammadan women; that radical reform in all the opinions of the latter involved inevitable change of front on the part of the entire coming generation; and that as a whole results would be further reaching, more thorough and more speedy,—the Catholic womanhood of France volunteered like another Jeanne d'Arc. "The moral superiority of the women", so Grussenmeyer the biographer of the cardinal tells us, "their self=denying kindness, their courage and devotion deeply impressed the unbelievers, who gazed at them with astonishment and admiration as if they belonged to a different order of beings and were something more than human". Lavigerie himself bore similar testimony. "I have", he stated, "seen them in the midst of their work. I have seen them surrounded by a motley crowd of men and children, Christians and Muhammadans, all clamoring for succor; begging them to cure their ailments, to relieve their poverty; with utmost veneration kissing the habit they wear. . . . One of the sisters, passing through the streets of a city, was accosted by an old Turk who with a mixture of curiosity and respect said: 'When you came from heaven, did you wear the dress in which we see you?'" Among the Arabs and Berbers there naturally sprang up an undying spirit of amazement and admiration for the dauntless courage of these missionary heroines, their medical knowledge and skill, their saintly steadfastness, their self=crucifying tenderness. From personal observation Sharp found that in Sidi=Okba, the Algerian Mecca, the sisters had not only entered but thriven. Yet it is not so long since no European woman, even with masculine escort, could visit this hot=bed of Musulman fanaticism without risk of violence. Many a white father, as one at Biskra informed Sharp, would instinctively shrink from the task fearlessly set themselves by the more daring sisters, who in moral courage are the superiors. In the face of insult, opposition and threats they persevered. Now they go to and fro in all Sidi= Okba, not unhindered only but saluted with honor by the Islamite.

The sisters experience few mishaps, strangely fewer than the fathers. Both have had martyrs, but the women lost life in ways little different from those that would have beset them in any alien clime. The Biskran father already cited was personally aware of but one tragical instance in the experience of women as Saharan missioners, though he had heard of others; and this martyrdom would not have occurred, had not the dismissed lover of the sister given the inhabitants of Tugurt occasion for misjudgment of the Christian missionary's character and calling.

The success of Christian women, Protestant as well as Roman, in so dangerous a sphere of African missions forms the climax to their grand work in other parts of Africa and in America. They who attempt great things for God are they who may expect great things from God. Human folly often proves itself to be divine wisdom, God choosing the weak to confound the strong and our extremity making His opportunity. When woman entered on the evangelization of Africa and the

American Negro, especially of their women, the tremendous task advanced far on the road to ultimate success. Female agency is now so independent, so large, so vital a factor in Christianizing and civilizing African peoples, that were woman's work to cease to-day, missions would end to-morrow. The women who from every Christian church go forth alone, without other weapon than the Bible or the crucifix, are clothed with the power of God. To Christian womanhood His angel hath said: Fear not, for thou hast found grace. . . . The Holy Spirit shall come upon thee, and the power of the Most High overshadow thee. Christian womanhood has answered: Behold the hand-maid of the Lord; be it unto me according to Thy word. It arises in these days, goes with haste into Christless countries, enters the house of Islam or of paganism, and salutes a womanhood without God and without hope. When such womanhood hears the salutation, it cries: Blessed is she that believed that there shall be a fulfillment of the things spoken to her from the Lord. Rightly may Christian women reply:

Magnificat anima mea Dominum!

CHAPTER 18

FOUNDING A MISSION

It is the practical Christian tutor, — who can teach people to become Christians, can cure their diseases, construct dwellings, understand and exemplify agriculture, turn his hand to anything, like a sailor, — that is wanted. Such a one, if he can be found, would become the savior of Africa.
H. M. Stanley

How much a missionary must know!
Mackay (in 1874)

How one must be jack=of=all=trades in a country where no trade is known, it is difficult to imagine unless on the spot. The natives expect the white man and, most trying, the same man to know everything and be ready to do any kind of work. . . It is next to impossible for you to realize the world we live in. . . I am so far from thinking my education wasted that I only wish I had double the amount, not only in book= learning but in practical skill. This is a field which offers scope for the highest energies. No man can know enough and be able to turn his hand to too many things to be a useful missionary in Central Africa.
Mackay of Uganda, 1878=90

Such a man was no mere industrial and civilizing missionary.
Eugene Stock

(I) ON THE ROAD TO THE FIELD AND LAYING THE FOUNDA- TIONS. GETTING READY. AFRICAN CURRENCY. A FEW GOODS. COSTLINESS OF CARRIAGE. AN IDEAL PREPARATION FOR THE MIS- SIONARY'S CAREER. A BULA=MATARI BEFORE STANLEY. ON THE MARCH. DIFFICULTIES AND HARDSHIPS. CHAOS AND COSMOS. (II) THE BLESSEDNESS OF DRUDGERY THE MISSIONARY'S ROUTINE. THE NECESSITY FOR MATERIAL MEASURES AND MEANS. CLERIC AND LAYMAN. MANY METHODS. THE SECULAR AND THE SPIR- ITUAL. MEDICAL WORK. CHRISTIAN INDUSTRIES. EDUCATION AND EVANGELISM. MISSIONARY=PROBLEMS. PRECEPT AND PRAC- TICE. EVIL VS GOOD. NATIVE DEMEANOR. A SPECIMEN DIFFICULTY.

I

On the Road to the Field and Laying the Foundations

The first step in Africa toward the founding of a mission formerly consisted in the equipment and organization of a caravan. The procedure and the requirements vary in the several sections of the continent, those, for instance, of East Africa differing from those of South Africa, and those of a mission in the barbarous interior being far greater than those of a post on the sea=board or within reach of civilization; but everywhere the details of preparation possess a generic likeness. "Ah! me", Stanley sighed in 1871, "what hard work it is to start an expedition alone! What with hurrying through the baking heat of the fierce, relentless sun from shop to shop, strengthening myself with far=reaching and enduring patience for the haggling contest with the livid=faced Hindi, summoning courage and wit to brow=beat the villainous Goan and match the foxy Banyan, talking volumes through the day, correcting estimates, making accounts, superintending the delivery of purchased articles, measuring and weighing them to see that everything was full measure and weight, overseeing the white men busy on donkey=saddles, sails, tents and boats — I felt when day was over as if limbs and brain well deserved their rest. Such labors were mine unremittingly for a month". Such toils were also Mackay's during 1876=77 and Livinhac's and Pascal's in 1878.

Even Arabia and Turkistan have means of travel that are royal in comparison with those of Africa. Coin and camel and horse can be employed there; but in eastern and inner Africa beads, cloth and wire constitute the currency, and naked men the beasts of burden. At Zanzibar in 1870 gold formed the sole money, and the result of this absence of all other mechanisms of exchange was that every dollar drawn on Europe cost twenty or twenty=five or thirty cents of additional expense! The porters could not carry more than seventy pounds at the most, but demanded at least fifteen dollars a man for carriage only so far as U=Nyanyembe, three hundred and sixty miles west. The conveyance of eleven thousand pounds requires about one hundred and sixty carriers, to say nothing of guards, and involves an expense of $2,500 for porterage alone*. Moreover, the European caravan in tropical and uncivilized Africa resembles the sailing=ship outward bound on a long voyage. Each must have a world of goods among its provisions and stores for the every need of its commander and crew. Yet, great as are the requirements of a commercial caravan or a mercantile settlement, those of a mission and its moving columns are still greater.

How much money is required? How many carriers? How many soldiers? How many beads? How much cloth; and what kinds for different tribes? How much wire? These and a thousand more queries plague the tiro and press insistently for answer. He learns that the bead neck=lace does duty for the copper cent; two yards of American sheeting for the silver half=dollar; and a fathom of thick, brass wire for gold coin. Stanley found that forty yards of cloth a day would purchase food for one hundred men, and accordingly bought sixteen thousand yards of American domestic sheeting, unbleached; eight thousand yards of Hindi blue cloth; and fifty=two hundred

---

*When Stewart in 1891 set out for Kibwezi, his caravan of two hundred and seventy=three men had to leave over two hundred loads. Could any other fact give so impressive, so vivid an idea of how every ounce has to be considered? A mule=road, to say nothing of the railway, would release thousands of natives now employed exclusively as carriers; revolutionize industries; and benefit Africa in myriad ways.

yards of mixed colored cloths (1871). These procured subsistence for two years. Next in importance after cloth came beads; and as tribes vary in their preferences for black, brown, green, red, white or yellow beads the traveler must calculate the probable duration of his stay in each district where one or other of these varieties is the sole currency. Stanley reckoned that for two years' traveling, spending fifty necklaces a day, he should require eleven varieties and twenty-two sacks of the best kinds, and purchased accordingly. Wire formed the third circulating medium, rating as gold in countries beyond the Tanganika*, but three hundred and fifty pounds proved ample.

The purchase of barter-goods is but the beginning of work. Ammunition must be procured; and bedding, boats, bagging, canvas, canned dainties, cooking-utensils, donkeys, equipments, fire-arms, hatchets, medicines, needles, presents for chiefs, provisions, rope,' saddles, slop-chest, tar, tents, tools and twine — to mention a few articles at random from the myriad of indispensable goods. The chaffer with steel-hearted Arabs, Banyans, half-castes and Hindis is most trying. When Stanley bought donkeys, he was obliged to beat the ass-dealers down from forty to fifteen dollars, and could not get a paper of pins without a five *per cent.* reduction, involving an amount of arguing deserving a nobler cause. He had also to invent and manufacture pack-saddles. The next thing was to enlist a faithful escort of soldiery. Each received three dollars a month, and was then equipped with bullet-pouch, flint-lock musket, hatchet, knife, powder-horn and two hundred rounds of ammunition. The entire equipment of an expedition weighs no

*Stanley "differs from Burton in spelling this word, as he deems the *y* superfluous".

FOUNDING A MISSION 629

less than six tons, and the amount of material often exceeds even this enormous total.

It is wiser and less costly to send a number of small companies than a single great caravan. Large companies are delayed by avaricious chiefs or invite attack; little caravans are more likely to pass unnoticed. Large or small, however, it is no easy task for a private caravan to obtain carriers. It required six precious weeks for Stanley (1871) to procure one hundred and sixty porters; and the cost of carriage for $1556.25 worth of goods would amount to $1850. Of course these expenses have increased since 1870, but the building of railroads between the salt and the sweet=water seas will eventually remove this difficulty. Another disadvantage under which missions struggled in those pioneering days consisted in the necessity of paying black=mail, euphemistically styled tribute, to scores or hundreds of petty potentates. The chiefs were not only avaricious but fastidious. They could not condescend to accept the flimsy, colored cloth of the carrier, but must receive high=priced, regal robings or crimson broadcloth. Between Bagamoyo, a maritime town twenty=five miles west of Zanzibar, and U=Nyanyembe the tribute for an expedition of nearly two hundred souls amounted finally to $330 in gold and a premium of $.25 on each dollar. Probably, however, the most trying drawback arose from the utter rascality of the middleman employed to hire porters. Under his marvelous manipulations $750 worth of work grew into a bill for $1500. No wonder that even as early as 1858 Burton and Speke's journey to Lakes Tanganika and Victoria cost over $15,000!

Stanley regarded Mackay of Uganda as "the best missionary since Livingstone". Accordingly we may study his career as fairly exemplifying the more modern missionary's experience in the founding of a new African mission and in the routine of daily life at his arduous post.

The son of a Scotch Free Presbyterian minister, himself an ardent student and able man, Mackay (1849-90) enjoyed a boyhood of extraordinary intellectual richness. At three he read the New Testament fluently. At seven his text-books were *The Decline and Fall of the Roman Empire, Paradise Lost,* Robertson's *History of the Discovery of America* and Russell's *History of Modern Europe.* Until the age of fourteen Mackay learned only from his father, who imparted a vast amount of knowledge. The boy's wonderful skill in map-drawing when but ten years old, his dextrousness in type-setting and the accuracy of his "proof" inspired no less a person than Sir Roderick Murchison with admiration. During the ensuing three years he busied himself with garden and glebe, household animals and machinery. The carding-mill, the carpenter-shop, the gas-works, the saddlery, the smithy became his haunts. Then literature reclaimed him, and he progressed rapidly in classics and mathematics. At school he spent the holidays in the photographic studio and the ship-yard. Above all, from his fifteenth year onward, the Bible became his armory and treasure-house, of whose every resource he was perfectly the master. At the normal college the youth added algebra, arithmetic, Biblical studies, drawing (ever a strong point), geography, geometry, Greek, history, school-management, skill in teaching and the theory of music to his equipment. The university gave him applied mechanics, engineering, higher mathematics, more classics and physical science. The man then crowned five years of study in Edinburgh with a course in fortification and surveying; filled the secretaryship of an engineering society; taught; worked at erecting, fitting and turning machinery and at model=making; attended lectures on chemistry, geology and similar subjects; and devoted his Sundays to worship in the morning and to religious work in the afternoon and evening. In 1873 he went to Germany for the purpose of mastering the language, and became a draftsman. He translated a German work on the calculus, and invented an agricultural machine that won the highest prize. . Presently he received promotion to the headship of the locomotive department, where he performed evangelistic work among the many employees, and gained the friendship of Baur, a minister at Berlin's cathedral=church and a royal chaplain. He mingled with the choicest Christian society, and in six weeks after leaving Scotland received the call of God to his true task. He immediately offered himself as an engineering missionary for Madagascar, but Providence had destined him for Uganda. The road was not open, the time not ripe, for Congregationalism to enjoy the privilege of his services. The Church Missionary Society issued an appeal (1875) for a civil engineer or other qualified layman; and though Mackay's enlistment was received too late to allow of placing him at Mombaz, the society's assignment of him to Lake Victoria (1876) arrived in the same mail that brought Doctor Duff's request that Mackay join one or other of the Scotch Presbyterian missions at Lake Nyasa!

During the two months of preparation in England and Scotland Mackay turned every hour to account. He designed a boiler of welded rings, each so light as to be carried by two men, in order that he might build a steamboat in Uganda. He purchased tools of all kinds, chiefly for iron and wood; and much else. He learned astronomy and the use of the sextant. He mastered the details of coal=mining and iron=puddling, printing, photography, the stethoscope and vaccination. In the spring=time of his genius, rejecting rare opportunities for the acquisition of power and wealth, this man,—who, in view of *all* the aspects and relations of his endowments, must be pronounced the most finely equipped man in body, mind and spirit that has yet devoted himself to Africa — went forth to years of toil, suffering and disappointment.

The glimpse at Stanley's trials enables us to infer the greater troubles that Mackay and his comrades went through in preparing their missionary expedition. It was divided into four parties, Mackay leading the third one with two hundred porters. Illness, however, prevented him from coming within hundreds of miles of the vision of the promised land (1876). He employed the intervening year in forwarding a relief caravan to his brethren at Lake Victoria and in cutting two hundred and thirty miles of road. His training in courage, experiment and forethought, with such materials as steam and steel, stood him splendidly in stead. Many a stately tree was felled for the first European bridge on the future highway, and the densest jungle yielded to the strokes of a score of sword=bayonets. Mackay armed forty men with American axes, British hatchets, picks, saws and spades. The utterance of him who cried in the wilderness: "Prepare the way of the Lord, make straight in the desert a highway for our God", received literal fulfillment. Mackay made the crooked straight and the rough places plain. In the more open country he distributed the men as thinly as the trees along the path, five or six felling a huge baobab, but on entering a jungle all hands worked in unison. Through the densest, thorniest thickets where porters had had to drag their bales and a donkey could not be pulled through, Mackay cleared a way broad enough to permit the largest bullock=wagons to pass two by two (1877). The Reverend Palmer Davies, director at Berlin for the British Bible=Society, rightly referred to the grandiose plans of the African International Association in this wise: "While commercial and scientific men are talking, the servants of the cross are acting; and while the former are fixing in words the problems to be solved, the latter are quietly solving them. I expect more from the Church Missionary Society in their field and the London mission on Tanganika and the Scotch mission on Nyasa than from the International for some time. What they [the Association] do will be accompanied by a flourish of trumpets and attract more general attention. Their Agamemnons will find scribes to make them known. Your Agamemnons will also not fail in such".

The pen=pictures painted by Livinhac and Pascal, two of Lavigerie's Roman missioners who followed Mackay in 1878, help us to see the caravan on the march. In front strode the guides and some of the soldiers, behind whom rode several of the white fathers. Then came the porters and the remaining priests. A second squad of guards, to bring stragglers along and to protect the rear, closed the procession. As this for the most part advanced in Indian file, a party of five hundred would form a lengthy train. The daily march is a very short stage, beginning usually at an early hour and continuing nearly to noon. The path traverses now a dense copse, then fields of maize or sugar=cane; now a swamp, now a virgin forest. The narrowness of the way, especially where the jungle or the wood chains and enlaces it with vines and compels it to zigzag like cattle=tracks or serpentine trails; the malarial air; and the murderous mid=day heat make the little journey most laborious. To linger behind is to invite loss of property if not of life. The halt for the night is most welcome. Huts are erected for the native, tents pitched for the European, property examined and protected, and dinner devoured. The after hours are occupied in bargaining with the residents, who, almost naked and reeking with rancid oil, crowd the travelers, mocking and jeering if of bad disposition or joking and laughing if good=natured; in receiving the chieftains or sultans; in settling the tribute; and in administering affairs for the following day.

Mackay's experience of the difficulties and hardships of African travel was even more painful. He had to sleep in all kinds of places — cattle=pens, hen=houses and straw huts as clean and commodious as kennels, where rain penetrated the mud=roofs and turned the earth on which he lay into liquid ordure. Not seldom he found himself compelled to repose in the open with only a blanket or two between him and the chill, disease=breeding dew. There was no walking under an umbrella, no riding on a donkey, for this small but sturdy Scot. He had twenty=six bullocks inspanned; and every man who has once driven a single yoke of oxen knows what a wealth of lashing and yo=ho=o=ing two dozen and more need. The Africans constantly brought the carts against rocks or trees or into holes, and not infrequently the vehicles upset. Then Mackay would seize the wheel, blackening his hands as if with soot and spotting his clothes with mud; and would span the entire ox=train to a single van; and yell till the woods rang. In crossing a river one animal would lie down, another run away and several more face the wagon! In order to make all pull together Mackay had to do so much bellowing that at

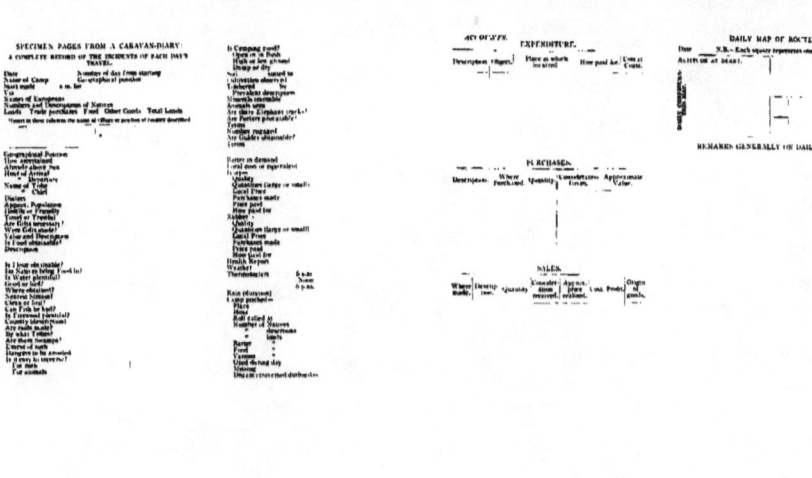

the end of the six hours' daily march he was always hoarse.

Such marching demands fine feeding; but food is not always obtainable and native cookery is execrable. Thick maize=porridge, scarcely boiled, tasting like ashes and sawdust and with a liberal allowance of sand, formed Mackay's daily bread one month. With the malign aid of his constant wettings it brought the man nigh to death. Had not he himself made a thin gruel of maize=meal and boiled it to a jelly, he would have lost his life.

Though Lake Victoria is only about seven hundred and fifty miles from the sea *via* the route pursued by the first missionaries, it cost the Protestant, now the sole African survivor of the original force, two years and more of misery to traverse this trifling distance. Mackay, however, would rather travel a hundred days than attempt to report the events of a single day. Yet new if not worse work confronted the worn hero (1878). Except articles already forwarded to Uganda, the supplies for the mission had been in the care of faithless freedmen and renegade slaves who had robbed and well=nigh ruined. "Piled in heaps promiscuously lay boiler=shells and books, cowrie=shells and candle=molds, papers and piston=rods, steam=pipes and stationery, printers' types and tent=poles, carbolic acid, cartridges and chloroform, saws and garden=seeds, trunks and toys, tins of bacon and bags of clothes, pumps and plows, portable forges and boiler=fittings; here a cylinder, there its sole=plate, here a crank=shaft, there an eccentric. Despair might well be found on my [Mackay's] features as I sat down to . . . look on the terrible arrangement". But it required only ten days of seemingly Sisyphean toil from dawn to dark on the part of this incarnate energy, in strife with Augean stables, to create cosmos from chaos. The boiler was ready for riveting, the steamer's engines stood complete to the last screw, and almost everything of the outfit was entire. Mackay also repaired the mission=boat, until this was in effect quite rebuilt. In order to make boards and planks he had to set up a pit=saw and run it with his own hands. Though he knew nothing of setting sail and steering, he taught himself the art of navigation. When wrecked on the voyage to Uganda, he rebuilt the schooner "as one would make shoes out of long boots". He cut out the center, and united stem and stern. This little job cost our much= enduring Odysseus of missions an eight weeks' stay at the very spot where Stanley had had a hair=breadth escape from massacre. But the explorer's Christian manliness in handling the Negro wrought miraculously in behalf of missions. He is most patient with the African, never allowing a single follower to oppress or even to insult a native*. Wherever Mackay "found himself in Stanley's track, his treatment of natives had invariably been such as to win the highest respect for a white man".

II

The Blessedness of Drudgery the Missionary's Routine

Ethiopia, cried the inspired seer and singer, shall suddenly stretch her hand to God. It is a sublime conception, this of a mighty and puissant people seeking for light and yearning for truth; but it is a spiritual ideal. The Ethiop hopes in reality to profit materially by the presence of Christian teachers, and his bearing toward

* *Mackay*, p. 397.

missions is that of a beggar, often that of an enemy and too frequently that of a suspicious man. The instances of genuine desire on the part of African pagans for moral and religious uplifting are not numerous enough to invalidate the accuracy of this statement as a general rule. Human nature accordingly compels the missionary to use the coveting for secular advantages as an opening wedge for spiritual interests. The first years of a mission are those of a pioneer subduing savage nature to tillage and the thousand other beneficent forms of men's obedience to God's primal command. It must fell the forest, fling cleansing flame through the jungle, drain the miasmal marsh and remove the rock. It must disarm distrust and gain confiding friendship. These preliminary tasks are as trying and wearisome as unavoidable; they make no show in statements; but in their success or failure lies the future of the mission for weal or woe.

Mackay has been characterized as the Paul of Uganda. The comparison is not wholly happy; yet it may be allowed to stand as indicating the leading position of him who believed that "Paul dictated epistles between stitches of tent-making", and who wrote: "Here we don't know anything about properly attired clergymen in black cloth and white tie, with sober countenance and hands undefiled with things of earth. Even the Romish priests with sacerdotal ideas were very industrious and industrial. . . . But a layman is at a great disadvantage. It is expected that preaching, teaching and translational work form the chief and peculiar employment of the *ordained* missionary, however qualified another may be to do such work. But secular work must also be done by some one".

The functions of an African mission are so varied as

to seem universal. They are secular and spiritual. They often though not uniformly bring industrial and medical work, education and evangelism within the scope of the activities of a single station. The extent to which one or other of these departments is pushed, varies with the denominational views of the mission and with the geographical situation or the social requirements; but in tropical Africa as a whole each post finds itself obliged to promote Christianity and civilization through every means at its command.

Mackay is in most minds identified solely with the industrial and material side of missions. Not every missionary is a craftsman and civilizer, but Mackay was such in superlative degree. Yet nothing is so unjust as to think of him entirely in that aspect. The secular was but his servant for the spiritual. He robed it in spiritual character and purpose. Manual labor and medical practice were as religious duties as catechising, pastoral work and preaching. This missionary toiled, as all should, in the spirit expressed by Herbert:

> A servant with this clause
> Makes drudgery divine:
> Who sweeps a room as by Thy laws
> Makes it and the action fine.

Mackay's experience shows that every missionary should have a good knowledge of medicine and surgery, or that some one at each station should be qualified to handle any accident and disease. Mackay even had to play the midwife, but he knew too little of surgery to like to treat accidents and wounds. Consequently he never volunteered to give medicine, practicing only when strenuously urged. Believing abstinence to be the secret of continued health in the tropics, he became an abstainer.

Mackay's first Ugandan industry was the erection of an iron=working shop whose anvil, blower, forge, grindstone, lathe and vice drew crowds. On the Sabbath he frequently taught how Christ's life evinces the dignity of labor. On week=days he was Jack of all trades and master of each. One day he would carve types to print reading=sheets. Hours of toil yielded only ten characters, but the font when completed produced good press= work, for with a toy=press and these types he printed two thousand pages. When the lack of a well made itself felt, Mackay rubbed the Aladdin's lamp of his wits. He found water between two strata of clay. He took levels, and saw that water could be drawn by sinking a shaft. He set natives to work with pick and spade. When the digger reached a depth too great for throwing dirt, Mackay rigged a trestle and hoisted clay, till water was reached at the exact depth predicted. The well= sinking had occupied more than a week. Now Mackay had to repair a battered pump. The whole procedure astounded the natives. They had never seen a deep well and, until they saw the liquid itself, would not believe that water could be had on a hill. When they saw a copious stream ascend twenty feet, and flow and flow so long as a man pumped, astonishment knew no bounds. "Mackay", they cried, "is the great spirit".

Mackay's residence consisted of a straw hut sorely decayed, and visited by venomous vipers, serpent= attracting rats and pythons. Circumstances finally obliged him to build a cottage, and the fame of this wonderful house traveled far. He combined barn, dispensary, printing=office, school=room and tool=shop under one roof. While O'Flaherty was in Uganda, Mackay characteristically did *not* live in this dwelling, but in a miserable tumble=down place which he consented to rebuild and make habitable only when its ultimate collapse appeared imminent. He claimed that a very small place would do for his wants, he having no furniture and liking to be near his boilers, engines and iron. About twelve boys always slept in the house. Some were frequently ill. Then the place was more like a hospital than aught else.

An amazing amount of boat=building fell to Mackay. In 1883 he spent three months as shipwright, cutting and shaping every plank, driving every nail, and launching and rigging the craft single=handed. One hour it was a book, another the anvil and sledge. Next year he fitted the boat with steam=machinery. By dint of hard work at forge and lathe and vice to restore the missing parts of a press, he also succeeded in setting this up. Four years later, at Usambiro, he built his third boat. This required him to fell timber twenty miles away, to make a four=wheeled wagon for hauling the logs entire, and to bake bricks for erecting a house in which to construct the steamship. Christians from Uganda had fled hither, and Mackay administered a most valuable discipline by compelling them to work for food and raiment.

Such instances of industrial mission=work stand for hundreds of others, and suffice to picture that phase of life.

Would that all missionaries, Mackay exclaimed, were taught to teach! The teaching he had received at his normal school he found of the greatest value, archly declaring that the national schools of Uganda needed more men from that excellent institution. For a part of one year he devoted more time to teaching than to anything else. Reading he taught by the look=and=say method, and prepared a Uganda series of sheets printed in large type. Some of the many candidates for baptism in 1883 read largely with him. The children and youth also made such progress that Mackay built a school=house, printed the Commandments, reading=sheets and Scriptures, and sent home for copy=books, maps, slates and similar articles. During the year ensuing he formed a class for the baptized, to prepare them to become communicants. In the belief that study of the life of Jesus would be of more benefit to people unfamiliar with the gospel than would sermons from isolated texts, Mackay began with this subject. In 1885 it was his habit to spend several of the morning hours in school and to give the larger part of every afternoon to translation. A host of difficulties presented themselves, and it may be long before any one translation can meet them. Four years later, while exiled, Mackay trained the best of his converts as evangelists and teachers. Some, since they read well, proved of great service in translation. Mackay rewrote his version of *John*, and much enjoyed giving instruction on the Scriptures to his dusky converts. It was quite a relief from the mundane matters that burdened so many of his hours.

In preaching to the pagan difficulties arise from the ignorance, peculiarities and vices of the native; from the missionary's knowledge and want of knowledge; and from circumstances outside the defects and faults of black men and white men, of the Christless and the Christly. When Mackay preached in 1877, he had not acquired the language and was compelled to have recourse to an interpreter. Interpretation, however, generally proves a broken reed, piercing the hand of him who trusts it. Mackay found that Mufta his spokesman had no understanding of the truth. If he thought Mtesa likely to take offense, he was most unfaithful in interpreting. On many occasions a Muslim would mouth out a terrific polemic against Christianity and its herald. Such arguments would be met quietly, and refuted by appeals to reason and the Scriptures. Mackay found it necessary to translate and use not the "apostolic" but the Nicene creed in order to cope with Islam. The shorter creed is not so explicit as the longer one on the Godhead of the Christ, nor does it guard sufficiently against the inference that Mary was the mother of God. The Nicene creed confutes the Muslim assertion that Jesus was only a prophet and the Roman claim that a human being was the parent of a divine nature. More effective, however, than any man=made article of faith was the Biblical statement of the Christ's own witnessing that He is the very God of God. As time went on, opportunities for evangelistic work at the court broadened beyond these controversies, and reached the peasantry. In Uganda as in Britain the commons proved better than the court.

On Sundays Mackay regularly held divine service at court, and all joined so far as they understood. Swahili was known, and in this language Mackay was at home. Though consistency in the observance of the Christian Sabbath is not always easy in Africa, it is always practicable, even when traveling, and Mackay, when Sunday came, dropped his every tool. "Why?" the natives asked. The missionary replied that God in His Word enjoins one day of rest in seven; and he taught the simplest truths of religion. Mackay longed for the time when he could spend every day in teaching the little ones. Such a class would form the nucleus of a training=college to furnish manifold seeds of life in place of the mere units that white men in Africa must ever be. Some would be trained for the ministry, and a citizen of Sukuma be bishop of Nyamwezi and a Ganda man primate

ALEXANDER M. MACKAY

for the lake=lands. Visionary as Mackay's ideal seemed fifteen years ago, it has already moved far toward perfect realization.

The Christianization of a people ebbs and flows. At one moment a mission seems entering on success; the next, native superstitions and wickedness regain the upper hand. White men, as an intelligent chief confessed to Livingstone, have no idea how wicked pagans are; and Mtesa was guilty of such foulness and villainy that only the hint of his actions may be made*. Sometimes the Scriptures thrust spiritual truth into souls apparently the least susceptible, and cause the missionary, exhausted in body and weakened in spirit, to thank God and take courage. Such an instance was the conversion of Dumulira through the Spirit blessing his reading of Mark. On his death=bed the lad had a friend, a devotee of witchcraft, sprinkle water on his, the dying boy's, brow, and name him the names of Father, Son and Spirit. So sure was Mackay of Dumulira's longing for God, that he believed this baptism written in heaven. Sometimes, however, despite years of preaching Christ and serving men, the missionary felt his heart riven with sorrow as the pagan chose the sorcerer instead of the Savior.

At religious services the general feeling is in favor of decorum, though the conception of this is often elastic. The reverence due to divine truth and divine worship does not come before conversion. It is, nevertheless, difficult to give any idea of the slight effect produced by teaching. No American, no European, can realize the degradation to which centuries of barbarism and ceaseless struggle for bare necessities have lowered the almost mindless pagan. Livingstone found the Kalahari people

* Mwanga was a worthy successor.

attentive, respectful listeners; "but", he added, "when we kneel and address an unseen being, the position and act often appear so ridiculous that they can not refrain from uncontrollable laughter. After a few services they get over this tendency. I was once present when a missionary sang among wild, heathen Chwana who had no music in their composition; the effect on the risible faculties was such that tears ran down their cheeks. . . . At public religious services in the *kotla* [a spot with a fire=place, near the center of each circle of huts] the Kololo women from the first, except at the conclusion of the prayer, always behaved with decorum. When all knelt, many of those who had children bent over their little ones. The children in terror of being crushed to death set up a simultaneous yell. This so tickled the assembly that there was often a subdued titter, turned into a hearty laugh as soon as they heard 'amen'. This was not so difficult to overcome as similar peccadilloes in women further south. Long after we had settled in Mabotsa, when preaching on the most solemn subjects, a woman might look round and, seeing a neighbor seated on her dress, give a hunch with the elbow to make her move. The other would return it with interest, perhaps with the remark: Take the nasty thing away, will you! Then three or four would hustle the first offenders, and the men by way of enforcing silence would swear."

Ten thousand such trifles happen, deserving mention only because without them we could form no correct idea of mission=work.

At Linyanti the number of natives attending Livingstone's religious service, whither Sekeletu's herald who acted as beadle summoned them, often amounted to seven hundred. Worship, necessarily held in the open air, consisted of reading a short Scripture and of an explanatory address not long enough to provoke inattention and weariness. As the associations of a *kotla* are unfavorable to solemnity, it is advisable to build a chapel or church as soon as feasible. As an aid toward securing the serious attention that religious affairs deserve, it is also important to treat the building with reverence. At Chonuane, one of Livingstone's posts, a bell=man was once employed to collect the people. Up he jumped, a gaunt, tall fellow, on a platform, and at the top of his voice shouted: "Knock that woman down! Strike her, she is putting on her pot. Do you see that one hiding herself? Give her a good blow. There she is, — see, see, knock her down!" All the women ran to meeting in no time, for each thought herself meant. But though a most efficient bell=man, Livingstone did not like to employ him!

CHAPTER 19

1795 = 1892

REPRESENTATIVE MEN: TWO TYPES OF THE AFRICAN APOSTOLATE

History is philosophy teaching by example.
Dionysius of Halicarnassus

(I) MOFFAT THE TYPICAL PROTESTANT MISSIONARY. PREPARATION AT HOME AND ABROAD. AFRIKANER. MRS MOFFAT. THE CHWANA. INCIDENTS AND EXPERIENCES. MISSIONARY MULTIFARIOUSNESS. THE TABILI. A WIND FROM THE SPIRIT. AT HOME ON FURLOUGH. THE SCRIPTURES TRANSLATED. MUSTERED OUT. SERVICE IN RETIREMENT. (II) LAVIGERIE THE REPRESENTATIVE ROMAN MISSIONER. THE FRENCH TRAINING. A LEVANTINE MISSION. THE BISHOP OF NANCY. THE ARCHBISHOP OF ALGIERS. REASONS FOR REMOVAL. CHURCH VS STATE. DIOCESAN MISSIONS. THE ALGERINE AND AFRICAN APOSTOLATES. LAVIGERIE IN UGANDA. WAS LAVIGERIE ACCOUNTABLE FOR THE ASSAULT ON ANGLICAN MISSIONS? LAVIGERIE THE CRUSADER. LAVIGERIE THE DREAMER AND SEER. (III) CONTRASTS AND PARALLELS. PERSONAL TRAITS IN MOFFAT AND LAVIGERIE. FRANK AND SCOT. MISSIONARY AND MISSIONER. SUCCESS WON BY EACH. SPIRITUAL LIFE IN CATHOLIC AND IN PROTESTANT. BRACQ ON LAVIGERIE. SCRIPTURE AS TO MOFFAT.

The layman represents the genius of the Protestant communion, the prelate that of the Roman church. Each gives the drift and tenor of his system as a whole. Robert Moffat as layman and as pastor was the ideal Protestant missionary. Cardinal Lavigerie stood as the incarnation of Rome's typical priestly missioner. So far as biography is history embodied, history in miniature, so far the characters and careers of these men express the philosophy of Protestantism and Rome in Africa, of Latin and Teutonic Christianity in missions.

I

Moffat the Typical Protestant Missionary

For African missions the year 1795 was *Annus Mirabilis*. The London Missionary Society came into being on September 21st, and on December 21st, sacred to American Congregationalists as the day when their forefathers first stepped on Plymouth Rock, Scotland gave birth to Moffat. The work and the worker entered the world together. Moffat's parents were hard=working, pious peasants, the folk of whom Burns in *The Cottar's Saturday Night* sang that they were the source of Scotia's grandeur. From them mainly the son drew the frugality, industry, mastery of his hands and shrewdness that Africa rendered invaluable. The trend of his life's purpose is clearly traceable to the mother. She trained the boy in the Scriptures, and told him of "Moravian" missions. It was inevitable that the youth when converted by the Wesleyans (1811) should remember the mother's missionary stories to the child, and resolve to devote himself to missions. It was providential that Mary Smith, who had not only been brought up religiously but had received her education at a "Moravian" seminary, became his betrothed. Through three years of engagement and fifty years of marriage this woman showed herself to be the truest of helps and his fellow=soul.

Moffat, though enjoying no opportunities for acquiring scholarship, possessed a twofold faculty as precious as Cambuscan's ring or the purse of Fortunatus. He had the gift of forgetting the secondary or the useless and of seizing the essential. In 1817 he arrived at Cape Town. Even as a stripling he manifested sagacity, self-reliance and tact. The governor, to protect the missionary while native disturbances were rife, withheld passports for nine months. The canny Scot quietly boarded in a Boer family and learned Dutch, thus increasing his efficiency as a missionary. On receiving passports, Moffat traveled to the Nama, who dwelt near the mouth of Orange River, three months' journey from the Cape. He struck twelve at the first stroke, and approved himself a strong man. He signalized the beginning of his career by an exploit that made his name shine among men. He won a victory of peace over an African Attila. He tamed the redoubtable Afrikaner.

The missionary was alone. He was a stranger among strange people. Even in his hut he was exposed to sun and storm, snakes, kine and dogs. He had to cook his own food — when he had any — to mend his clothing himself and to win consolation from the Psalms in Scotch and from the violin. He itinerated. He maintained day-schools. He preached regularly. He transformed Afrikaner and two of his brothers into efficacious helpers.

After being baker, carpenter, cooper, house-keeper, miller, smith and shoe-maker for a year as well as missionary, Moffat visited Cape Town for supplies, and restored Afrikaner to civilization. The task of piloting the outlaw through Dutch peasants who had not forgiven the man they had wronged, demanded nerve and tact. The colonial governor was so struck with the success of the missionary that he gave Afrikaner a wagon worth four hundred dollars. Miss Smith had come, and the brave man and perhaps braver woman became husband and wife about New Year's Day, 1820.

Mrs Moffat was one of those whose names belong to the peerage of faith. She was brave, like Moffat equal to every emergency, gifted with such powers of command as few men possess, patient, tender, and true to each of womanhood's claims. In superlative degree she justified Moffat in stating as the outcome of three years' African experience of bachelorhood that "a missionary without a wife in Africa is like a boat with only one oar. A good wife can be as useful as her husband in the Lord's vineyard". There was no adventure or enterprise, however perilous, in which Mary Moffat did not take part; no work that she did not share. She would not permit Moffat on her account to leave his tasks an instant. Again and again, escorted only by Chwana and Khoi=Khoin, she journeyed from Kuruman to Cape Town, a distance of seven hundred miles. Her ability to make the best of matters amounted to genius. When her husband itinerated from Kuruman, she for years made it her affair to accompany him. She wished not merely to ensure ordinary comfort for him but to master every detail of missions. She rose instinctively to his heights of unconscious greatness. If ever he needed to be inspired or reinforced, she was his inspiration.

The experiences in Cape Colony, among the Nama and at Griqua Town (1820) were stepping=stones to the true life=work. In 1821 was founded the memorable mission of Kuruman. It fell among thieves. The Chwana, according to worldly witnesses, were utterly degraded. Living in the dry district west of Vaal River, adjoining Kalahari Desert, they stood still in the first stages of barbarism. The people stole shamelessly. Grain could not grow to ripeness. Neither cattle nor sheep could be left in the fold. No tool might remain where work had been done. When canals were made, it was at the risk of the water being turned away before reaching the station. Many a time the home=makers, on returning from outdoor labors or preaching, found a stone in the pot instead of the meat they had left. The natives were thoroughly sensual. They robbed, murdered and lied without compunction so long as successful. Parents were so stubborn in adherence to ancient habit and custom, that they were afraid of the children becoming Dutchmen if instructed. Sin made the pagan undesirous of spiritual truth. Stupidity rendered the barbaric mind unteachable. The young missionaries, like the majority of supporters of missions, had expected that the Ethiopian would suddenly stretch his hand to God. The resultant reaction from the natives' contempt for Christianity deepened the Moffats' disappointment and saddened their spirit.

One day in 1822 the husband said: "Mary, this is hard work". The wife replied: "It *is* hard work, my love; but take courage. Our lives shall be given us for a prey". Robert answered: "But think, my dear, how long we have been preaching, and no fruits appear". Mary rejoined: "The gospel has not been preached *in their own tongue wherein they were born.* They have heard it only through interpreters, who have no just understanding, no love of the truth. We must not expect the blessing until you be able from your lips and in their language to bring it through their ears into their hearts".

From that hour Moffat gave himself with tireless diligence to learning the Chwana language. Its imagined barrenness and the imperfection of the interpreters caused the greatest difficulty, but he was too perseverant to lose courage. Since ability to speak Chwana was the first goal, the Moffats, in order to naturalize themselves to native speech and wean their tongues from using

Dutch with the assistants, took a wagon=journey.* Sometimes life was endangered. Once, when no rain fell, the missionaries were accused of causing drouth. At the spear's point they were told to leave. Fortified by the courage of the wife, who with her babe in her arms stood at the door of the hut, the husband threw open his vest and said: "If you will, drive your spear to my heart. We know you will not touch our wives and children". The intending murderers exclaimed: "These men must have ten lives, they are so fearless of death". As early as the close of 1822 Moffat could announce that the Chwana had dispensed with a rain=maker and had relinquished cattle=lifting.

Somewhat later the wrath of man turned to praise for God. A horde of marauders drew near. Nothing definite was known as to their object or strength. In order to ascertain these, Moffat with a few companions plunged into the wilderness. After perils innumerable, seeing nine lions in one day, he accomplished his purpose. Then he roused the Chwana. He gave such counsel, he exercised such ability and strategy, that he saved the people. His bravery, coolness, forethought and sagacity excited admiration, and led the grateful barbarians almost to adore him.

The tide turned. The outlook began to brighten. The Chwana felt that a man and woman who, instead of fleeing from death, had voluntarily shared their danger, must be unselfish seekers of others' good. Though language can not picture the difficulties at the new site, where the Moffats were daily obliged to toil at every kind of labor, the mission had garnered good=will, and forged slowly forward. Ten years passed without spiritual success. Life was ceaseless labor, difficulty and

*Moffat afterward declared that a language is not mastered until the learner *dreams* in the new tongue.

danger, fearlessly faced. Moffat was black=smith, builder, carpenter, dairy=man, ditcher — digging canal after canal to bring water to garden and field — gardener and thatcher by turns. Everything to which he set hand he did well, even darning and sewing. He was not a man of one idea. He was not wedded to preconceived methods or to a system. He was an opportunist in the best sense, adapting himself to conditions actually confronting him. He despised no means of gaining influence that would lead the pagan to better modes of living, to improved methods of agriculture and to thrift and settled habits. He acquired each art and industry demanded by the situation. His treatment of disease was a prediction of medical missions. Before Carlyle uttered the phrase, Moffat was a captain of industry. He gauged men's capacity with the eye of a master. He directed his every worker to the very task he was fit for. He also held him to it. His fearlessness and manhood, independence and tact enabled him always to appeal to the most open side of native character. He knew how to attach and govern men. During the decade of weary waiting he proved that he possessed an attribute of genius, a supreme test of strength. This is patience and persistence. The courage needed for facing formless perils is greater than that which nerves the soldier in the thrill of battle. Having done all, Moffat *stood!* Undespairing and untiring, assured that "they also serve who only stand and wait", with full faith that reward must come to those who work as well as wait and that they should see of the travail of their souls and be glad, — Mary and Robert Moffat toiled steadfastly.

Progress was made toward a Chwana literature. A catechism and spelling=book were prepared. In 1826, to become still more proficient in native languages, Moffat lived alone among the Rolong, and imparted Christian instruction. In 1829, at the instance of two envoys whom Umzilikatzi, chief of the Tabili, had sent to learn about the white man's teachings and ways, the missionary visited the tribe, quelled the terrible warrior, and made him feel this Christian indispensable to him. The Scotchman won so kind a reception, that he gained a hearing for the story of the resurrection.

Previously, however, the Spirit had breathed on the Chwana. Interest in spiritual affairs awoke without visible occasion. The chapel grew too small to hold the multitude that sought membership in the Christian church. The change in the inner nature of the former barbarian and pagan led to a change in the outer man. The naked became ashamed, and assumed decent clothing. Three years after Mrs Moffat, while there was no glimmer of day nor a single inquirer, had shown herself a spiritual heroine by writing home: "Send a communion=service; it will be needed" — one hundred and twenty Chwana communicants partook of the Sacrament, and used utensils that had arrived the very day before!

In 1830 Moffat finished the translation of *Luke*, and at Cape Town learned the art of printing. Like Raleigh he could toil terribly; and here he made himself ill. Next year, however, he returned triumphant with Chwana editions of *Luke* and a hymn=book, with a press and with liberal subscriptions for building a new church. As timber had to be brought two hundred and fifty miles to Kuruman, the structure was not ready before November, 1838. The following year saw the completion of the translation of the New Testament. In order to print it, the Moffats after two=and=twenty years of absence returned to Britain. They aroused unprecedented interest, and a tidal wave of enthusiasm for missions swept the land. Moffat added *Psalms* in Chwana to the Testament; sent six thousand copies of the new work to Kuruman; and wrote *Missionary Labors and Scenes*. The years at home (1839=42 inclusive) were as devoted to missions as those at Kuruman, and equally fruitful in results.

Space fails for detailing the long result of self=forgetful toil; for describing the labors manifold in exploration, civilization and Christianizing; the influence on Livingstone; or the grand achievement of translating the whole Bible and, as agent for the British Bible=Society, of circulating the Scriptures. The translation cost thirty years of toil. Moffat "felt it an awe=full thing to translate the Word. When he had finished the last verse (1856), he could hardly believe he was in the world, so difficult was it to realize that his work of so many years was completed. A feeling came over him as if he would die. . . . His heart beat like the strokes of a hammer. . . . His emotions found vent by falling on his knees and thanking God for His grace and goodness in giving strength to accomplish his task".

At an age when the average man draws out from the burdens of the day and the heat of conflict, this master=builder with his own hands laid another course in the foundation of the church of Christ in South Africa. Though sixty=two years old, the veteran pioneer of forty=one seasons accomplished an arduous and lengthy journey, and spent many months at Inyati, the mission of the British Congregationalists to the Tabili (1857=59).

In 1870 Mr and Mrs Moffat reluctantly accepted the invitation of their directors, and returned to England. The hearts of the Chwana were wrung with genuine sorrow. When the Moffats had arrived at Kuruman in 1843, some, whose hearts had sickened with hope de-

ROBERT MOFFAT, D.D.

ferred, asked again and again: "Do our eyes indeed behold you?" At this final parting the wail of woe was piteous; but Moffat's last preaching=service crowned an impressive career with an impressive close. In 1871 Mrs Moffat, as truly a gift from God to her husband as Eve of Eden to Adam, entered her eternal home. The dying words of the gifted and consecrated woman were a prayer that strength be given her bereft yoke=fellow for bearing his loss. The petition was answered with strength in him equal to her desire. To the day of death (1883) the aged saint labored unceasingly in behalf of the cause to which the youth had consecrated his life and powers.

These thirteen years of sunset splendor were the Indian summer of Moffat's high calling. The May of life had fallen into the sere and yellow leaf, but it owned all that should accompany old age: honor, love, obedience, troops of friends*. The church and the world rendered reverent homage to him who had not sought to be great, but simply strove to shepherd the flock. A Chwana training=school was named Moffat Institute. Twenty=five thousand dollars were given to the retired missionary who, had he been a self=seeker, could have become a mere millionaire. At the London mission=conference of 1878 the vast audience on discovering Moffat's presence rose spontaneously to their feet. The Reverend Doctor Thompson wrote: " 'Nothing but a missionary!' The man who gave that toss of the head and that half=scornful look should cast an eye down the hall. Whom see we coming up the aisle — a son of Anak in stature, erect, his features strongly marked, his venerable locks and long white beard adding majesty to his appearance? . . . A Wesleyan is in the midst of an address, yet

*Shakespere.

none heeds him till the patriarch has taken a seat. Who is the old man? Is it Beaconsfield? Is it Gladstone? There is but one other person in the realm, I take it, to whom in the circumstances so united and enthusiastic a tribute would be paid; and that because she is on the throne. This hoary=headed man is the veteran among South African missionaries. He went to the dark continent more than sixty years before. He is eighty=three. . . . With a voice still strong and musical he addresses the audience for twenty minutes. The man [Spurgeon] who preaches to a larger congregation than any other in London once said that when he saw Moffat he felt inclined to sink into his shoes"*.

II

Lavigerie the Representative Roman Missioner

Charles Martial Allemand Lavigerie was born at the Biscayan town of Bayonne, France, on October 31st, 1825. The boy was father of the man. The child delighted to give religious coloring to everything. His sports repeated the ceremonies he had seen at church. His calling toward the priesthood led his father to put him at fourteen into a seminary, and thirteen years were bestowed on academic and theological studies. Lavigerie's education was rhetorical rather than practical or philosophic, and qualified him for immediate but not lasting impression on intelligent audiences. The style of his oratory is emotional and theatric; not intellectual, logical, masculine in dignity or weight. The public addresses suffer from the artistic and literary defect of

*Compare *The Times*, London, Aug. 15th, 1883. Saul was among the prophets, for " The Thunderer" (quoted by *The Missionary Review* for January, 1888, vol. 1, no. 1, pp. 22=24) eulogized Moffat. Lack of space has rendered it impracticable to use this editorial.

monotony in language and narrowness in thought. As a speaker Lavigerie repeated not only his facts and ideas but his forms of expression and even his witticisms. Success in study secured him a professorate of ecclesiastical history at the Sorbonne, a Parisian university whose origins link it with Charlemagne. Here he paid his respects to Jansen the Gallican and Luther the Protestant. The theological position may be inferred from a French Catholic journal criticising the lectures on Jansenism with severity. Lavigerie was a firm upholder of papal dogma in its unity and a stanch champion of the claims of the Vatican. Probably no bishop has burned more incense before Peter's chair. Yet Lavigerie was as liberal as was then possible for Frenchmen within the Roman pale, and few bishops have manifested more personal independence of action in regard to the papal see. The lectures on Jansen (1854) formally avowed a belief in the infallibility of the pope; but in the Vatican council of 1870 Lavigerie held aloof from discussion of the opportuneness of the definition of papal infallibility. "For my part", said he to his clergy, "I only desire to be on the side of the pope and the majority of the bishops". [!] When the dogma was proclaimed, he laid his submission instantly at the feet of the pontiff, and as soon as possible convoked a provincial council in Algeria to ratify and promulgate the Vatican decrees.

Lavigerie was neither scholar nor thinker. He was a man of action and affairs, a born missioner, cramped by the professorate. When a society, formed among leading Catholics of Paris (for the purpose, Grussenmeyer and Clarke confess, of extending the political and religious influence of France in the Levant), decided that Lavigerie ought to direct and organize education in the east, the man of thirty-one, in obedience to the confessor's belief that it was God's will that he accept this providential opportunity for wider usefulness, followed the leading. This was the beginning of an apostolate that ended only with entrance into the higher activities of heaven.

The missionary course opened with an incident that was a prophetic omen. When the society had uttered its thanks, the committee handed over the accounts and an empty cash=box. Gagarin with a dry smile remarked: "You are afloat; it remains to see how well you can swim!" But Lavigerie belonged with the strong men whom difficulties delight instead of daunting. Financial embarrassments, from which, indeed, no part of the missioner's life gained entire exemption, called forth power and resourcefulness. In this school he learned the alphabet whose combinations unraveled pecuniary complications in Algeria.

The Muslim massacres of Christians in the Syrian Lebanon (1860), which, it is said, cost fifty thousand lives, introduced Lavigerie to Islam. Lebanon being a French protectorate, France sent a military force to save the remnant of the Syrian Christians. The [Franco=Roman] Society for the Promotion of Christian Education in the East felt it their mission to succor the victims. Lavigerie obtained over $400,000 and great quantities of goods, and spent six months in Beirut, Damascus and Lebanon. At Cairo as well as Constantinople, Damascus and Smyrna he in the course of seven years founded or supported hospices, orphanages and refuges. Africa, as if a dark or invisible planet, was already attracting Lavigerie unknowingly, though France was for years to hold the future satellite to his original orbit. A meeting with Abd=ul=Kader, the Algerine exile at Damascus, the Muslim protector of Christians, inspired Lavigerie with admiration for the natural virtues of Arab and Islamite.

The Levantine experiences initiated Lavigerie's interest in Islam and his insight, however shallow, into Arab character.

After eighteen months at the Vatican as domestic prelate of Pius IX and as a member of the highest tribunal of the Roman court, Lavigerie became bishop of Nancy (1863=66). The episcopal experience trained him in ecclesiastical administration, and qualified him for the proconsulship of Franco=Roman Africa. The scope of his activities constantly enlarged, but Lavigerie never allowed energy to mislead him into making changes merely for the sake of change. He might be a Gascon for impatience, but he could curb it into patience. If he proposed new measures, he put them forward moderately and pushed them with adroitness, diplomacy and tact. One of his reforms proved to be bread cast on the waters and returning after many days. He enlarged and improved the female religious associations; and several of these communities ultimately devoted themselves to African missions.

In 1867 at MacMahon's instance Lavigerie assumed the archbishopric of Algiers. It is claimed that "no motive of worldly ambition determined Lavigerie to accept the see. He was marked by public opinion as destined to fill the highest positions in the church in France itself. Yet at the call of duty he went into exile, giving up the splendid career, so far as all human probabilities were concerned, which opened at home". The prelate declared that his voluntary withdrawal was a painful sacrifice. If we, however, may draw inferences from certain developments of his Algerine life, mundane motives mingled with the spirit of self=devotion. Lavigerie had the instincts of a politician and the vision of a statesman. French influence was supreme in Egypt,

French interests of increasing importance in the Levant and North Africa. What might not a strong man do for his church and country in Algeria, in Mediterranean lands once Roman, now French? "Better", exclaimed Lucifer the sublime hero of *Paradise Lost*, "better to reign in hell than serve in heaven!" Lavigerie may never have read the Miltonic sentiment, but its temper was his. The masterful prelate was a visionary in the supreme sense, a seer before whose prophetic vision and spiritual eye shot auroral foregleams of the resurrection of the death=submerged continent from its slumber of ages.

> Let visions of the night or of the day
> Come as they will; and many a time they come,
> Until this earth he walks on seems not earth,
> This light that strikes his eye=ball is not light,
> This air that smites his forehead is not air
> But vision — yea, his very hands and feet —
> In moments when he feels he can not die,
> And knows himself no vision to himself,
> Nor the high God a vision, nor that One
> Who rose again. Ye have seen what ye have seen.*

Lavigerie's first pastoral letter to his Algerian clergy and people hints at his feelings and plan of action. He could perceive no undertaking among all carried on throughout Christendom preferable to the task that had fallen to him. "France", he wrote, "is calling to thee, O Africa! For thirty years she has been summoning thee to come from the tomb. . . . In His providence God has chosen France to make Algeria the cradle of a great and Christian nation. He is calling us to use gifts especially our own in order to shed the light of true civilization, which has its source in the gospel; to carry that light beyond the desert to the center of the conti-

---

*Tennyson, *The Holy Grail*, canto 56.

nent enshrouded in densest darkness, thus uniting central and northern Africa to the common life of Christendom. Such is our destiny. God expects us to fulfill it. Our country watches to see whether we show ourselves worthy. The eyes of the church rest upon us. Could any task be higher, any duty more honorable?"

The resources of the Algerine church scarcely sufficed for its needs. Funds were scant, clergy few, missions unachievable. Lavigerie at once took the entire administration of ecclesiastical matters as fully into his own hands as bureaucracy and red tape permitted. Facile though firm, he was as unyielding of will as kind of heart, and alike stubborn and suave. The archbishop filled the rôle of benevolent despot. From the first the evangelization of Islam was his self=assigned task. In order to reach this goal he trod down the government. In defiance of the colonial administration and its laws he exercised the right of liberty for the Christian apostolate *as he defined it.* He demanded the cessation of the system that divided the Algerians into an Arab and a French nationality. He pointed out that the natives were as hostile as on the day that Algiers had fallen; that tribes had been ruined; and that as the result of thirty=eight years of French influence the Muslim had acquired only the vices of civilization, and obstinately withstood progress. The colonist hailed Lavigerie as savior of Algeria. The hierarchy recognized that here was a fight for the supremacy of church over state and that here was a fighter. The pope stood by his man like a stone wall. Lavigerie showed himself a shrewd strategist and astute tactician. He foiled the attempt of the government to maneuver him from his position of vantage. Against his accusations they brought counter accusations. He repeated his, and ignored theirs. He interviewed Napoleon the Little in person. He extorted official orders that he be in no way interfered with.

This victory, the fall of the French empire, the rise of the republic and the supersedure of military rule by civil administration inaugurated a new era in French North Africa. Since 1871 the friction of races has lessened, and missions have laid foundations for Christianizing the Islamite.

Charity begins at home. He that careth not for his own is worse than an infidel. Lavigerie, while succoring Muslim orphans as a first step toward the Christianization of Africans, did not neglect home=missions. He immediately had sixty=nine new chapels or churches built; attempted to elevate the ethics of the colonial press; established a magazine; so furthered farming, the salvation of the colony, that the administration styled him Algeria's head=farmer; and purchased large tracts of barren soil. As apostolic administrator of Tunisia (1881) he revived and fostered its Christian life. Here his work was one, politically and religiously, with that in Algeria. There, according to an Italian journal of 1887, the prelate "possessed more authority and influence than any other agent of France, and had rendered greater services than any one else to the French power in Africa". In Tunis, Italian periodicals affirmed, "he rendered signal services to France, his presence being worth more to his country than that of an army". The construction of churches, hospitals, refuges and schools and the settlement of congregations and orders, some active, some cloistered, were merely a part of the activities of the cardinal. He prevented the French republic from enforcing in Algeria the decrees for the expulsion from France of religious communities and especially of educational orders. He persuaded Leo XIII, in recognition of the revival of the African church, to renew the metropolitan see of Carthage. Here, with an eye to dramatic setting and historic sentiment, the archbishop had in 1882 received the princely purple and title.

As early as 1868 Lavigerie had felt the necessity of founding a congregation of priests devoted exclusively to the evangelization of Africa. Five years later Providence bestowed three candidates and three nursing-fathers. This was the origin of The Society of Our Lady of Africa. As its achievements have already been chronicled*, we only need to note that, since Lavigerie had recently been appointed apostolic delegate of Sahara, the society's exemption from his authority as archbishop rendered it all the more his creature and tool. The authority of a bishop is checked by the mere existence of a clergy; the power of an apostolic delegate, on account of the absence of a considerable Christian community, stands without check or safeguard. Lavigerie the apostolic delegate was the power behind the throne. Deguerry became vicar, discharging the duties of superior-general, governing the work and managing the funds; but Lavigerie retained the general direction and superintendence in his vicelike grip. In 1877 when illness obliged the man to relinquish either his bishopric or his apostolate, he requested to be allowed to resign the episcopal dignity and its functions. Missions were the work that attracted him most powerfully. He yearned to consecrate himself wholly to those at the heart of the continent. But institutions dependent on an individual too often die with him. In order, therefore, to ensure the future of his Algerian enterprises, Lavigerie assigned the care of each to the new organization. This course

*Chapter 12.

made it after his death the virtual master of most if not all of the Roman missions in French North Africa.

The White Fathers were Lavigerie's other self. Their presence and procedure in Uganda were his. What, then, was the archbishop's accountability for the relations there between two branches of Christ's church? Was he aware that he was sending missionaries into a district already occupied? Did he learn of this occupancy before or after he dispatched his emissaries?

Cardinal Lavigerie and other Roman authorities and sources shall answer these inquiries.

In August, 1875, Stanley converted Mtesa of Uganda to Christianity, and in order to confirm the monarch in his new religion left a Protestant Negro at the court. On November 15th *The Daily Telegraph* of London, a newspaper read in Algiers where Lavigerie resided, published Stanley's appeal for a Christian mission to Uganda. Meanwhile Dallington, the Bible=reader from the Universities' Mission at Zanzibar, was promoting the Christian faith among the Ugandans. On November 18th the Church Missionary Society took the first step toward the establishment of the first Christian mission ever founded in Uganda. The news of this step was immediately published in every important journal and in a multitude of lesser periodicals. On April 25th, 1876, Protestant missionaries left for Uganda, arriving at Zanzibar May 29th, 1876, and at Uganda on June 30th, 1877. These arrivals and departures were announced in the press everywhere. In 1877, when Protestantism was already active at Lake Victoria, Rome instituted apostolic vicariats at the equatorial lakes. On March 25th, 1878, when Protestant missionaries had almost reached Lake Tanganika, Lavigerie's men set out. One band arrived in Uganda on February 22nd, 1879, the other at

Ujiji in November, 1878. Both sets of missioners had known beforehand that they would find Protestant missionaries working among the natives of the fields to which the representatives of Rome were journeying. On May 1st, 1878, Charmetant while at Zanzibar wrote thus to Lavigerie: "In the interior almost all the Protestant sects are already represented. At Ujiji an Anglican [? Congregational] mission is to be founded immediately. . . . Smith and other English missionaries have already established themselves in Uganda. They are sustained by Mtesa. . . . Wautier told me that the king of the Belgians had been happy to learn of the foundation of our mission in equatorial Africa, and would be happy to enter into relations with our missioners and would be in a position to render service to them. . . . On board our ship we had three Protestant delegates of the London missions [Church Missionary Society], who were journeying to Smith in Uganda"*. . .

Charmetant's letter to Lavigerie was communicated by Lavigerie himself to *Les Missions Catholiques*, a Roman missionary magazine published weekly at Lyons, France, by the Lyonese Society for the Propagation of the Faith. But *The Messenger of the Holy Heart of Jesus* had at an even earlier date published an article by Ramiere, in which the author declared that "Protestant sects are already preparing to send their emissaries into these countries [Uganda and the Ujijian region], and to occupy the most advantageous posts. In order to preserve the population from this pressing danger two things are needful: The apostles of the truth must hasten to announce the gospel to them [and] true Catholics must aid the workers".†

Les Missions Catholiques, July 19th, 1878, no. 476, p. 338, col. 1, lines 33, 40, 41, 47-50; also p. 339, col. 1, lines 7-12, 23-25.
† See *Les Missions Catholiques*, August 2nd, 1878, p. 367.

In 1882 Doctor Cust had a private conversation with the black cardinal as to the Anglican and Roman missions in Uganda. Doctor Cust said: "It is a shame that French and English Christians should go into Central Africa, and quarrel. There is room for both. My suggestion is a partition". Lavigerie, so Doctor Cust reports in a personal letter to the present writer, replied: "I agree entirely with you. My orders were to place a certain distance between our settlements and yours. I had no idea that you had settlements in Uganda till the king of the Belgians wrote to tell me so". Doctor Cust "understood that he [Lavigerie] agreed to the principle. Soon after, the Romish mission left the capital; but it came back".

Doctor Cust's letter was written after the death of the prelate. It was, therefore, composed with even greater Christian jealousy for the dead man's good name than if he were alive; in the spirit of love; and with scrupulous regard for historic accuracy and for truth. It can not be assailed as unfair, or impugned as unfaithful. Doctor Cust is a Protestant who dislikes injustice to Rome.

In the light, then, of the Catholic letters and testimony already cited, what becomes of Lavigerie's disclaimer of all knowledge (until Leopold informed him) that British Protestants were in Uganda? Can his profession of ignorance of the presence of Protesant missionaries before the arrival of his missioners withstand the search-light of investigation and the questioning of witnesses?

Sometimes queries receive their real and ultimate reply by asking other questions.

How could Lavigerie have helped becoming aware *before 1876* that Anglican missionaries were to occupy

TWO TYPES OF THE APOSTOLATE   667

Uganda; and before 1877 that British Congregationalists were to settle at the Tanganika? These things were not done in a corner. Their light was not hid in a basket. During 1876=79 all Christendom knew, from a thousand sources of information and through myriad channels of public communication, that British Protestantism was entering and evangelizing the Tanganikan and Ugandan peoples. The Belgian monarch may have informed Lavigerie as early as December, 1875, as to these enterprises; or he may not have informed him until as late as 1882; but in neither event did the action of Leopold relieve Lavigerie from accountability. If Lavigerie were for five years (or more) unacquainted with a fact known to every Christian community, such ignorance would be inexcusable. To avow non=acquaintance with it was to insult intelligence.

Lavigerie, before sending his missioners, was aware that Protestantism was at Lakes Tanganika and Victoria ere Rome arrived.

Did Lavigerie intend to harass or ruin these Protestant missions?

Again Catholic witnesses must be our source of knowledge.

Lavigerie alleged that he had ordered the placing of a certain distance between Protestant and Roman missions. *What* was the distance? One mile? One hundred miles? When was the order issued? In 1878 or 1882? The Algerian missioners left the Ugandan capital in the latter year, but they returned. Then came the trouble. In this connection Charmetant has explicitly disclosed the relation of Leopold, promoter of the Kongoan enterprise, to the Franco=Roman essay in Uganda. Accordingly it seems as if Catholic authorities and sources demonstrate that Lavigerie intended to break down the Anglo=Protestant mission at Lake Victoria. This was wholly spiritual in its purpose; but between the rulers of Belgium, France and the Roman church existed an understanding, if not a compact, that politics and papal Christianity should work together to win equatorial Africa. This goal could not be gained, unless Protestant missionaries were ousted.

There are circumstances in which silence is suicide, and suicide is confession. The circumstances as to Lavigerie in Uganda are of this character, and the silence of his biographers is a plea of guilt.

Lavigerie's work in Uganda suffered from the activity of the slave=hunter. The attempt to Christianize the Negro led the prince of the church to a crusade against the slave=trade. The necessity for protecting his missioners and their proselytes lifted the curtain on the prelate's far=reaching political and secular relations. His procedure and principles involved him in the most questionable positions of his public life. He considered it binding on him to interfere officially. He appealed to the European powers to compel the Zanzibari potentate to stop the atrocities. He might as sensibly have appealed to the peers of Pandemonium to have His Satanic Majesty curb his demons in their fiendishness. The ruler of Zanzibar was no demon; but, even if the European states could have acted in concert, he would have been powerless to enforce their decrees and to shape the course of events at the great lakes.

The impracticability of Lavigerie's proposition turned his attention to another scheme. Forgetting or ignoring that they that take the sword perish by the sword, he proposed to stop slave=stealing by the revival of such military religious orders of medieval Christianity as the Knights of Malta, of Lazarus, of Alcantara. These crusaders he would place under the authority of his own church, march them from place to place, and slay the slave=traffic with the sword. Adopting modern methods and serving as volunteers at the call of this or that government, they would move from district to district as need required. No enormous armies, Lavigerie asserted, were necessary. Fifty Europeans, acclimatized and well=armed, could in two weeks exterminate the three hundred brigands then (1888) terrorizing the region between Nyangwe and Ujiji.

Such a proposal for the inauguration of a holy war could originate only with one who had no personal experience of tropical Africa. The suggestion failed to commend itself to the judgment of those best qualified to pronounce on the merits of the scheme. Stanley scouted it as utter folly. Hore, for sixteen years a resident at Lake Tanganika, averred that it would simply divert the slave=traffic to other routes. Bracq asked: "Will not these volunteers be a danger to Protestant establishments? Catholic missioners have done much to wreck Protestant missions; will not this corps be animated by the same spirit? This is a question which the past of Catholicism brings home with increasing intensity".

Lavigerie maintained that the objection that the crusaders would merely kill a few brigands and leave but a wake of blood and hate rested on a misapprehension of his method. His idea, he asserted, was that every European power in whose African possessions the slave is hunted should place sufficient military forces in afflicted localities. If lack of means prevented this, he would revive the soldiers of the church.

As to this childlike willingness to devote modern military monks of the Roman communion to the service of the state, it appears enough to remark that no European power (France, perhaps, excepted) has availed itself of this generous offer.

Lavigerie achieved some remarkable results in his European campaign of anti=slavery education. He aroused papal peoples at last to the indispensability of annihilating the African slave=trade. He so affected public opinion in France that in its conquest of Dahomé, one of the chief strongholds of slavery, the government received popular support. He federated the majority if not all of the anti=slavery societies. Among thousands he kindled an enthusiasm for enlistment in the new soldiery. But he injured his cause and the advancement of Africa. In *Documents sur la Fondation de l'Œuvre Anti=Esclavagiste* Lavigerie, if referring at all to the achievements of Wilberforce, Sharpe, Wendell Phillips, the elder Macaulay, Livingstone, Lincoln, Gordon, Lloyd Garrison, Buxton and the British Anti=Slavery Society; or to the appeals of Britons to parliament; or to the effects produced by Protestant missionaries; or to the patient negotiations of European powers with oriental potentates — either alluded to his predecessors incidentally or minimized their success. Though Leo XIII, before the first results obtained by Lavigerie in his crusade, showed no special interest, the cardinal strove to have it seem as if the pope were the prime mover in the latest emancipation of Africa. Lavigerie scored his successes by the aid not of Catholics alone but of Protestants and rationalists; yet he attempted to monopolize all credit to himself, the pope and the Roman church for a movement whose most forceful factors consist of the material and moral elements of modern civilization and of the explorers, merchants, missionaries and statesmen of Protestantism.

Not content with this endeavor to rewrite the history of previous anti-slavery movements, the Roman hierarch exerted himself to make the present undertaking sectarian. An immense congress, ecumenical and international, was to have convened in 1889, but the cardinal perceived that the participation of Protestants, to the great number promised, would render it impossible to cramp the anti-slavery crusade within Catholic channels or to hold it within Roman pale. On the pretext that elections to occur in France six if not seven weeks *after* the conference would prevent France from sending full delegations, the ecclesiastical politician substituted a small convention, and wrested control to the Roman church over the new organization. This sectarianism has wrecked the practical usefulness of the papal anti-slavery societies. The real suppressal of African slaving, though the Belgians do something, is undergoing accomplishment at the hands of men of Teutonic blood and faith*.

It is noticeable that neither Keltie in *The Partition of Africa* nor White in *The Development of Africa* even mentions Lavigerie. If the omission of the very name be intentional, it seems significant. On the Roman side, however, there exists a more meaning silence. Clarke, the Jesuit editor and translator of Grussenmeyer's biography of Lavigerie, confesses the difficulty of refuting the charges of political and self-interested motives. The impossibility of refutation appears from the reverend father not attempting the task.

Though the White Fathers directed and still direct their most notable efforts in French North Africa against

---

* Though the Latin communion in Europe comprises millions on millions of members, its contribution one day for Lavigerie's crusade was only one hundred thousand dollars. To obtain the paltry sum of three hundred thousand dollars was the task of months. The Church Missionary Society alone has spent at least seven hundred and fifty thousand dollars for its East Africa mission.

the slave-trade, Lavigerie did not, as is claimed, do more than any other single individual to end this traffic of hell. For the conscience of papal Europe is at present palsied, and official France lags sadly behind the initiative of her generous son.

The imperial quality of Lavigerie the crusader brings into view Lavigerie the seer. New Carthage, so ran his dream, was to be the Christian capital of the orient and the south. He dreamed of establishing cathedrals in the coastal towns between Carthage and Tangier, and of dedicating them respectively to Augustine, Cyprian, Felicitas, Monica, Nymphanion, Perpetua, Tertullian and others. He dreamed of founding Arab Christian villages throughout Algeria and Tunisia. He dreamed of so vast expansion for Our Lady of Africa that her missioners should include representatives of every race and proselytes from every non-Christian faith. He dreamed more daringly and dearly of the Christianization and Gallicizing of the Kabyle, a race six hundred thousand strong. From this raw ore he hoped to forge a nation of missioners, a native army of the cross, whose spiritual strength should be as sinews of steel for the redemption of Islam.

These are great dreams. Despite self-styled "practical" men sneering at them as Quixotic and visionary, their grandeur, their compelling power over the historic imagination, over the seer's cloud-dividing vision of the future, endow such dreams with a faculty of self-fulfillment. Columbus was a visionary; but the outcome of his vision is America.

Rumor reports a remarkable if not significant vision to have been vouchsafed to Lavigerie when political and other reasons rendered it, in the judgment of the French republic and the Vatican, advisable that his missions temporarily retire from view. Delattre, a friend and fellow=worker, knew nothing [?] of the folk=tale, but his non=acquaintance with the alleged event would not affect the possibility of its occurrence, nor lessen its spiritual suggestiveness. One day the cardinal entered a Tunisian chapel to rest and pray. Alone, worn with anxiety, disappointment and fatigue, the man fell asleep. Suddenly he either woke or dreamed of waking. On the windows he beheld an unusual light; at the altar he saw Nymphanion, the first recorded martyr of Christian Carthage (A. D. 198). The saint addressed the priest as "his brother in Jesus Christ our Lord"; pointed to the south; and made a gesture as if embracing all between east and west. Lavigerie, if we may trust report, believed that he had received a vision portending the success of his vast African ambitions, believed that heaven had given sign that he was to persevere.

III

Lavigerie and Moffat: Contrast and Parallel

The contrasts between Lavigerie and Moffat are individual, racial, spiritual. The parallel rests on their common faith and works.

Lavigerie was the child of the mercantile, middle class; Moffat a plain=people's man. The former traced his line to Gaul and Roman; the latter, to Gael and Teuton. There was nothing ideal, nothing impressive in Moffat's personal presence while young, but Lavigerie possessed hereditary grace and was of stately appearance. In old age both looked patriarchs of eld. The appearance of Lavigerie altered little in his last twenty years, save for a more worn look in the striking face, save for the whitening beard. Moffat's bow abode in strength, and his natural force was but little abated. The eye, the revealer of the soul, was in Lavigerie so attentive and earnest as to be a *listening* eye, and always expressed energy and gentleness in union. Moffat's eye was commanding, penetrating, steadfast. The strong features, once as prosaic as a crag of gray granite, softened under the mellowing touch of time and shone with spiritual light.

Lavigerie sprang from her who had been mistress of the world; Moffat from her who is the mother of nations and a maker of destiny. Each man incarnated the British or the French type of national character. Destiny directed the Frenchman to the classic soil of North Africa; Providence pressed the Briton into the virgin wilds of South Africa. The Frank inherited the past, and worked where civilizations had waxed and waned; the Scot held the future in fee, and, like another Osiris of ancient African myth, sowed the seeds of culture and religion in waste and wilderness. The French subject crossed a narrow sea to a district within a few days of France and Rome, and resided in territory under the control of his government; the British citizen went to lands antipodal to his native clime, and dwelt in regions far beyond the shelter of the flag. Moffat reached Africa in the young dawn of Protestant missions, Lavigerie at the darkest hour before the new renaissance of Roman missions; but Moffat was pioneer and creator, Lavigerie entered into other men's labors and built on their foundations. These careers overlapped, Lavigerie arriving in 1867, Moffat departing in 1870; but the Scotchman was a missionary eight years ere Lavigerie was born and for half a century before the archbishop settled in Algeria, whereas the Frenchman served as a

CARDINAL LAVIGERIE
Prince of the Roman Church

missioner only twenty-five years. Moffat through thirteen seasons of retirement from active service remained a missionary; Lavigerie, though dying at the premature age of sixty-seven (1892), had nearly half a century of active life, and into it he put an amount of achievement that vindicates Tennyson's fifty years of Europe as better than a cycle of Cathay. The Protestant toiled in Africa during its sixty years of preparation; the Roman during the quarter-century of consummation. Moffat, though a loyal lover of the father-land, never lifted a finger to bring the Chwana country into a sphere of British interest; Lavigerie was so passionate a patriot that he employed every existent opportunity, and invented opportunities, for the aggrandizement of France. His great failing was his intrusion into politics and his yearning for secular power; and this fault, as the fact that the Huguenots recently were not ashamed to pray publicly for the success of the iniquitous French invasion of Madagascar demonstrates, was due to nationality and race rather than to religion. In the logic of events British influence has extended from the south into the north, French from the north toward the south. The unpurposed outcome of Moffat's work is the annexation of South Africa and much of Central Africa to Britain and Protestantism; but, though Lavigerie strove as strenuously to add North Africa and Uganda to France as to Rome, a Higher than man took Uganda from the French and may retake its Catholics from the Roman.

Moffat technically had no education; Lavigerie spent twenty years "in the still air of delightful studies". The school of practical life educated Moffat's naturally vigorous mind; the scholastic days of the student cramped Lavigerie's intellect.

The mission-work of either Christian affords a fair instance, according to the law of averages, of the results of Protestantism and Rome in Africa. Of course there are exceptions, and among so many individuals there must be exceptions, to the methods and principles of each creed and polity. Hence general statements can not apply to every representative of Latin and of Teutonic Christianity. Yet the following contrasts and parallels present (as justly, it is hoped, as the case allows) the generic type of both communions in Africa. They are intended as composite photographs.

Moffat fulfilled all personal relations; Lavigerie was "a eunuch for the kingdom of heaven's sake". The celibate lost power as missioner and priest, because the family, love and the wisdom of woman were absent from his private life; the parent, because a wife aided him and the presence of their children inspired trust among the natives, became a larger man, a more successful missionary, a truer pastor. The Protestant clergyman began at the bottom, built from the sole foundation, and worked on the barbaric pagan from within outward; the Roman churchman at the apex rather than the base, from the outside more than from within. Moffat after twenty-six years of experience in missions wrote that "evangelization must precede civilization. . . . The missionary has invariably found that to make the fruit good the tree must first be made good. Nothing less than the power of divine grace can re-form the hearts of savages. After this the mind is susceptible". Lavigerie had his missioners abstain from preaching openly, lay little stress on anything beside the basic ideas of Romanism, and frankly accept Muhammad as a minor prophet. Moffat made himself master of African tongues, and rendered the entire Word of God into a native vernacular; Lavigerie, though working in lands to which he owed the origin of Rome's version of the Scriptures, never, for aught that Clarke utters to the contrary, learned an African language, never translated the Bible. Both not only employed evangelization but enlisted industry and medicine in the service of missions. Moffat multiplied the agencies of missions a thousand=fold; Lavigerie's biographer fails to mention any creation of Christian literature or more than the rudiments of native agency. Intrinsically, the Protestant's work enjoys more likelihood of permanence; did it perish, this would befall through the extinction of the Chwana. The Roman's fabric rests on a false foundation, and suffers from structural weakness. Moffat for Christ's sake repeatedly took life in hand; Lavigerie never encountered personal peril in behalf of missions. It was the Protestant, not the Roman, who was the actual hero and potential martyr. In the relations to their respective communions the two exemplify the genius of Protestantism and of Rome; yet each illustrates the superiority of a strong man to a system. Moffat at his station stood at the circumference of an organization for the expansion of Christianity; Lavigerie in his own place was the center of an Algerian administration of missions and stood next to the center at the Vatican that controls all papal propaganda. The spirit of Protestantism — its individuality, freedom and centrifugal tendency, all informed by a higher and inner law of spiritual gravitation — expressed itself in Moffat; the spirit of Rome — its institutional character, subordination to a sovereign and universal sway toward a single center — received illustration in Lavigerie's empire within empire. Moffat unwittingly became bishop of South Africa; Lavigerie made himself pope in infidel lands.

Moffat was a practical nature,
Doer of hopeless tasks that praters shirk,
One of the still, plain men that do the world's rough work;
Lavigerie was diplomat, rhetorician and somewhat of a worldling. Moffat could have gained most of the results won by Lavigerie; but Lavigerie, though an excellent administrator, as when he estimated exactly the number of bricks necessary for a building, could hardly have accomplished the achievements wrought by Moffat. Put Moffat into the prelate's place; our Cadmus of South Africa can discharge its duties. Set Lavigerie at the missionary's post; the ecclesiastical literarian can not cope with its difficulties. Moffat, however, even if he spend a life in Lavigerie's environment, can scarcely, like the skilled politician, reconcile the papacy to the French republic or, if we may credit common report, help to shape the pope's favorable attitude toward democracy in America. These successes are the deeds of a statesman, who, so admirably was he qualified for action on the European stage, could have been president of France or supreme pontiff of Rome. Yet Moffat by virtue of his insight into African character, a virtue apparently not possessed by Lavigerie; by kingly mastery of men; and by Scotch canniness and Christian tact won diplomatic successes with barbaric pagans, that were no easier of attainment, no less deserving of admiration, no less lasting in result than those of Lavigerie.

As men among men both manifested greatness. Whether, individually, Lavigerie or Moffat were the greater, it were idle to attempt to determine; but as the maker is greater than the manager, so Moffat belongs with the first, Lavigerie with the second, order of great men. Though missions will always enlist men whose average of ability at least equals that of any other professional class, we may without disparagement to the African missionaries of to=day say: "There were giants in those days".

The contrast between Catholic and Protestant reveals itself in the character and spiritual life of Lavigerie and of Moffat. The Frank inherited Christianity in its Latin form; the Scot received the reformed faith that is one protest of the Teuton against Rome. Lavigerie's temper in boyhood was churchly, Moffat's mundane; but the fundamentally secular temperament of the Franco= Roman became externally rather than internally pious, and the essentially religious nature of the Keltic Teuton developed into spirituality. Not the Catholic but the Protestant was the holy man of God. Lavigerie grew up to missions; Moffat's Christian life began with missions. Lavigerie, a score of years after confirmation, was drawn by Providence and by others into the apostolate; Moffat, almost at conversion, consecrated himself to evangelization. Moffat first ascertained the will of God and then, though but fifteen years of age, acted from his own initiative; Lavigerie obeyed the divine will, but, though thirty years old, deferred to the decision of a confessor. Papal Christianity keeps men in leading=strings; Protestant Christianity makes men. No falsehood ever fouled Moffat's lip, no scandal dared to smirch his name; Lavigerie on his own showing convicted himself of uttering known untruth and of intending to deceive. Truth, the psychologist asserts, is one thing to man, means another thing to woman; if so, Catholicism and Protestantism, as far as the former is a more feminine, the latter a more masculine, form of faith, diverge in their views as to what constitutes veracity. The fibers of Lavigerie's moral nature unraveled during his African career. He speculated extensively in land.

He held lotteries, and failed to meet the conditions on which the government permitted them. He accepted a cantata, composed by one of his priests, which praised him constantly and several times called him the liberator. He arranged to have eighty of his pupils sing in the proposed congress at Lucerne, and requested Gounod to write the music. Into his anti=slavery documents the black cardinal inserted letters of praise for himself from the hierarchy. One bishop placed him among "the illustrious apostles of the church and unspeakable benefactors of mankind". Another made him a second Peter the Hermit and Urban II. Lavigerie in his volume allotted two pages to a statement of what others before him had done to end the slave=trade, but filled one hundred and thirty pages with letters about himself.

Clarke betrays the self=centeredness and theatricality of Lavigerie in his portrayal of the ceremony and state with which the cardinal prepared his tomb. At the dedication of the cathedral of Carthage he marched all his clergy thither, and in their presence blessed his final resting=place. He recited the formula without a sign of feeling, and afterward composed his own epitaph. In English it reads thus: "Here in the hope of infinite mercy rests Charles Martial Allemand Lavigerie, formerly cardinal=priest of the holy Roman church, archbishop of Algiers and Carthage and primate of Africa, now dust and ashes. Pray for him".

How sublime the simplicity of Moffat, in death as in life!

What, Bracq queried, could not the anti=slavery enterprise, had it remained unsectarian, have done to destroy slavery, improve the relations between all bodies of Christendom, uphold some of the best interests of mankind and civilization! It is with irrepressible melancholy that we contemplate possibilities thwarted by unscrupulous sectarianism. Lavigerie's addresses in Belgium, Britain, France and Switzerland sent horror through his audiences, as he related the harrowing scenes of barbarism and carnage attending the slave=trade. The cardinal stirred the feelings by appropriateness of utterance, the sympathetic glow that warms, the felicitous use of surroundings. Still, his pictures were from documents; it was easy to see that he has not witnessed the curse. Compare him with another anti=slavery orator [Henry Ward Beecher the Congregationalist] whose voice was heard in Britain a quarter=century ago [1863]. How witty, spontaneous, quick and brilliant was the American; how elaborate in method and restrained by religious forms is the French. How matter=of=fact was the Brooklyn preacher; how emotional and poetic is the primate of Africa. What singleness of purpose in the Plymouth pastor; what constant effort on the part of "the pastor of Africa" to win sympathy for his church, missioners and pope. What absence of personal concern in the American patriot; what frequent allusions to age, fatigue and self=sacrifice on the part of the Catholic philanthropist. The one how modern in address, how fond of democratic simplicity; the other how riveted to the past by his ideals, his ecclesiastical rank, his delight in aristocratic pretensions and high=sounding titles. The one must be humanitarian because a Christian; the other a Romanist because humanitarian. Both have great popularity, great zeal for the highest interests of the colored race. There are traits in Lavigerie we would not discuss. Great as have been his services to the anti=slavery cause, yet his anxiety to give the history of a work in which he is one of the chief factors; his parsimony in dealing with those who preceded him and prepared the ground; his *finesse* in making his enterprise Roman; and his self=glorification have led us to ask if Lavigerie has not much of Loyola in his spirit and something of Boulanger in his methods? Protestants would do well to reflect before giving the cardinal money or praises. Had he continued as he began, he would have deserved both*.

God once uttered through Isaiah a prophecy as to Cyrus His anointed that shows every man's life to be a plan of God. Stroke after stroke of this Scripture portrays Moffat. However much Lavigerie may have been a man of destiny, it remains true that Moffat was a providential man. We part from Moffat with these words: He is My shepherd, and shall perform all My pleasure, even saying to Jerusalem, thou shalt be built, and to the temple, thy foundations shall be laid. . . . His right hand have I holden, to subdue nations before him. I will loose the loins of kings, to open the two= leaved gates; and they shall not be shut. I will go before thee, and make the rugged places plain. I will break in pieces the gates of brass, and cut in sunder the bars of iron. I will give thee the treasures of darkness and the hidden riches of secret places. . . . I have even called thee by thy name; I have surnamed thee, though thou hast not known Me.

**The Missionary Review,* October, 1890, (vol. 3, No. 10), pp. 724=5, abridged and condensed.

CHAPTER 20

B. C. 225 = A. D. 1898

LOOKING BACKWARD — AND FORWARD

Mission=reports are said to be valueless; they are not half so value-less as anti=mission reports. Henry Drummond

So far from having failed, there is no work of God that has received so absolute, so unprecedented a blessing. To talk of the failure of missions is to talk like an ignorant and like a faithless man. Farrar

When the history of the great African states of the future comes to be written, the arrival of the first missionary will with many of these new nations be the first historical event. . . . This pioneering propagandist will assume somewhat of the character of a Quetzalcoatl — of those strange, half=mythical personalities that figure in the legends of old American empires, the beneficent being who introduces arts and manufactures, implements of husbandry, edible fruits, medical drugs, cereals and domestic animals. Sir H. H. Johnston

Wherever Christianity was taught, it brought the additional good of civilization. Sydney Smith

The missionary seems to me the best and truest hero this century has produced. Joseph Thomson

(I) MATERIAL AND SOCIAL EFFECTS. (1) GEOGRAPHY: ROMAN RECONNOISSANCES. PROTESTANT EXPLORATIONS. IN SOUTH AFRICA. ON THE KONGO. ALONG EQUATORIAL LAKES AND RIVERS. PRESBYTERIAN EXPLORERS IN NYASALAND. ARNOT ACROSS AFRICA. VALUE OF MISSION=EXPLORATIONS. LIVINGSTONE. (2) PHILOLOGY: MISSIONARY ORIGIN OF AFRICAN PHILOLOGY. SOME MISSIONARY PHILOLOGISTS. JUDGMENT OF SCHOLARS ON THEIR WORK. (3) NATURAL SCIENCE. (4) ART, COMMERCE AND INDUSTRY. (5) CIVILIZING AND COLONIZATION. CIVILIZATION AND CHRISTIANITY AS EVANGELISTS. (6) MISSIONS AS PEACE=MAKERS. MADAGASCAR. (II) ETHICAL AND SPIRITUAL RESULTS. (1) A STUDY IN STATISTICS: COMMUNICANTS. PROT-

ESTANT SOCIETIES. VARIETIES. CHARACTER OF THEIR AGENTS. THE FIELD=FORCE. ANALYSIS FOR AFRICA. ANALYSIS FOR MADAGASCAR. GAINS AND MEANINGS. THE PROTESTANT MISSION=PLANT. ROMAN STATISTICS. FRANCE THE CATHOLIC ORGANIZER OF VICTORY. PAPAL AND PROTESTANT CONTRASTS. ROME'S FATAL DEFICIENCIES. NEO=LATIN MISSIONER AND TEUTONIC MISSIONARY. PROVIDENCE VS ROME. (2) THE CHRISTIANITY OF THE AFRICAN: ADVERSE EVIDENCE. ITS VALUE. THE SPECTATOR AS DANIEL. FAVORABLE TESTIMONY. NATIVE EXAMPLES OF CHRISTIAN CHARACTER. (III) THE OUTLOOK FOR THE COMING CENTURY. (I) EUROPEAN MASTERY. (2) MUSLIM DECADENCE. (3) VITALITY OF PROTESTANTISM. LIABILITY TO INJURY FROM CIVILIZATION AND COMMERCE. RISING RATIOS OF GAIN. FEMALE MISSIONARIES. COLONIAL CHRISTIANS. NATIVE AGENCY. NEW METHODS. DIFFICULTY OF SELF=SUPPORTING MISSIONS. AMERICAN NEGRO CHRISTIANITY. A FORECAST OF COMING WAYS AND MEANS. GOD'S WILL, GOD'S WORK.

Modern Africa is a monument of Christian missions. To many this will be a hard saying. Yet in a large and real sense it is a faithful saying worthy of all acceptance. Examination of evidence will prove the statement true. Such an examination must begin at the beginning. This consisted in becoming acquainted with Africa.

I

Material and Social Effects

(1) As early as 1350, according to apocryphal accounts that may yet receive verification as authentic narratives of actual events, missioners had traversed Africa. If these two crossings really occurred, neither the medieval merchant nor soldier but the medieval missionary inaugurated exploration. If not, the modern missionary initiated the recovery of the lost continent, for the outlining of it by the Portuguese owed as much to the missionary motive as to the mercantile impulse.

In 1563 Orto spoke of a missioner having crossed Africa. Probably the unnamed traveler was a Jesuit, and the time between 1550 and 1560. In 1521 Manoel, king of Portugal, had dispatched Quadra to the Kongo with instructions to journey overland to Abyssinia; in 1526 and 1537 Castro and Pacheco had proposed a similar journey; and in 1546 João III had recommended that the Portuguese in Abyssinia cross to the mouth of the Kongo. Breto planned a series of stations between the eastern and western shores (1592). Araglio penetrated four hundred and twenty miles from Angola (1606). Godinho, a missioner, advocated an overland route (1663). Jarrie the Jesuit affirmed that according to his informants there was nothing to prevent passage from the northern Zambezi country to Angola. The Jesuits actually penetrated from the Toka plateau, north of Zambezi River, into the present Rutsi country above Victoria Falls. As the bird flies from the mouth of the Zambezi to that of the Kunene this is half the distance across Africa. Lacerda, who opened eight hundred and ten miles of new country between Mozambique and the southeastern lakes of the Lualaba (1798), was accompanied by a Catholic chaplain. Between 1500 and 1800 at least one missioner was among the crossers of Africa and anticipators of Livingstone.

Without referring to other African travels undertaken by Rome's representatives during the sixteenth and seventeenth centuries, their work on the Sûdanese Nile between 1848 and 1863 demands notice*. In 1849 Ignaz Knoblecher, then head of an Austrian mission, undertook what was really an exploring tour in behalf of evan-

---

*Paez, a Jesuit missionary in Abyssinia, claimed to have discovered the spring-head of the Blue Nile, which Bruce rediscovered one hundred and fifty years later (1770), but Bruce and Cooley discredit the claim. Paez was merely the first to describe what Portuguese residents had visited about 1595.

gelization. During this expedition up the Nile from Khartum to Gondokoro, the Jesuit reached the Logwek or Rijiaf hill (4° 45′ N.), and was the first to ascend it. Six years later, Beltrame, another missioner, traveled up the Blue Nile to Roseres. Duryak, Gossner, Kaufmann, Kirchner, Morlang, Mosgan and Vinco were also Jesuit explorers. Their journeys, researches for geography, meteorological observations and ethnographical and linguistic studies enlarged our knowledge of Nile lands and peoples. Petermann, a German scientist, declared that Duryak and Knoblecher "kept an annual hygrometrical and meteorological register with great precision and scientific regularity".

Massaia in 1878, through his influence with Menilek of Abyssinia, obtained permission for Antinori, an Italian explorer, to found a scientific station on the royal estate. The missioner was also a savant. In Algeria and Tunis Lavigerie was antiquarian and archæologist as well as apostle, and it was with his sanction that Delattre, an Algerian missionary, prosecuted a number of interesting discoveries and organized an invaluable museum.

About 1880 Duparquet made a journey from Walvisch Bay in German Southwest Africa to Omaruru and thence to the Ovampo between Kunene and Okavango Rivers. Francis Galton the scientist had with Andersson attempted in 1850-51 to explore their country, but the task seems to have been reserved for the Jesuit missioner. Ohrwalder, an Austrian Jesuit, escaping from the Mahdists, brought the first authentic news of events in Sûdan during the dark years following its closure to civilization in 1884.

All African missionaries have more or less been explorers. Long before Livingstone, Protestant missionaries had been the most active agents in adding to our knowledge of Africa. Livingstone, though the most remarkable and successful of missionary explorers, was far from being the first or last of such discoverers. The influence of the religious world, — so Brown averred in his history of African exploration, a work written purely in the interests of geographical science — has ever been all=powerful in opening Africa. It, above all agents, permeated society with a conviction that the white man would remain in arrears of duty, did he permit his black brother to acquire civilization through the Arab slaver and the European rum=seller. The Protestant factors in the African geographical movement entered in South Africa and Madagascar, opened explorations afterward in West Africa and East Africa almost simultaneously, and even effected something in North Africa. The Orange and Zambezi Rivers in the south; the Ogowai and Mobangi streams in the west; the Lualaba=Luapula system in the center; the inland seas and Nile sources in the east; and the uplands of Aybssinia are memorials of missionary enterprise*.

Missionaries entered Cape Colony in 1792, 1795 and 1799. Summerville and Trutter crossed Orange River in 1801 into the Chwana country. Campbell of the London Society was one of the most active among those who reached the remoter regions beyond the colony. In 1812 he determined the course of the Orange. In 1820, with Moffat, who himself did not a little of exploring, he reached the source=region of the Limpopo. Several of the American missionaries among the Zulu traveled from place to place, from the coast to the interior, over

* It has been claimed that though the British government sent Richardson to open commercial relations with Central Sûdan, it was his desire to found a Christian mission on Lake Chad that led him to cross Sahara (1850). The discovery of the Binwe and Shari Rivers and the after exploration of the Binwe by Crowther must be regarded, at least partly, as resulting from the missionary motive. The present writer has not been able, despite reference to authorities, to verify the claim as to Richardson.

mountains and wastes, till their acquaintance with ethnology and geography became extensive and accurate. Though South African missionaries, as a rule, did not take notable part in exploration, they contributed largely to our knowledge of the natives; and the early pioneers, sportsmen and travelers whose names are connected with the mapping of regions just beyond Cape Colony could never have been so successful had it not been for mission=stations protecting them when asylums were of utmost moment.

It is in Central, East and Northeast Africa that missions have most markedly linked themselves with exploration.

In West Africa Doctor Nassau, the American Presbyterian, revealed unknown reaches of Ogowai River and Grenfell, a British Baptist, discovered the Mobangi, the greatest tributary of the Kongo. Before his surveys of Africa's Amazon Grenfell had traveled thirteen hundred miles on foot in Kamerun (1874=78) and more than five thousand miles in canoe. Together with Comber he in a few years rendered service in the opening of Africa well worthy of comparison with those of their fellow= laborers. Comber like his colleague had been a missionary in Kamerun and had explored the district behind its mountain=range. In 1878 the missionaries, while at San Salvador, discovered Arthington Fall on Brije River in the Zombo Mountains. Before reaching Stanley Pool *via* the stream, Comber and Grenfell had attempted to gain it by leaving the lower river for the ancient capital of Portuguese Kongo, trying to strike thence east and north, and coming on the river above Livingstone Cataracts. The long stay was not fruitless for geography, and other interesting discoveries were made. After his establishment of his station at the Pool, one of Comber's first explorations was a voyage around this lake=like expanse of river. Even Stanley, so late as 1884, had not circumnavigated this water. Stanley in 1877 supposed it to be about nine miles long and from two to seven in breadth. Comber found a length of twenty=three miles, a width about equal and, in place of the area of about fifty=five square miles assigned to Stanley Pool by the discoverer, an area of three hundred and fifty square miles. Dover Cliffs were neither chalk, as Stanley had fancied, nor pipe=clay, according to a later legend, but silvery sands varied with brown and with black forests. Shortly after this expedition Comber was joined by Grenfell, and the river was more accurately investigated. They steamed up the Bochini, (which Stanley had called the Kwa), up the Kasai to the junction of the Kwango and Mfini Rivers and up the mighty Kongo itself to Ba=Ngala, nearly half=way from Stanley Pool to Stanley Falls. Another voyage by Grenfell added greatly to our knowledge of the northern tributaries of the giant stream, and revealed the noble Mobangi. Grenfell followed this up for four hundred miles, and, where he turned south again, (only a degree or two west of Junker's furthest on the same stream), found it still a broad, deep, open waterway and of such volume that Wauters, a Belgian scientist, demonstrated mathematically from the missionary's *data* that the Mobangi must be the Welle of Schweinfurth and the Makwa of Junker. On this trip, which occupied five months, Grenfell also entered the Lefini or Lawson, Lumami=Lubilash, Ma=Nagala, M=Bura, Nkenye, Ruki and Ukere Rivers for considerable distances. In the autumn of the same year (1885) he ascended the Lulanga and Ruki Rivers, the only two great southern tributaries between the Kasai and Kwango still unexamined, and found the

Juapa branch of the Ruki to be a most promising road for missions. In 1887 this brilliant series of explorations, which, be it remembered, were undertaken in behalf of missions, ended with the ascent of the Kwango to Kukunji Falls. The Royal Geographical Society in bestowing the patrons' medal in token of appreciation for these discoveries awarded nothing more than his due to Grenfell. Though not enjoying Livingstone's opportunities, he acquitted himself with Livingstonian sagacity and success. He has since distinguished himself in the difficult feat of defining the boundaries between Belgian and Portuguese Kongo.

Only the limitations of space can excuse mere mention of the travels of Anglican missionaries in Yariba, of United Presbyterians in Old Calabar and of others elsewhere. These journeys, though inferior in importance to those of the Baptists in Belgian Kongo, were not without interest for geography and for the opening of the regions examined. The London Society, had it done nothing more than send Vanderkemps, Kicheners, Campbells, Moffats and Livingstones to Africa and Ellises and Sibrees to Madagascar, would have performed a great work for exploration. Our knowledge of southern Abyssinia and northern Gallaland was increased by Krapf and Isenberg, the former learning of the existence of a pygmy race. While a missionary in Zanguebar, Krapf visited U=Sambara and U=Kamba, familiarized himself with the whole coast as far south as Cape Delgado, and (1849) discovered on the equator a snow=capped mountain nearly nineteen thousand feet high. Rebmann, his colleague, penetrated Taita and Chagga, mountainous districts, and (1848) sighted a still more extraordinary snow=mountain three and two=thirds miles in height. So astounding to arm=chair geographers and stay=at=home wiseacres was the information that in Africa about the equator stood mountains furrowed with glaciers and crowned with eternal snow, that Cooley, a commentator of no small eminence, relieved the trials of his theorizing mind by the gentlemanly allegation that the missionaries lied. Snow=topped mountains, such as Rebmann's Kilima=Njaro and Krapf's Kenia, could not possibly exist. Rebmann replied that he had lived in Switzerland, and knew glaciers, mountains and snow when he saw them. Time passed, and professional explorers justified the accuracy and truthfulness of the missionaries as to these equatorial yet loftier Jungfraus and Matterhorns. Krapf and Rebmann also gained among philologists a name almost as brilliant as their pioneer journeys had obtained among geographers.

In 1855 Erhard and Rebmann made a map of East Africa between the equator and 14° S. and for sixteen degrees inland from Zanzibar. On it figured a lake or, rather, an inland sea of whose existence they had learned from the natives. It was so portentous in size, so unseemly in shape, representing the salamander, that it swallowed about half the area. Yet this gigantic slug, according to the public statement of Speke, led the Royal Geographical Society to dispatch Burton on an exploring expedition to ascertain the actual facts. "The missionaries", Speke added, "are the prime promoters of this discovery. They put on the map that monster slug of an inland sea which caused our being sent to Africa". Though Marinus of Tyre and Ptolemy of Alexandria were aware of the existence of Nile lakes; though Lief=bin=Said in the thirteenth century mentioned a great midland lake, declaring "it well known by all people there that the river which goes through Egypt takes its origin from the lake"; though Portuguese missioners and travelers heard of this lake=sea; though Burton and Speke found that the vague native narratives had misled the German missionaries into making three widely separated lakes into one — yet the finding of Lakes Nyasa, Tanganika and Victoria is virtually an achievement of the Church Missionary Society and its Lutheran representatives. From the missionary travels of Krapf and Rebmann came the initial impulse toward the winning of the equatorial regions of East Africa. If Stanley in 1875 gave occasion for the coming of missions to Lake Victoria, missions had twenty, if not thirty, years before pointed out the path for Stanley.

New and Wakefield, British missionaries of the United Free Methodists in East Africa, likewise put geography and science in their debt. Wakefield greatly increased our acquaintance with distinct regions beyond the coast. New distinguished himself by ascending Kilima=Njaro (1871) higher than it had till then been climbed; and by acquiring so extensive a knowledge of languages that he was chosen a member of an intended expedition for the relief of Livingstone.

The Presbyterian missionaries on Lake Nyasa have rendered no unimportant service to exploration. Laws and Young in 1875 showed the lake to be, not, as supposed, only one hundred and fifty miles long but a hundred and twenty leagues (three hundred and fifty miles) from end to end. The voyages, a little later, of Laws with Stewart of Lovedale added extensively to our knowledge of the shores. In 1878 Laws and Stewart of India journeyed in the region west of Nyasa. At a later day the younger Stewart crossed from Nyasa to Tanganika, and in 1882 completed the survey of the Scotch=African loch. These explorations brought iron=mines, outcrops of coal and the presence of copper to light. They revealed at least fifteen different tribes immediately to the west, speaking as many languages. They showed Nyasaland to be, not a wilderness inhabited only by animals, but a land of villages, some of them with ten thousand residents. The pastoral districts of the cool western highlands possess a much larger population than many analogous regions in South Africa. Above all, the Scotch Presbyterian missionaries caused the construction of a road around Murchison Cataract on Shire River, and were mainly instrumental in the origination of the Stevenson route between Lakes Nyasa and Tanganika. The Established and the Free Church of Scotland shared equally the cost of Murchison Road. Stewart of India surveyed for Stevenson "Road". Stevenson of Glasgow paid the chief expense of the survey. The Blantyre and Livingstonia missions, representing respectively the Established and the Free Presbyterians, gave occasion for founding the African Lakes Company, a pioneer in promoting Christianity by means of colonization and commerce; and through its agency these missions, the successors of Livingstone, became the primary cause of Britain annexing his Nyasan lands. The Established Presbyterian taught the natives so to respect the British name, that a mere request was enough to prevent two chiefs on the eve of war from going to hostilities. The Free Presbyterians, with Glasgow merchants and planters, held their own before the British government arrived, and by force of arms first checked the Nyasan slaver. The services rendered to African civilization by Livingstonia Mission, another Lovedale, can not be exaggerated. When Europe's debt to Blantyre is placed in black and white, it will be admitted by the unfriendliest critics of missions that its influence makes for righteousness and well=being.

The year 1884 opened briskly for African exploration. Richards, an American Congregationalist, traveled from Inhambani to the Limpopo. Grenfell and Comber made their careful survey of the middle course of the Kongo and its Bochini tributary. Arnot, a Scotch undenominational missionary, completed a journey from Natal to Benguela, which, though not of geographical importance, excited the utmost attention. Arnot carried no lethal weapon more fatal than a walking=stick, and cumbered himself with so little baggage that difficulties with carriers, that hampered his forerunners, were almost unexperienced. The missionary, starting in August, 1881, worked his way from Durban, a Natalese port on the Indian Ocean, to Potchefstroem in Transvaal and to Shoshong, then the capital of Khama's kingdom. Thence he crossed Kalahari Desert to the junction of the Chobe=Kwando and Zambezi Rivers, arriving in August, 1882. After spending eighteen months among the Rutsi and breaking ground for Coillard, Arnot past up=stream to Lialui and thence to Bailundu and the harbor of Benguela, reaching it in December, 1884. While at Bihe, *en route*, he brought the chief, who had expelled and plundered the American Congregational missionaries, to his senses, and secured the renewal of the mission. From Benguela Arnot also traveled from June, 1885, to February, 1886, to Garenganze=Katanga, a region equidistant between the Atlantic and Indian Oceans. He discovered that not the stream flowing from Lake Dilolo but the branch called the Liba by Livingstone is the Zambezi; that its highest sources rise in the country west of Lake Bemba (Bangweolo); and that the southwestern sources of the Kongo lie so close to the northeastern one of the Zambezi that probably the furthest founts of each great river spring from the same hill.

The Royal Geographical Society in 1889 recognized the importance of Arnot's work, as also, afterward, of that performed by Sheppard, a Presbyterian missionary and Negro citizen of the southern United States who in 1891 explored the Kuba region of Belgian Kongo on behalf of missions. The transcontinental journey of Johnston of Jamaica, undertaken for missionary purposes, was in some respects of geographical note.

Joseph Thomson, a noble explorer who argued that, the more easily to win Africans, Christian teaching should lie level with Islam, particularized still another service of missions to exploration, when he wrote: "Nobody has more reason than I to speak well of missionaries and to rejoice that they have spread over the waste places of earth. In the heart of the dark continent I have been received as a brother, relieved when destitute, nursed when half=dead and time after time sent on my weary way rejoicing that there is such a profession as Christian missionaries". It was to Mackay of Uganda that Europe became indebted in October, 1886, for the first news since 1884 that Schnitzer (Emin Pasha) was alive and holding his own. It was Mackay who persuaded Mwanga to permit Junker, the great Russo=German explorer, to quit Uganda. It was by the help of still other missionaries that Junker reached civilization, and brought the information that initiated Stanley's expedition and its results for geography and politics. It was again Mackay whose kindness, according to Jephson, restored Stanley and his white comrades to health, gave them exactly what most they needed, and inspired them with fresh love and zest for their task.

It may be objected that this sketch of the exploring activity and achievements of African missionaries lacks perspective and proportion. There have been a thousand explorers of Africa, but the missionaries whose geographical work has been mentioned number less than a hundred. Are not the discoveries of merchants, military men and traders, of professional travelers and scientists ignored and undervalued?

Such an objection, if offered, could only originate in misapprehension of the object aimed at in the preceding account. The purpose is simply to show that several missionaries were the pioneers to whom exploration and science owe the forward movement in the recovery of tropical Africa. As subsidiary to this purpose should come a statement of the manner in which many missionaries have trod on the heels of the professed discoverer, and have completed his imperfect work. For this, however, space is wanting. William Dwight Whitney maintained that "religion, commerce and scientific zeal are the three instrumentalities rivaling one another in bringing new regions and peoples to light; and of the three the first is the most pervading and effective".

Livingstone's career affords the supreme instance of this principle. They are no few months' explorations that form the contents of his works. *Missionary Travels* cover sixteen years, half of his African life; *The Narrative of an Expedition to the Zambezi*, five years; *The Last Journals*, seven years. How many other explorers devoted even five years to an expedition? Very few.

Livingstone traveled twenty=nine thousand miles in Africa, and added one million square miles, one twelfth of its continental and insular area, to the known regions of the globe. His discoveries — Lake Ngami (1849), which wealthy, well=equipped explorers had failed to reach; the Zambezi in mid=continent (1851) and its course to the Indian Ocean and Victoria Falls (1856);

the two longitudinal ridges flanking the South=Central African valley; Shire River, Murchison Cataracts and Lake Shirwa (1859); and the rediscovery, virtually the original discovery, of the Nyasa — were never happy guesses or vague descriptions from native accounts. Each spot, however ill the man might be, was determined exactly. Livingstone fixed the true orientation of Lake Tanganika, whose length he was the first European to traverse; discovered Lakes Mweru (1867) and Bangweolo (1868) and the Lualaba stream of the Kongo; opened the Nyema country; and, seconded by Stanley, showed that the Tanganika did not empty northward and therefore could not feed the Nile.

Livingstone also investigated botany, geology, hydrography and zoölogy. His enjoyment of nature was as keen as his observation. He strove to form a right idea of the shape and structure of the continent. He was so painstaking and trustworthy in scientific matters that Arrowsmith, Fergusson, Frere, Herschel, Maclear, Murchison, Owen, Sedgwick and Stanley honored him. The more they knew him, the more they honored him. Nor did such explorers, scholars and scientists as Burton criticise him. When Burton would praise Speke, he affirmed that he had done what not even the dauntless, indefatigable Livingstone had excelled. "Of his intellectual force and energy", Frere wrote, "he has given such proofs as few could afford. No man ever attempted on a grander or more thorough scale to benefit and improve those of his race who most needed improvement and light. In the execution of what he undertook I never met his equal for energy and sagacity. Every year will add fresh evidence to show how well considered were the plans he took in hand, and how vast have been the results of the movements he set in motion".

German philologists who cared nothing for religion regarded Livingstone as the only man who understood races and how to deal with them for good. Herschel uttered a warm eulogy on the exactness and excellence of Livingstone's astronomical observations for latitude and longitude. Maclear in 1854 wrote: "No explorer has determined his path with the precision you have accomplished". In 1856 Maclear said publicly: "I never knew a man who, knowing scarcely anything of making geographical observations or laying down positions, became so soon an adept that he could take the complete lunar observation and the altitudes for time ["two thousand, eight hundred and twelve partial observations"] within fifteen minutes". The astronomer considered Livingstone's determinations of the Zambezi "the finest specimens of sound geographical observation he ever met with. . . What that man has done is unprecedented. . . . You could go to any point along Livingstone's track and feel certain of your position".

Astronomer, geographer, mercantile director, missionary, physician, traveler and zoölogist in one — few men ever sustain so many characters at once, and none ever performed the functions of each with greater success.

It has been charged that Livingstone sank the missionary in the traveler. Facts demonstrate this not to be the case. The journeys of 1840=56 were those of a poor missionary, and were undertaken solely in service to missions. The discoveries of this and the Nyasan period were the achievement of a Scotch Congregationalist endeavoring to enlarge and multiply opportunities for the evangelization and civilizing of barbaric pagans. The scientific journeys of 1866=73 were made

DAVID LIVINGSTONE

primarily in behalf of Christian civilization, and effected even more for missions than for geography. The end of the geographical feat, the Protestant missionary=statesman declared, is but the beginning of the Christian enterprise. "He could only feel in the way of duty by working as a missionary". He would not go simply as a geographer. The object of these explorations (1866=73) was to lead the British to Christianize and civilize Africa. For this purpose Livingstone, while traveling, taught Christianity to Africans and roused the conscience of Christendom against the slave=trade. The geographical result and the securing of Stanley, as he himself avers, with all its after wealth of blessing for Africa must be credited to the account of missions. Both as journeyman and as statesman of missions Livingstone was a pioneer of Christian civilization for races in darkness. Livingstone stands alone as the missionary=traveler.

How does Livingstone rank when contrasted to non=religious explorers?

Stanley says: "In the annals of exploration of the dark continent we look in vain among other nationalities for such a name as Livingstone's. He stands pre=eminent above all; he unites the best qualities of other explorers: the methodical perseverance of Barth, Moffat's philo=Africanism, Rohlf's enterprising spirit, Duveyrier's fondness for geographical minutiæ, Burton's literal accuracy, Speke's charming simplicity and seductive *bonhommie;* he is a rare human mosaic, a glory to Britain. But to Burton Germany can show Barth and France Duveyrier; to Speke the first can show Rohlf and the latter Caillé; to Cameron Germany can oppose Nachtigal and to Baker Schweinfurth, though two greater opposites can scarcely be imagined, and France can boast of Compeigne and Brazza [the Italian]. But Britain, after producing Bruce, Clapperton, Denham, the Landers and Park, excelled even herself when she produced the strong and perseverant Scotchman"*.

Livingstone, then, was the greatest of all African travelers. The transcontinental passages of Catholic missioners and Portuguese travelers during the sixteenth or seventeenth centuries failed of permanent effect. The hour had not struck, the man had not come. It was the trans=African journeys of Livingstone that inaugurated Africa's new era. He accomplished more toward her recovery and development than a multitude of men whose names are more intimately associated with the arduous undertaking. To Livingstone first and foremost among many belong (1) a renascence for African missions, (2) the reclamation of South=Central Africa from barbarism and sin and (3) the suppressal of a slave= trade that is "the open sore of the world". In the new world of tropical Africa Livingstone was a new and nobler Columbus. The Christliness of his character made him, makes him, a force in Christianizing Africans. No African ever uttered a syllable of scandal as to Livingstone. Missionaries who would explain to Muslim or pagan what constitutes practical Christianity need only point to the character and life of David Livingstone. Fergusson was right in regarding him as one of the greatest men of the human race; Florence Nightingale was not at fault in thinking him "what John the Baptist, had he been living in the nineteenth century, would have been", nor in thinking "his work finished, the most glorious work of our generation"

(2) Philology is only less a missionary science than geography. Lull, the African missionary, had in the thir-

* *The Congo*, v. 2, p. 385.

teenth century given a first impulse toward the study of oriental languages. Comparative philology took a medieval beginning in the fifteenth century through a comparison of translations of the Lord's Prayer. Boyle, the founder of the British Royal Scientific Society, declared that its special object was to propagate Christianity through literature and science. Leibniz planned that the Academy at Berlin should promote oriental learning *as* this concerned the propagation of Christianity. The same idea prevailed at the Halle, St Petersburg, Vienna and Wittenberg Academies. The American Board had Pickering, in 1820 an eminent philologist, construct a common alphabet and uniform spelling for Indian languages; and it applied this system in Africa. Venn, the scholar and statesman of the Church Missionary Society, with sagacious prescience brought a band of German scholars into the service of Anglican missions to elucidate the languages of West Africa. In 1848 he himself formulated rules for reducing unwritten languages to Roman characters, and these were applied to African languages. Lepsius the Egyptologist, at the instance of this Anglican mission=society, prepared a complete and standard alphabet of the same sort. Since he did this, he declared, for the sake of service to missions no less than to philology, the Berlin Academy, of which he was a member, carried out the purpose of Leibniz. The whole progress of African philology owes more to missionaries and societies for missions than to explorers, professed philologists and scientific societies together. Of seventy=seven persons named by Dr Cust as African philologists at least half were missionaries. British missionaries have of course accomplished the major portion of this achievement, though American and German scholars have seconded them, and the Church

Society printed the Lepsius alphabet. In 1847 Latham, then an acknowledged master of the science of languages and of men, composed a valuable monograph on African languages. Thirty=eight years later not only Latham's authorities but his own essay had become obsolete, because, according to Whitney the philologist, "the extraordinary activity of missions and geographical discovery had directed study toward African dialects. A great mass of material had been collected, and examined sufficiently to give a general idea of the distribution of races".

The known languages of Africa, including dialects, number at least six hundred. In 1891 missions were working among the speakers of one hundred and eleven of these languages, and the Scriptures had been entirely or partially translated into sixty=seven languages and dialects of the African continent*. These did not include those of Madagascar nor the Negro versions in the Americas. Other African languages have since received Scripture versions in whole or in part, and the total of modern versions of Africa and Madagascar together now numbers ninety=four. Of these the American Baptist Union, the [Particular] Baptist Missionary Society [British], the Basel Bible=Society, the Berlin Mission= Society [I], the Church Society, the Free Church of Scotland and the Gospel=Propagation Society each published one; the Society for Promoting Christian Knowledge and the Universities' Mission two each; the Baptist [?Bible?] Translation Society [British] four; the National Bible=Society of Scotland eight; the American Bible=Society nine; and the British Bible=Society sixty=

*See Cust, *Africa Rediviva*, pp. 101=104, for lists. Compare Cust, *Cyclopedia of Missions*, v. 2, appendix B., pp. 547=577. An appendix by the present writer contains other lists.

eight, more than twice as many as the other organizations together*.

A few African versions (though the great majority belong to the last half=century and Protestantism) run their roots deep into ancient Christianity, at least one, the Septuagint, antedating it. Alexandria gave Bashmur, Memphite and Sahidic variations of the Koptic version to Egypt; an Ethiopic translation to Abyssinia; its Greek to Armenian students of the Septuagint; and perhaps translations to Arabia (A. D. 632?). North Africa gave the first Latin version to Rome. This African vernacular version, this gift from a church that was itself the child of African missions originated by Greek=speaking Christians in Rome, lent life to the Vulgate, and yet lived independently in Scotland, Ireland and England for centuries.

Medieval missions yielded scarcely any result for African philology and Scripture=versions in addition to those of Lull. But with the entrance of modern Christianity both of these woke to new life. A Catholic missioner to the Nubians in the seventeenth century wrote a Barabra dictionary. Heyling the Lutheran missionary in Abyssinia between 1634 and 1636 translated the New Testament into Amharic. Dias the Jesuit in 1679 published a Mbundu or Angolan grammar. Vetralla, a representative of Rome, in 1699 wrote in Latin a grammar of the Kongo languages. In 1748 the Lord's Prayer was printed in seventy=five languages and one hundred and seventy=five dialects, of which only seven were African; in 1885 the totals had risen respectively to three hundred

*See my list of Bible=versions in the appendix. Several Bible=translations have been published by two societies, as the Zulu Bible by the American and Basel Bible=Societies, thus raising the total number in appearance, from ninety=four to one hundred. The above figures are approximations only. For exact statistics consult the appendices.

and thirty=one and to fifty=nine. In 1804=1805 Cannecattim the Capuchin issued a Mbundu dictionary and grammar. But The British and Foreign Bible=Society also came into being in 1804, and on the very day (March 7th) that is the saint's day of Perpetua, one of the first three women known to have died for Christ in Africa. The Septuagint translators, compared with this society and its congeners, and Jerome himself, in comparison with modern missionaries who render the Scriptures with scientific precision, both worked at hap= hazard.

It is manifestly impossible even to mention a tenth of the missionaries who have rendered service to African and Madagascarene philology. But the lay reader will, perhaps, not find it uninteresting to con the names of Macbrair, Hannah Kilham, Zimmerman, Christaller, Crowther, Townsend, Massaia, Gollmer, Goldie, Robb, Moffat, Shaw, Shrewsbury, Boyce, Casalis, Appleyard, Jones, Freeman, Mabille, Rebmann, Griffiths, Torrend, Steere, O'Flaherty and Pilkington. The work accomplished by such men forms a story of fascinating philological interest, and constitutes a structure of transcendent importance for the growth of language and literature in Africa. The missionaries have in fifty years done for African vernaculars what it took medieval Christian Europe five centuries to accomplish for itself. They have given shape and substance to the speech of great races. They have not only done this, thus preserving the life of many native languages, but they have baptized the speech and thought of the Arab, the Bantu, the Berber, the Malagasi and the Negro. What Wiclif did for the English language and for Chaucer, what Luther did for German and for Goethe, by rendering the Scriptures into their own speech — Krapf and Steere did for Swahili, Schoen for Hausa, Moffat for Chwana, Grout and Lindley for Zulu, Bentley for Kongoan and other missionaries for other African tongues. Each African translation of the Scriptures consecrates a new language with ethical, intellectual and Scriptural potencies undreamed of, and destines literatures unborn, the future children of religion and science, to be African heirs of the classic and the Christian ages.

It is instructive to note at least two or three instances of the estimation in which the secular world holds the work of African missionary=philologists. The French Institute conferred its gold medal on Schoen who revealed the Hausa language in dictionaries, grammars, reading=lessons and translations, and whose name, Livingstone declared, would live for generations after his had been forgotten. Koelle compiled a remarkable comparative vocabulary of the two hundred languages spoken in his day in Sierra Leone*. Crowther obtained European repute as a linguist no less than as a geographer. Krapf and Rebmann, though they themselves made next to no converts, enabled their successors to do their work a hundredfold better than if Krapf and Rebmann had not laid foundations and opened paths. Bentley unraveled many knotty points in Kongoan, and Mrs Bentley was also a fine scholar. Grout's grammar of Zulu is a classic, a work of genius. Wilson of Gabun, besides determining the relations of the neighboring tribes through affinities of language, showed how the tongues of West Africa reveal contacts with European speech. Grout independently worked out the Asian or Hamitic theory of the ancestry of the Bantu. Wilson, comparing such Bantu languages as Fan (Mpangwe) with such Negro tongues as Mande, came unaided to a prevalent

* A linguistic prize awarded to Koelle is asserted to have been founded by Voltaire. This seems an error.

view as to the unrelatedness of the Bantu and Negro families of speech. Chatelain, formerly of Taylor Mission and now chief of the Philafrican League, supplemented the African articles on geography in an American cyclopedia of names, and has done good work in Mbundu folklore and philology. Even the black freedman of the United States gave proof of what philology owes to African missionaries, for Ousley, once a slave of a brother of Jefferson Davis, translated the Bible into Sheitswa.

We close with three independent, mundane testimonies to the service of African missions to linguistic and philological sciences. Though papal missionaries made the earliest modern contribution to the science of African languages, Protestant missionaries have excelled them in quality and quantity.

Doctor Cust, whose literary and scientific services to missions it would be impossible to overestimate, has published this judgment: "Missionaries, in striking hard on the anvil of evangelization, their proper work, have emitted bright sparks of linguistic light which have rendered luminous a region previously shrouded in darkness. These sparks have kindled corresponding warmth in the hearts of great and, to them, personally unknown scholars working in their studies in Vienna, Berlin or some German university; scholars who, alas! cared little for the object of the missionaries' going forth, but rejoiced exceedingly at the wonderful, unexpected and epoch=making results of their quiet labors"*. Genial Sir Harry Johnston, who, unlike Doctor Cust, attaches little value to the religion planted by missionaries, warmly commends their gifts to science. He exclaims: "Huge is the debt which philologists owe to British mis-

*Modern Languages of Africa, v. 2, abridged and condensed.

sionaries! By evangelists of our nationality nearly two hundred African languages and dialects have been illustrated by dictionaries, grammars, translations of the Bible and vocabularies. Many of these tongues were on the point of extinction, and have since become extinct, and we owe our knowledge solely to the missionaries' intervention". William Dwight Whitney had an even higher opinion of missionaries. He said: "I have a strong realization of the value of missionary labor to science. The Oriental Society has been much dependent upon them [American missionaries] for its usefulness and importance. There would hardly be occasion for an *American* oriental society but for them. . . . The students of ancient languages and literatures well know their obligations to these devoted men. . . . I have heard the manager of one of the great oriental societies abroad speak with admiration of the learning, good sense and enterprise which their [American missionaries'] labors disclose, and lament that the men of his own people were so decidedly their inferiors".

(3) The natural sciences from the nature of the case can not stand so deeply indebted to African missionaries as are geography and philology. Yet Johnston avers that "indirectly, almost unintentionally, missionary enterprise has widely increased the bounds of knowledge. It has sometimes been the means of conferring benefits on science, the value and extent of which itself was careless to appreciate and compute. . . . Zoölogy, botany, anthropology and most of the other branches of scientific investigation have been enriched by the researches of missionaries who have enjoyed unequalled opportunities of collecting in new districts". Grout wrote a work upon Zululand in all its aspects and relations which *The North American Review* regarded as an

important contribution to the political and religious history of the times. *The New Englander* credited the book with "the accuracy of a photograph". Wilson the Carolinian made valuable contributions to our historical knowledge of Ashanti and Kongo. He has erroneously been credited with the modern rediscovery of the gorilla, but Doctor Savage, an American missionary had in 1847 found its skull, and the traders, to say nothing of Battell in 1589=1607, had long known the native accounts of it*. When specimens of this ape were worth one thousand dollars each, Walker of Gabun obtained a skeleton and a skin for Amherst College. Tyler of Zululand sent hundreds of invaluable specimens of rare African animals to the same institution. Champion, a man of remarkable mental and spiritual culture who gave not himself alone but his large fortune to the American Board and went to one of the hardest of mission=fields, wrote a monograph of great value on the botany, geology and topography of the regions environing the Cape. His career, though brief, shed luster on his Christian consecration and on science. Another representative of the American Board showed the superiority of seeing over unseeing eyes and of science over sciolism. It was asserted in the United States about 1865 that a race of men with tails had been discovered in Africa. Non= Christian circles reposed faith in the claim. But the missionary came close to these caudate persons, and ascertained that what the observer at a distance had supposed to be bodily tails were nothing more than coat= tails. The wearing of skins with the tails of the original owners hanging down from them still had caused the false impression.

It may turn out in like fashion that the monkeys

* Possibly Hanno, a Carthaginian explorer of West Africa in the sixth century before Christ, was the original discoverer.

SCENES FROM NATIVE LIFE

whom Schnitzer (Emin Pasha) professed to have seen carrying lighted torches were merely men seen afar by this half=blind scientist.

(4) The benefactions bestowed on the arts, industries and commerce by African missions can not be computed. Lack of space puts it out of question to mention more than three or four. The bringing of African rubber into the world's commercial staples was the achievement of Wilson the Presbyterian missionary at Gabun. His discovery is worth millions annually. The druggist owes valuable medicines to the African missioner, kola among them. Nassau, the American Presbyterian and medical missionary, introduced the Calabar bean, the kola nut and the strophanthus into our pharmacopœia. American agriculturists are indebted to a Congregational missionary among the Zulu for sorghum. In 1854 Wilder called attention in *The Journal of Commerce* to *imfi* as a syrup and sugar plant. He named and described over a dozen kinds of African sorghum, and also sent the seeds. An eminent horticulturist planted them and pronounced a favorable opinion on the sweetening power of the juice. Now the annual value of the American crop of African sorghum amounts to millions of dollars. Though Weay, an Englishman who for several years lived in Natal, afterward extended the cultivation of it in America, to Wilder the missionary belongs the credit of introducing it.

Missionaries did not, as claimed, first bring Kafir corn into the United States, a cereal admirably adapted to arid areas in the western states, but it has been asserted that on a map of South Africa made about 1750 [1850?] the words, *Here be diamonds*, are printed on the spot representing the very district where the diamond was found a century later. If the fact be as reported, it would seem as if the African missionary were the discoverer of the world's greatest diamond=fields. In that case civilization would owe a billion dollars for this item alone to Christianity and its African missions.

(5) The advantages derived by colonization, commerce and civilization at large from missions are so notable that the African potentate who complained that first came the missionary, then the merchant and finally the man of war was scarcely unjust. British Africa, east, south and west, at the Nile lakes and Zanzibar, at the Cape and in Zambezia, on the Niger and along the western coast, started on its career of expansion through the impulse originating in the information furnished by patriotic emissaries of Christianity. Ibea and Uganda; Cape Colony, Natal and South=Central Africa; Ashanti, Lagos, Liberia, the Niger territories and Sierra Leone owe the seed of European civilization among the natives to Protestant missions. To the same source the majority of these British spheres also stand indebted for the primal force that finally, though indirectly and unintentionally, made it possible for the colonist, the merchant, the statesman to dwell there and to erect the institutions of Christian Europe. No American, British or Scandinavian member of the Protestant mission=force, not even a Livingstone or a Mackay, has ever allowed himself to become a political agent for any European government. Some German Protestant missionaries have, however, been accused of exerting themselves in behalf of the aggrandizement and the secular interests of Germany in Africa. Not all Catholic missioners are guilty of prostituting their spiritual functions to the worldly wishes of administrators in papal states of Europe; but the French government, it has long been notorious, regards those, especially the Jesuits, in its colonial realms as part of its

political machinery, and annually appropriates funds from the public treasury for the promotion of their politico=sectarian projects. Protestant missions in Belgian Kongo, French Africa, Madagascar and the Portuguese and Spanish possessions can not count on favor from Catholic administrators. Roman missions in British, Dutch and German Africa will receive just if not generous treatment from Protestant rulers.

The attempts of colonial governments in South Africa to establish commercial intercourse with Kafir tribes were vain before Christian missionaries gained footing among them*. When Wilder went to Zululand in 1849, he "found only the rudest implements of farming. A clumsy hoe was used for breaking the ground, hoeing crops, etc. Thousands of oxen were idling away their useless existence on the hills. All the burden of agriculture came on the women, who were bought and sold as chattels. To yoke an ox to cart or plow was never dreamed of. They had neither carts nor plows. But the missionaries took plows and used wagons, trained oxen to the yoke and showed how much more valuable in breaking ground and transporting burdens was an ox yoked to cart or plow than a *woman*. Now the Kafirs own hundreds of American plows, and there are broken to the yoke tens of thousands of oxen by those who twenty=five years ago never saw a plow or yoked an ox. It is said that last year five hundred American plows were sold to the natives of Natal alone. Those plows were made in this country [America], and Natal is only one in a hundred markets opened in the heathen world by missionary labors. But not plows alone have been demanded by our native Christians. They all clothe

*The American consul at Zanzibar also averred that the commercial aid from this source had been most important. The date of Wilder's testimony is unknown to the present writer.

themselves in European style, creating a large, ever-increasing demand for the products of the loom. Furniture, cooking-utensils, wagons, carts, harness, saddles, books, maps are purchased by those who, but for Christianity, would be naked heathen living on the labor of the women they own. Nor to professed Christians only have these civilizing influences come; far away in regions beyond, among those who profess no regard for the gospel are the plow, the cart and the things of civilization sought because 'believers' have demonstrated their utility. The American plows sold last year brought more money than it costs to sustain the Zulu mission. This in addition to all other kinds of American manufactures which the gospel among the Kafirs has made a demand for".

The above instance of the civilizing power of Christianity on barbaric pagans is but one among many. It has been anticipated or repeated in Sierra Leone, Uganda and Yariba, among the Chwana and Malagasi, in Kongo and Nyasaland and a hundred other places. It brings us — and this is its greatest value — to the relative worth of Christianity and culture, of religion and science, in civilizing the Negro.

It is the view of an influential and large class that, in order to Christianize the heathen barbarian, missionaries must first civilize him. It is, so men maintain who regard themselves as intelligent and practical, impossible to inculcate the truths of spiritual religion in the non-Christian African before he has been equipped with material and mental endowments. First that which is natural, then that which is spiritual. Train the African into an artizan or farmer or other member of industrial society. Teach him to read. Then he will understand

and accept Christianity; and do so more intelligently and willingly.

This sounds as if it were a plausible theory. Is it a working hypothesis? Has it been tested? What are the facts of experience?

In 1795 Coke the Wesleyan united with men of several denominations for the civilization of the Fulbe in West Africa. This mission of culture was purely benevolent, wholly humanitarian and philanthropic. Wilberforce and other leading men lent their patronage, and great expectations were awakened. A number of well= disposed artizans with a surgeon, practically a medical missionary, at their head, went to Sierra Leone. They were to teach the arts of civilized life to the Fulbe, and then, after these had made progress in civilization, missionaries would come to preach the gospel. But the missionaries of culture never reached the Fulbe. Their courage failed. They became discontented. Soon they dispersed, and the survivors returned home.

It may be objected that the experiment failed on account of lack of adaptation on the part of the agents. The objection does not hold. The mechanics had been members of Methodist churches, some of them local preachers, and Coke recommended them to Zachary Macaulay. Their mission was to found a Christian colony and to form friendly relations with the Fulbe. But they failed to count the cost or else to understand their engagements. Their fundamental principle was not that ordained by Christ for the establishment of Christian missions. They had not the motive — the constraining love for souls — to push them among barbarians. The Wesleyan conference felt the rebuke. So far as the error was connected with the church, the conference promptly rectified it (1796). This body "unanimously judged that a trial should be made *on the proper missionary plan*"*.

Before 1795 modern missions had repeatedly demonstrated the helplessness of civilization as an apostle to bring men to Christ. The "Moravians" had once thought that they must first civilize and then evangelize the Eskimo. They found that they must first make him a Christian if they were to have any success in attempting to civilize him. The Roman missionaries in Portuguese Africa, especially in Angola, introduced civilization among the Africans, but, according to Catholic testimony, left them baptized pagans. Livingstone found great numbers of natives who could read and write but met with no Negro Catholics. Nominally Christian civilization has squatted along Atlantic Africa, between Sahara and the Kunene, since 1445; but how many converts to Christianity had civilization won? How many in East Africa? If European civilization along the western shore be so potent an elevating force, why have the Timni just rebelled against paying taxes to the British in Sierra Leone? In South Africa Dutch civilization had the field to itself from 1652 to 1795. What did it achieve? Governor Stell dressed a "Hottentot" in a military uniform with gold=trimmed hat, silk stockings and a sword. He learned Dutch and Portuguese in India. According to the hypothesis of the apostles of culture and the advocates for the Christianizing power of civili-

*Moister, *Memorials of Missionary Labors*, London ed., 1850, p. 31, appears to make Coke and the conference responsible for the whole undertaking. Other writers, possibly Thompson himself in *Moravian Missions*, p. 409, fell into the same misapprehension. But *The Missionary Magazine*, an Edinburgh periodical, in its issue for August, 1796, published the following statement: "We understand that the mission to the Fulah was not properly a Methodist mission, as the families that went with Mr Macaulay were not sent by the Methodist conference. We insert this note lest any, by attaching the common idea to the phrase *Methodist mission*, should conclude that these persons must have been missionaries sent by that body for the express purpose of preaching. They were neither so sent, nor was their mission so immediately to preach".

zation, he ought on his return to Cape Colony to have joined the Dutch Reformed Church. What this Khoi=Khoin actually did was to don his cloak of skins, enhance the effect of his *décolleté* costume with a cravat and sword and go back to barbarism. It was unregenerated human nature's reversion to type, to its animal inheritance from the brute. Natural law dominated, because spiritual life had not been implanted.

Hard facts and harsh experiences broke down the theory centuries ago, and will shatter it so long as human nature, barbaric or civilized, pagan or Christian, remains the same. The hypothesis fails on every side. It fails on this side; for where are the lovers of sweetness and light, of savage souls, who have taken the plow and press to pagan Africa before Christian missionaries entered? It fails on that side; for three hundred thousand pagan Zulu, though in touch with civilization for fifty years, are yet without furniture of any kind, whereas the Christian Zulu, as at Edendale, live like Europeans in houses with furniture and gardens, and have built a school and a stone church. The theory refuses to work at the European end, because mere culture is not a moral force. It declines to act at the African end, because aversion to the activities essential to progress inheres in paganism. Christian missions must civilize African peoples by bringing man after man into personal fellowship with God in Christ. As Christian belief and conduct, with their moral principles and religious practices, change the character and life of the African, he will crave civilization and its resources.

This is not theory. It is fact. Lindley has quaintly revealed the process and the psychology. Among the Zulu the first evidence of coming to the Christ is a sense of their nakedness. A convert obtains a calico shirt.

Next day he purchases duck pantaloons. He could not take comfort from that shirt unless he clad his legs. The third day he buys a three=legged milking stool, for he must not sit on the ground and soil his trousers! When that man wears that shirt and pair of pantaloons and sits on that stool nine inches high, — "he is nine thousand miles above the heathen round him".

Frere, whose experience of native races in India and South Africa still stands unsurpassed, long ago uttered the ultimate verdict on the relations between civilization and Christianity as evangelists. This civilian wrote: Civilization can not precede Christianity; the only successful way is to teach the gospel.

(6). Peace is an element of Christianity and civilization. Do missions and missionaries in Africa promote peace?

In Egypt the American mission, according to Schweinfurth the explorer and scientist, "has done an enormous amount of good". Gordon in Sûdan maintained that there could be no permanent amelioration in its condition, unless Christian missions were planted there. Schnitzer (Emin Pasha) requested missionaries for the Equatoria Provinces, and would have paid their expenses for the first five years, if he had obtained them. In Nyasaland it is the testimony of O'Neill, once a British consul at Mozambique, that "his experience of ten years in Africa had convinced him that mission=work was one of the most powerful and successful instruments for the pacification of the country and the suppression of the slave=trade". Lugard afterward expressed himself to the same effect, saying: "If we wish to benefit Africa, the first step is to introduce law and order. The establishment of each mission=station is singularly productive of this result. At Blantyre the Ngoni raids were turned aside at the earnest mediation of Mr Scott. At Bandawe the Tonga have for years been free from the same enemies, solely on account of Doctor Laws' influence and the promise won from Mombera". Thomson still more emphatically wrote: "Where international effort has failed, an unassuming mission, supported only by a small section of the British people, has been quietly and unostentatiously but most successfully realizing the program of the Brussels conference (1876). I refer to Livingstonia Mission. This has proved itself in every sense a civilizing center. By it slavery has been stopped, desolating wars put an end to, and peace and security given to a wide area. . . . Worthy also of all praise are the efforts of the London Society which have been so signally successful on Lake Tanganika, though working under even greater difficulties than their brethren on Nyasa. I can bear testimony from personal observation to the real, solid, civilizing work accomplished. The missionaries at Ujiji and Mtowa have won the confidence of the natives. With these missions continuing in the liberal spirit in which they commenced, there is a boundless sphere of hope and promise opened for the natives of East=Central Africa". Warren, lately governor of Natal and special commissioner for the pacification of Chwana and Zulu districts, declared that " for the preservation of peace between colonists and natives one missionary is worth more than a whole battalion of soldiers". Shenstone, a Natalese secretary of native affairs, attributed the unbroken peace of thirty years mainly to missionaries. Mitchell, governor of Natal in 1885, said publicly: "The shallow criticism which asserted that nothing was being done was an entire mistake. . . . The government had a hearty sympathy in the work of the American missionaries. . . The government and people knew full well that their work was of material assistance in enabling the government to rule the natives successfully". Maitland, when governor of Cape Colony (1844=47), had told Grout that he relied more upon the labors of missionaries than on the rifles of soldiers to keep savages quiet. Grout, an American Congregationalist among the Zulu, was returning home, his society having decided to withdraw. Maitland sent him back, and ensured his support. The society held on. Grout toiled on, and in 1865 could say that the success was a hundredfold more than he had ever dreamed of. From West Africa, where an American missionary trained the peaceable Abeokutans to withstand warlike Dahomé, comes testimony of the same tenor as to the condition of Sierra Leone. A parliamentary committee (1842) averred that "to the invaluable exertions of the Church Missionary Society more especially, as also to a considerable extent — as in all our African settlements — to the Wesleyan body the highest praise is due. By their efforts nearly one fifth of the population, a most unusually high proportion in any country, is at school; and the effects are visible in considerable intellectual, moral and religious improvement". In French North Africa the Lavigeriean missions, if we may believe Sharp, have done great good to "general health, individual physical well=being and the communal weal", and direct their most notable efforts against slaving. At Zanzibar the recent emancipation of two hundred thousand slaves is chiefly due to the bishop and staff of Universities' Mission.

Madagascar presents material and social results no less remarkable, probably more significant, than these victories of peace won by African missions. Between 1862 and 1882 no nation, except Japan, made such progress in civilization and showed such vigor of development as the Hova state. After it opened its doors to Christianity again, commerce increased steadily, the collection and cultivation of valuable products received a stimulus, and the demand for calicoes, cloths, hardware and prints of foreign manufacture increased constantly. The repeal of the law, closely connected with idolatry, that forbade the erection of any brick or stone structure in Tananarivo, gave so great an impetus to building that the capital has been quite rebuilt. Hundreds of handsome and substantial houses, most of them European in architecture, have replaced rush or timber with stone or sun=dried brick. Near the spot where the early martyrs died for Christ stands a fine stone church with beautiful towers. The erection of four memorial churches trained a guild of skilled artizans, and these builders, carpenters, glaziers, stone=masons and tilers carried the new architecture beyond the metropolis. In society the Christian spirit through its kindliness and mercy largely effected the abolition of the cruel customs and laws inherited by the pagan state. Phelps, the author of *The Island of Madagascar*, quotes the British envoy to Ranavalona III in 1882 as publicly expressing surprise "to find what manner of people the Malagasi were. He found Tananarivo a really splendid city with magnificent public buildings. The house he lodged at was as good as any in London. The prime minister, almost the astutest, cleverest, most intelligent man he had ever met, occupied a splendid official residence". Cousins maintains that the first men in Madagascar are the graduates of the Congregational missions and schools. Exception will be taken to this as the biased allegation of a "mere" missionary, but it receives confirmation from a military man. Phelps came to the conclusion that "Madagascar has passed from pagan barbarism to Christian civilization, in which it has taken a stand among Christian nations, chiefly through missionary agency".

II

Ethical and Spiritual Results

Social effects flow partly from moral and religious forces. They lead naturally to the ethical and spiritual successes won by missionary Christianity among African peoples. Such results are not to be judged by imposing tables of statistics, though there are enough of these for Africa, for Madagascar and for the Negro population of the Americas, but by the changed lives and Christian spirit of the converts from Islam and from paganism.

Communicants constitute the most concentrated basis for estimating the numerical success of missions, and furnish a crucial test of their spiritual influence. We begin our survey with native communicants, passing to the adherents, the force, the plant and the ultimate result*.

(1) Upon comparative study of such sources as Bainbridge; Bliss; Grundemann; Lowrie; missionary cyclopedias, handbooks and reports; *Missiones Catholicæ;* Newcomb and Vahl, it appears as if the grand total of Protestant native communicants in Africa and Madagascar (exclusive of adherents, Ethiopic and Koptic Christians and European=descended Africans) can not to=day be less than two hundred and fifty thousand souls, while the number of Roman converts from Islam and paganism (including

---

*The statistics investigated in the score of paragraphs following should be compared with the figures in the statistical summaries and tables of the appendices. Though the most recent of the statistics analyzed here are quite ten years old, comparison with those in an appendix may serve the student, as indicating the gains and losses of a decade and thus furnishing *data* for judgment as to the future.

adherents and church=members) must number at least three hundred thousand. Possibly the native Protestant communicants number twenty=five thousand more, the Roman "population" one hundred thousand more. Protestant missions distinguish between adherents and communicants, and regard as a convert only "one who gives credible evidence of personal renunciation of the past and of reception of the grace of God through Christ as Savior"; Rome classes adherents and communicants together as Catholic "population", and "the sacramentarian view that all baptized persons are Christians is the basis of all statistics of converts". If it be deemed advisable to attempt to compare the numerical successes of Latin and Teutonic Christianity in African missions, the bases must be either adherents or communicants. On the basis of native adherents the Protestant communion can boast eight hundred thousand, possibly one million, Africans and Malagasi within its influence; the Roman church four hundred thousand at most. On the basis of communicants, the Latin communion must deduct thousands upon thousands of children from its roll of adherents before we can approximate its true communicants; but even if we estimate the adult membership in full and regular standing belonging to Teutonic Christianity in Africa as only two hundred and fifty thousand, this exceeds that of Rome. The Catholic — despite the grand and imposing organization of his church; the great advantage of his African missions having begun two and a half centuries before those of Protestantism effected a permanent beginning; the numerical superiority of the Latin rite; and the rapid method of receiving larger numbers into communion — is in missions among African peoples (possibly excepting Algerians and Egyptians) behind the Protestant. Even on the low plane of mere numbers papal success is inferior to that of evangelical Christianity. Together these two branches of the church catholic, in Africa and Madagascar, have, according to our lesser figures, five hundred thousand communicants, and, in addition, influence one million adherents*. The results of Protestant missions since 1795, even numerically, surpass all that Coke, Johnson or Moffat dreamed. The religious future of Africa falls to the evangelical church.

This appears from the figures for 1852, 1882, 1886 and 1898. Newcomb in 1852 reported twenty=seven thousand, two hundred and forty=one communicants. Bainbridge thirty years later numbered one hundred and forty thousand, a gain of ninety thousand, seven hundred and eighty=three or one hundred and eighty=four *per cent.* since 1868. Two thirds, possibly four fifths of the growth 1868=82 occurred in Madagascar. Here in 1896 the London Society alone had sixty=two thousand, seven hundred and forty=nine adult Malagasi communicants, the Lutherans nearly forty thousand, and the Society of Friends nearly four thousand. In 1886 Grundemann reckoned African communicants as one hundred and sixty thousand, an increase of twenty thousand or fourteen *per cent.* since 1882. In 1898 the native Protestant communicants apparently number two hundred and fifty thousand, a growth of ninety thousand or fifty=six *per cent.* Oppel in 1887 claimed that since 1800 Christianity has each year gained ten thousand *adherents*. The Newcomb, Lowrie, Bainbridge and Grundemann statistics, on account of incomplete returns, err on the side of understatement.

*In 1898 Merensky stated that "omitting Madagascar, seven hundred and fifty thousand Negroes are connected with Christian churches and one hundred and forty thousand Negro children are in Christian schools". His numbers, though hardly permitting comparison with those above, seem to substantiate them as accurate or, if inaccurate, as erring by understatement. In Cape Colony alone, he adds, Protestant missions have five hundred and thirty thousand native converts, whereas Rome has but three thousand at most.

The force consists of over three hundred agencies and of fifteen thousand workers. The former constitute the bureau of military affairs in the administration of the church militant. The latter compose the troops in the field. Both seemingly large totals require analysis and explanation, if they are not to be misunderstood and thus work injury to the cause of African evangelization.

The Protestant organizations hail from America, the Antilles, Britain, Canada, Dutch Guiana (or Surinam), Egypt, Finland, France, Germany, Holland, Madagascar, Norway, South Africa, Sweden, Switzerland and West Africa. The Anglican communion is represented among Africans by more organizations than is any other Protestant body, but Presbyterianism pushes it hard. Next come Lutheran, Methodist, Baptist and Congregational societies.

Not all of these societies are directly evangelistic. Not all work for Africa alone. But in one way or another, directly or indirectly, in larger or less degree all exert themselves in behalf of the African at home or afar. Some send missionaries to preach Christ. Some are partly humanitarian, partly spiritual. As auxiliaries to evangelization the strictly missionary societies of Protestantism have associations for free distribution of the Scriptures and others for translating religious literature; international unions of missionaries; associations for planting Sabbath=schools abroad; alliances of theological schools and divinity students to promote missions; world=wide leagues of young people in every branch of the Protestant church; Young Men's and Young Women's Christian Associations; and the volunteering of students throughout America and Europe for service as missionaries. Some organizations send Christian literature and the Scriptures. Some aid mission=societies proper. Some simply educate, training either missionaries or proselytes. Some devote themselves to industrial missions or to medical missions or to secular adjuncts of African missions. Some work in Africa; others among the colored people of the United States; still others amidst the Negro populations of the West Indies. Some toil both in Africa and the Antilles, including South America; others in Africa and the American commonwealth; yet others in the United States and the West Indies. A few have their headquarters in the Antilles; a few more in Africa itself; many in America; the great majority in Europe and especially in Britain. Most are men's organizations, but not a few are women's and several are children's.

These agencies are of every church and of no church. A number are Catholic, but far the greater part are Protestant. Thirty represent Rome and continue her Franciscan and Jesuit tendencies. She also has diocesan hierarchies of secular clergy in French, Portuguese and Spanish Africa, in the Antilles and in America. The remaining organizations belong to Protestantism, and express its Anglican, Baptist, Congregational, Lutheran, Methodist, Presbyterian and undenominational creeds and polities. They also represent interdenominational federation, undenominational Protestantism and independent Protestants. These denominational distinctions rank among the efficient agents that have caused Protestantism in one hundred years to outstrip the Roman rival who in Africa had a start of centuries. Though in a few instances sectarianism, the illegitimate issue of denominational principles, has worked mischief, the prevalence of the evil has been grossly exaggerated. On the field, face to face with such common foes as Islam, paganism and savagery, the divisions of reformed Christianity are not marked. All the societies rest on the New Testament, and almost all work hand in hand. Protestant denominationalism has enhanced the holy emulousness of Christian brethren; provoked them to a blessed rivalry in good works; and enabled Protestant missionary societies to effect a hundredfold more for Africa and its peoples than could have been accomplished by a vast Protestant church enjoying formal and organic unity and possessing a single organization for missions that should duplicate Rome's Propaganda. When Protestant communions federate, centralization will advance the evangelization of Africa but only as it stimulates each mission=society's independent initiative and strengthens its efforts.

Representatives of these societies work in Africa, America, the Antilles, or Madagascar; but statistics of the field=force can be obtained only for Africa (including the isles). These agents comprise men and women; the married and the unmarried; members of the black, the brown, the copper=colored and the white races; foreigners and natives; laymen and priests; the old and the young; rich and poor; evangelists, educators, doctors, artizans and agriculturists; in short, Christian workers from every branch of Latin and Teutonic Christendom, from every class of society, from every condition of life. A large majority, in the judgment of *The Spectator*, a non=religious journal, are by inner disposition qualified for their duties. "Some are unfit; one or two in a thousand hopelessly unfit — bad persons; a majority well qualified in extremely varied ways for the burdensome duty. Many are teachers; many, preachers; many, like Moffat, born rulers of men. In all but a very few there is one quality rare in any other profession: absolute devotion to the work. If they can do it, living as quiet, hard=working pastors in the tropics, they do it so. If it require excessive toil, abstinence from all that is pleasant, incessant facing of physical danger, including moral certainty of death from torture — they accept those conditions, not boasting, not murmuring, as parts of the burden their consciences have placed on their necks. . . . The majority are not called on for his sacrifices, but everywhere they do their work, setting up an ideal which raises even heathenism, establishing Christian colonies, teaching native teachers — often in Africa horrible failures but often also the salt of entire districts — and everywhere spreading among barbarians the first ideas of a nobler and loftier life. We say distinctly, as the result of a life's experience, that this much is successfully done, and done frequently by men whom the world would account underbred. . . The profession conquers all, producing a horror. . . . of ceasing from direct labor, 'going back from the plow'. How it is possible for Christians to condemn such a profession with such results we can no more conceive than we can conceive how a Christian church can be fully alive yet never wish to proselytise."

Dr E. M. Bliss in 1891 enumerated the Protestant mission=force on the African continent and in the African archipelagoes as eleven thousand, nine hundred and three persons. In the Antilles, according to the same authority, who, however, was unable to present statistics of missions among the Negroes of South America or the United States, the Protestant mission=force numbered two thousand, two hundred and seventy=nine. Both sets of figures were confessedly incomplete, because some societies — notoriously one for the propagation of the gospel — did not dissever their statistics for Africa from those for other countries and thus rendered it impossible to state the numerical strength of their African and their Antillean field-forces. These are by no means slight. Accordingly the Bliss census, by no fault of its own, fell below the actual numbers. The size of the Protestant force engaged in missions among the Negro population of the United States can only be inferred from such facts as these: The American Missionary Association alone had four hundred and eleven agents, and since 1846 has had over three thousand, five hundred women as teachers in its Negro schools.

Analysis of the Bliss statistics for Protestantism yields the following results: Male white missionaries in Africa numbered eight hundred and eighty-one; female missionaries, three hundred and eighty-seven, of whom one hundred and fifty-three were single. In all, there were eleven hundred and sixty-eight American or European missionaries on the African continent. Only one hundred and seventy of the men were laymen, six hundred and eleven being ordained clergy. In 1895 Doctor D. L. Leonard stated that in Africa exclusive of Madagascar there were eighteen hundred American and European missionaries, over seven hundred of them ordained. If the difference of over six hundred between Doctors Bliss and Leonard be not due merely to greater completeness in the African statistics of the latter, perhaps it represents a great gain in the brief space of five years.

The native workers in Africa numbered five thousand, one hundred in 1891. Two hundred and nine constituted an ordained clergy; six hundred and sixty-five a battalion of teachers; and four thousand, two hundred and twenty-six the heavy brigade of other workers. Together the African force of foreign and native mission-agents consisted of six thousand, two hundred and sixty-eight men and women.

The figures (1891) for Madagascar were surprising. The European missionaries numbered only one hundred and ten, but the native force amounted to five thousand, five hundred and twenty=five. The foreign force was less than one tenth of that in Africa and its minor islands; the Malagasi auxiliaries outnumbered their African brethren by four hundred and twenty=five. Again, the European staff in Madagascar was less than one fiftieth of the number of native workers there. The Europeans comprised sixty=one men and forty=nine women. Only four of the former were laymen, only three of the latter were single women. The native staff included eleven hundred and sixty=six ordained ministers and four thousand, three hundred and fifty=nine other workers, but specified no native teachers. The foreign and native mission=agents for Madagascar numbered five thousand, six hundred and thirty=five. Finally, almost half of the European force and seven ninths of the native workers owed their initiative to British Congregationalism and its London Society.

The Malagasi statistics for 1896 were still more surprising. Christianity reported five hundred and eighty=four thousand, six hundred and thirty=two adherents. One hundred and thirty thousand were Catholics; four hundred and fifty=five thousand, Protestants. One sixth of the Madagascarenes were Christian. The London Society had sixty=two thousand, seven hundred and forty=nine adult communicants, seventy=five thousand scholars and two hundred and eighty=nine thousand adherents in addition to church=members. Ten hundred and forty=eight of the one thousand, three hundred and thirteen native Protestant clergy belonged to this Congregational agency, and eighty=eight thousand of the two hundred and forty thousand dollars contributed by native Christians came from its churches.

Combination of the African and the Madagascarene statistics, first as to foreign and then as to native missionaries, reveals interesting and significant points. The Americo=European force comprised twelve hundred and seventy=eight souls, only one third of the whole being women, only one third of the men being unordained workers. Their Africo=Malagasi assistants amounted to ten thousand, six hundred and twenty=five men (and women?), nine tenths of whom were lay helpers.

These comparisons afford discouragement and encouragement. They show that too few in Christendom regard evangelization as their personal affair, and that the laity are especially delinquent in volunteering. Twelve or eighteen hundred or two thousand white missionaries are not enough, even as leaders, for the Christianization of one hundred and twenty=five million pagans and forty million Muhammadans. But the statistics also show that Protestantism is moving in the right direction for the conversion of the heathen and the Islamite. Since 1854, when Newcomb specified the native workers as numbering one hundred and twelve, Protestant missions have multiplied this force a hundredfold. Teutonic Christianity has also strengthened its missions immeasurably by the enlistment of women. In 1854 Newcomb reported but forty=four women as working among African missions, whereas Bliss in 1891 could enumerate four hundred and thirty=six female missionaries. A force that multiplies itself by ten in thirty=seven years is a mighty power, and is destined to exert unimaginable influence in the twentieth century. But our admiration for the unmarried woman=missionary of to=day and to=

morrow need not blind us to the worth of the missionary's wife, for it is the Mary Moffats of yesterday who helped to make possible the African apostolate of single women.

The medical missionaries have increased from three to fifty=three*.

Race gifts and aptitudes reveal themselves as clearly in missions as in secular enterprises. Scotch missionaries in Africa deserve the encomium pronounced by Shaftesbury on American missionaries in Turkey. They are a marvelous compound of sanctity and sense. They excel in their sense of the situation, mastery of circumstances, plasticity and versatility. Second only to the canny, spiritual Scot, if indeeed second to any, come the Americans. The English missionary when unhurt by churchliness and conceit is steadfast and sweet, slow but sure, the right ruler for native races. The Dutch, the German, the Scandinavians are of more docile spirit, but injured sometimes by dogma or ritualism, sometimes by rationalism, and more liable, perhaps, to fall into ruts.

The African mission=plant of Protestants comprises church=edifices, hospitals, schools, stations and a score of other material appliances that defy classification and naming. Newcomb (1854) reported ninety=seven churches, two hundred and forty=five schools and two hundred and thirty=six stations; Bliss (1891) enumerated seven hundred and eight churches, seventeen hundred and fifty=four schools and twenty=six hundred and two stations. The churches and the schools both multiplied themselves by seven, the stations by ten. In 1854 the scholars numbered thirty=one thousand, five hundred and forty=seven; in 1891, one hundred and ninety thousand, an increase of sixfold. The Bliss statistics discriminate,

*The Medical Missionary Record in April, 1897, credited four female and forty male medical missionaries to "Africa", four medical men to Egypt and five to Madagascar.

as those of Newcomb did not, between the common and the higher school, between the week=day and the Sunday student, and are therefore correspondingly valuable. Bliss enumerated twenty=four schools for higher education, and seventeen hundred and thirty primary schools, but did not specify the number of Sabbath=schools. Africa had twenty=two of the secondary institutions, Madagascar eight hundred and ninety=one of the common schools. The Africans receiving higher education numbered a thousand, the Malagasi five hundred. Thirty thousand Africans, forty=five hundred Madagascarenes attended the Sabbath=school; but a hundred thousand Malagasi, only fifty=three thousand Africans, the common school. Fifty=nine thousand Malagasi, an army exceeding the African pupils of primary grade by six thousand, were enrolled in the eight hundred and sixty common schools of the London Society.

In 1891 the native contributions amounted to $184,050, but half of the societies failed to report as to this item. In 1886 Rome's Propaganda had received only $7,000 from Africa.

From Protestant we pass to Roman statistics. In 1886 *Missiones Catholicæ*, the official annual of papal missions issued by Propaganda, presented the following statement for Africa and all adjacent islands: Adherents, two hundred and ten thousand; chapels and churches, two hundred; elementary schools, six hundred and fifty=four; European missionaries, four hundred and seventeen, of whom two hundred and twenty=three were Jesuits; native missionaries, none; pupils, no statement. But Catholic societies reported two hundred and sixty=eight thousand, seven hundred converts. The discrimination between adherents and converts and the discrepancy between two hundred and ten thousand and two hundred and sixty=eight thousand must be explained by Roman authorities. In 1890 Propaganda published the following official figures of strictly missionary work in Africa and Madagascar: Native Catholic population, three hundred and ninety=eight thousand, nine hundred and forty; chapels and churches, seven hundred and forty=four; educational institutions, six hundred and ninety; priests, seven hundred and forty=five; stations, two hundred and ninety=two; and charitable institutions, one hundred and thirty=five. No statement appeared as to native missioners or the number of pupils. It is noteworthy, too, that Rome does not bring the opportunity for education to the African.

These two sets of statistics are almost impracticable for purposes of comparison; but if we could assume that such terms as adherent, convert, population express the same ideas for both communions, the figures would appear to convey information. They would seem to say that in five years the native population adhering to papal missions all but doubled; that the chapels and churches nearly quadrupled; and that the missioners multiplied by three fourths. Rome recognized the crisis in African missions, and strained every nerve for the conquest of Africa. Her celibacy and obedience may be as evil as Protestants deem them, but in missions they work wonders even if but temporarily. How large a force Rome will hereafter be able to throw into the conflict for a continent can not be stated and does not matter.

Among papal missioners in Africa, Belgians and Frenchmen stand preëminent. Xavier of Navarre when seeking assistants used to say: *Da mihi Belgas;* nor have they lost their facile genius. But the Frank bears the palm. His passionate patriotism and religious zeal render it impossible for him to refrain from intrigues for *la belle France* and schemes for his church; but the cheeriness, kindly sympathy, politeness and tact of the French make them ideal representatives for Rome.

Roman organizations for missions in Africa are entirely of European origin, and French Catholics do more than any of their continental brethren, though their fellows in the faith in Germany and Italy, Portugal and Spain are not wholly inactive for Africa. The Roman church in America accomplishes next to nothing for the African either in the new or the old world, for its home-missions are slight and without effect, while of its foreign missions Cardinal Vaughan of England said on January 3rd, 1893, to the American college at Rome: "Catholics of America have not yet done all they ought to do for the faith. They have done nothing yet, compared with other nations, to evangelize the earth. If they would widen their Catholic reputation, let them send missionaries to convert heathen Africa". In 1886 France furnished two thirds of the funds for *all* papal missions, Germany only a seventh of the amount contributed by France, and tiny Belgium a thirteenth. The Catholics of Italy, Britain, Holland and North America followed in the order named with petty and swiftly lessening sums. Those, for instance, of the United States, numbering six million communicants, contributed the magnificent amount of $20,000 for all missions of Propaganda. In 1890 France supported nine of the Roman agencies working in Africa; Germany two, Belgium, Ireland, Italy, Portugal and Spain one each; and the international orders four. It would accordingly seem that half of the effort exerted by Rome for the evangelization of Africa stands indebted for men and money to French Catholicism.

Though Roman plans for the conquest of Africa are

sublime, her day there is past. This appears from the contrast between certain features of Protestant and Roman missions.

Protestantism in 1890 had five times as many agencies as Rome for African evangelization; nearly twice her white missionaries in Africa and the islands; double her number of native adherents; and a larger total of adult native communicants. As the Roman church in 1854 claimed a population of one hundred and eighty=four million, while in 1880 Behm and Wagner estimated this as two hundred and sixteen million and allowed one hundred and thirty million to Protestantism, even the mere numerical superiority of Protestantism in African missions is remarkable. In 1854, according to Shea the Catholic scholar of America, the papal population of Africa was one million. In 1896 Professor A. H. Keane estimated it as but one million two hundred thousand. A church that gains only two hundred thousand in forty= two years can never hope to master Africa. The Protestant populations grew in the same period from less than five hundred thousand to over one and one half millions. Yet this phase of the success is the least significant one. The non=material factors of the problem constitute its most important elements.

Protestantism develops native agency to the utmost degree; Rome appears to distrust it. Latin Christianity makes no mention of Africo=Malagasi auxiliaries to its European missioners; Teutonic Christianity finds its ten thousand native assistants to be among African and Malagasi Protestants what the Ten Thousand Immortals of Xerxes and the Ten Thousand Greeks of Xenophon were to their fellow=soldiers. The loss incurred by Rome in its Christian endeavors for tropical Africans is incalculable.

Another injury inflicted by Propaganda itself upon papal missions is the absence of the Bible and other religious literature from among the converts. This is confessed by her own missioners. Bishop Le Roy of Kongo complained that "wherever he had been, he had met with Protestants of all nationalities armed with those wonderful instruments of propaganda — books. We have books, too, but not under the same conditions. We can not get books for nothing. Yet that is just what we want. We want a missionary=press like theirs, where we could produce our Bibles, catechisms, prayer=books, alphabets, grammars, sacred histories, dictionaries, etc".

On this contention the case may go to the jury. The Bible alone, minus man, has repeatedly shown itself to be a marvelous missionary. Rome, until she put a vernacular version into the hand of her every African convert, must fall to the rear of Protestantism more and more. On the other hand, to give the Scriptures to the laity is to remove the corner=stone and the foundation from beneath her system. The Ugandan furnishes an instance of this. His interest in the Bible is intense. His desire to possess it is irresistible. The Catholic missioners have been forced to translate. He compares their work with the Protestant version. He finds no Scriptural authority or evidence for the assumptions and claims of the Roman system. The outcome must be the loss to Rome of her converts in Uganda. This experience will repeat itself in varying degree and kind wherever in Africa papal and Protestant missions work side by side. Rome is on the horns of a dilemma. Each hurts.

A third disadvantage under which Rome labors is celibacy. The unmarried missionary, like the soldier without women, possesses superior advantages for over-running a country; but in the long run, when it must be mastered for missionary=occupancy and held permanently for Christian civilization, the celibate must yield to the husband and wife, the order to the home. The family is the unit of society, and the Christian home is a missionary whose absence from the African missioners of Rome lames her march. The monk and the nun, the brotherhood and the sisterhood, especially the latter, will long enjoy enlarging usefulness in Africa as new fields open. Protestantism as well as Rome needs mission=orders into which its unmarried men and women might be organized. The Kaiserswerth Deaconesses, the Red Cross Association, the Young Men's and the Young Women's Christian Associations point to paths of African service for single women. Through such or similar organizations their work as pioneers, as humanitarians, as auxiliaries can be made even more effective for Protestant missions than it now is. It also remains true that the marriage of missionaries before a period of work in the field might well receive more regulation from the societies than is at present general. The conditions and circumstances of African missions are exceptional and should subject missionary matrimony to exceptional treatment. But the married missionary is a *sine qua non.* Two Protestant men holding a lonely post together, two Roman women at a single station reinforce each other by mere companionship; but a wife strengthens the husband, the husband a wife, as no man can help the man, no woman the woman. Here Rome fails her missioner. Matrimony and parentage involve certain drawbacks, as, *e. g.,* increased expense, but their advantages outweigh those of celibacy. This is the conclusion of a century of African experience.

Comparison in Africa between Catholic missioners as

a class and Protestant missionaries as a body is scarcely feasible. What might hold good for one section of each or in one quarter of the continent might not prove true as to another. Generalization for the whole field and force is impracticable. The most that can be attempted is the statement of several salient contrasts.

The papal missionary is a cheap man, the Protestant comparatively expensive. It costs more to produce and sustain the latter, but the enhanced expense is recouped by the enlargement of efficiency. The Catholic missioner as a rule is less intelligent and practical, more poorly educated, than the Protestant. There are exceptions, notably among the French, but, taking all considerations into account, the superiority is on the Protestant side.

Sharp reports the following conversation with a Protestant missionary in Algeria as to the difference between Lavigerie's men and the equally indomitable Protestants. "We", the missionary is quoted as saying, "lack that particular quality of imagination or sympathy which enables *some* missioners literally to be all things to all men. We are, broadly speaking, always ourselves, always English, Scottish or American, always conscious of our Protestant calling, arrogance, aloofness. Naturally I believe that in the long run our compensating qualities tell and *predominate*, but at first and *for long* we are handicapped. The White Fathers are not primarily French [?] or Catholic priests, or missioners of this or that lord spiritual or temporal, but men preoccupied by burning zeal as heralds of a message of vital importance — a message independent of anything save its immediacy and paramount value. To a great extent this magnificent abnegation and discipline are due to Lavigerie, who never failed to impress on the missioners that the first thing was in all reasonable respects to conform to the manners, customs and habits of the Muslim people among whom they were to sojourn; to feel with them; see with their eyes; as much as possible judge with their minds. To this end he made the Fathers adopt a white robe similar to that worn by the Arabs; not only made them speak Arabic fluently and be familiar with the Quran and the chief writings on it, but insisted on adequate physical training in horsemanship and all kinds of physical exercise. When a Father goes among Arabs, he is in a way already one with them. This wins confidence to start with. When he expounds the Faith, he lays little stress on anything save the fundamental truths, that is, as he considers them. Above all, in what *he* teaches, and *we*, concerning the oneness of God — rather, in the way we teach that living doctrine — is a difference where the advantage is all on his side. The Arab with his intense faith in the absolute unity of Allah more readily follows one who does not confuse his hearer with different arguments regarding the trinity, but speaks clearly and logically of God, Christ and the *virgin* — than one who dwells upon a mystery altogether beyond Muslim comprehension or sympathy. Moreover, the priests do not as a rule say much against Muhammad; they accept him frankly as a minor prophet, whose faith became perverted in his lifetime, and whose influence has been mainly harmful"*.

At first it seems as if these comparisons made against all Protestant missionaries throughout Africa. In reality, however, they militate only against those in French North Africa; apply in favor of Lavigerie's men alone; and even for them hold true but temporarily. Americans, Britons and Germans are not so lacking in adapt-

* Abridged, condensed and italicised by the present writer from p. 226 of *The Atlantic Monthly* for August, 1894 (v. 74, no. 442).

ability, self-effacement or sense as the broad statement implied; nor is it the case for Africa at large, even if for Berber Africa, that "the greatest work is being achieved by the Roman church and, in particular, by the institutions and societies inaugurated and the specially trained emissaries sent forth by Lavigerie".

Wagner the tone-poet affords analogies from music that illustrate the spiritual contest between Protestantism and Rome in African missions. He often introduces a few notes from a leading melody as prelude and prediction of the *dénouement* toward which destiny is leading the action. In the drama of Christian evangelization, at the moments when ecclesiastical empires in Africa were rewarding the enterprise of Portugal and Rome, came a few brief notes from the north, the south, the west, freighted with ominous portent. The power for whom Providence had reserved the new African worlds of which the Latin church and the Portuguese state, sometimes so noble in aim, always so mistaken in method, were dreaming, regardless of Giant Pope, stretched a hand from her Teutonic home and touched the mountains of Abyssinia, the mouths of old Nile, the southern cape and the western shores. *This* contact of Protestant missions with Africa was but momentary, for the Lutheran in Ethiopia, the "Moravian" in Egypt, Cape Colony and the Gold Coast and the Anglican were then unable to make their occupancy effective. Long years had to pass before the consequences developed. But these were the eternal years of God; and the fateful notes that heralded the coming of Protestant supremacy sounded when Heyling translated the New Testament into Amharic (1636); when Dutch Presbyterianism (1652) and the Huguenot and the Waldensian planted themselves at the Cape of Good Hope (1688); when Dober and Nitschmann in the Antilles, Hocker in Egypt, Protten in Guinea, Richter in Algiers and Schmid in South Africa represented the Unity of Brethren (1732=83); and when Thompson and Quaque, the latter a Negro, inaugurated Anglican missions in Africa. The Roman propagandist of those days, had he had ears to hear and eyes to see, would have felt his spirit smitten with a sense of impending doom, as is the heart of the rapt listener when in Lohengrin's bridal chamber there suddenly steals upon the ear the sound of the distant Grail motive. Not for the knight=errant of Rome, but for the lowly=minded spiritual Protestant, was the African quest for the Holy Grail.

This brings us to the passage from the wilderness of statistics to the promised land, the spiritual city of communicants. The Christian character and career of the native converts are the Holy Grail of African missions. On this center the search and the struggle of Christianity in Africa. The question as to the African's Christliness is a moot controversy, not to be settled by allegation on one side and denial from the other, but only through hearing the testimony of both sides and sifting their evidence.

(2) Brown states that in Sierra Leone "the manners of the bumptious black men are not calculated to win the affections of white folk. . . . All of them treat with supreme contempt the unfortunate white man. For in Freetown it is 'white niggahs an' black gentlemen', and the former fares very badly if he treat the impertinence of the latter as it deserves. For the injured man will hale the white before a black justice, and, fortified with a score of voluble witnesses, lay such a tale before his honor that nothing save an enormous fine will meet the demerits of the case. As a portion of the fine goes

into the pocket of the wronged person, there are citizens who earn a precarious livelihood by insulting strangers and levying blackmail when these find they must either lose passage or pay. . . . Yet, though the 'Sa= Leone' Negro, despite certain improvements of late years, is the most insufferable, insolent, vain and arrogant of his species, he is intensely proud of his nationality. . . . Religious and philanthropic societies have dotted the place with schools, colleges and half=finished churches, all much too large. . . . 'These Negroes', an acute critic explained (and his remark applies to all West Africa), 'are not sufficiently honest; *i. e.*, not sufficiently intelligent; *i. e.*, not sufficiently educated to take positions of confidence and trust. Trial by jury in civil cases is at present impossible in Sierra Leone. Verdicts would be given, damages awarded, according to the nationality and color of the parties' ".

J. Scott Keltie, H. H. Johnston and A. Silva White confirm these judgments. Doctor Keltie, who holds "that there are other ways of rousing the native from his low estate beside preaching at him", declares that "missions have not had the effect hoped for". Sir Harry formerly expressed himself more specifically and severely, maintaining that "it is not on the spread of Christianity that missions can base their claims to gratitude, respect or support. Judged from a purely Christian point of view, they have not been successful. In many important districts where they have been at work for twenty years, they can scarcely, in honest statistics, number twenty sincere Christians, — *i. e.*, twenty natives understanding in any degree the doctrines they have been taught and striving to shape their conduct to their new principles. In other parts, principally British possessions, where large numbers of nominal Christians exist, their religion is discredited by numbering among its adherents, all the drunkards, liars, rogues and unclean livers of the colony. In the oldest of our African possessions [Sierra Leone] the unrepentant Magdalens of the chief city [Freetown] are professing Christians. The most notorious one would boast that she never missed going to church on a Communion=Sunday. . . . The immediate success of British missionaries in spreading their religion is doubtful; the average type of their converts seems an unsatisfactory product of so much labor and expenditure of lives and wealth"*. Mr White considers the "success more or less problematical. If their efforts had not been discounted by the immoral and subversive effects arising out of European political rivalries and commercial greed, the success of missions in West Africa would have been much more marked; but it is not the missionaries who should be held morally responsible for this abortive action. South Africa may be now regarded as a Christian land. . . . The missions in Madagascar and South Africa have made good progress; in West Africa, moderate progress; in East Africa, little progress; in North Africa no [?] progress. . . . We do not expect the missionaries to assimilate with the natives and thereby sacrifice so many centuries of civilization; we expect them to make greater allowance for native prejudice and depravity and, whilst living an industrious, educative and exemplary life, to endeavor to instil the principles and practices rather than the (to natives) incomprehensible dogmas of Christianity. We have no right [?] to expect of natives the miracle of sudden conversion by the power of faith or the intelligence to grasp the abstract truths of Christianity; we must pursue the most direct and intelligent course to their hearts and minds".

*British Protestants spend over one million dollars a year for African missions. Cf. *British Central Africa* (Methuen & Co., London, 1887), pp. 202=204.

These are the testimonies of intelligent gentlemen, who, though of secular temper, appreciate and sympathize with African missionaries. Now listen a moment to mundane minds of another spirit.

Huebner made much of the fact that out of two thousand scholars at Lovedale fifteen reverted to heathenism. Lenz announced that African missions were failures. Winwood Reade stated that the Baptist missionaries at Victoria, Kamerun, accomplished nothing, and that their station was quite useless. The Natalese superintending=inspector of schools for 1889 declared that "from personal observation I have been impressed with the uselessness of much that is taught. Parrot=like repetition of grammatical rules and of isolated facts in astronomy, physiology and ancient Hebrew history is not education but a travesty. The time spent in enumerating the plagues of Egypt and in unraveling the intricacies of patriarchal relationships would be more profitably employed in leveling the breakneck roads and repairing the treacherous drifts that make a visit to many of the stations more a penance than a pleasure. . . . With one exception these schools belong to missions, and the end of the missionary's work is to make converts. The children are taught to read primarily that they may study their Bibles and learn their catechism. The whole life of a mission is ecclesiastically concentric". Lichtenstein about 1805 said of the "Moravian" Khoi=Khoin: "They could sing and pray, be heartily penitent for their sins, and talk of the Lamb of the atonement; but none was really better for this specious appearance". Reclus holds that "since the fall of Carthage and the decadence of Egyptian culture the most important event in African history has been the Muslim invasion. . . . Christianity has attempted to dispute the field with its Muhammadan rival; Protestant missionaries have even obtained some little success, especially in South Africa; but, compared with the apostles of Islam, they stand at a great disadvantage, for they are unable except in a figurative sense to announce themselves as brethren of their black proselytes. The messenger of good tidings can not give his daughter in marriage to his Christian Negro convert. Color keeps them apart. Both remain men of different race and caste"*.

What, now, are the qualifications of these critics for judging the character of African Christians or the success of missions?

Reclus is an anti=theistic scientist who contemns Christianity and all its works, and lacks scientific knowledge of African missions. Lichtenstein had been in the Dutch service, and had imbibed the ignorance and prejudice of the Boer as to missions. The Natalese school= inspector regarded the Christianization of Africans as "mistaken sentimentalism", and represented the typical colonist in his attitude toward the natives. The average European in Africa, the bulk of the white populations, holds that Africans and Malagasi ought forever to be hewers of wood and drawers of water. Here is an anti=

*Grenfell (white) married a Negro lady of Kamerun, whose abilities and Christian character are the admiration of all. Fred Douglass (Negro) married a white woman. Portuguese and Dutch Christians have frequently taken Negro wives. Dods and Dumas, two distinguished Frenchmen, were of Negro ancestry. Reclus' assertion requires qualification. In a later portion (v. 4, p. 117) of his wonderful work this great geographer in 1890 thus modified his preceding statement: "In no African region have missionaries been more zealous and successful than in Cape Colony. At present nearly two hundred thousand natives in Cape Colony and about three hundred and fifty thousand in the whole of Austral Africa south of the Zambezi profess the Christian religion". Merensky in 1898 reckoned all native converts in Cape Colony as five hundred and thirty=three thousand. If the numbers enumerated by Reclus be the figures for 1888 and if his "professors of religion" be the class meant by Merensky's "native converts", it would seem as if, even in so brief a span of time as a single decade, the native Christian population of Cape Colony had doubled; had, indeed, not merely doubled but had all but increased two and a half times. In any event the Christianization of Cape Colony, within a century, by means of colonization and missions is really one of the most momentous events of history and the miraculous marvels of evangelization. It seems almost impossible of comprehension that to=day Cape Colony alone has more native Christians, by nearly two hundred thousand, than did all Austral Africa so recently as 1888. Verily a nation is in the loom.

mission bias to start with. As a rule it is quite the last to yield to facts and their stern logic. To it is due the feeling against the Christianization of "lower" races, and underlying it there is invariably more or less of dislike for the African and of a sneer at missionaries, for the Christian native can no more be the stupid, ignorant, bear=to=be=kicked creature that the raw native was. Winwood Reade began life with a strong anti=theological bias; published an impeachment of Christianity; and worshipped mud=gods. In reply to Reade, Saker stated that his station could hardly be considered entirely useless; it had saved Negro women from the drunken attacks of the traveler's friends. Lenz condemns the missionary's very object, and also expresses himself as to African missions in a non=scientific spirit. He visited a few missions on the Kongo and those on Lakes Nyasa and Tanganika. The death=rate had been unusually large, the establishment of the enterprises too recent for great and varied results. Yet Lenz, though not near any other mission, drew unscientific and untruthful deductions from insufficient *data*. *The Times* thundered against Lenz. The independent and unimpeachable testimony of impartial and unprejudiced witnesses, it said, is quite opposed to that of Lenz, adding: "There are mission=villages in Central Africa that would compare favorably in conduct with many English hamlets. The picture Farler draws of his station is corroborated by a body of independent testimony".

So much as to the worthlessness of the testimony volunteered by the enemies of missions. What of the evidence furnished by such friends of missions as Messrs Johnston, Keltie and White?

White has studied African missions, but not from a spiritual standpoint. Keltie surveyed them from the secular point of view, and did not study the religious partition of Africa. Johnston was misinformed and misled. His impeachment of the Christianity of the native communicants and other converts, though unquestionably true, is only true in a limited degree. It can not apply to African missions in general. It is applicable to the western coast and such places as Alexandria, Cape Town, Johannesburg or Zanzibar. West Africa has for centuries been an Alsatia of Christendom, made such by the Christianism of Europe and its nominally Christian representatives; and many black men who never accepted Christianity naturally imitate white men in styling themselves Christians in distinction from the Islamite and the pagan. Again, mining centers and sea=ports notoriously draw the moral scum of heathendom and civilization. Genuine Negro Christians are thus discredited by hypocrites and liars who falsely claim affiliation with missions or churches. More extensive and intimate acquaintance with mission=work would have enabled Johnston to judge as sympathetically and wisely of its moral and spiritual results as of its scientific success. Young, "having seen a good deal of the missions of different churches in Cape Colony and Natal, makes bold to say that such a state as Johnston describes has no existence there, nor would it be tolerated a single day".

The negative evidence as to the vital Christianity of African converts has been summarized by *The Spectator* thus: "The plain truth about missionary=work we believe to be this: . . . 'But,' [it is objected] 'then these results are not conversions?' Yes, [*The Spectator* replies], they are, as much as Augustine's. We no more believe that the majority of converts are men raised to the level of English clergymen than that Augustine's were. They are nothing of the kind. Ordinary intellectual acquiescence in Christianity as truer than any other faith will no more turn a savage into a civilized man than a Bengali into an Englishman. It took more than one generation or three to kill the brutality of Saxons; it will take many to kill the special predispositions of tropical races toward evils — incontinence — which oftentimes they only dimly see to be evils. There is always the difficulty, too, which, *pace* Canon Taylor, has nothing to do with Christianity, that tropical man when he drinks longs to be drunk, and that the missionary, unlike Manu, Gautama and Muhammad, is unable to say that drink, apart from drunkenness, is inevitable damnation. But there are genuine converts, as complete and sincere as any made by the apostles. . . . We appeal to hostile critics to answer whether they have ever known a Christian native church in the tropics in which there were *not* one or two whom they excepted from doubts or censures, whom they felt to be utterly unlike all around, whom they could trust implicitly in all circumstances, who were of themselves positive proof that there is nothing in race, climate, circumstance which should ultimately in any corner of the world prevent the triumph of Christianity. The work is hard. It is not hopeless".

Positive testimony as to the Christian character and conduct of African converts is milk and honey for spiritual-minded men. Drummond from his personal experience gives us this fragment: "I had a black man with me on a tour in Tanganika. He could not speak a word of English. I wanted one in whom I could place confidence. Doctor Laws had succeeded in influencing six or seven lads. He gave me the worst. I remember, the first night, lying in the tent after I thought the men had gone to bed. I heard a strange noise from one of the camp=fires. I peered out. I saw Mulu kneeling, around him a group of Bandawe who understood his language, and he was having prayers as Laws had taught him. I tried to catch the accents. I could rake out this petition for what to him was the whole known earth. He prayed for Bandawe, Blantyra, Tanganika and 'Engalandi'. That to me proves the mission a genuine thing. This man was not what you call a pious convert; he was a common=place black. I trusted him with every thing; I tested him in many critical ways, on many adventurous occasions; but Mulu's character never broke down".

So much for an average, fairly typical, individual Christian. What of the native church and community?

Let Livingstone's experience for sixteen years (1840=56) answer:

"My first impressions were that the accounts of the effects of the gospel had been too highly colored. I expected a higher degree of Christian purity and simplicity than exists among them or ourselves. I expected character such as we imagine the primitive disciples had — and was disappointed"*. "When I passed to true heathen in countries beyond missionary influence, and could compare people there with Christian natives, I came to the conclusion that if the question were examined in the most severe or rigidly scientific way the change effected by the missionary=movement would be considered unquestionably great. We can not fairly compare these poor

---

*"The popular notion, however, of the primitive church is not accurate. Those societies especially which consisted of converted Gentiles — men accustomed to the immoralities of heathenism — were certainly anything but pure. In spite of conversion some carried the stains and vestiges of their former state from the temple to the church. If the instructed and civilized Greek did not all at once rise out of his former self and understand and realize the high ideal of his new faith, we should be careful in judging of the work of missionaries among savage tribes not to apply to their converts tests and standards of too great severity. If Lucian's account of Peregrinus the impostor may be believed, we find a church probably planted by the apostles manifesting less intelligence even than modern missionary=churches. Peregrinus, a notoriously wicked man, was elected to the chief place; Romish priests backed by the power of France could not find a place at all in the [Protestant] mission=churches of Tahiti and Madagascar".

people with ourselves who have an atmosphere of Christianity and enlightened public opinion, the growth of centuries, around us to influence our deportment; but let any one from the natural and proper point of view behold the public morality of Griqua Town, Kuruman and other villages, and remember what even London was a century ago; he must confess the Christian mode of treating aborigines incomparably the best. . . . Now these people come to church in decent clothing, and behave with a decorum superior to what seems to have been the case in the time of Pepys in London. Sunday is well observed. Even in localities where no missionary lives religious meetings are regularly held and children and adults taught to read by the more advanced of their fellow country-men. No one is allowed to make a profession of faith by baptism, unless he knows how to read and understands the nature of the Christian religion. The Bechwana [Chwana] mission has been so successful, that when coming from the interior we always felt on reaching Kuruman that we had returned to civilized life. But I would not give any one to understand that they are model Christians, in any degree superior to members of our country churches. They are more stingy and greedy than the poor at home, but in many respects the two are exactly alike. On asking an intelligent chief what he thought of them, he replied [that] . . . 'a pretty large number profess because they are really true believers' ".

In other passages Livingstone added that the idea of making model Christians of young Africans need not be entertained; that "we should not indulge in overwrought expectations as to the elevation which those who have inherited the degradation of ages may attain in our day. The principle might even be adopted that one missionary's lifetime of teaching should be considered an ample supply of *foreign* teaching for any tribe in a thinly peopled country, for some never will receive the gospel, while in other parts when Christianity is once planted the work is sure to go on. . . . Protestant missionaries agree that no mere profession is sufficient to entitle converts to the Christian name. They are anxious to place the Bible in the hands of natives. With ability to read this there can be little doubt as to the future. . . . Of the effects of a long=continued course of instruction there can be no reasonable doubt".

With these words of Livingstone's, published exactly forty years ago, compare Bryce's views, published in 1897: "The native congregations are usually small, the careers of converts not always satisfactory. This is so natural it is odd to find Europeans, especially those whose life is not a model of morality, continually sneering at missionaries because not all converts turn out saints. . . . The Kafir are not such bad Christians as the Frank warriors for three generations after the conversion of Clovis. We must wait for generations before we can fairly judge the influence of his new religion on a Kafir whose ancestors had no [?] religion, and were ruled by the lowest forms of superstition. These facts are better recognized by the missionaries than sixty years ago, and they have made changes in methods. They are no longer so anxious to baptize, so apt to reckon success by the number of converts. They are more cautious in ordaining native pastors. The dogma of the equality of the black and the white has been dropped [?]. . . . The missionaries devote themselves more than formerly to secular instruction, and endeavor to train the natives in habits of industry. The work of education is entirely in their hands. . . Polygamy is so bound with heathen customs, and exerts so entirely baneful an influence on native society, that it must be at all hazards resisted and condemned. . . . Within Cape Colony and on its borders they [the missionaries, "especially those of the London Society"] for the first sixty years of the century were the leading champions of the natives. Outside the colony they were often the principal advisers of native chiefs. . . . But for missionaries, natives would have lacked all local protection, and only through missionaries could news of cruelty or injustice practiced on a native reach the British government. . . . Notwithstanding the slowness of progress, the extinction of heathenism may be deemed certain at no distant date. In forty years there will probably be no pagan rites in Cape Colony; in eighty years none in Matabililand. . . . Although the Kafir have shown rather less aptitude for assimilating Christian teaching than have some other savage races, there is nothing to discourage the hope that such teaching may prevail. . . . The gospel and the mission=schools are the most truly civilizing influences which work upon the natives, and upon these influences more than on any other agency depends the progress of the colored race*"

The African Christian, then, lives out his religion. Bishop Crowther; Archdeacon Crowther; the Reverend James Johnson, law=maker and moral shepherd of Lagos; the native Bible=women at Gabun; Bokwe of Lovedale; Khama, the Alfred of Africa; Afrikaner; Sechele; Tiyo Soga; Yona, the Zulu Harriet Newell; Wilhelmina, the "Moravian" Kafir and even the men who bore Livingstone's body, to name but a few at random, are men and women whose Christianity, in its devotion to duty and daily drudgery, its devoutness, its missionary activity,

* *Impressions of South Africa*, pp. 387-393, abridged and condensed.

its self=sacrifice in service to Christ would hardly suffer from comparison with that of the average church=member in America and Europe*. The Malagasi, though pitifully poor, formerly gave $233,360 annually, between 1877 and 1888 contributing nearly one million dollars for missions. The native communicants in Africa as a rule take high ground against polygamy, refusing church= membership unless the candidates accept marriage as the union of one man and one woman. In West Africa, on ground originally none of the best, the moral tone has of late years been lowered, but the Christian church may be trusted to master polygamy even here. Throughout Africa as a whole the testimony of such men as Warren, an ex=governor of Natal; Baxter, Mason and Cairns of the British parliament; Mrs Baker; General and Lieutenant=Governor Cunynghame; Donald Ross, inspector of schools for Cape Colony in 1882; the official Kafir commission of the colonial administration; Charles Brownell, lately minister of native affairs in Cape Colony; and the editors of *The Cape Times*, *The Port Elizabeth Telegraph* and *The South African Methodist* — is that the moral and the spiritual life of the native Christians are sterling †.

Greater love, said Jesus, hath no man than this: that he lay down his life for the life of his friend. Perhaps the crucial test for the genuineness of the African's Christianity is his endurance of persecution, his readiness for martyrdom. The Berber in Algeria, the Kopt in Egypt, the Hova in Madagascar, the Nyasa, Uganda and Zanzibari Christians, the Zulu, the Kafir, the Khoi=

---

* David Susi, one of Livingstone's men, did not become a Christian till more than twenty years after he had first met with Livingstone. See *The Story of Africa*, v. 2, pp. 265 and 280.

† The evidence is far too voluminous for citation, but is easily accessible in Liggins' *Great Value of Missions*, published by Baker and Taylor of New York City, and in Young's *Success of Missions*, published by Hodder and Stoughton of London.

TWO NATIVE CHRISTIANS

Khoin and the Chwana, the Kongo converts, the Gabunese, the Calabarans, the Niger proselytes and the Negro communicants of Guinea have furnished followers of the Christ. They bore His cross in lives of suffering or died in loyalty to their divine Friend. Madagascar, Uganda and Yariba stand among the historic names that leap to the lip when Christianity is asked whether the African, at the risk of death, will cleave to the Christ. With Stanley we say: "What can a man wish better for a proof that Christianity is possible in Africa? . . . I take this powerful body of native Christians in the heart of Africa, who prefer exile for the sake of their faith to serving a monarch indifferent or hostile to their faith, as more substantial evidence of the work of Mackay than any number of imposing structures clustered together and called a mission=station would be. These Africans have endured the most deadly persecutions. Stake and fire, cord and club, sharp knife and rifle=bullet have all been tried to cause them to reject the teachings they have absorbed. Stanch in their beliefs, firm in their convictions, they have held together stoutly and resolutely".

III

The Outlook for the Coming Century

The present conditions are difficult to state. The problem of evangelization has geographical, ethnical, philological, political and religious factors. Africa, by and large, is known and is a result of missions. The linguistic and racial elements are well along toward being understood. We know the chief ethnic stocks and their relative values; we see the great language=groups and their potencies of service. The American, Antillean, Bantu and Sûdanese Negro; the Abyssinian and Arab, the Jew and Kopt; the Boer, the British Afrikander and the Malagasi are natives of the once lost and hopeless continent who are already supplementing the effort of Americans and Europeans. Christian Jews are evangelizing Hebrews, former Muslims are seeking the Islamites, and former heathen preach to the pagans. Industrial and normal institutes, medical missions and woman are adding incalculable potencies. The world=wide organizations of young lay=workers form dynamos and motors of missions. One hundred and one African languages, including dialects, have missionary Bible=versions in whole or in part, and have thus received baptism with pentecostal power. The continent as a whole, despite the skirmishing between the outposts of savagery and civilization, is quieting down as Christendom, law and strong=armed peace take possession. Within twenty=five years Gallaland, Somalia, Sahara and Sûdan will be mastered. They can not be Christianized then, but they can be evangelized. Paganism has no coherence and crumbles in the environment of civilization. In Cape Colony, for instance, it will, when 1950 arrives, have ceased to exist, even if only half of the aborigines be Christians. But several large facts bear upon the outlook. Though not without somber shadows, it is one of sunny skies. In any discussion of mission=ary=problems these facts may be accepted as axioms.

(1) Africa, by and large is in the grip of Christendom. Europe has made Africa a political appanage, is achieving somewhat toward the suppressal of slavery, and breaks the backbone of the slave=trade. This means the saving of millions of lives annually; the protection of missionaries and the promotion of missions; and the multiplication of native agents.

(2) The partition of Africa strikes the sword from the hand of Islam. We can not ignore the Mahdist movement, the existence of the Senusiya, the fierceness of Maroccan Muhammadanism; but Marocco is a crumbling empire, the Senusiya lacks capacity for political cohesion through areas so vast and scattered as Mediterranean Africa, Sahara and Sûdan, and Mahdism will have become a thing of the past ere long. Since 1890 Islam south of the equator has received such blows that there it can never again lift its heel against Christianity. Between the equator and the tenth degree north [east of Adamawa] it is more than ever a waning force. The solidarity and strength of Bagirmi and Bornu have sustained severe shocks. The suffering subjects of the khalifa welcome any foreigner who can enforce peace and restore prosperity. Only on the Niger and in Guinea can be found a form of Islam at all hopeful. In North Africa Islam is symbolized by the mosques that Richardson found throughout Sahara. These consist simply of small stones outlining the ground=plan of a mosque. Unfinished, unsurrounded by human habitations, these prayer=places typify African Islam itself. In West Africa, however, the Negro Muslims are interested in the Bible; and through vernacular versions for Guinea and the Arabic version for Egypt Christianity will gain a leverage for Muslim missions in Atlantic and Mediterranean Africa during the twentieth century. Among the Sûdanese Muslims, however, the progress of Christianity can at best be but slow, and the Saharan Islamite may withdraw jealously into inaccessible fastnesses; but Islam is no longer a competitor for the control of the coming continent, and, unless the Senusiya cross swords with Britain or France, the movement of the Sûdanese messiahs will be the last African attack of

Islam upon Christianity. But Canons of the church, if Christians are to occupy the newly opening strategic centers with missions, must cease arguing that Islam is better suited than Christianity for African races of low development, must stop their fire from the rear upon the advance=guard of Christian civilization.

(3) For the first time, then, in fifteen hundred years, Christian missions among Africans are to have a fair chance and an open field. The warfares of theologians from the fourth century on; the entrance of Islam and its eclipse of the cross; the living death of the Koptic and Ethiopic churches; the struggle of European Christianity against Saracen and Turk through a millennium; our ignorance of Africa; the infancy of Protestantism; the impotence of Rome to create lasting communities of living churches in tropical Africa; the liquor=traffic and the slave=trade; the immorality and unreligiousness of nominal Christians, papal as well as Protestant; the lack of stability in native society; and the recency of the entrance of Protestantism=at=large have, some of them successively, some simultaneously, barred out aggressive, pure and vital Christianity. Now these giants are mostly fallen into the past. Paganism will crumble in the atmosphere of civilization. The waning crescent slowly sinks toward eternal night. Protestantism moves to federation. Rome revives; and, as in the sixteenth century she reformed her clergy, in the twentieth century she will reform her European laymen. Britain has swarmed into the cardinal coigns of African vantage. In Egypt and South Africa she holds an axis of the continent, and in East and West Africa rests on such corners of the quadrilateral as Ibea and Nigeria. Germany, our fellow= Protestant power, flanks the British position, but, Boer and German notwithstanding, the best portions of Africa

for men of Saxon stock are in British hands. Evangelical Christianity in Africa is better situated than is Rome. The ultimate issue of the differences between Britain and Transvaal; Egypt and Sudan; Italy and Abyssinia; and of France with Nigritia and Sahara must make for the advancement of Christian missions. America and Britain, Germany and Scandinavia, the Protestant and Teutonic powers wielding the moral headship of humanity, are the Christian countries most richly endowed for the betterment of African peoples, are those enjoying the greatest influence in their spiritual regeneration. Despite backsets here and eddies there, so that sections of the continent will lag behind the Christian progress of others, the historian of African missions in 1996 will not be discouraged by the result, for the steadfast tide of Christian energy, directed by God and Godlike men, will have everywhere made for righteousness.

The supreme danger for the future of African missions rises from political complications and from the secularism of European civilization. The development itself of Africa brings peculiar difficulties. Intertribal wars may end, but Europe's international rivalries take their place. The slave=trade and even domestic slavery wane, but the liquor=traffic, if unthrottled, will wreak at least as much ruin. The passing of the heroic, the martyr, the romantic age of missions may lessen interest in the prosaic, routine stage now at hand and immeasurably important. Islam, in virtue of the grain of truth at its heart and of its social power as a free=masonry, may persist for centuries. The devil of heathenism and savagery may be cast out; but, if his place be not filled by the spirit of Jesus, and if the worldliness and fellow= fiends of civilization take his place, the latter estate of the African will be worse than the former. The Negro is at least as worldly as the white man, and African Christianity has to show whether its fiber can withstand sapping by ease and material prosperity.

The Hova afford the best evidence now available, both negative and positive, from their past and present, as to the outcome. The Reverend James Sibree in March, 1896, wrote from Tananarivo as follows: In many villages there was a distinct return to heathenism. . . . But there was little call for wonder at this reversion to old superstitions, when we remember the small amount of teaching a large proportion have yet had. . . . More recently, since the return of the Roman priests and their co=workers, new difficulties have arisen. Many have been led to believe they must become Catholics, since the French have conquered. This idea has been industriously spread. With large numbers "French" is synonymous with "Catholic", "English" with "Protestant". It is not wonderful that with an ignorant and timid people the dominant idea is, not which is the true religion, but which is to be the strongest. As they think Romanism the French religion, therefore it will be safest for them to be of that religion. Doubtless there are many difficulties looming ahead in the near future from this quarter. Great efforts are made to get the children from our schools and the young people from our congregations. Our brethren in the southern province are feeling this already. So are our Norwegian friends in Central Madagascar. General Duchesne gave at once the fullest assurance of religious liberty, and Resident=General Laroche has promised a proclamation on the subject. Laroche is a Protestant, and will therefore fully carry out the agreement between England and France as to religious freedom. Many of the leading officials are also liberal and enlightened men, in full accord with their chief on this point. . . . Of course there are attendant evils which seem inseparable from the presence of a large number of soldiers. There is, we fear, a great increase of drinking among the Malagasi as well as licentiousness; and there is now much Sunday trading in the capital, a thing not known for twenty=five years. The Resident=General has, however, already struck a blow at one of the chief blots on Malagasi civilization, and has stopped the sale of slaves in the markets. We may hope that other measures may eventually be taken, so that slavery itself may gradually come to an end. On the whole, although there are many discouragements arising from the time=serving character of the Malagasi and their want of moral back=bone and courage in doing right, as well as difficulties arising from religious differences, there are many cheering features. The French authorities are trying to promote justice and religious equality. The people seem to have quietly acquiesced in the new political arrangements. Protestant missionaries loyally accept the new régime, and will work heartily with those in power to promote in every way the well= being of the Malagasi.

The French treatment of Protestant missionaries in Algeria and Gabun hitherto and the German attitude toward British and French missions cause the present writer to prefer suspense of judgment as to the future of non=papal missions in the African possessions of France and Germany. The most he deems it well to say, in the light of the developments during 1898, is that in Madagascar the French administration wears a face of friendliness to Protestant missions and that it looks as if, in the end, the Jesuit might prove *not* to be a power behind the throne. The Paris Society has assumed charge of secular education in the London

Society's elementary schools, the British Congregationalists continuing religious instruction, and has also received about half of the country districts of Imerina and two districts in Betsileo.

The rum=trade also menaces missions with increasing injury as railroads and steamers multiply.

Not only do the results of Protestant missions in Africa and Madagascar from 1795 to 1895 surpass all that Carey, Coke, Johnson and Moffat could have dreamed of, but the rate of gain is rising and they are receiving reinforcements. The Christian womanhood of America and Europe, the British and Dutch Christians of Cape Colony and Natal, the Orange State and Transvaal and the Negro churches of Africa and the Americas have begun to double the Protestant force. Its Africo=Malagasi missions may enter the twentieth century with twenty=five hundred American and European missionaries, over fifteen thousand native mission=workers and, among the native communicants, a Gideon's band of twenty=five thousand chosen and consecrate. When The South African Republic has composed the variances of Boer and foreigner, the stalwart Dutch will furnish pioneers to lock hands in Christian service with their fellow=Protestants or to push Christian missions in tropical Africa. The Spirit of God will yet choose Him missionaries from the Transvaal Dutch*.

Now that the Muslim and pagan populations of northern and tropical Africa are more and more opening to women, Catholic and Protestant womanhood will render still greater service than in the past. The Kaiserswerth

---

*The Free State in 1896 had thirty=six Dutch congregations. These, one or two excepted, sustain missions among the aborigines, the Boer deacons or elders and pastors being in charge. Nearly every native congregation has a school for their children, very often an evening school for adults. Eight churches had nearly thirteen hundred native members and four hundred native school=children, and the missionary=spirit is stronger each year.

deaconess, the Protestant woman=missionary and the Roman nun or sister have enlarging parts in evangelization*.

The Anglican, Congregational, Presbyterian and Wesleyan clergy of Cape Colony and Natal are no less alert to meet the need of the natives than of colonists. So are some ministers of the Dutch Church, notably Andrew Murray. South Africa's white population, numbering seven hundred and thirty thousand, supports at least sixteen local agencies for African missions. Cape Colony can, humanly speaking, accomplish the Christianization of Austral Africa before the year 2,000.

Native agency affords another occasion for hopefulness. Much has already been accomplished by Africans once heathen, Muhammadan or slave that no other instrumentality could have attained. The Church Society long ago made its Negro Christians in Sierra Leone an independent Anglican church. So is that of Lagos; and the Anglican missions in Yariba seem at least to be semi= independent. The British Wesleyans have made their mission in Cape Colony a separate conference. The Presbyterian Church of South Africa proclaims independence. The United Presbyterians in Egypt will soon set up the Presbyteries of Asiut, the Delta, Middle Egypt and Thebes, and unite them in the Synod of the Nile. Liberia's Negro Baptists, Methodists and Presbyterians have grown into independence. The Hova have a national church of their own. These organizations of native Christians number thousands upon thousands of communicants. The native missionary=societies of Negro Anglicans in Lagos and Sierra Leone, of Malagasi Congregationalists, of Egyptian Presbyterians are instances of Christian aggressiveness on the part of the Protestant African.

*Cf. *British Central Africa*, pp. 198=200. Commissioner Johnston's reasoning as to the influence of native animalism is not so right and seemly as it should be.

Even Abyssinian and Koptic Christians can not remain impervious to spiritual light and vitalizing truth. The Musulman will be won by proselytes from Islam, the pagan by Negro Christians. Though on the whole testimony has borne against the Negro as a missionary, the fault lies not with the people but with the individual. Time and culture are removing the vices, the infirmities, the difficulties of an imperfectly cultured, unripe race. The truth of the equality of the black and the white must not be dropped, but be held and pushed to the fullest reach of its validity. The Negro genius has an original and unique contribution for Christianity*.

(4) New applications of old methods constitute a fourth ground for hope. Evangelization will remain the sole human agency for God to inspire the African with life, but the preacher or teacher will be more and more aided by the craftsman, the doctor, the farmer and the Christian trader. Industrial institutions, however, will in future have to guard more carefully than in the past against secularism swamping spirituality. So will societies that engage in agriculture or commerce in order to support missions.

The self=sustaining white missionary in tropical Africa belongs to the far future. The Jesuit and the "Moravian", a hundred years and more before Doctors Simpson and Taylor were born, had been forced by experience to surrender the theory of self=supporting missions. When a Tesla or some succeeding wizard has so mastered electricity that men may modify climatic conditions, Americans and Europeans will be enabled to Christianize the natives and also to support themselves in the tropics†.

*An enthusiast has gone so far as to say: "The Negro, more than other races, exemplifies the beauty and consistency of his Christianity".

† *Our Day*, October, 1893, p. 317, l. 29 *sq.* *The Century*, April, 1895, p. 933, l. 10.

The fact that nine tenths of the success have been attained by less than fifty societies, but five of which in turn are non=denominational, demonstrates that the bulk of the work will continue to be accomplished by strong church=societies and through salaried missionaries.

The American Negro has so far lacked interest in African missions. But it was unreasonable to expect this of a race just out of bondage. The first two generations born in freedom must pass away before the bulk of our black Christians can rise to the realization of their racial obligations and providential privileges as to Africa. A little, however, has already been effected in this direction. The Protestant Negro of the United States and West Indies has rewarded his Christianizers. The Anglican, Baptist, Basel, Congregational, Episcopal, Methodist and Presbyterian missions in Africa, have enjoyed his services. Six Negro Baptist, five Negro Methodist, bodies engage in missions among African peoples. The Protestant communions in the United States number ten times as many colored communicants as Protestantism in Africa. On the principle that "evil is good in the making", American slavery was an instrumentality in the origination of missions, and thus, in a sense, Christianity stands indirectly in debt to "the sum of all villainies" for certain of its greatest and most remarkable gains. Except for five hundred and twenty=five thousand American Negro Protestants in 1861, the result is the outcome of but thirty=three years. In one third of the time that European societies have been active in Africa, missions among our freedmen and their children have accomplished tenfold as much. Since America's black Baptists and Methodists comprise three million communicants, they can be held to stricter account for the Christianization of the Negro than may any other Christian church. Not even the Anglican communion is weighted with heavier African responsibilities. The Negro Christian is awaking to his peculiar duty in regard to Africa and its peoples. The growing interest, evidenced by discussion and investigation, promises that fifty years hence black Baptists and Methodists will annually send hundreds of Negro missionaries to Africa. Stewart Mission=Foundation, if it train students to distinguish science from sciolism and to replace rhetoric by reason, sentimentality by sense and shrewdness, will render yeoman service. If Negro Baptists and Methodists concentrate on African missions, those of intertropical Africa should advance ten times more swiftly*.

A final reinforcement for African missions is to come from the Lutheran, Methodist and Roman communions in America. When these sleeping giants — asleep as to Africa — rouse themselves, their communicants, who in 1890 numbered over twelve millions, will contribute men and means in no slight degree. The American Methodist and the European Jesuit have been Christianity's failure in African missions; but the day is destined to arrive when the American Catholic and the Methodist will exert themselves to retrieve the disaster.

The twentieth century can then carry out the ideas of Krapf and Mackay. The German contemplated a series of supporting stations across Africa; the Scot, the utilization of the ideals and methods of the normal school. The Lutheran's plan has already partly realized itself east and west; the Presbyterian's is in partial play at Lovedale and its fellow=schools. When mission=posts cross the continent from north to south, thus planting

---

*Transvaal Negroes have formed "The Ethiopic Church", and President Kruger is quoted as assuring Bishop Turner (the first of Abraham Lincoln's Negro chaplains) that the African Methodist Episcopal Church has his sympathy. Bishop Turner is reported to believe that this, his church, has a greater future in South Africa than in Liberia.

spiritual light=houses along *all* the great rivers and lakes, the missionary=societies of the next century will put new Lovedales at scores on scores of strategic centers. They will be placed in Muslim, and not alone in pagan, Africa. Arabia as well as Africa and America; Aden and Maskat no less than Alexandria; Algiers, Khartum and Zanzibar will be made recruiting fields of native missionaries to the Arab and Berber, the Galla and Somal. Carefully chosen Africans will receive thorough training, partly industrial but chiefly educational and spiritual. Such schools in America as Calabar, Codrington and Fisk will also prepare Negro missionaries. Some of the African seminaries must be planted at easily accessible points. All must be unstintedly supported and well=manned. Teaching must be in a language that is the English speech of great regions or many tribes. The native individuality must be respected, and no effort exerted to create white men from colored men. Such methods, if pushed — and pushed hard — for century after century, will eventuate in a Christian Africa.

To make Europe Christian, even nominally, has required eighteen centuries. To prepare a way for the Lord in Africa has been a millennial and terrible task. Though the next hundred years will determine the religious trend for generations afterward, will set the streams of spiritual tendency flowing either toward the City of God or the kingdom of Satan, it is not to be believed that God intends Christendom, even when aided by science, even if unhindered by civilization, to Christianize the myriad millions of a tropic continent in so brief and inadequate a time as the next hundred years. The twentieth century may prove a crisis in the Christianization of Africa, calling for the church to give her choicest children, for consecrated wealth to spend supremely; yet even if Africa in bulk be not a Christian continent in A. D. 2000,—missions will *not* have failed.

But if we attempt great things for God, we may expect greater things from God. If we greatly grant, we shall grandly gain.

For missions are God's work. They are Christ's work and the Holy Spirit's. They are the business, the supreme business, of Christ's church. They are the personal affair of Christians in the mass and as individuals. But it is the Almighty Himself who is the Master=Workman and the Captain of the Lord's host. The annals of missions are chronicles of the King. The marvels and miracles of African missions; the existence of as many native Christians in them to=day as in the world at the close of the first century; and the unprecedented progress of the Negro in America prove God's presence and power in the Christianization of Africa. Again His pillar of fire leads the advance. *From* Africa, then; *into* Africa, now. If America and Europe render Christly service to Ethiopia, if Britain and France in Sûdan are completing that task of crushing Islam's political power which the United States initiated at Tripoli in 1801, — it is because Our Father has long stretched His hand to Africa and her children, and has sounded the silver trumpet that never calls retreat. Sahara's desert=ranger shall yet kneel, not to Allah, but to God; the Ethiopic stranger shall come from Nigritia and Bantuland to His glory; and the African isles of the eastern and western seas that wait His law shall yield dominion unto Him who is King of Kings and God over all. For HIS are the kingdom, the power and the glory forever. *Amen!*

STATISTICAL SURVEY OF PROTESTANT MISSIONS

AMONG

AFRICAN PEOPLES IN AFRICA, THE ANTILLES AND MADAGASCAR

COMPILED BY FREDERIC PERRY NOBLE

FROM A

"STATISTICAL SUPPLEMENT TO 'CHRISTIAN MISSIONS AND SOCIAL PROGRESS'"

BY

THE REVEREND JAMES S. DENNIS, D.D.

EDUCATIONAL STATISTICS

1

COLLEGES AND UNIVERSITIES

Location	Name	Date of Founding	Church or Society
AFRICA			
Asyut, Egypt............	Mission Training=College ..	1867	Am. Un. Pr.
Blythswood, Kafraria.....	Institution................	1877	Sc. Fr. Pr.
Cape Coast, Gold Coast...	Collegiate School		Br. Wes.
Cline Town, Sierra Leone.	Furah Bay College.........	1827	Ch. Miss. Soc.
Cuttington, Liberia	Hoffman Institute	1868	Am. Epis.
Grahamston, Cape Colony.	St Andrew's College.......	1855	S. P. G. (Ang).
Grahamston, Cape Colony.	Kafir Institution...........	1860	S. P. G.
Kiungani, Zanzibar........	St Andrew's College	1884	Un. Miss.
Lovedale, Cape Colony....	Lovedale Miss. Institution..	1841	Sc. Fr. Pres.
Pieter Maritzburg, Natal..	St Alban's Training College	1883	S. P. G.
Riebeck, Cape Colony	Riebeck....................		
Rondebosch, Cape Colony.	Diocesan College, The.....	1849	S. P. G.
Wellington, Cape Colony.	Huguenot Female College..	1874	Nondenom.
Zonnebloem, Cape Colony.	Kafir Institution...........	1860	S. P. G.
THE ANTILLES			
Barbados.................	Codrington College	1710	S. P. G.
Bethlehem, Jamaica	Training College		Un. of Br.
Fairfield, Jamaica	Training College		Un. of Br.
Kingston, Jamaica.......	Calabar College	1843	Eng. Bap.
San Fernando, Trinidad...	Presbyterian College.......		Can. Pres.
MADAGASCAR			
Ambatoharanana	St Paul's College...........		S. P. G.
Tananarivo...............	College		L. M. S.

2

THEOLOGICAL SEMINARIES AND TRAINING SCHOOLS

AFRICA			
Akropong, Gold Coast	Theological Seminary......		Basel Miss. Soc.
Aliwal North, Cape Colony	Training School.		Prim. Meth.
Amanzimtote (Adams), Natal	Theological School		Am. Board
Amedschovhe, Slave Coast	Theological Seminary.....	1864	North Germ. Soc.
Asmara, Eritrea...........	Theolog. and Train. School.		Swed. Nat. Soc.
Bandawe, Nyasaland......	Preachers' Class...........		Sc. Free Pres.
Banza Manteke, Kongo State..................	Training School............	1894	Am. Bapt. Union
Batanga, Kamerun........	Theol. Training Class......	1891	Am. Pres. (Northern)
Bensonvale, Kafraria	Training Institution........		Br. Wesleyans

EDUCATIONAL STATISTICS

Location	Name	Date of Founding	Church or Society
AFRICA—Continued			
Bensonvale, Kafraria	Training School		Undenom.
Blair Ochil, Nyasaland	Training Institute		Zambezi Indust. Mission
Blantyre, Nyasaland	Training Schools		Estab. Ch. of Scotland(Pres.)
Bloemfontein, Orange	Theol. Depart. St A. Col.		S. P. G.
Bonaberi, Kamerun	Training School		Basel (Und.)
Botschabelo, Transvaal	Teachers' Seminary	1884	Berlin (Luth.)
Cairo, Egypt	Theological Seminary	1864	Am. Un. Pres.
Cape Coast, Gold Coast	Training Institution		Brit. Wesleyans
Cape Town, Cape Colony	Trinity Church School		Anglican (?)
Clarkebury, Cape Colony	Training Institution		Undenom.
Cunningham, Kafraria	Elders' and Deacons' Class		Sc. Free Pr.
Cuttington, Liberia	Theological School	1868	Am. Episc.
Duke Town, Old Kalabar	Hope Waddell Train. Inst	1895	Sc. Un. Pres.
Durban, Natal	St Alban's Train. School		S. P. G.
Emgwali, Cape Colony	Boarding and Train. School	1840	Sc. Un. Pres.
Engcobo, Kafraria	Augusta Memorial Train. Inst	1882	Scotch Episc.
Fort Peddie, Cape Colony	Train. School for Teachers		Br. Wes. Wom. Aux.
Freetown, Sierra Leone	Training and High School		Br. Wesleyans
Freretown, Brit. E. Africa	Divinity Class	1894	Ch. Miss. Soc. (Ang.)
Gnadenthal, Cape Colony	Training College	1838	Un. of Breth.
Healdtown, Cape Colony	Training School		Undenom.
Impolweni, Zululand	Theological Class	1896	Sc. Free Pres.
Isandhlawana, Zululand	Mackenzie Train. College		S. P. G.
Keiskamma Hoek, Cape Colony	Normal School for Girls	1897	Wom. Assoc. of S. P. G.
Kibunzi, French Kongo	Train. Sch. for Evangelists and Teachers	1892	Swed. Miss. Un. (Cong.)
Kiungani, Zanzibar	Theological College	1887	Univ.Miss.(Ang.)
Kuruman, Bechuanaland	Moffat Institute	1873	London Soc. (Cong.)
Lagos, Yariba	Training Institution	1871	Ch. Miss. Soc.
Leribe, Basutuland	Theological School	1882	Paris Soc. (Pres.)
Lesseyton, Cape Colony	Girls' Training Institution		Br. Wesleyans.
Lesseyton, Cape Colony	Theol. and Train. Institute		Br. Wesleyans.
Lialui, Barutsiland	Evangelists' Train. Class	1895	Paris Soc.
Livingstonia, Nyasaland	Training School	1894	Sc. Free Pres.
Lovedale, Cape Colony	Theol. School (Dep't of the Institution)	1884	Sc. Free Pres.
Mbweni, Zanzibar	Train. Class for Nat. Teachers, and High School		Un. Miss.
Mengo, Uganda	Training School		Ch. Miss. Soc.
Morija, Basutuland	Bible School	1872	Paris Soc.
Morija, Basutuland	Theol. and Train. School	1868	Paris Soc.
Okabe	Watney Train. Inst	1897	Ch. Miss. Soc.
Onitsha, Nigeria	Girls' Train. School	1895	Ch. Miss. Soc.
Oyo, Yariba	Training Institute	1896	Ch. Miss. Soc.
Pieter Maritzburg	Evening Train. School		Wom. Miss. Ass. of S. P. G.
Pretoria, Transvaal	Kilnerton Train. Ins	1896	Br. Wes. Soc.
Pretoria, Transvaal	Train. College for Men	1897	S. P. G.
Rotufunk, Sierra Leone	Training School		Am. Un. Br. in C. (Anglican?).
Sea Point, Cape Colony	All Saints' School		Am. Un. Br. in C.
Shaingay, Sherbro, S. L.	Clark Train. School		Br. Wesley. (?)
Shawbury, Cape Colony	Training School		
Stellenbosch, Cape Colony	Bloemhof Theol. Sem	1859	Dutch Pres.(Boer)

EDUCATIONAL STATISTICS 771

Location	Name	Date of Founding	Church or Society
AFRICA—Continued			
Thaba Bossiu, Basutuland.	Girls' Train. Inst..........	1876	Paris Soc.
Thlotsi Heights, Basutuland....................	St Mary's Train. College for Schoolmasters........	1894	S. P. G.
Tripoli, Tripolitana.......	Training Home...........		Cent. Sudan Miss.
Umtata, Cape Colony.....	St John's Theol. College...		Sc. Episc.
Wellington, Cape Colony..	Miss. Train. Inst......		Undenom.
THE ANTILLES			
Bethlehem, Jamaica.......	Training College..........	1861	Un. of Breth.
Ebenezer, Jamaica........	Theological School........	1852	Jam. Pres. Ch.
Fairfield, Jamaica........	Theological School........	1861	Jam. Pres. Ch.
Fairfield, Jamaica........	Training College..........		Un. of Breth.
Fairfield, Jamaica........	Normal Train. School.....		Un. of Breth.
Kingston, Jamaica........	Theological College.......	1863	Jam. Ang.
Kingston, Jamaica........	Theological School........		Br. Par. Bapt.
Kingston, Jamaica........	Theological Seminary.....		Jam. Un. Pres.
Niesby, St. Thomas......	Training College..........		Un. of Breth.
St. John's, Antigua.......	Training College..........	1869	Un. of Breth.
York Castle, Jamaica.....	Theological School...		Brit. Wesley.
	Training Home...........		Am. Friends
MADAGASCAR			
Ambohimandroso.....	Training Ins. for Teachers..		London Soc.
Ambolijatovo.............	Training Sch. for Teachers.		Br. Friends
Fianarantsoa	Training School for Teachers		London Soc.
Fianarantsoa	Training School for Students' Wives...........		London Soc.
Fianarantsoa....	Train. Sch. for Preachers and Teachers..........		Norse M. S. (Luth.)
Isoavina......	Training Class............		London Soc.
Masinandreina............	Training Seminary,........		Nor. Miss. Soc.
Tamatave....	Training School...........		London Soc.
Tananarivo..............	Normal Training School....		London Soc.
Tananarivo..............	Theological School........		London Soc.
Tananarivo.......	Special Classes for Preachers		London Soc.
Tananarivo..............	Theological Seminary.....	1871	Nor. Miss. Soc.
Tananarivo..............	Training School for Girls...		London Soc.
Vonizongo...	School of Theology for Pastors and Teachers.....		London Soc.
MAURITIUS.			
	Theological School.		S. P. G.

3

BOARDING SCHOOLS, HIGH SCHOOLS AND SEMINARIES

AFRICA			
Abetifi, Ashanti...........	Boarding Schools		Basel
Abokobi, Gold Coast......	Boarding Schools		Basel
Aburi, Ashanti...........	Boarding Schools....		Basel
Aburi, Ashanti...........	Boarding School........		Br. Wesleyans
Adams (Amanzimtote). Natal......	High School or Seminary...		Am. Board
Ada, Gold Coast..........	Boarding Schools..........		Basel

EDUCATIONAL STATISTICS

Location	Name	Date of Founding	Church or Society
AFRICA—Continued			
Adams, Natal............	Ireland Home for Runaway Kraal Girls............	1894	Am. Board
Akropong, Ashanti.......	Boarding Schools.........		Basel
All Saints...............	Augusta Boarding School..		Sc. Episc.
Anuni, Ashanti..........	Boarding Schools		Basel
Asyut, Egypt............	Pressley Mem. Inst.......		Am. Un. Pres.
Bandawe, Nyasaland.....	Boarding School..........		Sc. Free Pres.
Batanga, Kamerun.......	Boarding School..........		Am. Pres. (N.)
Begoro..................	Boarding Schools		Basel
Benito, French Kongo....	Boarding Schools (2).....		Am. Pres. (N.)
Blythswood, Kafraria....	Seminary................	1877	Sc. Free Pres.
Burnshill, Kafraria.......	Seminary................		Sc. Free Pres.
Cairo, Egypt............	Boarding School..........		Am. Un. Pres
Cairo, Egypt............	Girls' Boarding School....		Ch. Miss. Soc.
Cape Palmas, Liberia....	Seminary................		Am. Meth. (N.)
Chisamba, Benguela.....	Clara Wilkes Currie Mem. Sch...................		Am. Board
Christiansborg, Gold Coast	Boarding Schools		Basel
Clay Ashland, Liberia....	Alexander High School....	1867	Am. Episc.
Cunningham, Kafraria ...	Seminary................		Sc. Free Pres.
Cuttington, Liberia......	Hoffman Ins. and High Sch.	1868	Am. Episc.
Domasi, Nyasaland......	Boarding School..........		Es. Ch. of Scotland
Duff, Kafraria...........	Seminary................		Sc. Free Pres.
East London, Kafraria....	Seminary................		
Efulen, Gabun (?).......	Boarding School..........		Am. Pres. (N.)
Fort Peddie, Cape Colony.	Boarding School..........		Br. Wesleyan
Freetown, Sierra Leone...	Grammar School..........	1845	Ch. Miss. Soc.
Freetown, Sierra Leone...	Annie Walsh Inst.........	1844	Ch. Miss. Soc.
Impolweni, Natal........	Girls' Institution........		Sc. Free Pres.
Inanda, Natal...........	Lucy Lindley Sem........	1869	Am. Board
Keiskamma Hoek, Cape Colony................	Boarding Schools (2).....		S. P. G.
Kilimani (?) or Quelimane (?)............	Boarding School..........		Un. Miss.
Kiungani, Zanzibar......	High School..............	1872	Un. Miss.
Kologwe	Boarding School..........		Un. Miss.
Kyebi, Ashanti...........	Boarding Schools.........		Basel
Lagos...................	Grammar School..........	1859	Ch. Miss Soc.
Lagos...................	Girls' Seminary..........	1868	Ch. Miss. Soc.
Likoma, Nyasaland......	Boarding Schools (2).....		Un. Miss.
Macfarlan, Kafraria......	Seminary................		Sc. Free Pres.
Madschame, Ger. E. Africa	Boarding School..........	1894	Leip. Soc. (Luth.)
Magila, Ger. E. Africa....	Boarding School..........		Un. Miss.
Main, Kafraria	Seminary................		Sc. Free Pres.
Mamba, Ger. E. Africa...	Boarding School..........	1895	Leip. Soc.
Masasi, Mozambique.....	Boarding School..........		Un. Miss.
Mbweni, Zanzibar.......	Boarding School..........		Un. Miss.
Misozwe, Ger. E. Africa..	Boarding School..........		Un. Miss.
Mkuzi, Ger. E. Africa....	Boarding School..........		Un. Miss.
Mlanji, Nyasaland.......	Boarding School..........		Sc. Est. Ch.
Monrovia, Liberia........	College of West Africa....	1897	Am. Meth. (N.)
Moschi, Brit. E. Africa...	Boarding School..........	1896	Leip. Soc.
Mount Silinda, Gazaland..	Boarding School..........		Am. Board
Newala, Mozambique.....	Boarding School..........		Un. Miss.
New Hermannsburg, Natal	High School..............	1862	Her. Soc.
Odumase, Gold Coast....	Boarding Schools		Basel
Pirie, Kafraria...........	Seminary................	1832	Sc. Free Pres.
Shawbury, Kafraria......	Boarding School		Br. Wesley.
Somerville, Kafraria.....	Seminary................		Sc. Free Pres.
Taveta, Ger. E. Africa....	Mahu Boys' Boarding Sch.		Ch. Miss Soc.
Thaba Bossiu, Basutuland	Boarding School..........		Par. Soc.

EDUCATIONAL STATISTICS

Location	Name	Date of Founding	Church or Society
AFRICA—Continued			
Tsolo, Kafraria............	Boarding Schools (2).......		Sc. Episc.
Umzumbe, Natal..........	Umzumbe Home..........		Am. Board
Unangu, Portuguese Nyasa	Chitala / Nielesa } School for Boys.		Un. Miss.
Usaba, Gold Coast........	Boarding Schools..........		Basel
Wathen, Belg. Kongo.....	Boarding School for Girls...		Br. Baps. (Par.)
West Africa.............	Boarding Schools (14)......		Am. Episc.
White Plains, Liberia......	Seminary................		Am. Meth (N.)
MADAGASCAR			
Ambatonakanga............	High School..............		Br. Friends
Ambatonakanga..........	High School..............		London Soc.
Mandridrano..............	High School..............		Brit. Friends

(No returns for the West Indies)

TOTALS OF BOARDING SCHOOLS AND PUPILS

Location	No. of Schools	Number of Pupils
Africa....................	70	4,727 (Fem. 2,488; Males, 2,239)
Madagascar	8	494 (" 430; " 64)

(No returns for the West Indies)

TOTALS OF DAY SCHOOLS AND PUPILS

Location	No. of Schools	Number of Pupils
Africa....................	1,588	90,948 (Fem. 40,655; Males, 50,293)
Antilles, The.............	358	31,973 (" 13,647; " 18,326)
Madagascar	855	120,490 (" 67,398; " 53,092)

4

INDUSTRIAL SCHOOLS AND WORK

Location	Name	Date of Founding	Church or Society
AFRICA			
Adafo.....	Mercantile Establishment..		Basel
Agboa....................	Industrial Mission........	1896	Colwyn Bay Ins.
Ailsa Crag, Nyasaland....	Industrial Work (Coffee-planting)...............	1892	Zambezi Miss.
Akra, Gold Coast.........	Mercantile Establishment..		Basel
Aliwal North, Cape Colony	Trade Classes.............		Br. Prim. Meth.
Amanzimtote, Natal.......	Industrial Dep't of Boys' Sch.....		Am. Board
Amedschove, Slave Coast..	Industrial School..........		No. Germ. Pres.
Bandawe, Nyasaland	Industrial Work (agriculture, carpentry, printing).		Sc. Free Pres.
Banni, Fernando Po.......	Industrial Work...........		Br. Prim. Meth.
Baraka, Gabun........	Industrial Work (coffee-culture......		Am. Pres. (N.)
Beabu, West Coast........	Industrial Work (Coffee-culture).....		Am. Meth. (N.)?

EDUCATIONAL STATISTICS

Location	Name	Date of Founding	Church or Society
AFRICA—Continued			
Blair Ochil, Nyasaland....	Industrial Work (Coffee-plantation)	1893	Zambezi Miss.
Blantyre, Nyasaland......	Industrial Schools.........		Sc. Es. Ch.(Pres.)
Blue Barra, Liberia.......	Industrial Work (Agriculture)................		Am. Meth (N.)
Blythswood, Kafraria......	Industrial Class (Carpentry, laundry and sewing).....	1884	Sc. Free Pres.
Bolobo, Belg. Kongo......	Industrial School..........	1889	Br. Baptists
Bonny, Niger-mouth......	Industrial School..........		Delta Pastors
Brass, Niger Delta........	Industrial Class...........	1897	Ch. Miss Soc.
Brooks Station, West Coast	Industrial House..........		Am. Meth. (N.)
Bugama, New Kalabar....	Alfred Jones Institute (in existence?)............	1893	Colwyn Bay Ins.
Burnshill, Kafraria........	Spreull Indust. School.....		Sc. Free Pres.
Cape Mount, Liberia......	Industrial Department.....	1878	Am. Episc.
Cape Palmas, Liberia.....	Industrial Work (Agriculture)		Am. Episc.
Cape Town, Cape Colony..	Poor Boys' Indust. Home...		So. Af. Mission
Christiansborg, Gold Coast.	Industrial Workshop.......		Basel.
Chilingani, Nyasaland....	Industrial Work (Coffee-farm)................	1892	Zambezi Ind.Mis.
Chinde, Nyasaland........	Industrial Work (Telegraphy)................	1892	Zambezi Ind.Mis.
Chisamba, Benguela.....	Industrial Department.....		Am. Board
Cunningham, Kafraria....	Industrial Class...........		Sc. Free Pres.
Cuttington, Liberia.......	Industrial Work (Coffee-culture).............		Am. Episc.
Doko....................	Industrial Work...........	1893	Zambezi Ind.Mis.
Domasi, Nyasaland.......	Industrial Work (Bootmaking, brick-making, carpentry, laundrying)...		Sc.Est.Ch.(Pres.)
Duff, Kafraria............	Women's Classes..........		Sc. Free Pres.
Duke Town, Old Kalabar..	Hope Waddell Indust. Department (Carpentry)....	1895	Sc. Un. Pres.
Dumbole.................	Industrial Work...........	1893	ZambeziInd. Mis.
Ebenezer, Liberia.........	Industrial Work (Agriculture)................		Am. Meth. (N.)
Efulen, Gabun............	Industrial Education......		Am. Pres. (N.)
Ekwendini, Kafraria......	Industrial Work...........		Sc. Fr. Pres.
Emgwali, Kafraria........	Indust. Dept. of the Girls' School................	1893	Sc. Un. Pres.
Engcobo, Kafraria	Trade-Classes.............		Sc. Episc.
Entakamin, Kafraria.....	Industrial Work		Miss. to Kafirs (Eng. and undenom.)
Eublokey, Cavalla, Liberia	Industrial Work		Am. Meth. (N.)
Fordsburg, Transvaal.....	Present Help League, etc ..		(?)
Freetown, Sierra Leone....	Industrial School	1896	Ang. Ch. of S. L.
Freretown, Br. E. Africa ..	Industrial Work...........		Ch. Miss. Soc.
Fwambo, Tanganika, Br. Cen. Africa............	Industrial Work...........		London Soc.
Garraway, Liberia........	Industrial Work (coffee-culture)................		Am. Meth. (N.)
Gnadenthal, Cape Colony..	Indust. Dep. Train. Col. (baskets, chairs and plaiting)		Unity of Breth.
Gordon Memorial, Natal..	Manse Boys' Home........	1874	Sc. Free Pres.
Gordon Memorial, Natal..	Zulu Girls' Home.........	1874	Sc. Free Pres.
Harding, Natal (?)........	Industrial Work...........		Young Men's Soc. (Und.)
Hora, Natal (?)...........	Industrial Work...........		Sc. Free Pres.

EDUCATIONAL STATISTICS

Location	Name	Date of Founding	Church or Society
AFRICA—Continued			
Ibuno, Niger Delta (?)	Indust. Train. School		Qua Ibo Miss. (Irish Pres.?)
Ikorofiong, Old Kalabar...	Industrial School...........		Sc. Un. Pres.
Ikwezi Lamaci, Natal.....	Indust. Work (six schools) .		Young Men's Soc.
Impolweni, Natal	Industrial Institution.......	1877	Sc. Free Pres.
Inanda, Natal.............	Indust. Dept. of Seminary..		Am. Board
Isangila, Belg. Kongo	Industrial Institution.......		Am. Meth. (N.)
Jacktown, Liberia.........	Industrial Work............		Am. Meth. (N.)
Kambole, Bechuanaland (?)	Industrial Work............		London Soc.
Kamondongo, Benguela...	Farm School................		Am. Board
Keiskama Hoek, Kafraria.	St. Matthew's Indust. Inst..		S. P. G.
Kologwe, Usambara, G. E. A................	Industrial Work............		Univ. Miss.
Lagos, West Africa	Native School..............		Colwyn Bay Inst.
Leloalong, Basutuland	Industrial School...........	1879	Paris Soc.
Leopoldville, Belgian Kongo	Manual Training	1887	Am. Bapt. (N.)
Likabula, Nyasaland......	Industrial Mission		Nyasa Ind. Mis.
Likoma, Nyasaland........	Industrial Work (book=binding, etc.).............	1887	Univ. Miss.
Lisungwe, Br. Cent. Af....	Industrial Work (coffee= culture)..................	1893	Zam. Ind. Miss.
Livingstonia, Nyasaland..	Livingstonia Ind. Inst.	1894	Sc. Free Pres.
Livingstonia Village, Nyasaland.................	Industrial Work............	1892	Zam. Ind. Miss.
Lovedale, Cape Colony....	Industrial Dept. (book=binding, carpentry, laundrying, printing and sewing).		Sc. Free Pres.
Magila, Usambara, G.E.A	Industrial Work............		Univ. Miss.
Maliya, Nyasaland........	Industrial Work (coffee= culture)..................	1892	Zam. Ind. Miss.
Mbweni, Zanzibar	Industrial Schools..........	1887	Univ. Miss.
Mengo, Uganda...........	Industrial Work (carpentry and printing)............		Ch. Miss Soc.
Mitsilo, Nyasaland (?)...	Industrial Work............	1892	Zam. Ind. Miss.
Mkunazini, Zanzibar......	Home for Artizan Apprentices....................		Univ. Miss.
Mlanji, Nyasaland........	Industrial Work............		Estab. Ch. of Scot.
Monrovia, Liberia........	Ricks Indust. Inst..........	1887	Colwyn Bay Inst.
Monserrado, Liberia.......	Industrial School...........	1893	Colwyn Bay Inst.
Morija, Basutuland	Apprentices' Training Sch. (binding and printing) ...	1841	Paris Soc.
Muhlenberg, Liberia	Industrial Work............	1870	Am. Luth. Gen. Syn.
Muhlenberg, Liberia	Emma V. Day Sch. for Girls		Am. Luth. Gen. Syn.
Niamkolo, Tanganika, B. C. A.................	Industrial Work (carpentry)		London Soc.
Ntonda, Nyasaland	Industrial Work............	1893	Zam. Ind. Miss.
Okat, Niger Delta (?).....	Industrial Branch of........		Qua Ibo Miss.
Okrika, Niger Delta......	Industrial School........ ..		{ Ch. Miss Soc.(?) { Delta Pastor. (?)
Opobo, Niger Delta.......	Industrial School...........		{ Delta Pastor. (?) { Ch. Miss.Soc.(?)
Onitsha, Nigeria..........	Industrial Class............		Ch. Miss. Soc.
Patima, Nyasaland........	Industrial Work	1892	Zam. Ind. Miss.
Pemba, Br. East Af.......	Industrial Work	1897	Br. Friends
Pesseh, Liberia	Industrial Work (coffee=culture)..................		Am. Meth. (N.)
Phalapye, Bechuanaland..	Industrial School...........		London Soc.
Pieter Maritzburg, Natal..	St. Alban's Col. Ind. Dept.		S. P. G.
Pieter Maritzburg, Natal..	Industrial Training School..		S. P. G. Wom. Miss. Ass.

EDUCATIONAL STATISTICS

Location	Name	Date of Founding	Church or Society
AFRICA—Continued			
Pirie, Cape Colony........	Ross Industrial Home......		Sc. Free Pres. / Women's Soc.
Rotufunk, Sierra Leone...	Industrial School..........		Un. Breth. in C.
San Carlos Bay, Fernao Po	Industrial Work (cocoa= farm)...................		Br. Prim. Meth.
Sass Town, Liberia	Industrial Work (coffee=culture)..................		Am. Meth. (N.)
Sefula, Ba=Rutsiland.....	Industrial School..........	1896	Paris Soc.
Talagonga, Ba=Rutsiland..	Industrial School..........		Paris Soc.
Taveta, Br. East Af.......	Industrial Dept. of Boys' Boarding School.........	1893	Ch. Miss. Soc.
Tsolo, E. Grikwaland	St. Cuthbert's Ind. Dept....		Sc. Episc.
Umtata, Cape Colony.....	St. John's Col. Indust. Dept.		Sc. Episc.
Umzinga, Natal..........	Industrial Work...........		Sc. Free Pres.
Umzumbe, Natal	Trade Class...............		Am. Cong.
Veh Mission, Cape Mount, Liberia................	Industrial Work (coffee= culture)................		Am. Meth. (N.)
Wah Land, Liberia........	Industrial Work (agriculture)..................		Am. Meth. (N.)
White Plains, Liberia.....	St. Paul River Industrial Mission (farm)..........		Am. Meth. (N.)
Wissika, Liberia..........	Industrial Work (coffee= culture.)................		Am. Meth. (N.)
Wynberg, Cape Colony....	School of Industry.........		?
Zonnebloem, Cape Colony.	Kafir Col. Indust. Dept		S. P. G.
THE ANTILLES			
Port-au-Prince, Haiti.....	Industrial Work (school= farm)....................		Am. Episc.
MADAGASCAR			
Isoavina.................	Industrial School..........		Br. Cong.
Tananarivo..............	Girls' Sch. Indust. Dept....		Br. Friends

5

MEDICAL AND NURSING SCHOOLS

AFRICA

Cape Town, Cape Colony..	Nurses' Home.............		So. Af. Gen. Miss.
Freetown, Sierra Leone....	Train. Class for Nurses.....		Diocese of S. L.
Lovedale, Cape Colony....	Nurses' Training Class.....		Sc. Free Pres.
MADAGASCAR			
Analakely................	Medical Academy..........		Br. Friends
Isoavinandriano..........	Nurses' Training Class.....		Br. Fr. and Cong.
Isoavinandriano..........	Medical Academy..........		Br. Fr. and Cong.
Tananarivo...............	Nurses' School............		Br. Fr. and Cong.
Tananarivo...............	Medical Dept. of College...		Br. Cong.
Tananarivo...............	Nurses' Training Class.....		Br. Fr. and Cong.

No returns for the Antilles

6
KINDERGARTENS

Location	Name	Date of Founding	Church or Society
AFRICA			
Amanzimtote, Natal,	Kindergarten		Am. Board
Bailundu, Benguela	Kindergarten		Am. Board
Blythswood, Kafraria	Kindergarten Class		Sc. Free Pres.
Chisamba, Benguela	Kindergarten	1897	Am. Board
Ikwesi Lamaci, Natal	Kindergarten Class		Young Men's Soc.
Kamondongo, Benguela	Kindergarten		Am. Board
Lovedale, Cape Colony	Kindergarten	1888	Sc. Free Pres.
Phalapye, Bechuanaland	Kindergarten		London Soc.
Pretoria, Transvaal	Kindergarten Class		Br. Wes. Soc.
Sakanjimba, Benguela	Kindergarten	1897	Am. Board
Wellington, Cape Colony	Kindergarten		Undenom.

No returns for the Antilles or for Madagascar

LITERARY STATISTICS

1

BIBLE=VERSIONS

This List is compiled by Mr. Noble from those of Doctors Cust, Dennis and Edmonds.

Language or Dialect	Location	Publication	Date	Publisher
AFRICA				
Akba, Akra or Ga..	Eastern Gold Coast.	Bible, entire.......	1844	Br. Bible Soc.
Akunakuna.........	Old Kalabar.......	Luke.............		Nat. Bib. Soc. Sc.
Akwapem (See Ashanti)				
Amharic...........	Abyssinia	Bible, Revised Version		
Arabic............	Africa, *passim*.....	Bible; also, in part, for the blind.......		{ Am. Bib. Soc. { Br. Bib. Soc.
Ashanti or Otshi....	Ashanti and Gold Coast...........	Bible.............	1870	Br. Bib. Soc.
Ashanti or Fanti....	Cape Coast Castle .	New Testament....	1884	Br. Bib. Soc.
Bangi.............	Belgian Kongo.....	Matthew, Mark, Luke and John...		Bap. Miss.Soc.
Benga.............	Gabun............	Psalms and New Testament.......		Am. Bib. Soc.
Berber (? Kabail)...	Algeria and Tunisia	Luke.............	1883?	Br. Bib. Soc.
Bilin or Bogos......	North. Abyssinia...	Mark.............	1881	Br. Bib. Soc.
Bondei............	North. Zanzibar....	Matthew and Luke.	1888	Br. Bib. Soc.
Bopoto (See Poto)				
Bule..............	Gabun............	Gospels (all)		Am. Bib. Soc.
Bullom............	Sierra Leone (near).	Matthew....	1815	Br. Bib. Soc.
Bunda or Ki=Mbunda	Angola...........	Luke and John.....	1888	Br. Bib. Soc.
Busembi	Belgian Kongo.....	Matthew, Mark and Luke............		Bap. Miss.Soc.
Chagga.	Kilima=Njaro......	Matthew....	1892	Br. Bib. Soc.
Chinyanja (See Nyanja)				
Chuana or Si=Chuana	Chuana and Tabili.	Bible.............	1856	Br. Bib. Soc.
Chuana or Si=Rolong	Bechuanaland	New Testament....		Gospel=Prop. Soc.
Dama or Damara (See Herero)				
Di=Kele (See Kele).				
Dualla	Kamerun	Old Testament (in part)............ Bible	1870	{ Br. Bib. Soc. { Bap. Miss. Soc.
Efik...............	Old Kalabar.......	Bible.............		Nat. Bib. Soc. Scot.
Ethiopic, Gheez or Giz.............	Abyssinian Church.	New Testament and Psalms.........		Br. Bib. Soc.
Evhe (Anlo)........	West. Gold Coast..	{ New Test. and parts of O. T..... { New Test. by Bremen Bible Soc. ..	1874	{ Br. Bib. Soc. { No. Ger.Miss. Soc.

LITERARY STATISTICS

Language or Dialect	Location	Publication	Date	Publisher
AFRICA—Contin'd				
Evhe (Popo).......	Dahome...........	Genesis, Psalms and N. T........	1884	Br. Bib. Soc.
Fadidja (See Nubian)				
Falasha=Kara (for Jews)............	Kara, Abyssinia...	Mark.............	1885	Br. Bib. Soc.
Fan, Fang or Pa=Huin............	Gabun............	Genesis and Matthew...........	1893	Br. Bib. Soc.
Fiot or Fyot (See Kifiot or Ki=Fiot)				
Galla (Bararetta)...	Gallaland,.........	John.............	1888	Br. Bib. Soc.
Galla (Ittu)........	Harar.............	Matthew..........	1886	Br. Bib. Soc.
Galla (Shoa)	Gallaland....	New Test. and parts of O. T..	1867	{ Sw. Ev. Nat. Soc. { Brit. Bib. Soc.
Ganda or Lu=Ganda.	Uganda...........	Bible.............	1887	Brit. Bib. Soc.
Giryama............	Mombaz...........	Acts, Luke and Matthew.........	1892	Br. Bib. Soc.
Gogo,.............	Ger. East Africa...	{ Jonah, Luke, { Matthew and Ruth	1887	Br. Bib. Soc.
Grebo.............	Liberia...........	Parts of New and Old Tests.......		Am. Bib. Soc.
Gwamba	{ Limpopo River and { Transvaal......	Gospels (all)	1888	Br. Bib. Soc.
Hausa.............	Nigeria...........	{ Genesis, Exodus, Psalms, Isaiah and New Test.	1857	Br. Bib. Soc.
Herero or Ova=Herero	Damaland, G. S. A.	New Testament and Psalms...	1877	Br. Bib. Soc.
"Hottentot" (See Nama)				
Ibo or Isuama.......	Niger Delta	{ New Test. (A. V.) in part.......... { New Test. (R. V.) in part..........	1877	Br. Bib. Soc.
Ibo....	Upper Niger River.	New Test. (to Hebrews) and Psalms	1860	Br. Bib. Soc.
Idzo or Ijo.........	Niger=mouth.......	Gospels...........	1896	Br. Bib. Soc.
Igara....	Niger=mouth......	New Testament....		Ch. Miss. Soc.
Igbira.............	Binwe and Niger confluence.......	Matthew	1891	Br. Bib. Soc.
Isubu..............	Kamerun....	Genesis and Gospels		Bap. Miss. Soc.
Jolof or Yolof or Wolof............	Bathurst, Gambia..	Matthew	1882	Br. Bib. Soc.
Kabail or Kabyli....	Algeria and Tunisia	Acts and Gospels...	1883	Br. Bib. Soc.
Kafir, Khosa or Xosa (?)..........	Kafraria, Cape Colony	Bible (Revised Version)...........	1888	Br. Bib. Soc.
Kaguru....	U=Sagara, G. E. A	{ John, Jonah, Luke, { Matthew and Ruth.	1885	Br. Bib. Soc.
Kele or Di=Kele.....	Gabun........	John		Am Bib. Soc.
Khoi=Khoin (See Nama)				
Ki=Bondei (See Bondei)	Magila, G. E. A...	John.............		Un. Miss.
Kifiot (Fyot or Kabinda)...	Belgian Kongo.....	New Testament....		Sw. Miss. Un.
Kingondo or Ki=Ngondo (See Ngondo)				

Language or Dialect	Location	Publication	Date	Publisher
AFRICA—Contin'd				
Kongo............	Belgian Kongo.....	New Testament....		Bib.Trans.Soc.
Koptic.............	Egypt............	New Test. and parts of O. T. (?)......	1852	S. P. C. K. Br. Bib. Soc.
Kuana (See Si=Kuana)				
Kuanyama or Kwenyama............	North.Ovamboland, G. S. A.........	Gospels (all)	1893	Br. Bib. Soc.
Makua or Kua......	Mozambique.......	Matthew....		Un. Miss.
Malagasi........	Madagascar.......	Bible (R. V.)......		Br. Bib. Soc.
Maltese....	Malta............	Acts, John,Matthew		B. B. S. ?
Mambwe or Ki=Mambwe..........	Tanganika, B. C. A.	Mark............	1893	Br. Bib. Soc.
Mananja or Nanja..	Shire, Nyasaland..	Gospels (4) and Epistles (3)......		Nat. Bib. Soc. Scot.
Mande or Mandingo.	Gambia...........	Matthew...........	1838	Brit. Bib. Soc.
Mashona(See Shuna)				
Matabele (See Tabili)				
Mauritian Creole....	Mauritius..........	Luke, Mark and Matthew.........	1885	Br. Bfb. Soc.
Mende	Sierra Leone (near)	Acts, Gospels (4) and Romans.....	1871	Br. Bib. Soc.
Mongo	Equatoria, Belg. Kongo	Matthew..........	1897	Br. Bib. Soc.
Mpongwe (See Pongwe)				
Mwamba....	Nyasaland	Mark.............		Nat. Bib. Soc.
Nama, Khoi=Khoi or Hottentot......	Great Namaland, G. S. A..........	New. Test.; O. T. preparing; and Psalms..........		Br. Bib. Soc.
Ndonga (See Ovambo)				
Ngondo....	Livingstonia, Nyasaland...........	Gospels (all)		Sc. Free Pres.
Ngoni (Nyasan Zulu)............	West. Nyasaland..	Mark.............		Sc. Free Pres.
Nubian.............	Dongola. Egypt....	Mark.............	1885	Br. Bib. Soc.
Nupe....	Nigeria,Cent.Sudan	Gospels (all)	1861	Br. Bib. Soc.
Nyamwezi..........	Unyamwezi,G.E.A.	Luke, Mark and Matthew.........	1896	Br. Bib. Soc.
Nyanja.............	Lake Nyasa and Shire River......	Nehemiah......... New Testament...	1895	Nat. Bib. Soc. Br. Bib. Soc.
Nyika or Ki=Nika...	Mombaz, B. E. A...	Luke and Matthew.	1850	Br. Bib. Soc.
Ovambo or Ova=Mbo	Ovamboland or Damaland........	Matthew...........	1892	Br. Bib. Soc.
Pedi or Si=Pedi	North. Transvaal ..	New Testament....	1888	Br. Bib. Soc.
Pokomo....	Witu, B. E. A	Mark.............	1894	Br. Bib. Soc.
Pongwe or Mpongwe	Gabun............	Bible (in great part)		Am. Bib. Soc.
Poto or Bopoto......	Belgian (?) Kongo.	Luke.............		Bap. Miss.Soc.
Riff, Rifi or Shilha..	Marocco..........	John and Matthew.	1884	Br. Bib. Soc.
Ronga.............	DelagoaBay,P.E.A.	First Corinthians and John.........	1894	Br. Bib. Soc.
Sagalla.............	B.E.A. and G.E.A. (boundary)......	Mark.............	1892	Br. Bib. Soc.
Sena	Shire and Zambezi confluence......	Mark....	1897	Br. Bib. Soc.
Shambala	German East Africa	Genesis and Mark (in parts)........		"Berlin III."

LITERARY STATISTICS

Language or Dialect	Location	Publication	Date*	Publisher
AFRICA—CONCL'D				
Sheitswa............	Zululand, Natal....	Acts, Luke, Mark and Matthew.....		Am. Bib. Soc.
Shuna or Ma-Shona.	Rhodesia, B. S. A..	Mark.............	1897	Br. Bib. Soc.
Siga or Tonga......	Tongaland (N. of Zululand)........	New Testament....		Am. Bib. Soc.
Sukuma............	Lake Victoria, G. E. A.........	Gospels (all)......	1895	Br. Bib. Soc.
Sus (? Shlu ?)......	Marocco...........	Luke (in part).....		Br. Bib. Soc.
Susu....	French Guinea.....	New Testament....		Soc. Chr. Knowl.
Sutu or Si-Sutu.....	Cape Colony, Orange and the Sutus	Bible.............	1850	Br. Bib. Soc.
Swahili (Mombazi).	Mombaz, B. E. A..	John and Luke.....	1892	Br. Bib. Soc.
Swahili (Zanzibari).	Zanzibar, B. E. A..	Bible.............	1862	Br. Bib. Soc.
Tabili or Ma-Tabele	Rhodesia, B. S. A..	Luke.............	1897	Br. Bib. Soc.
Taveta.............	Kilima-Njaro, G. E. A.........	John, Luke and Matthew........	1892	Br. Bib. Soc.
Teke....	Belg. and French Kongo...........	Mark.............		Am. Bap. Union
Temne or Timni....	Sierra Leone (near)	Hist. Books, Pentateuch, Psalms and New Testament...........	1866	Br. Bib. Soc.
Tigre or Tigrai.....	East. Abyssinia....	Gospels (all)......	1865	Br. Bib. Soc.
Tonga (not Siga)...	Nyasaland........	Mark.............		Sc. Free Pres.? Nat.Bib.Soc.?
Tumbuka....	West. Nyasaland..	Mark.............		Sc. Free Pres.
Umbundu..........	Benguela..........	John and Mark....		Am. Board
Umon or Yala......	Old Kalabar.......	Mark and part of Matthew.......		Nat. Bib. Soc.
Wanda....	Betw. Lakes Nyasa and Tanganika..	Jonah and Mark...		Sc. Free Pres.
Yao	East. and South. Nyasaland.......	New Testament (to James).........	1880	Br. Bib. Soc.
Yariba	Yariba, Cent. Sudan	Bible (Rev. Vers.).	1850	Br. Bib. Soc.
Yiddish (Hebrew dialect............	Algeria,Tripolitana, Tunisia.........	Luke.......	1896	Br. Bib. Soc.
Zulu....	Natal.............	Bible.............	1869	Am. Bib. Soc. BaselBib.Soc. Br. Bib. Soc.
ANTILLES AND SOUTH AMERICA				
Creolese............	Danish West Indies	N. T............. Mark.............	.	Dan. Bib. Soc. Am. Bib. Soc.
Curacoan...........	Dutch West Indies.	Mark and Matt....		
Dominican (French patois)............	Dominica, Grenada, St. Lucia and Trinidad.........	Mark.............		Brit. Bib. Soc.
Negro-English......	Dutch Guiana or Surinam.........	Psalms and N. T...		Brit. Bib. Soc.

*The dates of publication are not intended to be regarded as absolute. From the nature of the case only approximations to the date can be stated. *The Encyclopedia of Missions* gives exact dates, and also adds many interesting and valuable details both as to the versions named here and as to tentative or unknown translations.

NON=MISSIONARY BIBLE=VERSIONS

These are used either by inhabitants of Africa who are not aborigines or by Africans outside of Africa itself. Among African missionary=versions might almost be included the Baluch, Hindi and Osmanli=Turki translations of the Bible in whole or in part, for it can not but be either that those respectively are used by Christian missionaries among the Baluch and Sikh soldiery of the British possessions on the East Coast and among the Banian traders or Hindi laborers of Mauritius, Natal, Trinidad and Zanzibar, or that this is read among the Turkish=speaking inhabitants of Egypt and Tripolitana. For Spanish Jews in North Africa a Judeo=Spanish version is available.

Language of the Version	Location or Peoples
Dutch	Boers throughout South Africa
English	Throughout Africa, the African Islands and the Americas
Finn	Finn missions in Ger. Southwest Africa
French	North, South and West Africa, Egypt, Madagascar, Mauritius, Reunion and the West Indies
German	German East Africa, Kamerun, German Southwest Africa, Togo and German missions
Greek	Egypt, Tripolitana, etc
Hebrew	Egypt, North Africa and South Africa
Italian	Eritrea, the Levant, Malta, Tripoli and Tunis
Latin	The Roman Church
Norse and Swedish	Scandinavian missions in Madagascar and South Africa
Portuguese	Angola, Azores, Bissao, Cape Verd Is., Madeira, Mozambique and Sao Thome
Russian ?	Abyssinian Christians?
Spanish	The Antilles and, in Africa, the Canaries, Ceuta, Corisco, Sahara, etc.

STATISTICS OF AFRICAN LANGUAGES AND PEOPLES POSSESSING BIBLE=VERSIONS

These are compiled from Doctor Cust's two Lists in *The Encyclopedia of Missions*

Language	Family	Alphabet	Number of Speakers	Duration of Language
Akba, Akra or Ga	Negro	Roman	100,000	Permanent
Akunakuna	Negro	Roman	Unknown	
Amhara	Shemitic	Amharic and Roman	2,000,000	Permanent
Arabic	Shemitic	Arabic and Roman	50,000,000 in the world	Permanent
Ashanti	Negro	Roman	3,000,000 (?)	Permanent
Baluch	Aryan	Arabic	1,500,000 in Baluchistan	Permanent
Bangi	Bantu	Roman	Unknown	
Benga	Bantu	Roman	Unknown	
Berber	Hamite	Roman	Several millions.	Permanent
Bilin or Bogos	{ Hamite ? Shemitic?. }	Amharic	10,000	Permanent
Bondei	Bantu	Roman	Unknown	Permanent
Bopoto (See Poto)	Bantu	Roman	Unknown	Permanent
Bule	Bantu	Roman	Unknown	Permanent
Bullom	Negro	Roman	1,000	Dying
Bunda	Bantu	Roman	Unknown	Permanent
Busembi	Bantu	Roman	Unknown	Uncertain

Language	Family	Alphabet	Number of Speakers	Duration of Language
Chagga	Bantu	Roman	Unknown	Uncertain
Chuana	Bantu	Roman	Unknown	Permanent
Creolese	Aryan	Roman	Unknown	Uncertain
Curacoan	Aryan	Roman	Unknown	Uncertain
Dominican	Aryan	Roman	Unknown	Uncertain
Dualla	Bantu	Roman	Unknown	Permanent
Dutch	Aryan	Roman	3,500,000	Permanent
Efik	Negro	Roman	90,000	Permanent
English	Aryan	Roman	200,000,000	Permanent
Ethiopic or Ghiz	Shemitic	Ethiop	A few priests	Dead
Evhe	Negro	Roman	Unknown	Permanent
Falasha=Kara	Hamite	Amharic	20,000 "Jews"	Permanent
Fan, Mpangwe or Pa= Huin	Bantu	Roman	200,000	Permanent
Finn or Suomi	Ural=Altaie	Gothic	2,250,000	Permanent
Fiot or Kabinda	Bantu	Roman	Unknown	Permanent
French	Aryan	Roman	40,000,000	Permanent
Galla	Hamite	Amharic and Roman	4,500,000	Permanent
Ganda	Bantu	Roman	5,000,000	Permanent
German	Aryan	Gothic and Roman	45,000,000	Permanent
Giryama	Bantu	Roman	Unknown	Uncertain
Gogo	Bantu	Roman	Unknown	Permanent
Grebo	Negro	Roman	Unknown	Permanent
Greek	Aryan	Greek and Roman	3,000,000	Permanent
Hausa	Negro	Roman	15,000,000?	Permanent
Hebrew	Shemitic	Hebrew	8,000,000?	Permanent
Herero	Bantu	Roman	Unknown	Permanent
Hindi	Aryan	Arabic and Roman	85,000,000	Permanent
Ibo	Negro	Roman	Unknown	Permanent
Idzo or Ijo	Negro	Roman	Unknown	Permanent
Igara	Negro	Roman	Unknown	Permanent
Igbira	Negro	Roman	Unknown	Permanent
Isubu	Bantu	Roman	Unknown	Permanent
Italian	Aryan	Roman	29,000,000	Permanent
Jolof	Negro	Roman	Unknown	Permanent
Judeo=Spanish	Aryan	Hebrew	Unknown	Uncertain
Kabail	Hamite	Roman	Unknown	Permanent
Kafir	Bantu	Roman	250,000	Permanent
Kaguru	Bantu	Roman	Unknown	Permanent
Kele	Bantu	Roman	100,000?	Dying?
Kongo	Bantu	Roman	Unknown	Permanent
Koptic	Hamite	Koptic	A few priests	Dead
Kuana, Secoana, Si= Kuana	Bantu	Roman	Unknown	Permanent
Kuanyama or Kwenyama	Bantu	Roman	Unknown	Permanent
Latin	Aryan	Roman	Clergy of Rome	Dying
Makua or Kua	Bantu	Roman	Unknown	Permanent
Malagasi or Hova	Malay=Polynesian	Roman	3,500,000	Permanent
Maltese	Hamite and Shemitic	Arabic (?)	170,000	Dying
Mambwe	Bantu	Roman	Unknown	Uncertain
Mande or Mandingo	Negro	Roman	8,000,000	Permanent
Mende	Negro	Roman	Unknown	Uncertain
Mongo	Bantu	Roman	Unknown	Uncertain
Mpongwe (See Pongwe)				
Mwamba	Bantu	Roman	Unknown	Uncertain
Nama	Khoi=San	Roman	Unknown	Dying
Ndonga (See Ovambo)				

Language	Family	Alphabet	Number of Speakers	Duration of Language
Negro=English	Aryan and Negro	Roman	Unknown	Uncertain
Ngondo	Bantu	Roman	Unknown	Uncertain
Ngoni	Bantu	Roman	Unknown	Dying
Norse	Aryan	Gothic and Roman	4,000,000	Permanent
Nubian	Hamite? Negro?	Arabic and Roman	1,000,000	Permanent
Nupe	Negro	Roman	Unknown	Permanent
Nyamwezi	Bantu	Roman	Unknown	Permanent
Nyanja	Bantu	Roman	Unknown	Permanent
Nyika	Bantu	Roman	50,000	Uncertain
Osmanli	Ural=Altaic	Arabic	5,000,000	Permanent
Ovambo, Ndonga or Mpo	Bantu	Roman	120,000	Uncertain
Pedi	Bantu	Roman	Unknown	Uncertain
Pokomo	Bantu	Roman	Unknown	Uncertain
Pongwe, Mpongwe or Ayogo	Bantu	Roman	Unknown	Dying?
Portuguese	Aryan	Roman	5,000,000	Permanent
Poto	Bantu	Roman	Unknown	Uncertain
Riff or Shilha	Hamite	Roman	Unknown	Permanent
Ronga	Bantu	Roman	Unknown	Uncertain
Russian	Aryan	Cyril's	75,000,000	Permanent
Sagalla	Bantu	Roman	Unknown	Uncertain
Shambala	Bantu	Roman	Unknown	Uncertain
Sheitswa	Bantu	Roman	Unknown	Permanent
Shuna	Bantu	Roman	Unknown	Uncertain
Siga or Tonga	Bantu	Roman	Unknown	Uncertain
Spanish	Aryan	Roman	16,000,000	Permanent
Sukuma	Bantu	Roman	Unknown	Uncertain
Sus (? Shlu ?)	Hamite	Roman	Unknown	Permanent
Susu	Negro	Roman	Unknown	Permanent
Sutu	Bantu	Roman	220,000	Permanent
Swahili	Bantu	Arabic and Roman	1,000,000 ?	Permanent
Swedish	Aryan	Gothic and Roman	4,000,000	Permanent
Tabili	Bantu	Roman	200,000 ?	Uncertain
Taveta	Bantu	Roman	Unknown	Uncertain
Teke	Bantu	Roman	Unknown	Uncertain
Tigre	Shemitic	Amharic and Roman	2,000,000	Permanent
Timni or Temne	Negro	Roman	200,000	Permanent
Tonga or Thonga	Bantu	Roman	Unknown	Permanent
Tumbuka	Bantu	Roman	Unknown	Uncertain
Umbundu	Bantu	Roman	Unknown	Permanent
Umon	Negro	Roman	Unknown	Permanent
Wanda	Bantu	Roman	Unknown	Uncertain
Yao	Bantu	Roman	Unknown	Dying
Yariba	Negro	Roman	3,000,000	Permanent
Yiddish	Shemitic	Hebrew	Unknown	Uncertain
Zulu	Bantu	Roman	300,000	Permanent

DIGLOTS AMONG AFRICAN PEOPLES
(From Doctor Cust's List.)

Amhara; in A. and Ethiopic.
Arabic; in A. and English, Ethiopic, French, Hausa, Koptic or Syriac.
Bangali; in B. and English.
Bullom; in B. with English.
Dutch; in D. with English.
English; in E. with Arabic, Bangali, Bullom, Dutch, French, German, Greek, Hebrew, Italian, Osmanli or Spanish.
Ethiopic or Ghiz; in E. with Amharic.
French; in F. with Arabic, English, Greek, Hebrew, Maltese or Osmanli.
German; in G. with English, French, Hebrew or Italian.
Greek; in G. with English, French, German or Latin.
Hebrew; in H. with English, French, German, Italian, Osmanli or Spanish.
Italian; in I. with English, French, German, Hebrew, Latin, Maltese or Osmanli.
Latin; in L. with Italian, Osmanli or Spanish.
Norse; in N. with English.
Russian; in R. with Hebrew.
Spanish; in S. with English, Latin or Hebrew.
Swedish; in S. with English.
Syriac; in S. with Arabic.
Turkish; in O. with English, French, Hebrew or Italian.

AFRICAN VERSIONS IN PREPARATION

Benga: Gen., Prov., Ecc., Is. and Dan.
Gogo: Acts, John and Mark.
Nama: Old Testament.
Ngondo: Old Testament (a few chapters).

2
CIRCULATION OF THE SCRIPTURES, BY BIBLE AND TRACT SOCIETIES, IN 1895

	Bibles	Testaments	Portions	Totals
American Bible Society				
Africa (including Egypt)	2,030	4,563	13,023	19,777
Arabia	14	63	664	771
Totals	2,044	4,626	13,687	20,548
British and Foreign Bible Society				
Abyssinia and Arabia	397	488	3,262	4,147
Africa	6,091	44,313	34,672	85,076
Madagascar	1,338	4,535	4,308	10,181
Totals	7,846	49,336	42,242	99,404
(This society in Africa has sixty-six auxiliaries.)				
National Bible Society of Scotland				
Africa	1,733	1,817	1,252	4,602
Antilles, The	224	100		324
Totals	1,957	1,917	1,252	4,926
Grand Totals	11,847	55,879	57,181	124,878

3

MISSION PUBLISHING HOUSES AND PRINTING PRESSES

Location	Society
AFRICA	
Asmara	Swed. Nat. Soc.
Blantyre	Estab. Ch. of Scotland
Bolobo, Belgian Kongo	Br. Par. Bapt.
Bonny, Niger Delta	C. M. S.
Cape Mount, Liberia	Am. Episcopal
Chumie	Sc. Free Pres.
Domasi, Nyasaland	Estab. Ch. of Scotland
Duke Town, Old Kalabar	Sc. United Pres.
Freretown, B. E. A.	?
Gnadenthal, Cape Colony	Unity of Breth.
Heluan, Egypt	C. M. S.
Kambole, Tanganika	L. M. S.
Kamondongo, Benguela	Am. Board.
Lagos, Yariba	C. M. S.
Likoma, Nyasaland	Univ. Mission

Location	Society
AFRICA—Continued	
Livingstonia, Nyasaland	Sc. Free Pres.
Londe, French Kongo	Swed. Miss. Un.
Lovedale, Cape Colony	Sc. Free Pres.
Luba	C. M. S.
Magila, B. E. A.	Univ. Miss.
Main, Kafraria	Sc. Free Pres.
Mkunazini, Zanzibar	Un. Miss.
Morija, Basutuland	Paris Soc.
Onitsha, Niger River	C. M. S.
Taveta, B. E. A.	C. M. S.
Wathen or Ngombe	Br. Part Bap.
MADAGASCAR	
Tananarivo	F. F. M. A.
Tananarivo	L. M. S.
Tananarivo	Norse Luth.
Tananarivo	S. P. G.

(No returns for the West Indies).

4

PERIODICAL LITERATURE

Place of Publication	Name of Periodical	Publisher
AFRICA		
Bethany	Moshupa=Tsella (Monthly)	Hermannsburg
Blantyre	Kalilole (Monthly)	Es. Ch. of Sc.
Blantyre	Life and Work in British Central Africa (Monthly)	Sc. Estab. Church
Bolobo	Sparks of Fire (Monthly)	Br. Par. Bap.
Botschabelo	Mogoera on Basutho (Monthly)	Berlin Soc.
Cairo	Murshid (The Guide) (Weekly)	Am. Un. Pres.
Cape Town	The Link (Monthly)	S. A. Gen. Miss.
Cape Town	The Pioneer (Monthly)	S. A. Gen. Miss.
Gnadenthal	De Bode (The Messenger)(Bimonthly)	Un. of Breth.
Gnadenthal	Children's Friend (Monthly)	Un. of Breth.
King William's Town	Imvo Neliso Lomzi (Opinion and Eye of the Town) (Weekly)	?
Kiungani	Msimulizi (The Reporter) (Weekly)	Univ. Miss.
Kuruman	Sichwana Monthly Magazine	London Society
Livingstonia	Aurora: a Journal of Miss. News and Christ. Work (Bimonthly)	Sc. Free Press.
Londe	Almanac; also, Messenger of Peace (Monthly)	Swed. Miss. Union
Lovedale	Christian Express (Monthly)	Sc. Free Pres.
Lovedale	Lovedale Literary Soc. Magazine	Sc. Free Pres.
Lovedale	Lovedale News	Sc. Free Pres.
Magila	Habari za Mwezi (Monthly News)	Univ. Miss.

Place of Publication	Name of Periodical	Publisher
AFRICA—Continued		
Main..................	Indaba Zamabandla (News of the Churches) (Quarterly)............	Sc. Free Pres.
Mengo.................	Ebifa Munsi (Monthly)............	Ch. Miss. Soc.
Morija.................	Leselinyana (Monthly)............	Paris Society
Sierra Leone...........	Sierra Leone Messenger...........	
South Africa...........	Ys and Otherwise (Quarterly)......	W. C. T. U.
South Africa...........	Christian Student (Quarterly)......	Y. M. C. A.
Taveta................	Taveta Chronicle (Occasional).....	Ch. Miss. Soc.
Tunis.................	Monthly Bulletin.................	Y. M. C. A.
Wellington............	Mission Newsletter (Monthly).....	Independent
Wellington............	White Ribbon for South Africa (Monthly)....................	W. C. T. U.
Zululand..............	Torch Light.....................	?
	Niger and Yariba Notes..........	Hausa Ass.
MADAGASCAR		
Tananarivo............	Church and School...............	Brit. Friends
Tananarivo............	Children's Friend................	Brit. Friends
Tananarivo............	Antananarivo Annual.............	London Society
WEST INDIES		
Kingston, Jamaica......	Jamaica Moravian (Monthly)......	Unity of Brethren

MEDICAL STATISTICS

1

HOSPITALS AND DISPENSARIES

Location	Designation	Date of Founding	Society or Church
AFRICA			
Abeokuta	Dispensary	1890	Ch. Miss. Soc.
Alexandria	Kaiserswerth Deaconesses' Hospital and Dispensary	1857	Deaconess=Order of Rhen. Westphalia
Alexandria	Dispensary		No. Af. Miss.
Amanzimtote	Hospital and Dispensary		Am. Board
Amedschovhe	Dispensary Work		No. Germ. Soc.
Asiut	Hospital and Dispensary	1868	Am. Un. Pres.
Awyaw (Oyo)	Hospital and Dispensary		Am. Bapt. (So.)
Bailundu	Dispensary Work		Am. Board
Bandawe	Dispensary		Sc. Free Church
Banza Manteke	Hospital and Dispensary		Am. Bap. Un. (N.)
Batanga	Mary Laffin Hospital and Dispensary	1895	Am. Pres. (North)
Belloso	Dispensary		Swed. Nat. Soc.
Benguela	Dispensary		Am. Board
Benito	Dispensary		Am. Pres. (N.)
Blair Ochil	Hospital and Dispensary	1897	Zambezi Ind. Miss.
Blantyre	St Luke's Hospital		Sc. Estab. Church
Blythswood	Dispensary		Sc. Free Church
Bolengi	Medical Work		Am. Bap. Un. (N.)
Bolobo	Dispensary		Br. Par. Bap.
Bompeh	Dispensary		Un. Breth.in Christ
Cairo	Hospital and Dispensary	1889	Ch. Miss. Soc.
Cairo	Victoria Hospital	1884	Deaconess=Order
Cape Mount	Dispensary Work for Women		Am. Episcopalians
Cape Palmas	St Mark's Hospital		Am. Episcopalians
Casablanca	Dispensary		No. Af. Miss.
Chisamba	Dispensary		Am. Board
Creek Town	Goldie Memorial Hospital	1896	Sc. Un. Pres.
Domasi	Dispensary		Sc. Estab. Church
Duke Town	Hospital and Dispensary	1896	Sc. Un. Pres.
Durban	Dispensary		S. P. G.
Efulen	Hospital and Dispensary	1896	Am. Pres. (N.)
Ekwendeni	Dispensary		Sc. Free Church
Emgwali	Dispensary Work	1885	Sc. Un. Pres.
Emuremura	Dispensary		Sc. Un. Pres.
Equatorville	Dispensary		Am. Bap. Un. (N.)
Fez	Victoria Dispensary for Jews	1888	No. Af. Miss.
Freetown	Princess Christian Cottage Hospital	1892	Sierra Leone Ch.
Fwambo	Dispensary		London Society
Hohenfriedberg	Dispensary Work		" Berlin III "
Ibadan	Dispensary	1896	Ch. Miss Soc.
Ikau	Dispensary		Colwyn Bay Miss.
Ikoko	Hospital and Dispensary	1895	Am. Bap. Un. (N.)
Ikorana	Dispensary		Sc. Un. Pres.
Ikorofiong	Dispensary		Sc. Un. Pres.
Irebu	Dispensary		Am. Bap. Un. (N.)

MEDICAL STATISTICS 789

Location	Designation	Date of Founding	Society or Church
AFRICA—Continued			
Kamondongo or Bihe....	Dispensary..............		Am. Board
Karonga....	Hospital and Dispensary...		Sc. Free Church
Kavungu.....	Dispensary (in charge of Dr. Fisher)............		Independent
Kifwa...............	Dispensary..............		Am. Bap. Un. (N.)
Kisokwe	Dispensary..............		Ch. Miss. Soc.
Leopoldville	Dispensary..............		Am. Bap. Un. (N.)
Likoma....	Hospital and Dispensary...	1894	Universities' Miss.
Lokoja.....	Dispensary..............	1890	Ch. Miss. Soc.
Lourenco Marquez......	Dispensary (in charge of Mr. Loze)............		?
Lovedale.............	Victoria Hospital.........		Sc. Free Church
Luba...............	Dispensary..............		Ch. Miss. Soc.
Luebo..........,.....	Dispensary..............	1894	Am. Pres. (S.)
Lukunga	Dispensary..............		Am. Bap. Un. (N.)
Magila......	Hospital and Dispensary...		Universities' Miss.
Marakesh............	Hospital and Dispensary...	1891	So. Marocco Miss.
Massawah............	Dispensary..............		Swed. Nat. Soc.
Mazagan..............	Dispensary..............	1891	So. Marocco Miss.
Mengo...............	Hospital and Dispensary...	1891	Ch. Miss. Soc.
Mequinez...	Dispensary..............		Mildmay Miss.
Miller...............	Dispensary..............	1887	Sc. Un. Pres.
Mitsidi....	Hospital...............	1896	Zambezi Ind. Miss.
Mkullo........... ...	Hospital...............		Swed. Nat. Soc.
Mkunazini............	Hospital and Dispensary...	1893	Universities' Miss.
Mlanji...............	Dispensary..............		Sc. Estab. Church
Mombaz....	Hospital and Dispensary...		Ch. Miss. Soc.
Mpwapwa........	Hospital and Dispensary...	1894	Ch. Miss. Soc.
Mt Silinda............	Dispensary..............		Am. Board
Muhlenberg......... ..	Hospital and Dispensary...	1897	Gen.Syn.Am.Luth's
Mukimbungu	Hospital and Dispensary...	1891	Swed. Miss. Union
Mukimvika....	Sanitarium, Hosp. and Disp.		Am. Bap. Un. (N.)
Niamkolo.....	Dispensary..............		London Society
Njuyu...............	Dispensary..............		Scotch Free Church
Nkanga....	Dispensary..............		So. Af. Gen. Miss.
Ntonda..............	Dispensary..............	1893	Zambezi Ind. Miss.
Nzawi...............	Dispensary..............	1896	Af. Inland Miss.
Obusi...............	Dispensary..............	1896	Ch. Miss. Soc.
Odumase	Hospital and Dispensary...		Basel Miss. Soc.
Onitsha..............	Hospital and Dispensary...	1890	Ch. Miss. Soc.
Rabai............	Dispensary..............		Ch. Miss. Soc.
Rabat...............	Hospital and Dispensary...		Cent.Marocco Miss.
Rotufunk.............	Dispensary..............		Un. Breth. in Christ
Safi.................	Dispensary..............	1892	So. Marocco Miss.
Sakanjimba...........	Dispensary Work.........		Am. Board
Sao Salvador..........	Dispensary..............		Par. Bap. Soc. (Br.)
St Barnabas...........	Dispensary..............		S. P. G.
Senegal..............	Dispensary..............		Paris Soc.
Susa.................	Dispensary..............		No. Africa Miss.
Tangier..............	Tulloch Memor. Hospital...		No. Africa Miss.
Tangier..............	Women's Hospital.........	1895	No. Africa Miss.
Tangier..............	Dispensary..............		Mildmay Miss.
Tetuan......	Dispensary..............		No. Africa Miss.
Tetuan..............	Dispensary..............		Mildmay Miss.
Toro................	Dispensary..............	1897	Ch. Miss. Soc.
Tripoli.....	Dispensary..............	1889	No. Africa Miss.
Tunis................	Dispensary..............	1883	No. Africa Miss.
Umsinga.....	Gordon Memor. Hospital...		Sc. Free Church
Umtali...............	Hospital...............		S. P. G.
Umtata..............	Hospital...............		S. P. G.
Umtata..............	Hospital...............		Sc. Epis. Ch.
Unangu	Dispensary..............		Univ. Miss.

Location	Designation	Date of Founding	Society or Church
AFRICA—Continued			
Unwana	Dispensary	1887	Sc. Un. Pres.
Urambo	Hospital		London (?) Soc.
Wathen or Ngombe	Dispensary		Par. Bap. Soc. (Br.)
ARABIA			
Sheikh Othman, near Aden	Hospital	1887	Sc. Free Church
MADAGASCAR			
Ambohipotsi	Dispensary	1893	Br. Cong. and Friends
Analakely	Dispensary		Br. Cong. and Friends
Antsirabe	Hospital		Norse Miss. Soc.
Fianarantsoa	Cottage Hospital		London Soc.
Ilazaina	Dispensary		Br. Cong. and Friends
Imerimandroso	Cottage Hospital	1887	London Soc.
Isoavinandriano	Hospital		Br. Cong. and Friends
Mandridrano	Dispensary		Br. Friends
Tananarivo	Hospital		Norse Miss. Soc.
Tananarivo	Hospital for Infectious Cases	1894	Br. Cong. and Friends

No returns for the Antilles

HOSPITALS FOR LEPERS

AFRICA			
Ake, Abeokuta	Leper Camp		Ch. Miss. Soc.
Emjanyana	Leper Asylum		{ S. P. G. or Sc. Episc. Ch.
Mosetla	Leper Colony		Hermannsburg
Mzizima	Leper Settlement		Ch. Miss. Soc.
Niamkolo	Leper Home		London Soc.
Robben Island	Leper Hospital	1846	Ind. (?)
MADAGASCAR			
Antsirabe	Leper Asylum		Norse Miss. Soc.
Fianarantsoa	Home for Lepers	1895	London Soc.
Isoavina	Leper Asylum		London Soc.

PHILANTHROPIC AND REFORMATORY STATISTICS

1

FOUNDLING ASYLUMS, HOMES FOR INFANTS AND ORPHANAGES

Location	Designation	Date of Founding	Church or Society
AFRICA			
Appelbosch	Orphanage		Swed. Church
Bonny,	Orphanage		Delta Pastorate (?)
Canandua	Children's Home		Am. Meth. (N.)
Cape Town	Orphanage		So. Af. Gen. Miss.
Cape Town	St George's Orphanage		S.P.G. Women's Ass.
Dely=Ibrahim	Orphanage	1844	German Lutherans
Durban	Orphanage		?
Ekutuleni	Orphanage		Swed. Church
Eschol	Industrial Orphanage		No. Af. Miss.
Harper	St Mark's Orphan Asylum		Am. Episcopalians
Hoffman	Brierley Mem. Orphan Asylum		Am. Episcopalians
Luebo	Children's Home	1895	Am. Pres. (S.)
Mukimvika	Sanitarium		Am. Bap. Un. (N.)
Oskarsberg	Orphanage		Swed. Church
Port Louis	Rose Belle Orphanage		Ch. Miss. Soc.
MADAGASCAR			
Tananarivo	Orphanages (2)		Friends' Ass. and London Soc.
Tananarivo	Orphanage		Norse Miss. Soc.

No returns for the Antilles

2

SCHOOLS FOR DEFECTIVES

AFRICA
Worcester, Cape Colony. | Deaf and Dumb Ins....... | | So. Af. Gen. Miss.

No returns for Madagascar or the West Indies

3

ORGANIZATIONS FOR TEMPERANCE

AFRICA

Banza Manteke	Strictly Temperance Church	Am. Bap. Un. (N.)
Blythswood	Temperance Society	Sc. Free Church
Blythswood	Band of Hope	Sc. Free Church

Location	Designation	Date of Founding	Church or Society
AFRICA—CONTINUED			
Cape Town............	Gospel Temperance Mission		Col. and Cont. Soc. (Ang.)
Cape Town............	Band of Hope............		W. C. T. U.
Cradock....	Band of Hope............		S. A. B. M. S.
Creek Town	Band of Hope............		Sc. Un. Pres.
Freetown	Total Abstinence and Purity Society................		Ch. Miss. Soc.
Harding...............	Bands of Hope (3)........		Young Men's Soc.
Kokstad................	Church Temperance Society		Sc. Epis. Church
Lovedale.............	Temperance Work........		Sc. Free Church
Lukunga.....	Total Abstinence Society...		Am. Bap. Un. (N.)
Mount Frere...........	Band of Hope............	1896	Sc. Free Church
Pirie...................	Band of Hope......	1896	Sc. Free Church
South Africa...........	Young Women's Temperance Unions (27)........	1890	W. C. T. U.
South Africa...........	Women's Christ. Temperance Unions (55)		W. C. T. U.
MADAGASCAR			
Tananarivo	Women's Christ. Temperance Union.............		W. C. T. U.
WEST INDIES			
Jamaica....	Temperance Work........		Sc. Un. Pres.
Jamaica.....	Loyal Temperance Legion..		W. C. T. U.
Nassau, Bahama........	Women's Christ. Temp. Union	1890	W. C. T. U.

4
REFUGES

AFRICA			
Adams (Amanzimtote)..	Refuge for Kraal Girls.....		Am. Board
Cairo..................	Home for Freed Women Slaves		Br. Antislavery Soc.
Cape Town............	Home for Inebriates.......		Salvation Army
Creek Town...........	Classes for Slaves.........		Sc. Un. Pres.
Frere Town............	Freedmen's Settlement.....		Ch. Miss. Soc.
Gordon Memorial.......	Girls' Home..............		Sc. Free Ch. Wom. Soc.
Hoffman...............	Refuge for Fallen Women..		Am. Episc.
Kichelwe...............	Freed Slave Settlement.....		Univ. Miss.
Kilindini.....	Work Among Freed Slaves.		Ch. Miss. Soc.
Kisserawe.............	Home for Freed Slaves.....		"Berlin III"
Mbweni.....	Slave Rescue.............		Univ. Miss.
Pieter Maritzburg	Girls' Home..............		Wom. Soc. Sc. Free Ch.
Tangier................	Free Night=Refuge for Homeless Men...........		No. Africa Miss.

No returns for the Antilles and Madagascar

5
VARIOUS SOCIETIES

Location	Designation	Church or Society
AFRICA		
Alexandria	Sailors' and Soldiers' Institute	?
Algiers	Seamen's Mission Room. (The German Seamen's Mission in Foreign Harbors conducts this.)	
Cape Palmas	Mary Magdalene Society	Am. Episc.
Cape Town	Seamen's Mission	Ind.
Cape Town	Seamen's Home and Sailors' Rest	So. Af. Gen. Miss.
Cape Town	Soldiers' Home	So. Af. Gen. Miss.
Cape Town	Nurses' Home	So. Af. Gen. Miss.
Domasi	Young Men's Guild	Sc. Estab. Church
Durban	Work for Sailors	So. Af. Gen. Miss.
Emgwali	White Cross Society	Sc. Un. Pres.
Freetown	Evangelical Reform Association	Ch. Miss. Soc.
Funchal	Sailors' Rest	{ Am. Seamen's { Friend Society
Lovedale	Students' Volunteer Association	Sc. Free Church
Lovedale	White Cross Society	Sc. Free Church
Mbweni	Guild of the Good Shepherd. (This aids women trained as teachers in the Girls' School	Univ. Mission
Mengo	Gleaners' Union for Women	Ch. Miss. Soc.
Pieter Maritzburg	Soldiers' Home	So. Af. Gen. Miss.
Port Said	Seamen's Rest and Strangers' Welcome	?
Salt River, Cape Colony	Rescue Home	W. C. T. U.
Wynberg	Soldiers' Home	So. Af. Gen. Miss.
MADAGASCAR		
Fianarantsoa	Prison Visitation	London Soc.

No returns for the West Indies

CULTURAL STATISTICS

1

SOCIETIES FOR THE YOUNG

(1) Young People's Society of Christian Endeavor

Location	Young People's	Senior	Junior	Totals
Africa	89	12	9	110
Bermuda	7			7
Egypt	3		1	4
Madagascar	93			93
West Indies	73		11	84
Totals	265	12	21	298

South Africa in 1897-98 had the greatest proportionate increase in the number of societies.

(2) The Methodist Episcopal Church reports chapters of The Epworth League in *all* its mission-stations. Doctor Dennis has not been able to secure statistics, but reports one hundred and seventy senior and eleven junior leagues in the foreign missions of the Methodist Church and the Methodist Church South. If The Epworth League has branches in *all* the missions of the former church, it would seem as if these branches, by inclusion, must exist in Africa and among American and Antillean Negroes.

(3) Young Men's Christian Association.*

Location	Associations	Membership
Africa	24	2,160
Antilles	8	101
Madagascar	2	

(4) Young Women's Christian Association.

Location	Associations	Membership
Africa	6	172

(5) The Daughters of the King have two organizations in the Antilles.

(6) Various Societies for Children

Location	Designation	Society
AFRICA		
Cape Town	Boys' Brigade	Sc. Free Church
Cape Town	Boys' Brigade	Col. and Cont. Ch. Soc.
Durban	Boys' Brigade	Sc. Free Church
Gordon Memorial	Boys' Brigade	Sc. Free Church
Pretoria	Boys' Brigade	Sc. Free Church
Africa (*passim*)	Children's Scripture Union (This has many branches and 3,000 members)	Ch. Miss. Soc.
ANTILLES		
Port au Spain, Trinidad	Boys' Brigade	Sc. Free Church

*Cf. *Fifty Years' Work of the Y. M. C. A.*, p. 306, pp. 308-310.

2
WORLD'S FEDERATION OF CHRISTIAN STUDENTS

In Africa this has The South African Students' Christian Association. The Student Christian Movement in Mission=Lands is perhaps included.

3
SISTERHOODS

Location	Designation	Society
AFRICA		
Alexandria.....	Kaiserswerth Deaconesses.....	Deaconess=Order of Rhen. Westphalia
Cairo..........	Kaiserswerth Deaconesses.....	Deaconess=Order of Rhen. Westphalia
Grahamston....	Sisters of Uva...............	Wesley. Miss. Soc.
Johannesburg...	Deaconesses' Home..........	So. Af. Gen. Miss.

No returns for the Antilles and Madagascar

4
BIBLE=WOMEN

Africa, including Mauritius and the Seychelles Islands........................... 5
Egypt.. 20

No returns for Madagascar and the West Indies

5
ZENANA=VISITORS

Africa.. 63
Madagascar... 20

No returns for the Antilles

6
MISCELLANEOUS ORGANIZATIONS

Location	Designation	Church or Society
AFRICA		
Freretown.................	Council of Mothers.................	Ch. Miss. Soc.
Pretoria....................	Christian Workers' Association......	Wesley. Miss. Soc.
Sheikh Othman (in Arabia)	Keith Falconer Memor. Library......	Sc. Free Church
MADAGASCAR		
Ambohimandroso.........	Harvest Thanksgiving.............	London Soc.

No returns for the West Indies

NATIVE ORGANIZATIONS

Location	Designation	Object
AFRICA Durban............	African Christian Union.................	To unite Christians in the name of the Christ and to pray and work for Africa becoming a Christian land.
Kimberley..........	(There is an organization, name unknown, of native Christians among the diamond-mines. Its aims and methods, in general, are those of Christian reform.)	

No returns for the Antilles and Madagascar

RETURNS FOR SUNDAY=SCHOOLS IN 1896

Location	Number	Scholars	Teachers
Africa...................	4,246	161,394	8,455

No returns for Madagascar and the West Indies

AFRICAN MISSION=BOATS

Location	Name	Owner
Batanga.............	Nassau	Am. Pres. (N.)
	The Chain Memorial	Am. Pres. (N.)
Cross and Old Kalabar Rivers.............	David Williamson...................	Sc. Un. Pres.
Kongo River.........	Good Will	Br. Bapt.
Kongo River (upper) ...	Henry Reed......................	Am. Bap. Un. (N.)
Kongo River..........	Peace............................	Br. Bapt.
Kongo River (upper) ...	Pioneer (1889)	Kongo=Balolo Miss.
Nile River.............	Ibis (1867)........................	Am. Un. Pres.
Nile River.............	?	Kaiserswerth
Nyasa Lake...........	Charles Janson (1885)..............	Un. Miss.
Nyasa Lake...........	Charlotte	Un. Miss.
Nyasa Lake...........	Ousel............................	Un. Miss.
St Paul River	? (1891)	Am. Luth.Gen.Syn.
Tanganika Lake.......	Good News	London Soc.
Tanganika Lake.......	Morning Star (1884)................	London Soc.
Victoria Lake	Ruwenzori (1896)..................	Ch. Miss. Soc.

No returns for the Antilles and Madagascar

Doctor Dennis ended here the statistics which he so kindly furnished to Mr Noble.

DIRECTORY OF AGENCIES
FOR THE
CHRISTIANIZATION OF AFRICAN PEOPLES
IN
AFRICA, AMERICA, THE ANTILLES AND MADAGASCAR.
BY
FREDERIC PERRY NOBLE

DIRECTORY OF MISSION-AGENCIES

CLASS A

ALPHABETICAL LIST OF SOCIETIES AMONG ALL AFRICAN PEOPLES*

Name of Society	Polity of Adherents	Nationality of Supporters	Sphere of Operations†
Aborigines' Protection Society	Nondenominational...	British.......	Auxiliary
Africa Inland Mission.........	Nondenominational..	American (United States)	East Africa
African Christian Union	Undenominational ...	Negroes.....	Natal
African Institute..............	Nondenominational..	British	Sierra Leone
African Lakes Society........	Nondenominational..	Scotch.......	Auxiliary
All Saints' Sisterhood	Anglican............	English......	Cape Colony
All Hallows College.........	*Roman*............	*Irish*........	*Auxiliary*
American Baptist Home-Mission Society.................	Baptist............	American ...	Freedmen
American Baptist Missionary Union....................	Baptist............	American ...	Belgian Kongo
American Baptist Publication Society....................	Baptist............	American ...	Religious Literature
American Bible Society.......	Interdenominational .	American ...	Religious Literature
American Board of Commissioners for Foreign Missions	Congregational......	American ...	Angola, Zululand, Transvaal
American Church Missionary Society.....................	Anglican............	American ...	Freedmen and Cuba
American Colonization Society	Nondenominational..	American ...	Liberia
American Missionary Association	Congregational......	American ...	Freedmen
American Tract Society.......	Interdenominational .	American ...	Religious Literature
Amsterdam Auxiliary of the Rhenish Mission..........	Lutheran...........	Dutch (European).....	Auxiliary
Ansgar Union of East Gothland....................	Lutheran...........	Swedish.....	Galla
Antigua Diocesan Mission....	Anglican...........	British Antilleans......	Freedmen
Arnot Mission to Central Africa‡.....................	Interdenominational .	Scotch	Katanga
Association for Cape Town Missions......	Anglican...........	British	Cape Town....
Association for the Free Distribution of the Scriptures.....	Interdenominational .	English	Religious Literature
Association for the Furtherance of Christianity in Egypt	Anglican...........	English.	Kopts

*Catholics in italics, Protestants in Roman type.
†In case of societies not engaging directly in missions, the kind of work is indicated, being substituted for the sphere of operations.
‡The Brethren's Mission to Garenganze seems to be the new title of Arnot's Mission.

DIRECTORY OF MISSION=AGENCIES

Name of Society	Polity of Adherents	Nationality of Supporters	Sphere of Operations
Association for the Propagation of the Faith	Roman	English	Auxiliary
Association of the Good Shepherd	Roman	Italian	Central Africa
Bahama Baptist Union........	Baptist	Antilles, British	Freedmen
Baptist Book Society	Baptist.............	English	Religious Literature
Baptist Congregation.........	Baptist (*colored*)...	African	Kamerun
Baptist Foreign Missions Convention	Baptist (*colored*)...	American...	Liberia
Baptist General Association	Baptist (*colored*)...	American ...	Kongo
Baptist Missionary Society (See Particular Baptist)....			
Baptist Union of Liberia......	Baptist (*colored*)...	African	Negroes
Baptist Union of South Africa.	Baptist.............	British	Cape Colony
Baptist Young Peoples' Union	Baptist.............	International	Africa
Barbados Diocesan Mission...	Anglican...........	Antilles, British	Freedmen
Bassa (Shiloh) Mission*......	Nondenominational..	American ...	Liberia
Bible=Christian Missionary Society.......................	Methodist	English	
Bible=Lands Missions' Aid Society.......................	Undenominational...	British	Egypt
Bible=Translation Society.....	Baptist.............	English	Religious Literature
Bishop White Prayer=Book Society.....	Anglican...........	American ...	Religious Literature
Bloemfontein Diocesan Mission†.....................	Anglican...........	British	Orange Free State
Board of Education of Presbyterian Church	Presbyterian (North)	American ...	Freedmen
Board of Foreign Missions of Presbyterian Church........	Presbyterian (North)	American ...	Gabun; Liberia
Board of Foreign Missions of Southern Baptist Convention	Baptist (white)......	American ...	Yariba
Board of Home Missions of Southern Baptist Convention	Baptist (white)......	American ...	Freedmen
Board of Missions for Freedmen	Presbyterian (north).	American ...	United States (South)
Board of Missions of Presbyterian Church South.........	Presbyterian (south)	American ...	Kongo; Cuba
Board of Missions of Scotch Episcopal Church	Anglican...........	Scotch	Kafraria
Board of Missions of United Presbyterian Church........	Presbyterian........	American ...	Egypt
Board of Missions of Seventh= Day Adventist Church......	Adventist...........	American ...	South Africa
Bodelschwingh [or Bielefeld] Deaconesses	Lutheran...........	German.....	East Africa
Boer Farm Mission...........	Presbyterian........	African Dutch	Transvaal
Bremen Bible Society.........	Interdenominational .	German.....	Religious Literature

*The American Church Missionary Society (United States Episcopalians) holds the property by deed of trust in perpetuity for missions.
†Vahl mentions an Anglican Bloemfontein Missionary Union. Is this the Diocesan Mission?

DIRECTORY OF MISSION-AGENCIES 801

Name of Society	Polity of Adherents	Nationality of Supporters	Sphere of Operations
British Anti-Slavery Society..	Nondenominational..	British......	Auxiliary
British and Foreign Bible Society.....................	Interdenominational.	British......	Religious Literature
British and Foreign School Society.....................	Nondenominational..	British......	Sierra Leone
British Guiana Mission......	Anglican (?)........	British......	Colored Races
British Methodist Episcopal Church....................	Methodist (Negro)..	Canadian....	Antilles; Guiana
British Society for the Propation of the Gospel among the Jews*.....................	Interdenominational.	British......	North Africa
Canada Congregational Woman's Board...............	Congregational......	British......	Benguela
Canadian Missionary Society..	Congregational......	British......	Benguela
Cape Colony Evangelical Voluntary Union.............	Interdenominational.	British......	Cape Colony
Cape Town Diocesan Mission.	Anglican...........	British......	Cape Colony
Capuchins (Fratres Minores Capuzini)................	Roman.............	International	East and North Africa
Central Marocco Medical Mission.....................	Undenominational...	Scotch......	Marocco
Children's Medical Missionary Society...................	Nondenominational..	English.....	Auxiliary
Children of the Heart of the Immaculate Virgin Mary	Roman.............	Spanish.....	Fernando Po
Christian Woman's Board of Missions (Disciples).......	Congregational......	American...	Jamaica
Christian Reformed Church Missionary Society†........	Presbyterian.........	African Dutch	South Africa
Christian and Missionary Alliance (Simpson Self-Supporting Mission)	Nondenominational..	American...	Kongo State
Church of England Book-Society...................	Anglican...........	English.....	Religious Literature
Church Missionary College....	Anglican...........	English......	Auxiliary
Church Missionary Society....	Anglican...........	English.....	Africa; Antilles
Church of Norway Mission....	Lutheran...........	Norse.......	Madagascar and Zululand
Church of Scotland (Established) Committee for Propagation of the Gospel........	Presbyterian.........	Scotch......	Nyasaland ✓
Church of Sweden Mission....	Lutheran...........	Swedish.....	South Africa
Colonial Bishops' Fund.......	Anglican...........	British......	Auxiliary
Church-Women's Association.	Anglican...........	Scotch......	Auxiliary
Colonial Committee of Church of Scotland (Established)...	Presbyterian........	Scotch......	Antilles, Guiana, Mauritius
Colonial Missionary Society..	Congregational......	English.....	Transvaal
Committee of Evangelization of the Presbyterian Church South...................	Presbyterian	American ...	Freedmen
Colonial and Continental Church Society.............	Anglican...........	English.....	Africa and Negroes in Canada

*This is not the London Society for Promoting Christianity among the Jews.
†The Christian Reformed Church of Holland, a Free Presbyterian body from which grew this Boer society, entered Transvaal in 1858, Surinam in 1863.

DIRECTORY OF MISSION-AGENCIES

Name of Society	Polity of Adherents	Nationality of Supporters	Sphere of Operations
Commission for Catholic Missions	Roman...............	American ...	Freedmen
Colonial and Continental Committees [2] of Free Church..	Presbyterian	Scotch.......	African natives, et al.
Colwyn Bay Institution.......	Undenominational...	British	West Africa
Committee on Missions of Scotch Free Church.........	Presbyterian.........	Scotch.......	Kafraria and Nyasaland
Continental Board of United Presbyterian Church........	Presbyterian.........	Scotch	African Natives, et al.
Continental Committee of Presbyterian Church.............	Presbyterian	English	African Natives, et al.
Congo=Balolo Mission. (See East London Institute for Home and Foreign Missions)			
Congregational Union of Jamaica....................	Congregational......	British.......	Colored People
Congregational Union of Madagascar....	Congregational......	Hova	Madagascar
Congregational Union of South Africa........	Congregational......	British......	Native Races
College of Verona..........	Roman...............	Italian	Education
Congregatio de Propaganda Fide..................	Roman	Italian	Africa
Congregation of African Missions	Roman..............	French	North and West Africa
Congregation of Algerian Fathers (Notre Dame de l' Afrique)...............	Roman...............	French.......	North and East Africa
Congregation of Armed Brethren of Sahara.......	Roman..............	French	North Africa
Congregation of Benedictines	Roman..............	German.....	German East Africa
Congregation of Brethren of Christian Schools.........	Roman...............	French	North and West Africa
Congregation of Dominicans....................	Roman...............	Irish*.......	South Africa
Congregation of Eudists....	Roman...............	French	Antilles
Congregation of Franciscans (Fratres Minores)..	Roman............	International	East and North Africa
Congregation of the Holy Ghost and the Heart of Mary.....................	Roman	French	East, South and West Africa
Congregation of Issoudon...	Roman	French	South Africa
Congregation of Lazarists (Fathers of the Mission)..	Roman	International	East and North Africa
Congregation of Marists (Society of Sacred Hearts of Jesus and Mary)			
Congregation of Oblats of Mary......	Roman...............	French	South Africa

*The order is international, but the branch working for Africa seems to be Irish.

DIRECTORY OF MISSION=AGENCIES

Name of Society	Polity of Adherents	Nationality of Supporters	Sphere of Operations
Congregation of Oblats of St Francis de Sales	Roman	French	South Africa
Congregation of Pallotin	Roman	German	Kamerûn
Congregation of Pious Mothers of Nigritia	Roman	French	West Africa
Congregation of the Ploermel Fathers	Roman	French	?
Congregation of Scheut les Bruxelles	Roman	Belgian	Kongo
Congregation of St Vincent Paul	Roman	French	North Africa
Congregation of Sisters of St Joseph	Roman	French	?
Congregation of Trappists (Ordre de Citeaux)	Roman	French	Algeria; Natal
Consolidated American Baptist Convention	Baptist (colored)	American	Haiti; Liberia
Coral Missionary Fund	Anglican	English	Auxiliary
Cork Society	Roman	Irish	?
Cowley Brotherhood (Society of St John the Evangelist)	Anglican	English	South Africa
Deaconess=Order of Rhenish Westphalia	Lutheran	German	Egypt, et al.
Department of Missions	Unity of Brethren	German	Africa; Antilles
Dutch Lutheran Association	Lutheran	AfricanDutch	Cape Colony
Dutch Reformed Church Mission*	Presbyterian	AfricanDutch	Nyasaland; South Africa
Dutch Protestant Missionary Society	Presbyterian	European Dutch	?
East Africa Scotch Mission	Nondenominational	Scotch	Ibea
East Friesland Missionary Society	Lutheran	German	Africa†
East London Institute	Nondenominational	English	Lololand; Kongo State
Echo of Service [?]	Plymouth Brethren	England	Africa and Guiana
Edinburgh Medical Missionary Society**	Nondenominational	Scotch	Auxiliary
Epworth League	Methodist	International	Africa
Ermelo Missionary Society	Presbyterian	European Dutch	Egypt
Evangelical Mission at Hermannsburg	Lutheran	German	Transvaal,et al.
Evangelical Missionary Society at Basel	Interdenominational	GermanSwiss	Gold Coast
Evangelical Missionary Society at Leipzig	Lutheran	German	East Africa

*Vahl named the Cape Colony Synod of the Dutch Reformed Church and the South African Dutch Reformed Church as missionary agencies. But are not these and the Dutch Reformed Church Mission all one and the same?
†This body, though auxiliary to Gossner's Union (Berlin II) independently supports a Hermannsburg station either among the Chwana or the Zulu.
**Vahl mentions an Edinburgh Missionary Society as an organization distinct from the Medical Society.
††This is often called "Berlin III".

Name of Society	Polity of Adherents	Nationality of Supporters	Sphere of Operations
Evangelical Missionary Society for German East Africa††...	Lutheran............	German.....	East Africa
Evangelical National Society..	Lutheran............	Swedish.....	Eritrea
Evangelical Mission to the Zambezi...................	Presbyterian.........	French......	Ba=Rutsi
Fellow=Workers' Union [Women]..................	Presbyterian.........	Scotch	Auxiliary
Finland Mission=Society......	Lutheran.....	Finn	German Southwest Africa
Foreign Mission of the United Presbyterian Church........	Presbyterian	Scotch	Kafraria, Jamaica, Old Kalabar
Foreign Missionary Society of the Lutheran Church in the United States	Lutheran (General Synod)............	American ...	Liberia
Foreign Christian Missionary Society [Disciples of Christ]	Congregational.....	American ...	Belgian Kongo
Foreign Sunday=School Association...................	Interdenominational .	American ...	South Africa
Freetown Auxiliary to the Religious Tract Society	Interdenominational .	British......	Sierra Leone
Freedmen's Aid and Education Society of the Methodist Episcopal Church	Methodist (North)...	American ...	Freedmen
Free Church of Norway's Mission......................	Congregational......	Norse.	Zululand
Friends' Board of Missions....	"Quaker"...........	American ...	Freedmen
Friends' Industrial Mission...	"Quaker"	English.....	Pemba, East Africa
Friends' Missionary Association	"Quaker"...........	English.....	Madagascar
Gabun and Corisco Presbytery	Presbyterian.........	African	French Kongo
General Missionary Board of the Free Methodist Churches	Methodist	American ...	Inhambani ?
German Evangelical Synod...	Methodist	American ...	Sierra Leone
Ghent Clergy..............	Roman..............	Belgian.....	Belgian Kongo
Ghent Sisters of Charity ...	Roman..............	Belgian.	Kongo State
Grahamston Association*.....	Anglican............	English......	Cape Colony
Guiana Diocesan Church Society......................	Anglican............	British	British Guiana
Hanover and Hermannsburg Free=Church Mission	Independent Lutheran	German.....	Africa
Hartford Mission=School (in existence?).............	Anglican............	American ...	Auxiliary
Haüsa Association (Harris Central Sudan Mission).....	Anglican......	English	Sudan
Helgelse Förbindung i Nerike	Lutheran (?)........	Swedish.....	South Africa
Huguenot Female Seminary Missionary Society.........	Interdenominational .	Boer and British	South Africa
Hvita Bergets Mission........	Lutheran (?)	Swedish.....	North Africa

*A Glasgow African Society and the Glasgow Missionary Society are omitted here, as having passed away.

DIRECTORY OF MISSION=AGENCIES   805

Name of Society	Polity of Adherents	Nationality of Supporters	Sphere of Operations
Independent Baptist Church...	Baptist.............	AfricanDutch	Transvaal
Institute for Education of Converted African Youth.......	Baptist.............	English.....	Auxiliary
International Bible=Reading Association	Interdenominational.	British......	Auxiliary
International Missionary Union	Interdenominational.	American...	Auxiliary
International Medical Missionary and Benevolent Association.....................	Undenominational?..	American...	Auxiliary
International Medical Society.	Interdenominational.	American...	Auxiliary
Jamaica Church=Ladies' Association..................	Anglican...........	English.....	Jamaica
Jamaica Diocesan Mission....	Anglican...........	British......	Jamaica
Jamaica Missionary Society...	Anglican...........	British......	Colored Race
Jamaica Missionary Union ...	Baptist (colored)....	British......	Central America, Cuba, Haiti
Jerusalem Mission=Fund......	Anglican...........	British......	Egypt
Jesuits (Societas Jesu)	Roman.............	International	Africa, Madagascar, and Antilles
Jewish Mission of Church of Scotland..................	Presbyterian.........	Scotch	North Africa
Jewish Mission of Presbyterian Church	Presbyterian.........	English.....	North Africa
Joyful News [Champney's] Evangelists................	Methodist...........	English.....	?
Kamerûn Missionary Union..	Baptist.............	German.....	Kamerûn
Kimberley Union of Native Christians....	Undenominational...	Negro.......	Diamond=mines
Kongo Children's Friends.....	Congregational......	Swedish.....	Education
Kongo Training Institution....	Undenominational...	English.....	Education
Ladies' Association for the Christian Education of Jewish Females*...............	Presbyterian.........	Scotch.......	Egypt
Ladies' Association for Promoting Female Education among the Heathen**.......	Anglican...........	English.....	South Africa
Ladies' Association for Missions†	Presbyterian.........	Scotch	Nyasaland
Ladies' Auxiliary of Wesleyan Missionary Society.........	Methodist...........	English.....	South Africa
Ladies' Committee of the London Society	Congregational	English.....	Africa and Madagascar
Ladies' Continental Association††.....................	Presbyterian.........	Scotch.......	South Africa
Ladies' Kafrarian Society‡....	Presbyterian.........	Scotch	Kafraria

*With Established Church of Scotland Committee.
**With Gospel=Propagation Society.
†With Established Church of Scotland Committee.
††With Scotch Free Church Mission=Committee.
‡With Scotch United Presbyterian Mission=Board.

Name of Society	Polity of Adherents	Nationality of Supporters	Sphere of Operations
Ladies' Negro=Education Society (Ladies' Society for Promoting Education in the West Indies)	Anglican?	English	Antilles
Ladies' Society for Female Education in South Africa*	Presbyterian	Scotch	South Africa
Lady Huntingdon Connexion Society for the Spread of the Gospel	Congregational	English	Sierra Leone
Lady Mico Charity	Undenominational	British	Education†
Lagos Missionary Society	Baptist (*colored*)	Negro	Lagos
Liberian Missionary Society	?	African	Liberia
London Association in Aid of Brethren's Missions	Nondenominational	English	Auxiliary
London [Missionary] Society	Congregational	English	Africa, Madagascar
London Society for Promoting Christianity among Jews	Anglican	English	North Africa
Luther League	Lutheran	International	Africa
Lyons College	Roman	French	Auxiliary
Mackenzie Memorial Mission	Anglican	English	Zululand
Madagascar Diocesan Mission	Anglican	English	Madagascar
Madras Auxiliary Bible=Society	Interdenominational	British	Mauritius
Malagasi Missionary Society	Congregational	Hova	Madagascar
Malines Fathers	Roman	Belgian	Kongo State
Maritzburg Diocesan Mission (1869)	Anglican	British	Natal
Maritzburg Mission (1880)	Anglican	English	Natal
Matschappij Vereenigung	Presbyterian	European Dutch	Surinam Negroes
Mauritius Auxiliary Bible=Society	Interdenominational	British	Mauritius
Mauritius Church Union	Anglican	British	Mauritius
Mauritius Diocesan Mission	Anglican	British	Mauritius and Seychelles
Mauritius Tract Society	Interdenominational	British	Mauritius
Mauritius Union for Evangelization	Roman	Mauritian	Mauritius
Medical Missionary Association	Nondenominational	English	Auxiliary
Mildmay Mission to Jews	Interdenominational	English	Marocco
Mission for Kabylia	Presbyterian	French Swiss	Algeria
Mission of Free Churches of French Switzerland	Presbyterian	Swiss	Transvaal
Mission of French Wesleyans	Methodist	French	Kabylia
Mission to Muhammadan Malays‡	Anglican (?)	British	Cape Colony
Missionary=Board of African Methodist Episcopal Church	Methodist (*colored*)	American	Africa, Antilles, United States
Missionary=Board of African Methodist Episcopal Zion Church	Methodist (*colored*)	American	Liberia

*With Scotch Free Church Mission=Committee.
†Mico College at Kingston, Jamaica, is sustained by this society, and trains young men of African descent to become missionaries to West Africa.
‡Hesse says this is defunct. Does he mean the English organization of 1861? Is there such a society in Cape Colony?

DIRECTORY OF MISSION=AGENCIES 807

Name of Society	Polity of Adherents	Nationality of Supporters	Sphere of Operations
Missionary=Board of the Canada Methodist Episcopal Church	Methodist	Canadian	Bermudan Negroes
Missionary=Leaves Association	Anglican	English	Auxiliary
Missionary Society of the Methodist Episcopal Church	Methodist (north)	American	Angola, Liberia, Rhodesia
Missionary Society of the Protestant Episcopal Church in the United States	Anglican	American	Liberia
Missionary Society of United Free Methodist Churches	Methodist	British	Africa, Antilles
Missionary Society of the Wesleyan Connexion	Methodist	American	West Africa
Muslim Missionary Society	Anglican	English	Egypt
Nassau Diocesan Mission	Anglican	British	Bahamas
Natalese Missionary Committee	Presbyterian	African Dutch	South Africa
National Bible Society	Nondenominational	Scotch	Religious Literature
"The Net" Collections	Anglican	English	Auxiliary
Netherlands Missionary Society	Presbyterian	European Dutch	Surinam
Neuendettelsau Missionary Establishment	Lutheran	German	Educational Auxiliary
Neukirchen Missionary=Society	Lutheran	German	East Africa
New York Bible Society	Anglican	American	Religious Literature
Norse Medical Mission	Lutheran	Norwegian	Madagascar
Norse Mission=Society	Lutheran	Norwegian	Madagascar and South Africa
North Africa Mission	Interdenominational	English	North Africa
North Carolina State Convention	Baptist	American	Africa
North German Missionary Society	Presbyterian	German	West Africa
Nyasa Industrial Mission	Undenominational	British	Nyasaland
Oriental Women's Education Society	Interdenominational	British	South Africa
Paris School Society	Presbyterian	French	Africa
Parochial Mission to Jews	Anglican	English	Funds to Egypt
Particular Baptist Society for Propagating the Gospel among the Heathen	Baptist	English	Angola and Kongo State
Philafrican Liberators' League	Nondenominational	American	Benguela
Prayer=Book Society	Anglican	English	Auxiliary
Preachers' Missionary Union	Presbyterian	Cape Colony Dutch	Nyasaland
Presbyterian Church in Canada	Presbyterian	British	Trinidad*
Presbyterian Church in Jamaica	Presbyterian	British Antilleans	Old Calabar

*Negroes and Coolies.

DIRECTORY OF MISSION-AGENCIES

Name of Society	Polity of Adherents	Nationality of Supporters	Sphere of Operations
Presbyterian Women's Missionary Society of the Northwest.*	Presbyterian (north).	American...	Auxiliary
Presbytery of Egypt	Presbyterian	Koptic	Egypt
Pretoria Diocesan Mission	Anglican	British	Transvaal
Primitive Methodist Missionary Society	Methodist	English	South Africa and FernanPo
Protestant Episcopal Education Society	Anglican	American...	Negroes, *inter al.*
Pure Literature Society	Interdenominational.	English	Religious Literature
Qua Ibo Mission	Presbyterian?	Irish	Old Calabar
Reformed Presbyterian Church	Presbyterian	Scotch	East Africa
Reformed Presbyterian Church in United States	Presbyterian	American...	Kongo State
Religious Book Society	Interdenominational.	Scotch	Auxiliary
Religious Tract Society	Interdenominational.	English	Auxiliary
Rhenish Mission Society†	Lutheran	German	South Africa
Rock Fountain Mission	Friends	English	Cape Colony
Saint Chrischona Pilgrim Mission	Lutheran	Swiss	Egypt
Saint John Diocesan Mission	Anglican	Scotch	Kafraria
Saint Joseph College	Roman	American...	Freedmen
Salvation Army	Nondenominational.	British	South Africa
Scandinavian Missionary Alliance	Congregational	American...	South Africa
Scotch Society for the Conversion of Israel	Interdenominational.	Scotch	North Africa
Sierra Leone Auxiliary Bible Society	Interdenominational.	Negro	Religious Literature
Sierra Leone Church Missions. (?Sierra Leone Diocesan Mission)	Anglican	African	Sierra Leone
Sierra Leone Mission-Society	Anglican	African	Sierra Leone
Sisterhood of St John the Divine	Wesleyan	English	Auxiliary
Sisterhood of the Resurrection.	Anglican	British	Natal
Sisterhood of St Michael	Anglican	British	Cape Colony
Sisterhood of St Raphael	Anglican	British	Cape Colony and Orange
Sisters of our Lady of Namur	Anglican	British	Cape Colony
Sisters of Uva	Roman	Belgian	Belgian Kongo
Slesvig-Holstein Union	Methodist	British	Kafraria
Society at Berlin for Missions.	Unity of Brethren	Danish	Danish Antilles
Society [at Bethlehem, Pa] for Propagating the Gospel	Lutheran	German	Transvaal
	Unity of Brethren	American...	Antilles

*With the Board of Foreign Missions of the Presbyterian Church.
†The Barmen Society and the Missionary Society of the Rhine and Westphalia are other names by which this society is also known.

DIRECTORY OF MISSION=AGENCIES

Name of Society	Polity of Adherents	Nationality of Supporters	Sphere of Operations
Society at Paris for Evangelical Missions among non=Christian Peoples*	Presbyterian	French	South and West Africa
Society for Female Education in the East	Interdenominational	English	South Africa
Society for Promotion of the Christian Faith	Anglican	British	Religious Literature
Society for the Gospel in Surinam	Presbyterian?	European Dutch	Negroes
Society for Promoting Christian Knowledge	Anglican	English	Religious Literature
Society in Scotland for Christian Knowledge	Presbyterian	Scotch	Religious Literature
Society for the Propagation of the Gospel	Anglican	English	Africa, Antilles and Madagascar
Society for Prevention of Liquor=Traffic	Nondenominational	British	Auxiliary
South Africa General Mission†	Interdenominational	British	South Africa
South African Book=Society	Interdenominational	British	Religious Literature
South African Tract=Society	Interdenominational	British	Religious Literature
South African Wesleyan Missionary Society	Methodist	British	South Africa
Stuttgart Kamerûn Union	Lutheran	German	Kamerûn
Stewart Mission=Foundation	Methodist (north)	American	Education‡
Sunday=School Missionary Union	Presbyterian	AfricanDutch	South Africa
South Marocco Mission	Presbyterian	British	Marocco
Sûdan Pioneer Mission	Nondenominational	American	West Africa
Sunday=School Union of the Methodist Episcopal Church	Methodist (northern)	American	Africa
Swedish Missionary Union	Congregational	Swede	Algeria, Kongo
Swedish Women's Mission	Congregational	Swede	Algerian Women
Tophan Hospital	Nondenominational	BritishHindi?	Zanzibar
Trinitarian Bible=Society	Interdenominational	English	Religious Literature
Trinidad Diocesan Mission	Anglican	British	Negroes
Tropical Training School	Methodist	American	Barbados
Union of Evangelical Associations	Interdenominational	French	Algeria

*Vahl not only mentions the Paris Missionary=Society, but specifies "the French Reformed Church" and "the French Evangelical Mission=Society" as independent organizations active in African missions. But is not the Evangelical Society the Paris Society? Is not the society the instrument, despite an individual existence, of this Huguenot church? Or, else, does this Presbyterian state=church work in Africa apart and aside from the society?
In the Paris Society I do not include the French Zambezi Mission.
†In 1779 there was a South Africa Missionary Society.
‡This is in Gammon Theological Seminary, Atlanta, Georgia, U. S. A., and has "Friends of Africa" and "Missionary=Bands" associated with it.

DIRECTORY OF MISSION-AGENCIES

Name of Society	Polity of Adherents	Nationality of Supporters	Sphere of Operations
Union for Spreading the Gospel	Presbyterian	European Dutch	Egypt
United Brethren in Christ	Methodist	American	West Africa
United Norse Church in United States	Lutheran	American Norwegians	Madagascar
United Presbyterian Jewish Mission	Presbyterian	Scotch	Marocco
Universities' Mission (Cambridge, Oxford, Durham and Dublin Universities' Mission to Central Africa)	Anglican	English	Nyasaland and Zanzibar
Wachovia Society for Propagating the Gospel	Unity of Brethren	American	Auxiliary
Waldensian Church, The	Presbyterian	Italian	South Africa
Wesleyan Missionary Society	Methodist	English	South and West Africa
West Africa Presbytery	Presbyterian	African	Liberia
West Indies Church of England Missionary-Society	Anglican	British	Rio Pongo
West Indies Methodist Conference (east)	Methodist	British	Antilles and Guiana
West Indies Methodist Conference (west)	Methodist	British	Jamaica and Haiti
[Wettergren's] Free Norse Mission	Undenominational	Norwegian	East Africa
Whately School and Hospital	Anglican	English	Egypt
Winchester Deaconesses	Anglican	British	Kaffraria
Woman's Auxiliary to Protestant Episcopal Society	Anglican	American	Liberia
Woman's Baptist Society *	Baptist (north)	American	Kongo State
Woman's Baptist Society of the West	Baptist (north)	American	Kongo State
Woman's Board**	Congregational	American	South and West Africa
Woman's Board of the Interior†	Congregational	American	South and West Africa
Woman's Christian Temperance Union	Nondenominational	Afrikander	South Africa
Woman's Missionary Society††	Presbyterian	American	West Africa
Woman's Missionary Society of Reformed Episcopal Church	Anglican	American	Liberia
Woman's Missionary Association‡	Presbyterian	English	North Africa
Woman's Missionary Association of United Brethren in Christ	Methodist	American	West Africa
Woman's Missionary Society of the General Synod	Lutheran	American	Liberia
Woman's Missionary Society of the United Presbyterian Church	Presbyterian	American	Egypt

*With American Baptist Missionary Union.
**With American Board.
†With American Board.
††With Presbyterian Board, North.
‡With English Presbyterian Mission Committee.

DIRECTORY OF MISSION-AGENCIES

Name of Society	Polity of Adherents	Nationality of Supporters	Sphere of Operations
Woman's Missionary Society*.	Presbyterian...........	Scotch	South Africa
Woman's Mission=Union**....	Baptist (white)	American ...	West Africa
Women's Mite Missionary Society African Methodist Episcopal Church...............	Methodist (*colored*).	American ...	Haiti
Woman's Oriental Union.....	Lutheran............	German.....	Egypt
World's Federation of Christian Students†............	Interdenominational..	International	Africa
Young Men's Association in Aid of the Baptist Society...	Baptist.............	English	Auxiliary
Young Men's Christian Association....................	Nondenominational..	International	Africa and Freedmen
Young Men's Mission=Society of Birmingham............	Nondenominational..	English	Natal
Young People's Missionary Society	Interdenominational.	American ...	Somalia
Young People's Societies of Christian Endeavor.........	Interdenominational.	International	Africa, Freedmen, Madagascar
Young Women's Christian Association..................	Nondenominational..	International	Africans
Young Women's Christian Temperance Union	Nondenominational..	Afrikander..	South Africa
Zambezi Industrial Mission..	Nondenominational..	British	Nyasaland
Zeist Missionary Society [for Surinam]	Unity of Brethren....	European Dutch.....	Auxiliary
Zenana Mission of Scotch United Presbyterian Church	Presbyterian.........	Scotch.......	Old Calabar
Zulu Missionary Society......	Congregational	Zulu	Gazaland
Zululand Diocesan Mission...	Anglican............	British	Zululand

NAMES RECEIVED TOO LATE FOR CLASSIFICATION

American Christian Convention	Congregational (?)...	American...	?
Morris Christian School......	Undenominational (?)	American ...	West Africa
Self-supporting Industrial Mission......................	Undenominational....	American ...	Nyasaland
Woman's Union Missionary Society	Interdenominational.	American..	Egypt

TOTAL NUMBER OF AGENCIES FOR MISSIONS................................... 310

*With Scotch United Presbyterian Board of Missions.
**With Southern Baptist Convention.
†This includes the following organizations that promote the evangelization of African peoples: in America, the Student=Volunteer Movement for Foreign Missions; in Britain, the Student=Volunteer Missionary Union; in Germany, the University Christian Alliance; in Scandinavia, the University Christian Movement; in South Africa, the Students' Christian Association; and, perhaps, the Student Christian Movement in Mission=Lands. The official statement as to the Federation and the Movements leaves it uncertain whether these should not be entered separately in this list as independent and national organizations. If it be an error to enumerate the Federation and the Movements as one body instead of seven, it seems better to err by understatement than by overstatement. In the case of the German, Scandinavian and South African Movements, it is feared that their mission=department has not here received its technically correct title, if, as with the American and British Movements, it has a specific name.

NOTE

In addition to these corporate or organized agencies for missions, there are individuals of different denominations working as independent missionaries. It is manifestly impossible to ascertain their names, number or place, but there are known to be representatives of the Anglican and Lutheran communions and of the Plymouth Brethren promoting individual missionary efforts, as well as other free=lances of no denomination or of several. Some chaplains of the British government do African missionary work, and thus the British empire in its official capacity might be regarded as an actual missionary. So far as the Belgian, French, German, Portuguese and Spanish administrations (papal) in Africa and its islands have governmental chaplains (priests) who also act as missionaries among the natives, these governments likewise would assume a missionary character.

The Dennis statistics mention local organizations within a mission, such, *e. g.*, as the Boys' Brigade at Gordon Memorial, a station of the Scotch Free Presbyterians. As this Brigade owes its origin and support to missionaries and their home=society, it is not an organization for the promotion of missions. So with other bodies dependent on a church or a society that sustains missions: they are parts of missions rather than missions themselves. The *Statistical Survey* that constitutes the first appendix mentions many such, and is a significant revelation of the multifarious activities within an African mission.

CLASS B

Classified Catalog, according to Creed or Polity, of Church=Bodies in Africa (Associations, Dioceses, Synods, Unions)

ANGLICAN

Diocese of Bloemfontein
Diocese of Cape Town
Diocese of Cape Palmas (with the Protestant Episcopal Church)
Diocese of East Central Africa (Ibea, U=Ganda and Zanzibar)
Diocese of Grahamston
Diocese of Lebombo
Diocese of Likoma (Nyasaland)
Diocese of Madagascar
Diocese of Ma=Shunaland
Diocese of Mauritius
Diocese of Pieter Maritzburg
Diocese of Pretoria
Diocese of Saint Helena
Diocese of Sierra Leone
Diocese of West Central Africa (Lagos, Niger Territory, Sudan)
Diocese of Zululand

BAPTIST

Baptist Church at Kamerun (Negro)
Baptist Union of Liberia (Negro)
Baptist Union of South Africa (White)
Independent Dutch Baptist Church in Transvaal (White)
These Baptist church=bodies in Africa also act as African mission=societies.

CONGREGATIONAL

Congregational Union of Madagascar (Hova)
Congregational Union of South Africa (British)
Both of these Congregational church=bodies in Africa also act as African mission=societies.
It is believed that in Sierra Leone there is a native Lady Huntingdon Connexion, independent of the missionary society sustained by that church in England.
Zululand Association of Congregational Churches (Native)

KOPT

The Koptic church in Abyssinia and Egypt forms two church=bodies with administrative divisions and organizations of their own.

LUTHERAN

Dutch Lutheran Association of Cape Colony (white)
This is believed to do mission=work.
Synod of North Transvaal (Organization formed by the Berlin Society)
Synod of South Transvaal (Organization formed by the Berlin Society)
It is questioned whether these synods have independent existence.

DIRECTORY OF MISSION=AGENCIES 813

METHODIST

Liberian [now African] Methodist Conference (Negro)
  Does this promote missions?
Sierra Leone Church=District (including Gambia Mission, now independent)
South African Wesleyan Conference (White)

PRESBYTERIAN

Christian Reformed Church in the South African Republic (Boers)
Dutch Reformed Church in Cape Colony (Boers and Kafirs)
Dutch Reformed Church in Natal (Boers)
Dutch Reformed Church in Orange Free State (Boers)
Dutch Reformed Church in South African Republic (Boers)
  Individual laymen, ministers and parishes among these Dutch Presbyterians promote missions.
Gabun and Corisco Presbytery (With the Presbyterian Church in the United States, north)
Presbytery of Egypt (With United Presbyterians of the United States)
Synod of South Africa (Organization of the Free and the United Presbyterians, (Scotch)
West Africa Presbytery (Liberian Negroes with the Presbyterian Church in the United States, north)
  The native presbyteries of Egypt, Gabun and Liberia promote missions.
  The union of Presbyterian churches in Cape Colony and Natal promotes missions in its character of a colonial church=body.

ROMAN

Alexandria, Patriarchate of
Apostolic Delegation: Egypt and Arabia
Apostolic Prefectures: Basutuland, the Gold Coast, the Lower Niger and the Orange River
Apostolic Vicariats:
  Abyssinia
  Benin
  Cape of Good Hope (three divisions)
  Egypt (Koptic and Latin Rites)
  Gallaland
  Guinea
  Ivory Coast
  Kongo State (four subdivisions)
  Madagascar
  Natal
  Orange Free State
  Sahara
  Senegambia
  Sierra Leone
  Sûdan
  Tanganika
  U=Nyanyembe
  Upper Nile
  Victoria Nyanza (two subdivisions)
  Zanguebar
Archbishoprics:
  Algiers
  Carthage (A metropolitan see, its bishop the primate of Africa)
Bishoprics:
  Angola, Lower Guinea (Suffragan of Lisbon)
  Angra, Azores Islands (Suffragan of Lisbon)
  Ceuta
  Constantine (Suffragan of Algiers)
  Funchal, Madeira Islands (Suffragan of Lisbon)
  Hippo=Oran (Suffragan of Algiers)
  Port Louis, Mauritius (Suffragan of the Holy See)
  Port Victoria, Seychelles (Directly subject to the Holy See)
  Saint Denis, Reunion Island (Suffragan of Bordeaux)
  San Cristoval da Laguna, Canary Islands (Suffragan of Seville)
  Sao Thome, Gulf of Guinea (Suffragan of Lisbon)
  Santiago, Cape Verd Islands (Suffragan of Lisbon)
Koptic Rite:
  Koptic Vicar=Apostolic
  Latin Vicar=Apostolic

Gross Total of Agencies for the Christianization of African Peoples (both church=bodies in Africa and missionary=societies included) 406
Counted twice 14

Net Total.. 392

NUMERICAL RECAPITULATIONS

Number of Protestant and Roman Societies Working in Africa and Madagascar*... 285
Africa 274
Madagascar 44
Mauritius 6

Number of Societies Working Among Freedmen** 44
In Antilles 29
In Canada 1
In South America 6
In United States 16

Gross Total 52
Working in two or more fields 8

Net Total 44
Number of Protestant Societies among all African Peoples† 285
Number of Roman Societies among all African Peoples 34
Number of Protestant Church=Bodies in Africa and Madagascar 37
Number of Roman Church=bodies in Africa and Madagascar 48
Protestant Societies of Strictly Missionary Character operating in Africa and its Islands†† 140
Protestant Societies of Auxiliary Character operating in Africa and the Islands 96
Protestant Educational Societies operating in Africa and Islands 12
Protestant Literature Societies 29
Protestant Medical Societies 8
Protestant Sunday-School Societies 3
Protestant Unclassifiable Societies (Chiefly Raisers of Funds) 9
Protestant Women's Societies 34
Protestant Women's Societies classified‡
  Auxiliary 22
  Independent (including Anglican sisterhoods and Luthero=Presbyterian deaconesses) 12

RECAPITULATIONS, ACCORDING TO CREED AND POLITY, OF THE MISSION=SOCIETIES FOR AFRICA AND MADAGASCAR‡‡

Anglican|| (and Episcopal) 49
Baptist 21
Congregational 22
Interdenominational (union of two or more denominations) 30
Lutheran 23
Methodist 22
Nondenominational (societies not of strictly spiritual scope) 31
Presbyterian 48
Roman 34
Unity of Brethren 5

*Auxiliaries included, church=bodies excluded.
**Auxiliaries are excluded.
†Auxiliaries are included.
††Women's auxiliary societies are excluded, women's independent societies included.
‡With these may be classed, in addition, four children's organizations of various kinds. There are also five societies for the Christianization of the Jews, that work in Africa.
‡‡Auxiliaries included.
||This and its Protestant sister=communions are represented in Africa by the following denominations:
The Anglican communion comprises the Church of England (established); the Church of England (?Episcopal Church) in Cape Colony (disendowed); the Church of England in Natal (disendowed); the Church of England in Sierra Leone; in Lagos; the Church of England in the West Indies; the Protestant Episcopal Church in the United States; and the Scotch Episcopal Church.
The Baptist order is represented in Africa through the following branches: the

DIRECTORY OF MISSION=AGENCIES 815

Baptist churches (Calvinist) of England; a Baptist congregation (Boer) in Transvaal; a Baptist congregation (*colored*) in Kamerun; the Baptist churches (*colored*) of Jamaica; the Baptist Foreign Missionary Convention (*colored*) in the United States (north); the Baptist General Association (*colored*) in the United States (north); the Baptist Union (*colored*) of Liberia; the Baptists of Lagos (*colored*); the Baptist Union (colonists) of South Africa; the Northern Baptists (white) of the United States; and the Southern Baptist Convention (white) of the United States (south). Among American Baptist bodies is included the North Carolina State Convention, though its denominational connection is unspecified.

The Congregational faith and order have the following representatives working in Africa: The Congregational Churches of Canada, of England, of Madagascar, of South Africa (colonists) and of the United States; together with the American Disciples, the Free Churches of Norway and of Sweden, the Lady Huntingdon Connexion in Great Britain (and also? in Sierra Leone?), the Scandinavian Alliance in the United States, and the Zulu Congregational Churches (native).

Interdenominationalism is represented by such organizations as the Basel Society, the Christian Endeavor Societies, the International Missionary Union, the Religious Tract Society and the Young Men's and Young Women's Christian Associations. Strict analysis and exact numbering are here impracticable.

The Lutheran bodies working in Africa comprise the Dutch Lutheran Association of Cape Colony; the Established Church of Norway; the Established Church of Sweden; the Finnic Lutheran Church; the General Synod of the Evangelical Lutheran Church in the United States; the Lutheran Church in the German Empire (including the United Evangelical Church of Prussia?) and the United Norse Church in the United States.

The Methodist denominations that interest themselves in African missions are the African Methodist Episcopal Church (*colored*) in the United States; the African Methodist Episcopal Zion Church (*colored*) in the United States; the Bible=Christians of Great Britain; the Free Methodists (white) of the United States; the Liberian Conference (*colored*); the Methodist Episcopal Church in the United States; the Plymouth Brethren (?) of England; the Primitive Methodists of England; the Seventh=Day Adventists (?) of the United States; the Sierra Leone Church=District; the United Brethren in Christ in the United States (not to be confused with the Unity of Brethren or "Moravians"); the United Free Methodist Churches of Great Britain; the Wesleyan Church in England; the Wesleyan Methodist Church of South Africa; the Wesleyan Connexion in the United States; and the Wesleyans of France.

Nondenominational organizations include such bodies as the African Lakes Company, the Medical Missionary Association, the Salvation Army (whose non=observance of the sacraments makes it an order instead of a church) and the Society of Friends (which is self=confessedly not a church). Exact accuracy of enumeration is impracticable.

The Presbyterian polity promotes African missions through the following denominations: the Christian Reformed Church in South Africa; the Dutch Reformed Church in Cape Colony; in Holland; in Natal; in the Orange Free State; and in the South African Republic or Transvaal; through the Established Church of Scotland; the Free Church of Scotland; the Free Churches of French Switzerland; the Presbyterian Church in England; the Presbyterian Church in Jamaica; the Presbyterian Church in the United States (north) with presbyteries in Gabun and Liberia; the Presbyterian Church (south) in the United States; the Reformed Church (Huguenots) of France; the Reformed Church in Germany (with native branches in Transvaal?); the Reformed Presbyterian Church in Scotland and in the United States; the United Presbyterian Church of Scotland (with presbyteries in South Africa?); the United Presbyterian Church in the United States (with an Egyptian presbytery); and the Waldensian Church of Italy.

The Roman communion works in Africa through the Catholics of Austria, Belgium, England, France, Germany, Ireland, Italy, Portugal and Spain. The Roman Catholics proselytized from the Ethiopic, Greek, Koptic and Syriac rites might possibly be included.

The Unity of Brethren ("Moravians") works in Africa through the English, German and West Indian provinces.

Total Number of Communions: 8; Total of Denominations: 74.

DIRECTORY OF MISSION-AGENCIES

RECAPITULATIONS, ACCORDING TO NATIONALITY, OF MISSIONARY SOCIETIES OPERATING IN AFRICA*

Belgium (papal societies) 7
The British Empire. (Societies supported by British subjects) 144
   African (Bantu-Negro) 3
   Afrikander (Boer and British colonists) 14
   Antillean (British colonists and Negroes) 4
   Canadian 2
   English (Two Catholic organizations) 79
   Hindi 2
   Irish (One Presbyterian (?) society, three Roman societies) 4
   Mauritian 4
   Scotch 30
Denmark (Protestant society) 1
Finland (Protestant society) 1
France (Six Protestant, sixteen Roman, societies) 23
Holland (Protestant societies) 6
Germany (Three Roman societies) 20
International (Five Catholic orders, five Protestant organizations) 10
Italy (Two Catholic bodies, one Protestant organization) 3
Norway (Protestant societies) 5
Portugal .... ?
Spain (Roman) .... 1?
Sweden (Protestant societies) 9
Switzerland (Protestant societies). One of these is Franco-Swiss; two are German Swiss) 3
United States (Protestant societies) 59

MISCELLANEOUS RECAPITULATIONS OF MISSION-SOCIETIES

Societies supported by African Negroes 10
Societies sustained by American Freedmen 4
Societies sustained by Negroes in West Indies 4
Societies sustained by Canadian Negroes 1
Koptic Societies .... (2 ?)1
Malagasy Societies 2
South African Societies** 20

*Auxiliary Societies and Madagascar are included. Work among any American Negroes is excluded.
**This enumeration differs from that under the heading, "British Empire," sub-headings, "African" and "Afrikander." That excluded the Boers of Orange Free State and the South African Republic; this, in order to show the full extent of missionary activity among all Afrikanders in South Africa, includes the Dutch republics as well as the British colonies.

NOTE

None of the organizations mentioned in this directory has been listed until and unless authenticated by apparently reliable authority. Where doubt existed, exclusion, not inclusion, has been practiced, societies being actually omitted. Some, too, have been named but not numbered. The recapitulations understate. Organizations belonging to more than one class, or exercising several kinds of functions, appear two or more times. Hence apparent error and a seeming failure of the totals to tally. Only an approximation to substantial accuracy appears attainable.

October, 1898.

NATIVE ADHERENTS AND COMMUNICANTS

IN

AFRICAN (INCLUDING MALAGASI) MISSIONS

NOTE

These, though based on official returns, are published only as approximations. But they are the outcome of critical and, it is hoped, thorough investigation among *all* accessible sources, and these are not few. It is, accordingly, believed that the following approximate figures are below, rather than above, the true totals. These estimates are given tentatively as a contribution toward the realization of Dr Warneck's and other mission-statisticians' desire that the statistics of missions may become more than "a pious aspiration". These figures should be compared with those in the text, *passim*, for which see the index of subjects, *s. v.*, statistics and the entries of missions; and they can, also, the present compiler trusts, be further verified.
Adherents exclude communicants.

Church-System	Adherents	Communicants
Anglican	?	25,000
Baptist	?	4,500
Congregational	302,245	66,000
Lutheran	82,000	60,000
Methodist	106,600	75,000
Presbyterian	17,000	25,000
Roman	?	250,000
Undenominational (Basel Society, Friends, North Africa Mission, *etc*)	?	10,000
Unity of Brethren	10,000	3,500
Totals	517,845	519,000

ERRATA

P. 801, Church of Norway Mission: *for* Madagascar and Zululand *read* Zululand.
802, Congregation of Marists: *add* Roman, French and South Africa.
803, East Friesland Society: *see* note two.
803, Note four: *see* Evangelical Missionary Society, p. 804.
804, Evangelical Society for East Africa: *see* note four, p. 803.
807, Norse Medical Mission: *see* Norse Mission-Society.
807, The North German Society is also known as the Bremen Mission.
809, Society for Prevention of .... Liquor Traffic: *read* Society for the Prevention of the Demoralization of Native Races by the Liquor-Traffic.
809, Note two: *for* 1779 *read* 1799.
811, Total: *for* 310 *read* 355.
813, Gross total: *for* 406 *read* 451.
Net total: *for* 392 *read* 437.
814, Numerical recapitulations:
for 285; 274; 44; 6; 44; 29; 6; 16; 52; 8; 44; 285; 34; 140; 96; 29; 34; 22 and 12
read, respectively,
298; 280; 10; 8; 50; 30; 10; 18; 59; 9; 50; 310; 38; 142; 102; 25; 46; 26 and 20.
814, Recapitulations according to creed: *for* 49; 21; 22; 30; 23; 31; 48; 34; 5 and five
read, respectively, 51; 22; 19; 50; 29; 52; 42; 36; 2 and ten.
816, *For* 7; 144; 3; 14; 79; 4; 23; 6; 20; 5; 1; 9; 59; 4 and 2
read, respectively,
5; 157; 5; 18; 69; 5; 20; 4; 19; 4; 2; 8; 56; 6 and 1.

PRINCIPAL AUTHORITIES
FOR
THE REDEMPTION OF AFRICA

PRINCIPAL AUTHORITIES

PREFATORY NOTE

It is desired to call attention to the fact that many periodicals, reports of societies and works of travel, though used, remain intentionally unnamed. To specify each would have swelled this list to undue proportions. A hundred books by African travelers have been employed, including those from Herodotus to Miss Kingsley, but few proved of value for the present purpose. It is a source of regret to the present writer that he could not in the text avail himself of several authorities whom it would have been a privilege to consult. One is Johnston, whose *British Central Africa* came too late to meet such needs; another is Lawrence; a third, Thompson. A glance at Lawrence's *Modern Missions* showed this to be built on lines so similar to those independently blocked out by myself, that I could not, before writing, have read his work without involuntary imitation and plagiarism. So of Thompson's *Dawn of Protestant Missions*, which traverses ground independently investigated by me for the excursus to the chapter on mission=environments. During publication additional authorities were consulted, and some of these are named, either in the footnotes to the body of the book or in the present list. Atlases of specific historical or scientific value, books of travel for missionary purposes and the signed articles of specialists in reference=works receive mention; because the statements of such authorities, when interpreted and revised in the light of our broadest and most recent knowledge, become original sources. To indicate the Protestant or the Roman relation of the respective authors, the names of Protestants are printed in roman type, of Catholics in capitals. Titles are given in the briefest form that seems advisable.

Names of Authors	Titles of Works
Adams, Cyrus C.	Africa as a Factor in Civilization.
Alder	Wesleyan Missions.
Allen and McClure	Two Hundred Years: History of the S. P. C. K., 1698=1898.
Allman	Ptolemy.
ALZOG, J. B.	Manual of Church=History; English ed.
American Board, The	Historic Sketch of Missions in Africa.
Anderson, M.	Presbyterianism: its Relation to the Negro.
Anderson, Rufus (ed.)	Memorial Volume of the American Bd.
Anderson, Rufus	Foreign Missions.
Arnold=Forster	Heralds of the Cross.
Arnot, F. S.	(1) Bihé; (2) Garenganze; (3) What Africans Have Done to Develop Africa.
Ashe	Two Kings of U=Ganda.
Atterbury	Muhammadanism in Africa.
Bachman	Moravian Missions.
BAESTEN (Belgian Jesuit)	Précis Historiques.
Bainbridge	Around=the=World Tour of Missions.
Baird	Religion in America.
BALUFFI	Charity of the Church; Eng. edition.
Bancroft	History of the United States.
Barnard and Guyot (eds.)	Johnson's Cyclopedia.
	The Biblical World, (ed. by Harper).
Blaikie	Personal Life of David Livingstone.
Blair	(1) Prosperity of the South Dependent on the Negro; (2) What is the Southern Problem?
Bleby	Romance without Fiction.
Bliss, E. M. (ed.)	Cyclopedia of Missions.
Blumhard	Christian Missions; ed. by Barth.
Blyden	Christianity, Islam and the Negro.
Boegner	African Missions of French and Swiss Presbyterians.
Bowen, J. E.	Conflict of East and West in Egypt.
Bowen, T. J.	Central Africa.
Brackett	Negro in Maryland, The.
Brown, Robert	(1) Bibliography of Marocco; (2) Story of Africa.

Names of Authors	Titles of Works
Brown, Wm.	History of Propagation of Christianity.
Browne, Geo.	History of the British Bible Society.
Bryce	Impressions of South Africa.
Buhl	*Basler Missionen auf Gold=Kueste.*
Burkhardt	*Kleine Mission's=Bibliothek.*
Butler	Ancient Coptic Churches.
Campbell	Maritime Discovery and Missions.
Carroll (ed.)	Report on Statistics of Churches in U. S., 11th Census, 1890.
Carlyle	South African Mission=Fields.
Centenary Conference on Protestant Missions, 1888: Report.	
CERRI	Account of the State of the Roman Religion.
CHALIPPE	Life of Francis of Assisi (Eng. trans.)
CHALLONER	Missionary=Priests.
Chapin	Missionary Gazetteer.
Charlesworth	Africa's Mountain Valley.
Chicago Congress on Africa, 1893:	Addresses and Essays.

(*The papers and speeches of this world=congress at the Columbian exposition include more than one hundred unpublished manuscripts. They remain in the care of the secretary of the African congress; and he has enjoyed access to them in the preparation of the present work*).

Choules and Smith	Origin of Missions.
Christlieb	Foreign Missions.
Church Missionary Society	Church Missionary Atlas.
Church Missionary Society	Mercy and Truth.
Clark (*et al.*)	Voice of Jubilee (Narrative of Baptist Missions, Jamaica).
CLARKE (English Jesuit), ed. and trans.	Cardinal Lavigerie.
Clowes	Black America.
Cox	The Crusades.
CRAMOISY	History of Events in Ethiopia (French trans. from Italian letters of 1620=24).
Croil	The Missionary Problem.
Crowther and Taylor	The Gospel on the Niger.
Cust	(1) *Africa Rediviva;* (2) Articles in Magazines; (3) Letters; (4) Missionary Map of Africa; (5) Modern Languages of Africa; (6) Notes on Missionary Subjects.
Daggett, Mrs. L. H. (ed.)	Historical Sketches of Woman's Missionary Societies.
DAIGNOULT (S. J.)	Mission of the Zambezi.

Names of Authors	Titles of Works
Darmesteter	The Mahdi.
D'Aubigne	History of the Reformation.
Davies	Illustrated Hand=book on Africa. (The title is a misnomer. The book devotes itself to Taylor's missions).
Dawson	History of Bp. Hannington's Life and Work.
Denison	Foreign Work of Episcopal Church.
Dorchester	(1) Christianity in the United States; (2) Problem of Religious Progress.
Dunelm (ed.)	Reports of Boards of Missions of Canterbury and York, 1894.
Eaton	Twenty=five Years of Negro Education.
Edwards, Bela B.	Missionary Gazetteer.
Elliott	New England History.
Ellis	(1) History of Madagascar; (2) The Martyr Church; (3) Three Visits.
Felkin	(1) Disease and Medicine in Africa; (2) Geographical Distribution of Tropical Diseases in Africa.
Fisher, Geo. P.	(1) History of the Christian Church; (2) Discussions in History and Theology.
Flickinger and McKee	Missions of the United Brethren in Christ.
FOLEY	Records of the English Province of the Soc. Jesu.
Geddes	Church=History of Ethiopia.
Gibbon	History of the Decline . . . of the Roman Empire; with notes by Milman.
Gobat	Journal in Abyssinia.
Good	(1) Ba=Ntu Theology; (2) Negro Nature=Religions.
Gracey	Manual of Missions.
Gracey, Mrs. J. T.	Woman's Work for African Women.
Great Britain: Parliament: Com.	Report on Aboriginal Tribes.
Green	Presbyterian Missions; with notes by Lowrie.
Grout	Zululand.
Grundemann	(1) *Allgemeiner Missions=Atlas;* (2) *Neuer Missions=Atlas.*

Names of Authors	Titles of Works
GRUSSENMEYER	*Vingt=cinq annees en France et Afrique;* Englished and enlarged by CLARKE as Cardinal Lavigerie and the Slave=Trade.
Guericke	Manual of Church=History; trans. by Shedd.
Guinness, jr., H. G.	African Missions of English Baptists.
Guizot	History of Civilization.
Gundert	*Evangelische Mission, 3te auflage.*
H., Mrs. J. W. (née Mackay)	A. M. Mackay.
Haines	Islam as a Missionary.
Hallam	View of the . . . Middle Ages.
Hammond	What American Negroes owe Africa.
Hannington	Last Journals.
Harrison	The Gospel among the Slaves.
Hase	History of the Church; trans. by Blumenthal and Wing.
Hartzell	Freedmen's Work of American Methodists.
Hawkins	Historical Notices of the Missions of the Church of England in the North American Colonies Previous to Independence.
Haygood	(1) Our Brother in Black; (2) Pleas for Progress.
Heanley (ed.)	Central Africa.
Headland	Brief Sketches of [Anglican] Missions.
Heeren	Historical Researches.
Helps	Life of Columbus.
Henderson	African Colonization by American Negroes.
Hepburn	Twenty Years in Khama's Country.
Herivel	Haiti and the Gospel.
Hervey	The Story of Baptist Missions.
Herzog	Religious Cyclopedia; ed. by Schaff.
Hesse	*Missiongesellschaften.*
Hewitt	Sketches of English Church=History in South Africa.
Hodder (editor)	Conquests of the Cross.
Hole	Early History of the Church Society.
Holley	Christendom's Debt to the Black Republics of the Antilles.
Holsey, Bishop	Autobiography.
Hoole	Year=Book of Missions.
Hore, Capt. E. C.	Lake Tanganika.
Horne	Story of the London Society.
Houghton	Women of the Orient.
Hughes	Dark Africa.
Humboldt	Cosmos; trans. by Otté and Dallas.

Names of Authors	Titles of Works
Hunter	History of the Missions of the Free Church of Scotland.
Hurlburt, W. H.	Muhammadanism [The Encyclopedia of Missions, Volume II, pp. 112=125.]
	ILLUSTRATED CATHOLIC MISSIONS.
Imes (American Negro)	The American Negro: His Duty to Africa.
	Independent, The.
International Congregational Council	Authorized Record.
Isenberg and Krapf	Journals.
Jackson	Christianity in Egypt and North Africa.
Jackson, S. M.	Bibliography of Missions.
JACOBINI	The Propaganda.
John, I. G.	Handbook of Methodist Missions.
Johnson, A. N.	African Missions of English Congregationalists.
Johnston, H. H.	British Central Africa.
Johnston, James	Missionary Landscapes.
Johnston, James (Dr.)	Reality vs. Romance.
Johnston, Keith	Africa.
JOUVANCY	*Historia Societatis Jesu.*
Kay	(1) Abyssinia; (2) Algeria.
Keane	(1) Negro, The; (2) Synoptic Table of the Races of North=East Africa; (3) Ethnology.
Keltie	(1) Partition of Africa, The; (2) Statesman's Year=Book.
Kerr, Rob.	Pioneering in Marocco.
Kidder	Missions.
Kletzing and Crogman	Progress of a Race.
Krakenstein	*Kurze Geschichte der Berlin Mission.*
Krapf (See Isenberg)	
Krueger, F. H.	[Africa], Gundert's *Evangelische Mission*, 3d ed., pp. 58=183.
Lane=Poole, S.	(1) Barbary Corsairs; (2) Moors in Spain.
Lange	Commentary on the Scriptures; ed. and trans. by Schaff.
Langford	African Missions of American Episcopalians.
Langston	The Negro in Latin America.
Lansing	Egypt's Princes.
Leavens	(1) African Missions of American Presbyterians; (2) Planting the Kingdom.

Names of Authors	Titles of Works
Lenker	Lutherans in all Lands.
Liggins	The Great Value of Missions.
Little	Madagascar.
Littledale	(1) Council of Trent; (2) Jesuits; (3) Monachism.
Liverpool Conference on Missions	Report.
Livingstone	(1) Cambridge Lectures; (2) Missionary Travels; (3) Narrative of an Expedition to the Zambezi.
Lloyd	North African Church.
Lord	Compendious History of Missions.
Lovedale Mission=Institute	Report, 1890=93 inclusive.
Lowe	(1) Medical Missions; (2) Historical Sketch of the Edinburgh Society.
Lowrie	Manual of Missions of the Presbyterian Church, U. S. A.
Macaulay, Lord	Complete Works.
McCarter	Dutch Reformed Church in South Africa.
McClintock and Strong	Cyclopedia.
Macdonald	(1) Religion in Africa; (2) Religion and Myth [in Africa].
Mackenzie	(1) Austral Africa; (2) Day=Dawn; (3) Light in Dark Places.
Mackinnon	South African Traits.
Maclear	Missions.
Mallard	Plantation Life before Emancipation.
MARSHALL, T. W. M.	Christian Missions.*
Marvin	Life of Cotton Mather.
Mason	Zululand.
Mears	Story of Madagascar.
Merensky	Erinnerungen aus Missionsleben in Transvaal.
Merriam	Historical Sketch of the American Baptist Missionary Union.
MICHAUD	The Crusades.
MIGNE (ed. and pub.)	Dictionnaire des Missions Catholiques; par Lacroix et Djunkovskoy.
Mildmay Conference on Missions	Report.
Milman	Complete Works.
	Missionary Herald; ed. by Strong.
	Missionary Review of the World; ed. by Pierson and others.

*"Marshall's lying book is a sort of Catholic Bible. . . . Marshall has gathered the garbage". (*The Independent*, Dec. 2, 1897). The use of such a book by Roman writers on Protestant missions, a book also half a century behind the times, impugns both their integrity and their intelligence.

Names of Authors	Titles of Works
	MISSIONS CATHOLIQUES.
Mitchell	Foreign Missions.
Moffat, John S.	Lives of Robert and Mary Moffat.
Moffat, Robert	(1) Missionary Scenes; (2) A Life's Labor.
Moister	History of Wesleyan Missions.
Mombert	(1) History of Charles the Great; (2) The Crusades.
Mommsen	(1) History of Rome; (2) Roman Provinces; (3) *Aufklaerungen ueber . . . Afrika* (in Trans. of Saxon Society of Sciences, v. 4, s. 213 *sq.*)
Moore, Mrs E. M.	Negroes' Mission=Work.
Morgan, T. D.	Freedmen's Work of American Baptists.
Morrison	Fathers of the London Missionary Society.
Muir	Rise and Decline of Islam; also, other works on Islam.
Murdock	Mission=Jubilee of the American Baptist Missionary Union.
Myers (ed.)	Centenary of Baptist Mission=Society.
Nassau	Medical Missions in Africa; (2) Bantu Fetish=Worship; (3) Bantu Theology
Nassau *and others*	Historical Sketches of [Presbyterian] Missions.
Neander	General History of the Christian Religion and Church; trans. by Torrey; 6th Am. ed.
Newcomb	Cyclopedia of Missions.
Noble	(1) African Slave=Trade of To=Day; (2) An African Devil's=Mission; (3) Africa's Claim; (4) Captain Great= Heart and His Holy War; (5) Development of Africa; (6) Natural Religion Prophetic of Revelation; (7) Oem Paul: A Representative Boer; (8) Outlook for African Missions; (9) Story of the Chicago Congress on Africa; (10) Missions and Missionaries: an Essay toward a Bibliography. [Bound manuscript volume of seventy=nine pages in Newberry Library]; (11) Evangelical Christianity and Africa; (12) Current Events in Africa: Their Bearing on Christianity; (13) Evangelical Christianity and Africa.
Otken	Ills of the South.

Names of Authors	Titles of Works
Palfrey	History of New England.
Palgrave	West and Central Arabia; (2) Arabia.
Palmer (ed. and trans.)	*Al Qur'an.*
Peschel	Races of Man.
Pitman, Mrs.	Female Missions.
Playfair	(1) Bibliography of Algeria; (2) Scourge of Christendom.
Poole, E. W.	Arabian Society.
Poole, R. S.	(1) Egypt; (2) Cities of Egypt.
Prescott	(1) History of Ferdinand and Isabella; (2) History of Philip II.
Prout	Madagascar.
Pruen	Arab and African.
Quatrefages	(1) The Human Species; (2) The Pygmies; trans. by Starr.
Rankin	Handbook of Presbyterian Missions.
Rappard	*Fuenfzig Jaehre der Pilger Mission.*
Reclus	(1) Africa; ed. by Keane; (2) Ethnography and Ethnology.
Reid	Missions of the Methodist Episcopal Church.
Religious Tract Society	(1) Handbook of Missions; (2) Short Biographies.
Robertson	History of Charles V (with Prescott's Account of His Life after Abdication).
Rowley	(1) Story of the Universities' Mission; (2) Religions of Africa.
Sabatier	Life of Francis of Assisi; trans. by Houghton.
Satterfield	Freedmen's Work of American Presbyterians.
Saunders	The Healer=Preacher.
Schaff	(1) Creeds of Christendom; (2) History of the Christian Church.
SCHREIBER (*Societas Jesu*)	Life of Father Law, S. J.
Schreiber	*Zur Rheinischen Mission.*
Schultze	*Fetichismus.*
Scotland, Free Church of: Ladies' Society	Woman's Work.
Seebohm	Era of the Protestant Revolution.
Seelye	Christian Missions.
SHEA	(1) The Church of Rome; (2) History of the Catholic Church in the United States; (3) Missions of Rome.
Sibree	Madagascar.

Names of Authors	Titles of Works
Slater	Philosophy of Missions.
Slatin	Fire and Sword in Sudan.
SLATTERY	Freedmen's Work of American Catholics.
Smith, Bosworth	Muhammad and Muhammadanism.
Smith, E. R.	African Missions of American Methodists.
Smith, George	African Missions of Scotch Presbyterians.
Smith, Henry Boynton	History of the Christian Church in Chronological Tables.
Smith, Judson	African Missions of American Congregationalists.
Smith, Philip	History of the Christian Church.
Smith, S. F.	Missionary Sketches.
Smith, Wm. Joseph	Anglican Missions in Africa.
SOCIETAS JESU	[*Africana* and other writings.]
Speckmann	*Hermannsburger Mission in Afrika.*
Spencer, Herbert	Descriptive Sociology.
Stanley, A. P.	(1) Lectures on the Eastern Church; (2) Lectures on the Jewish Church.
Stanley, H. M.	(1) How I Found Livingstone; (2) Through the Dark Continent; (3) The Congo; (4) In Darkest Africa.
Steiner	(1) *Reise=Eindruecke in Kamerun;* (2) *Blatt aus Brueder Mission auf Gold=Kueste.*
Stephens	Portugal.
Stevens	Freedmen's Work of the Reformed Episcopal Church.
Stevenson	Dawn of the Modern Mission.
Stewart, Dr	Lovedale Past and Present.
Stock	Story of U=Ganda.
Stowe	The Missionary Enterprise.
Stowell	Mission=Work of the Church.
Student=Volunteer Movement	The Student Missionary Appeal.
Taylor, Wm.	(1) Christian Adventures; (2) Self=Supporting Missions; (3) Story of My Life; (4) The Flaming Torch.
Theal	(1) History of the Boers; (2) Story of South Africa.
Thomas, T. M.	Eleven Years in Africa.
Thompson, A. C.	Moravian Missions.
Titterington	Century of Baptist Missions.
Tomkins	Abraham and His Age.
Townsend	Madagascar.
Tracy (and others)	History of American Missions.

Names of Authors	Titles of Works
Tucker	Under His Banner.
Tunsi, Muhammad al	Journey to Wadai (French version by Perron).
Tupper	African Missions of American Baptists.
Tylor	Anthropology.
Vahl	(1) Classbook of the History of Evangelical Missions [in Danish]; (2) *Missions=Atlas;* (3) Scandinavian Missions to Africa; (4) Statistical Review of Missions.
VIVIEN DE ST=MARTIN	*Le Nord de l'Afrique.*
Walsh	Christian Missions.
Wangemann	(1) *Evangelische Missionsarbeit in Sued Afrika;* (2) *Lebensbilder aus Sued Afrika.*
Warneck	(1) *Mission=Stunden;* (2) *Mission und Cultur;* (3) Outline of Protestant Missions, trans. by T. Smith.
Warren	These for Those.
Watson, Andrew	The American Mission in Egypt, 1854=96.
Weil	Introduction to the Qur'an.
WELD (S. J.)	Mission of the Zambezi.
Wellhausen	Muhammad and Muhammadanism.
Wheeler, Mary S.	First Decade of the Methodist Episcopal Women's Missionary Society.
White, A. Silva	Development of Africa, The.
White, J. C.	Livingstonia Mission.
Williams, E. F.	(1) Freedmen's Work of American Congregationalists; (2) Christian Life in Germany.
Williams, George W.	History of the Negro in America.
Wilson, J. L.	Western Africa.
Wingate	Ten Years' Captivity in the Mahdi's Camp.
Winsor	Christopher Columbus.
Wise	Our [Methodist] Missionary Heroes.
Wood, Norman B.	White Side of a Black Subject.
Wood, Richard	Freedmen's Work of American Friends.
Woodworth	Problems in the Education of the American Negro.
Woolsey (and others)	First Century of the Republic.
Worman	(1) Muhammadanism; (2) Muhammadan Sects.

Names of Authors	Titles of Works
Young, Robert	(1) Light in Darkness; (2) Modern Missions; (3) Success of Missions; (4) Trophies from African Heathenism.
Yule	Prester John.

SUMMARIES

American Authors *named*	99
British " "	122
Other " "	50
Total "	271
Papal Authorities named	23
Protestant " "	260
Secular " "	60
Total	343

In these summaries a distinction is made between an author and an authority. For the sake of discrimination an author is in the two tables, above, regarded as the writer, an authority as the thing written. As a number of the authors named wrote two or more books, the number of authorities exceeds that of authors by seventy=two.

INDEXES

The mouse-hunt and ferret of an index.
                                    Milton

INDEX OF PERSONS

Protestants and others in romans, Catholics in italics.

Abraham: 1, 2, 6, 9, 39, 41, 79.
Abd=allah: 47.
Abd=el=Kader (Abd=ul=Qadir): 53, 58.
Abelard: 111.
Adams, C. C. (quoted): 189.
Adams, Pres. John: 4.
Adelard: 110.
Afrikaner: 267, 648.
Ahmad Gragne: 51.
Ahmadu: 53, 169.
Akbah: 8, 47, 138.
Albrecht, Mrs: 610.
Alexander the Great: 6, 14, 21.
Alfonso the African: 133.
Alzog (quoted): 364, 394, 396.
Amaury: 91.
Amenhotep: 10.
Amru: 46, (quoted) 87.
Anderson (of Old Kalabar): 345.
Apollos: 9, 21.
Araglio: 685.
Arius: 34.
Arnold, T. W. (quoted): 176 *note;* also *passim.*
Arnot: 524, 694.
Arthur, Mary: 589.
Aser: 332, 334.
Athanasius: 2, 24, 33.
Augustine: 2, 32, 35, 86.

Backhouse: 515.
Bacon, Roger (quoted): 148.
Baesten (quoted): xxiv, 373, 381.
Baillie (of Old Kalabar): 346.
Bainbridge (quoted): 726.
Baize: 412.
Baker, Sir Samuel (quoted): 62, 71.
Barnabas: 18.
Baumann (on Islam): 68.
Behm and Wagner (quoted): 158, 734.
Beltrame: 686.
Benson: 232.
Bentley: 705.
Bergier (quoted): 105.
Bermudez: 377.
Bernard of Clairvaux (quoted): 105.
Bessieux: 395.
Bickersteth: 240.
Bilal: 43.
Bismarck: 4, 188.
Blerzey (on Islam): 66.
Bliss, E. M. (quoted): 726.
Bliss, I. G: 544.

Blunt, W. S. (quoted): 64.
Blyden on Islam: 60, 62, 68, 71.
Bogatzky: 213.
Booth, Wm. (quoted): 527.
Boyle: 212, 230, 601.
Bracq (quoted): 680=2.
Bradford, Wm. (quoted): 586.
Braun: 427.
Breto: 685.
Brown, R. (quoted): xi, 14, 687, 740.
Brown, Wm: xii.
Bruce, James: 179, 685 note.
Brun=Renaud on Islam: 69.
Bryce, James (quoted): 438, 750.
Buchanan: 340.
Buckland (quoted): xvii.
Burns, Bishop Francis: 306.
Burton, Sir Richard, on Islam: 62; (on Livingstone) 182.

Ca da Mosto: *See* Mosto, Ca da.
Caedmon (quoted): 2.
Cam: 3.
Campbell: 687.
Cannecattim: 704.
Capers: 495.
Carey, Wm: 215.
Carlyle, Thos. (quoted): 576.
Casalis: 382.
Casas: 139.
Castro: 685.
Cerri (quoted): xiv.
Cervantes: 104.
Chalippe (on Francis of Assisi): 95.
Charlemagne (Charles the Great): 2, 83, 87, 88, 110.
Charles V: 3.
Charmetant (quoted): 665.
Chatelain: 561, 705.
Church, Dean, on Islam: 67.
Clarkson: 4.
Claver: 501.
Clement of Alexandria: 23.
Coillard: 334, (quoted) 534.
Coke: 299, 713.
Coker: 305.
Colenso: 575, 592.
Columbus: 3, 136.
Comber: 688.
Cophetua: 6.
Cotterill: 230.
Covilham: 136.
Cox (quoted): 299, 305.

835

Cromwell, Oliver: 4, 213.
Cross: 155, 556.
Crowther: 21, 241, 590.
Cumming on Moffat: 266 note.
Cust (quoted): xii, xxiv, xxv, 188, 234, 257, 410, 522, 666, 705.
Cyprian: 2, 22.

Daniel: 9.
Dante: 37, 81.
David: 9, 11, 12, 14, 207.
Davies: 498.
Davies, Palmer (quoted): 633.
De Baize: See Baize, De.
Dias: 703.
Diaz: 3, 136.
Dionysius of Halicarnassus (quoted): 646.
Dober: 421.
Doellinger (quoted): 38, 360.
Dominic: 3.
Donatus: 2, 32.
Drummond (quoted): 683, 747.
Dudley (quoted): 482.
Duff: 23, 339.
Duparquet: 686.
Duryak: 686.
Dyke: 333.

Edgerly (of Old Kalabar): 348.
Edward VI of England (quoted): 210.
Edwards, Jonathan: 4, 214.
Eliot, John: 213, 488.
Elmslie (quoted): 160 note.
Emerson (quoted): xi, 168.
Emin Pasha: *See* Schnitzer, Eduard.
Erasmus: 3, (quoted) 150.
Erhard: 691.
"Ethiopian, The": 19.
Eymeric: 141.
Eyo: 346.
Ezekiel: 9, 13.

Felkin: 155.
Ferdinand: 139.
Ferry: 278.
Fliedner: 586.
Fox: 514.
Francis of Assisi: 3, 83, 93, 96, 107, 110.
Francke: 212.
Frere (quoted): 577, (on Livingstone) 697, 716.
Freycinet: 278.
Frumentius: 25.

Gama: 3.
Gambetta: 4.
George, Saint: 6.
Gezo: 169.
Gibbon (quoted): 1 note, 24, 29.
Gibbons, Cardinal (quoted): xxiv.
Glenny (quoted): 522.
Gobat: 245.
Goldie (of Old Kalabar): 345.
Gordon, "Chinese" (quoted): 62, 716.
Gossner: 686.
Gray: 229, 236, 592.
Grenfell: 688=690, 744 note.
Grey: (quoted): 577.

Grotius: 213.
Grout: 705, 707, 718.
Grundemann (quoted): 722.
Grussenmeyer (quoted): 622.

Haig: (quoted): 356, 359.
Haines on Islam: 69.
Hallbeck: 473.
Hamilton: 430.
Hanlon: 410.
Hannington: 408.
Harris on Abyssinia: 173.
Harris, W. T., (quoted): i, 480 (note).
Hartzell: 311 *sq.;* (quoted) 498.
Hastie: 515.
Haven: 306.
Hay, Wm. (quoted): 511.
Hemans: 270.
Henry the Navigator: 3, 127=32.
Hesse (quoted): 158, 448 note.
Heyling: 158, 703.
Hinderer, Mrs: 241.
Hocker: 448.
Holley: 234.
Holliday, Miss: 616.
Homer: 5.
Honorius III: 110
Hopkins: 478, 488.
Hore: 269.
Hosea: 16.
Houghton on Islam: 76.
Huebner (quoted): 574, 743.
Hukoff: 447.
Humboldt on Lull: 119.

Ibn Batutah (quoted): 30 note
Ibn Khaldun: 47.
Isabella: 139.
Isaiah: 9, 12, (quoted) 438.
Isles: 427.

Jackson (quoted): 428.
James the Less: 18.
Jarrie: 685.
Jefferson, Thomas: 4, 184.
Jeremiah: 9, 13.
JESUS THE CHRIST: 16, 17, 41, (quoted) 251.
Joao III: 685.
Job: 9, 12.
John of England, King: 3.
John the Perfect: 133=5.
John, Saint: 9, 15.
Johnson on Islam: 78.
Johnson, James: 751.
Johnson, W. A: 240.
Johnson, H. H. (quoted): xxii, 519, 578, 683 *sq.*, 706, 707, 741.
Johnston, James (quoted): 334.
Joseph: 9.
Joshua: 13:
Joshua, Book of (quoted): 213.
Josiah: 9.
Joubert: 412, 416.
Justinian: 27, 29.

Keane (quoted): 64, 158, 159, 166, 169.
Keltie: xi, (quoted) 189, 741.

INDEX OF PERSONS

Ketchwayo or Cetewayo: 169.
Kilham, Mrs: 515, 614.
King, John: 426.
Kirchner: 685.
Knoblecher: 685.
Khama: 267, 387.
Khu=en=aten: 10.
Koelle: 705.
Krapf: 245, 246, 320, 611, 690.

Lacerda: 685.
Lane=Poole (quoted): 197.
Lavigerie: 4, 63; on Islam 78; 187, 397=414; (quoted) 622; 656=82, 686.
Law (quoted): 387.
Laws: 339, 556, 692.
Leavens (quoted): 325.
Lechmere: 488.
Leibniz: 213, 701.
Leitner: 450.
Lenz (quoted): 62, 69, 71, 743, 745.
Leo Africanus: 48.
Leonard (quoted): 727.
Leopold of Austria: 106.
Leopold of Belgium: 4, 183, 186.
Lepsius: 701.
Le Roy (quoted): 735.
Lichtenstein (quoted): 743.
Lincoln: 4.
Lindley (quoted): 715.
Lisle: 255.
Livingstone: xv; (quoted) 61, 63, 146; 187, 216; (quoted) 260; 267; 284; 339; (quoted) 373, 381; 600; (quoted) 644; 696=700; 748.
Livinhac and *Pascal* (quoted): 583, 634.
Lobengula: 390.
Loch (quoted): 577.
Louis IX of France (St Louis): 3, 83, 87, 97=102.
Louis XIV of France: 4.
Lourdel (quoted): 405.
Loyola: 369, 377.
Lugard (quoted): 706.
Luke: 9, 17, 19, 552.
Lull: 3, 83, 109=26, (quoted) 141, 148; (writings) 117; 701.
Luther: 210.

Macaulay: 4.
Machabees: 9.
Mackay: 231, 248, (quoted) 625; 630=43, 695.
Mackenzie: 236, 593.
Maclear on Livingstone: 697.
McMurtrie (quoted): 620.
Madison: 184.
Mage on Islam: 77.
"Mail, The" (quoted): 159.
Maitland (quoted): 718.
Malan (quoted): 331.
Maltzahn (quoted): 523.
Manoel the Great: 137, 685.
Maples: 238.
Mark: 18.
Marshall: (quoted): 137, 376, 418.
Martyn: 440.
Maspero (quoted): 200.

Massaia: 686.
Mather: 212.
Matheson (quoted): 38 note.
Matthew: 9, 18, (quoted) 459.
Mehemet Ali: 4, 179.
Mendez: 378.
Merensky (quoted): 722 note.
Metternich: 4.
Migne (quoted): 415.
Mills: 265.
Milton (quoted):x, 69, 82, 83.
Miriam: 9.
Mitchell (quoted): 717.
Moffat: 647=56, 673=9, 682, (quoted) 551.
Monica: 580.
Monroe: 4.
Montesino: 139.
Montgomery: 428.
Moore, Joanna: 596.
Moran (quoted): 415.
Morlang: 686.
Moses: 2, 6, 8, 10.
Mosgan: 686.
Mosto, Ca da (quoted): 132.
Msidi or Msiri: 525.
Mtesa: 247.
Mueller, F., on Islam: 73.
Mueller, Max (quoted): 74 Note.
Muhammad XIX, xxii note, 1, 6, 12, 29, 37, 38, 39, 40=45, 57, 58, 61, 75, 176.
Muhammad Ahmad: 53, 57.
Muhammad al Tunsi: 52, 59, 69, 73.
Muhammad Uthman: 55.
Murray: 534, 618.
Mwanga: 408.

Napoleon the Great: 4, 80, 85, 179, 184.
Nassau: 555, 619, 688, 709.
New: 692.
Newcomb (quoted): 722, 729.
Newell: 263.
Nightingale on Livingstone: 700.
Nitschmann: 421.
Nolasco: 104.

Obeid: 195.
Ohrwalder: 686.
O'Neill (quoted): xvii note.
O'Neill (quoted): 716.
Oppel (quoted): 722.
Origen: 24.
Orto: 685.
Othello: 4.
Ouseley: 705.

Pacheco: 685.
Paez: 685 note.
Palgrave on Islam: 75.
Pantænus: 23.
Paris, Matthew (quoted): 108.
Paul: 23.
Paul, Vincent: 4.
Paulitschke (quoted): 54 note.
Peschel (quoted): 157.
Peter: 18.
Petrarch: 3.
Phelps (quoted): 711.
Philip, Dr: 284.

837

838 INDEX OF PERSONS

Philip the Evangelist: 19.
Philo: 15, 23.
Pickering: 701.
Pinkerton and Volney (quoted): 158.
Pliny: 6.
Plutarch (quoted): 198, 576.
Polo, Marco: 31, 50.
Prester (or, Presbyter) John: 3, 135, 150.
Prochet: 332.
Protten: 286, 446.

Quadra: 685.
Quaque: 228.

Radama: 276.
Railton on Salvation Army: 527.
Rameses: 10.
Ramiere (quoted): 665.
Ranavalona: 277, 282.
Ravenstein (quoted): 64.
Reade (quoted): 743, 745.
Rebmann: 247, 690.
Reclus: xi; on Islam, 67, 69, 70; (quoted) 744 and note.
Reed (quoted): 307.
Reichard: 171.
Renan on Islam: 66, 69 note, 71.
Reutlinger: 329.
Rhodes: 188.
Richards: 694.
Richardson: 687 note.
Richelieu: 4.
Richter (quoted): 297.
Riis, 287.
Roberts: 206.
Rolland: 332.
Rousseau: xvi.
Roy: 491.

Sabatier (quoted): 108.
Saker: 256, (quoted) 745.
Saladin: 3, 66, 92.
Salisbury: 278.
Samory: 53.
Savage: 708.
Schaff (quoted): 364 note, 513.
Schmid: 431, 435-7, 454-6.
Schnitzer (Emin Pasha): 57, 62.
Schoen: 705.
Schreiber (quoted): 257.
Schreiber (quoted): 388.
Schweinfurth (quoted) 62, 77 (on Islam), 588, 716.
Scott: 306.
Sechele or Setshele: 267.
Segued or Susneus: 379.
Selous: 167.
Senusi: 45.
Shakspere (quoted): 4.
Sharp (quoted): 523, 718, 737.
Shea (quoted): 108.
Sheppard: 328, 695.
Sibituani: 169.
Sibree (quoted): 785.
Sicard: 380.
Simon of Cyrene: 16.
Simon Zelotes: 18.

Sims: 258, 553.
Slattery: xxiv, 502, 504, 510, (quoted) 501 note.
Smith, B., on Islam: 71.
Smith, Captain John: 4.
Smith, E. R. (quoted): 307, 316.
Smith, Geo., on Lull: 120.
Smith: H. P: 42 note.
Smith, Sydney (quoted): 683.
Smythies: 238.
Solomon: 9, 11, 19.
"Spectator, The" (quoted): 746.
Speke (quoted): 184.
Spitta: 73.
Stanley, A. P. (quoted): 27, 42.
Stanley, H. M., on Islam: 77; on Livingstone: 267 note, 285, 699; 186, 187, 221; (quoted) 236, 254, 257, 259, 395, 625, 626, 753.
Steere: 237.
Stell: 714.
Stevens: 483.
Stevenson: 269.
Stewart, John: 304.
Stewart, Lt. Col. (quoted): 175.
Stewart of Liberia (quoted): 234.
Stewart of Lovedale: 529, 556, 569, 692.
Stock (quoted): 625.
Stompjes: 613.
Stowe, Mrs: 581.
Summers: 557.
Summerville: 687.
Swedenborg: 4.

Talleyrand: 4.
Taney: 501.
Taylor, Canon: xix; (quoted) 68.
Taylor Wm: 306, 308, 313, 618; (quoted) 564, 617.
Tennyson (quoted): xvi, xxv, 120, 152.
Tertullian: 2.
Theodora: 27.
Theodore of Abyssinia: 174, 193, 245, 380.
Theophilus of Sokotra: 30.
Thomas: 18, 31.
Thompson (quoted): 453, 463, 655.
Thompson, Mrs. Crowther: 618.
Thomson on Islam: 68, 72; (quoted) 683, 695, 717.
Thornton: 529 note; (quoted) 235.
Tilly: 520.
"Times, The" (quoted): 745.
Tiyo Soga: 349.
Tozer: 236.
Truth, Sojourner: 581.
Trutter: 687.
Tshaka or Chaka: 169.
Tyler: 708.

Umar II of Egypt: 80.
Umar of Sudan: 53, 56.
Uthman-Dan-Fodie: 52, 53.

Vanderkemp: 280.
Van Orden (quoted): 501 note.
Vaughan: 410; (quoted) 733.
Venn: xiv, 701.
Vergil (quoted): 360.

INDEX OF PERSONS

Vetralla: 703.
Vinco: 686.

Waddell: 343.
Wahab: 52.
Wakefield: 320, 692.
Walker, 515, 708.
Warneck (quoted): 520 note.
Warren (quoted): 717.
Welz: 212; (quoted) 286.
Wesley: 481, 493.
Whately: 245, 593.
White (quoted): 742.
Whitney (quoted): 696, 707.
Whittier (quoted): 477.
Wilberforce: 4.
Wilder: 709, 711.

Wilkins, Ann: 612.
Wilson: 325, 705, 708, 709.
Woodrow: 592.
Wolfall: 211.
Wordsworth (quoted): 102, 122.
Wright (quoted): 477.

Xavier: 3, 372.
Ximenes: 3, 65, 138.

Young (quoted): 692, 746.

Zephaniah: 13, 19.
Zinzendorf: 4, 420 *sq.*, 447, 463, 464, 468, 470.
Zoeller on Islam: 71.
Zuccelli (quoted): 393.

INDEX OF PLACES

Abyssinia: xiv, xviii note, 2, 6, 12, 25, 37, 156, 172=4, 179, 192, 217, 221, 245, 292, 377, 690.
Adamawa: 50, 60.
Aden: 217, 246, 341.
Africa: *See* Index of Subjects, *s.v.* Africa and East, North, South and West African missions. *See*, also, names of countries in this index.
Alexandria: 14, 23.
Algeria: 3, 262, 333, 396, 406, 448, 622, 660=3.
Algiers: 659.
America: 138=9, 465, 480=99, 503, 763.
Americas, the: 478.
Angola: 310, 313, 376.
Antigua: 427.
Antilles: xviii, 228, 251, 299, 421=31, 465, 481, 485, 489, 492, 503, 550, 620.
Arabia: 28, 37, 45, 52, 246.
Ashanti: 70, 517.
Azores: 22 note, 138.

Baboon Glen (Baviansklaof): 435.
Bagirmi: 50, 69.
Bahr=al=Ghazal: 57.
Balololand: 521.
Bantuland: 217, 766.
Banza Manteke: 553.
Barbados: 428.
Barbary: 45, 65.
Barotseland: 334.
Bassa: 234, 253.
Basutoland: 219, 229, 331.
Bechwanaland: 218, 229, 297.
Belgian Kongo: 222, 223, 251, 252, 254, 257, 262, 266, 310, 313, 328, 333, 373, 393, 520, 524, 596, 685, 688, 697.
Belgium: 157, 182.
Benguela: 222, 265.
Bihe: 262, 265.
Blantyre: 222, 340.
Bornu: 49.
Brazil: 426.
Britain: 157, 184, 465.

Calabar: *See* Kalabar and Old Kalabar.
Cameroons: *See* Kamerun.
Canary Islands: 6, 138.
Cape Colony: 51, 217, 218, 219, 220, 222, 292, 294, 302, 303, 309, 330, 433=46, 449, 618.
Cape Verd Islands: 6, 138.
Cayenne: 503.

Central America: 431.
Chad States: See Bornu, Sudan, etc.
Congo: *See* Angola; Belgian, French and Portuguese Kongo; and Kongo.
Corisco: See Gabun.
Cuba: 252.

Dahomé: 70.
Damaraland: *See* German Southwest Africa.
Darfur or Dar=Fur: *See* Fur.
Demerara: 431.
Draa: 82.

East Africa: xxiv, 47, 48, 52, 66, 156, 157, 217, 221, 222, 247, 287, 320, 382, 394, 448, 554.
Egypt: 1, 2, 5, 7, 13, 16, 18, 22=5, 27, 29, 33=5, 37, 46, 58, 82, 92, 179, 191, 217, 220, 244, 292, 351, 357, 358, 448, 548.
England: *See* Britain.
Equatoria: 57.
Eritrea: 156.
Ethiopia: *See* Abyssinia.

Faredgha: 54.
Fernando Po: 220, 221, 256, 319.
Fezzan: 168.
Finland: 288.
France: 83, 157, 158.
French Kongo, Gabun and Ubangi: 333, 373, 393.
Fur, Dar=Fur or Darfur: 49.

Gabun: 219, 222, 264, 325, 395, 555. *See* French Kongo.
Gallaland: 50, 171, 221, 289, 295, 532, 690.
Gambia: 304.
Gao: 48.
Garenganze: 222, 525.
Gazaland: 336. *See* Rhodesia.
German East Africa: 222, 287=8, 448.
German Southwest Africa: 289, 293.
Germany: 157, 178, 465.
Gnadenthal: 439.
Gold Coast: 3, 218, 303, 331, 446, 516, 553.
Grain Coast: *See* Guinea and Liberia.
Great Britain: *See* Britain, Ireland, Scotland.
Guiana: *See* Cayenne (French Guiana), Demerara (British Guiana), Surinam (Dutch Guiana).
Guinea: 45, 219, 446, 518, 563. *See*, also, its territorial divisions.

INDEX OF PLACES 841

Haiti: 234, 251, 318-9.
Harar: 50.
Hausaland: 232.
Hindustan (India): viii, 23.
Holland: 178.

Ilorin: 53.
Inhambani: 314.
Italy: 83.

Jaghbub (Jarabub): 54.
Jamaica: 255, 320, 342, 427.
Jinne: 49.

Kabylia: 333, 522.
Kafraria: 218, 230, 232, 337, 349, 443.
Kamerun: 220, 222, 256, 519.
Kanem: 49.
Katanga: 222, 525.
Katsena: 49.
Kibwezi: 530.
Kimberley: 56.
Khartum: 50.
Kondeland: 448.
Kongo and Kongo Independent State. *See* Angola; Belgian, French and Portuguese Kongo; and Gabun.
Kongo River: 3, 186.
Kordo, Kordo-Fan or Kordofan: 50, 70.
Kufra (Cephro): 22, 51.
Kuruman: 649.

Lagos: 53, 217, 221, 242. *See* Slave Coast and Yariba.
Levant: 658.
Liberia: 185, 218, 219, 221, 233, 251, 253, 255, 263, 288, 305 *sq.*, 318, 324, 554, 563.
Libya: 9, 29.
Livingstonia: 222, 339.
Loanda: *See* Angola.
Loango: *See* French Kongo.
Lovedale: 565.
Lualaba and Luapula: *See* Kongo River.

Madagascar: 50, 217, 221, 230, 233, 271, 291, 333, 515, 549, 554, 555, 718, 728, 732, 758.
Madeira: 6, 130, 138, 558.
Magila: 559.
Malta: 22 note, 246.
Marocco: 18, 31, 47, 63, 349, 536, 558.
Mascat: 51.
Mauritania: *See* Marocco.
Mauritius: x note, 217, 231, 246.
Mediterranean: 7, 15.
Mobangi-Welle or Ubangi: 57, 688.
Mosquitia: 431.
Mozambique: 380-2.

Namaland: 300. *See* German Southwest Africa.
Natal: 219, 220, 221, 264, 290, 294, 296, 338, 516, 519, 563. *See* Zululand.
Niger River: 242.
Nigeria and Nigritia: *See* Sudan.
Nile River: 686, 691, 697.

North Africa: 2, 22, 30, 47, 49, 52, 53, 58, 63, 65, 222, 522, 555, 617, 622.
Nubia: 27, 29, 45, 50, 292.
Nyasaland: 221, 237, 330, 339, 535, 556, 557, 692, 697, 716.

Old Kalabar: 220, 343.
Ophir: 5, 9, 11.
Orange Free State: 219, 294, 330, 760 note.
Orange River: 687.

Pongo River: 220, 228.
Portugal: 83, 90, 157, 177, 186.
Portuguese Kongo: 310, 313, 373, 393. *See* Angola, Kongo.

Qua Ibo: 808.

Red Sea: 37.
Rhodesia: 218, 229, 265, 380, 382-91
Rio Pongo: *See* Pongo River.
Rome: 15, 22, 33.

Sahara: 2, 45, 48, 49, 63, 687 note.
Saint Croix: 424.
Saint Kitt: 424, 429.
Saint Thomas: 421.
Senaar: 50.
Senegal: 333.
Seychelles Islands: 217.
Sheba: 9, 11.
Sierra Leone: 53, 217, 218, 220, 221, 239, 255, 261, 300-304, 318, 319, 320, 321, 336, 489.
Silla: 48.
Simbabye: 11.
Slave Coast: 220:
Sokotra: 30.
Sokotu: 49, 60, 68, 72.
Somalia: 5, 11, 45, 47, 50.
Sonrhai: 49.
South Africa: 156, 158, 228, 251, 262, 268, 300-303, 318, 533, 563. *See* territorial divisions.
South African Republic: 218, 219, 221, 262, 294, 330, 335.
South America: 426, 431.
Spain: 83, 157, 178.
Stellaland: 218.
Sudan: 1, 2, 45, 56, 62, 69, 74, 76, 79, 535, 686. *See* Britain, Egypt, France, Germany and the territorial divisions, Bornu, Equatoria, Wadai, *etc.*
Surinam: 425, 440 (text and note), 471.
Swaziland: 218, 229.

Tanganika: 411, 412.
Tibesti: 49.
Timbuktu: 48, 60, 80.
Tobago: 429.
Togo: 331, 517.
Transvaal: *See* South African Republic.
Tripolitana: 45, 47.
Tunis: 3, 100, 112.
Turkey: 177.

Ubangi: *See* French Kongo and Mobangi=Welle.
Uganda: xi, 71, 217, 248=50, 404=410, 664=8, 735.

Victoria Nyanza or Lake Victoria: 692.

Wadai: 49, 55, 60.
Welle: *See* Mobangi=Welle.
West Africa: 138, 156, 158, 300, 688. *See* Belgium and the other European powers and, also, the territorial divisions.

West Indies: *See* Antilles.

Yariba: 200, 217, 218, 241, 255.

Zambezia: 221, 222, 380=91.
Zambezi River: 186.
Zanguebar: *See* Zanzibar.
Zanzibar: 45, 66, 221, 236, 558.
Zeila: 50.
Zululand: 218, 219, 221, 229, 290, 553, 563, 575, 608, 711, 715.

ly, those of Roman societies in italic, type.

INDEX OF PRINCIPAL SOCIETIES

Societies are recorded here only when their work receives more than mere mention in the body of the book. For additional details and for names of societies not here mentioned consult the appendices and other indexes. Names are entered in this list according to their familiar form, and those of non=Catholic organizations are printed in roman, those of Roman societies in italic, type.

African M. E. Church: 318, 319, 494, 507, 612.
American Baptist Miss. Union: 222, 252, 254, 259, 553, 596, 702.
American Bible=Society: 544, 709.
American Board: 219, 222, 263=5, 553, 563, 608, 709, 711, 715, 718.
American Miss. Association: 220, 261, 489, 609.
"American [United Presbyterian] Mission" (in Egypt): 220, 351=96, 761.
Amirghani: 56.
Association for Furtherance of Christianity: 230.

Baptist Home=Missionary Society: 486, 597.
Baptist Miss. Society: xxi, 219, 222, 255=8, 553, 702.
Baptist Union: 252.
Barmen Mission: *See* North German Society.
Basel Society: xxi, 218, 287, 516, 553, 563, 702.
Berlin Miss. Society ("Berlin I"): xxi, 219, 222, 288, 294, 554, 702.
"Berlin III" (German East Africa Society): 222, 287.
Bible=Lands' Society: 547.
Boer Missions: 222, 330.
Bremen Mission: *See* Rhenish Society.
Brethren's Mission (Arnot's): 222, 524.
British Bible=Society: 539, 702, 704.

Canadian Society: 262.
Capuchins: 392, 393.
Central Sudan (Hausa) Association: 232.
Christian Endeavor Societies: 549.
Christian Faith Society: 231.
Christian Knowledge Society: 231, 702.
Church=Book Society: 232.
Church Miss. Society: xxi, 217, 223, 227, 238=50, 482, 554, 610, 631=43, 691, 702, 718, 753, 761.
Church of Scotland: xxi, 218, 222, 336, 339, 349, 350, 620, 692, 716, 745.
Church=Women's Association: 232.
Colonial Society: 231, 262.
Colored Methodist Church: 494, 508, 511.

Consolidated Convention: 252.
Coral Fund: 232.
Cowley Fathers: 232.

Dominicans: 93, 108, 146, 503.
Dutch Reformed Church: 221, 222, 330, 760.

East Africa Mission: 529=33.
Edinburgh Medical Society: 545.
Episcopal Miss. Society: 219, 233, 235, 482, 554.

Finland Mission=Society: 221, 289, 554.
Foreign Convention: 251.
Franciscans: 106, 146, 581.
Free Churches of French Switzerland: 221, 335, 556.
Free Churches of Norway and Sweden: 262.
Freedmen's Aid Society: 497.
Free Methodists: 318.

General Association: 251.
Gospel=Propagation Society: 216, 220, 221, 228=30, 238, 481, 702, 740.

Hermannsburg Mission: xxi, 220, 295=7, 554.
Holy Spirit Mission: 394.
Huguenot Miss. Society: 618.

International Medical Association: 546.
International Medical Society: 546.
International Missionary Union: 547.

Jesuits: xx, 367, 369=91, 503, 685.

Kaiserswerth Deaconesses: 584, 587=9.
Kharijites: 58.
Knights=Hospitaller, Knights of St. John, Knights of Malta: 105.
Knights=Templar: 105.
Kongo=Balolo Mission: 521, 554.

Ladies' Association: 232.
Leipzig Society: 221, 228.
Livingstone Mission: 520.

844 INDEX OF PRINCIPAL SOCIETIES

London Miss. Society: xxi, 217, 222, 260, 266=71, 280=5, 554, 648=54, 690, 696, 698, 717, 719, 728, 731, 745, 748, 751, 758, 761.
London Society for Jews: 232, 260, 263, 266=70, 280=5.
Lutheran Miss. Soc. of the General Synod (U. S.): 221, 288, 563, 611.

Mercedarians: 104.
Methodist Church South: 495.
Methodist Miss. Society: 304=307, 311, 315, 317, 495, 497, 508, 612, 761.
Methodist Zion Church: 318, 494, 507.
Missionary=Leaves: 232:
"Moravians": xx, 217, 419=74, 480, 613, 740.

National Bible=Society: 545, 702.
National Miss. Society: 221, 289.
Negro Baptist organizations: 485, 507, 761.
"Net, The": 235.
Neukirchen Mission: 222, 288.
North Africa Mission: 222, 522, 555, 617.
North German Society: xxi, 220, 330.
Norwegian Miss. Society: 220, 221, 290, 555, 611, 728.

Our Lady of Africa: See "White Fathers and Sisters".

Paris Society: xxi, 219, 222, 331=5.
Parochial Missions: 235.
Presbyterian Board: 222, 324, 329, 498=9, 509, 555, 619, 709, 761.
Presbyterian Church South: 223, 324, 328, 498, 509.
Primitive Methodists: 221, 319.
Propaganda: xxiv, 365=9, 731.

Qadriya: 56, 80.
"Quakers": 221, 492, 514.

Reformed Episcopal Church: 235, 483.
Religious Tract Society: 538.
Rhenish Mission=Society: 218, 293.

Saint Chrischona Mission: 292.
Saint Joseph Seminary: 505, 510.
Salvation Army: 526.
Scotch Episcopal Church: 230.
Scotch Free Church: xxi, 218, 222, 336=42, 350, 556, 620, 692, 702, 716, 745.

Scotch United Presbyterians: xxi, 218, 220, 336, 338, 342=9, 351, 352.
Senusiya: 45, 50, 54, 55, 72.
Seventh=Day Adventists: 252.
Shiloh or Bassa Mission: 524.
Sierra Leone Society: 235.
"Simpson's Mission": 524.
Society for Christian Faith: *See* Christian Faith Society.
Society for Female Education: 582, 613.
Society for Promoting Christian Knowledge: *See* Christian Knowledge Society.
Society for Propagation of the Gospel: *See* Gospel=Propagation Society.
South Africa General Mission: 533.
South African Miss. Society: 218, 303, 563.
Southern Baptist Convention: 218, 255, 484.
Student=Volunteer Movement: 527=9.
Sudan Pioneer Mission: 535.
Swedish Church Mission: 290.
Swedish. Miss. Society (Congregational): 222.

"Taylor Missions": 223, 308, 313, 316, 557, 563, 564, 617.
Teutonic Knights: 106.
Tijaniya: 56.
Trinitarians: 104.

United Brethren in Christ: 220, 321, 557, 618.
United Free Methodists: 221, 320, 692.
Unity of Brethren: *See* "Moravians".
Universities' Mission: xxi, 221, 236=8, 557, 558, 702, 718.

Wesleyan Connexion: 319.
Wesleyan Miss. Society: 218, 299=304, 319, 563, 612, 713, 761.
West Indies Church of England Pongo Mission: 220, 228.
Whately Hospital: 557.
"White Fathers" and "White Sisters": 399=414, 620=3, 663, 668, 718, 737.
World's Gospel=Union: 536.

Young Men's Christian Association: 527, 535.
Young Men's Miss. Society: 519.

Zambezi Industrial Mission: 535.
Zenana=Mission: 350.

INDEX OF SUBJECTS

See, also, appendices, with indexes of persons, places and principal societies. Individuals, localities and missionary organizations are generally omitted here, though churches, nations and races are included. Countries and men that received special or topical treatment will be found in this index as well as in their more appropriate one.

Missions recorded under countries are indexed under several heads. American missions, *e.g.*, missions promoted by the people of the United States, are indexed as among freedmen, as in Africa (including Madagascar) and as in the Antilles. These Freedmen's, African and Antillean missions, each, are again classified as Anglican, Baptist, Congregational, Lutheran, Methodist, Presbyterian, Roman, undenominational and Unity of Brethren. To ascertain what American Episcopalians are doing among freedmen, see "American missions", subhead "among freedmen" and subtitle "Anglican". Missions recorded under denominations are also indexed in like fashion. Anglican missions, *e.g.*, are entered as among freedmen, as in Africa and as in the Antilles. These fields are each classified by nationalities or races, as American, English, Negro or others, Entries of missions under countries of their supporters enable investigators to see what a people, in all its churches, is doing among Africans. Entries under denominations help to show what a church, in all its national or racial branches, is accomplishing.

Missions in a country, such as Algeria or Cape Colony, *i.e.*, in states, are indexed in names of places. Those in such geographical divisions or mission=fields as East Africa are entered here.

For pages before p. 475 see Volume One; for pages after p. 476, Volume Two.

A=: 161 note.
Abyssinians: 18=20, 25=9, 37, 42, 45, 50, 56, 78.
Adherents: 817.
Africa: development, 160=90; etymology, 5 (note); history, 177=9, 183=5; influence, 8, 14; influenced by Europe, 188=90; missionary=occupation of, xi, xiii, xx, 17=36, 93=151, 217=456, 514=766; mythology, 5, 6; place in history and culture, 1=4; population, 158; size, xxiii, 696; spheres of missions, xviii, 156=8.
African Christendom (non=missionary): Abyssinian, 20, 24=8, 172, 192, 245, 377=9; Egyptian, 2=4; 88, 159, 190, 762; North African, 31, 86, 89 (note); Nubian, 29, 50 (note).
Afrikander: *See* Boer and South African missions.
Akpoto: 244.
American Anglicans: *See* American missions, Anglican missions, *etc.*
AMERICAN (*i.e.*, UNITED STATES) MISSIONS: *among freedmen*, xviii, 477= 512, 763; Anglican, 480=3; Baptist, 483=7, 596=600; Congregational, 487= 91, 609; Friends, 492, 614; Lutheran, 480, 610; Methodist, 299, 311, 493=8; Presbyterian, 499; Roman, 500=505; *in Africa:* Anglican, 219, 228, 233, 235, 554; Baptist, 218, 222, 251=5, 259, 553; Congregational, 219, 220, 222, 261=5, 322, 376, 553, 563; Lutheran, 221, 288, 291, 764; Methodist, 219, 223, 304=19, 321, 555, 618, 764; Presbyterian, 219, 220, 222, 223, 324=9, 555, 619, 688, 695, 709, 716, 739; Roman, 733, 764; undenominational, 222, 524, 535, 537, 544, 546; *in the Antilles*, 220, 228, 234, 427, 429, 485.

Amharic: 538, 703.
Ancient missions: apostolic, 18=21; ecclesiastical, 22; failures, 33; lessons, 34=6; spheres, xx, 18; successes, 3=4.
Anglican bishoprics in Africa: 220, 229, 812.
ANGLICAN MISSIONS: *among freedmen*, 480=3; *in Africa*, 216, 217, 219, 220, 221, 223, 227=50, 253, 260, 261, 287 299 (note), 332, 337 (note), 358 (note), 405, 408=10, 440, 552, 554, 557=8, 589= 96, 630=43, 690, 691, 695, 701, 702, 704, 718, 723, 735, 739, 740, 753, 761, 763, 768=96 *passim*, 799=817 *passim; in the Antilles*, 481; American, 210, 233=6, 482, 554; Antillean, 220, 228; English, 216, 217, 220, 221, 223, 227= 50; Negro, 220, 221, 228, 229, 235, 241, 242, 509, 510, 740, 761, 763; Scotch, 230; South African, 229, 231.
Anglo=American interdenominationalism: 548.
ANTILLEAN MISSIONS (those sustained by West Indians): *among Freedmen*: 234, 252, 255, 299, 343, 430, 763, 769, 771, 781, 785, 787, 792, 794, 799, 802, 805, 809; *in Africa:* Anglican, 228; Baptist, 255; Congregational, 270; Presbyterian, 343; Unity, 430, 431.
ANTILLEAN MISSIONS (those *in* the West Indies): American, 220, 234, 252, 255, 318, 427, 485, 489; British, 288, 252, 255, 299, 342, 428; Canadian, 343 (note); Dutch, 471; German, xviii, 421=9; Anglican, 228, 234, 481; Baptist, 252, 255, 485; Congregational, 489; Friends, 492, 614; Methodist, 299, 493 (note), 495 (note); Presbyterian, 342, 343 (note); Roman, 501, 503; Unity, 420=31.

Apostle Street: 270, 292.
Apostles: 18.
Arabic: 43, 148, 176=7.
Arabs: 36, 44=51, 59, 65, 66, 70, 71, 77, 89, 129, 132, 153, 174=6, 184, 397.
Arts, native, and industries: 167=9, 175.
Ashanti: 70, 163, 708.
Asylums: 791.
AUSTRIAN MISSIONS: 395, 685=6.
Azhar (Cairo University, The Splendid Mosque): 66, 73, 529 (note).

Ba=: 161 note.
Bambara: 69.
Bantu languages: xxiii, 160.
Bantus, the: 46, 48, 51, 134, 164=9, 171, 199=202, 215, 229, 236, 246=50, 254, 256=9, 264=70, 288, 291, 294=7, 303, 310, 313, 326, 330, 332, 334=42, 350, 373, 380, 383, 393, 402, 405=12, 443, 448, 516, 520, 525, 530, 534, 565=78, 626=45, 650=4, 711, 715, 750.
BAPTIST MISSIONS: *among freedmen*: 483= 7, 507=9, 553, 597; *in Africa*: American: 218, 251=5, 259, 553, 596, 763; Antillean, 252, 255; English, 252, 256=9, 553, 688=90, 702; Liberian (Negro), 253; South African, 252; *in the Antilles*: 252, 255, 485.
Bara: 283.
Bari: 70.
Barotse (Ba=Rotse): *See* Rutsi.
Basa: 244.
Bassa: 234, 453.
Basuto (Ba=Suto): *See* Sutu.
BELGIAN MISSIONS (Roman): 384 (note), 392, 732, 804.
Benga: 326, 544.
Berbers: 13, 14, 22, 31, 47, 66, 80, 84, 85, 86, 89, 132, 169, 170, 222, 262, 398, 400, 522, 539, 617, 622, 672, 739, 752, 765.
Bible in missions: 14, 19, 34, 43, 79, 144, 163, 211, 215, 231, 252, 264, 281, 329, 353, 374, 376, 418, 539=45, 577, 641, 650, 654, 676, 702=705, 735, 750, 754.
Bible=versions: 418, 653=4, 676, 703=5, 735, 750, 754, 755, 778=85.
Biblical view of woman: 580.
Bibliographical authorities (mentioned in *footnotes**): 18, 30, 35, 38, 42, 45, 46, 50, 51, 54, 69, 74, 82, 89, 94, 103, 105, 109, 116, 117, 119, 121, 127, 138, 150, 162, 166, 172, 174, 183, 198, 200, 223, 238, 239, 240, 241, 247, 261, 268, 271, 286, 295, 303, 313, 318, 322, 335, 343, 358, 364, 373, 415, 425, 438, 440, 449, 480, 501, 502, 504, 505, 529, 535, 552, 589, 596, 609, 610, 636, 656, 665, 700, 702, 706, 714, 738, 751, 752, 762.
Bibliographical authorities (mentioned in text): xi=xvi, xxiv, 15, 18, 19, 21, 24, 33, 38, 42, 47, 52, 60, 61, 62, 63, 64, 66, 67, 68, 69, 70, 72, 73, 77, 78, 94, 95, 105, 108, 121, 147, 150, 155, 158, 159, 177, 189, 210, 234, 236, 256, 257, 259, 260, 297, 305, 307, 308, 311, 325, 335, 356, 363, 375, 376, 381, 387, 393, 401, 416, 482, 510, 511, 513, 519, 523, 527, 534, 551, 560, 576, 577, 585, 589, 591, 592, 596, 611, 612, 622, 625, 633, 635, 655, 664, 665, 670, 680, 683, 686, 691, 695, 697, 707, 708, 716, 717, 719, 720, 725, 733, 743, 747, 750, 758, 820=31 (principal authorities).
Bird's=eye view of freedmen's missions: 580.
Boarding= and high=schools: 771.
BOER MISSIONS: 51, 178, 185, 213, 221, 222, 297, 330, 339, 433, 441, 529, 535, 618, 761, 795, 803, 805.
Boers (Afrikanders or African=born Dutch): 185, 219, 264, 267, 284, 297, 432, 436, 438, 440, 549, 648.
Bohemian Protestantism: 460.
Bongo: 70.
BRITISH MISSIONS: *See* Antillean, Canadian, denominational, English, Irish, Scotch and South African missions.
Bu=: 161 note.
Bule: 326.
Bullom: 235, 240.
Bushmen: *See* Sans.

CANADIAN MISSIONS: *in Africa*, 262, 343 (note); *in the Antilles*, 343 (note), 495 (note); Congregational, 262; Methodist, 495 (note); Presbyterian, 343 (note).
Capuchins: 393, 396.
Caravan: 384=6, 626, 629, 632=4.
Census, United States, 1890: 506=10.
Characteristics of German missions: 297; of medieval missions, 82=5, 90, 93, 104, 126, 131, 140=9; of mission=spheres, 157.
Chicago Congress on Africa: 491, 549.
Chronology of Islam: 80.
Chwana: 297, 302, 332, 387, 527, 601 *sq.*, 644, 649=54, 717, 749.
Civilization as Christianizer: 575, 676, 712=6.
Climate: 154.
Colleges and universities: 527, 769.
Colonization and missions: 14, 48, 128=34, 177=9, 211, 236, 253, 266, 295, 300, 302, 305, 324, 383, 397, 425, 468, 474, 504, 530=2, 675, 688, 710, 713, 744 (note).
Comity: 216, 239, 258, 292, 297, 318, 327, 332, 337, 342, 352, 363, 387, 403, 405, 409, 467, 411, 548, 664=8, 725.
Commerce and missions: 29, 126=33, 135, 137, 139, 177, 180=3, 185, 187, 211, 221, 243=4, 258 (note), 275, 294, 478, 518=9, 627, 629, 693, 710=2, 719, 756, 760.
Communicants: *among freedmen:* 479, 482, 483, 494, 497, 499, 505, 506=10, 763; *in Africa*, xvi, 134, 159, 191, 218, 720=2, 734, 741, 744 note, 752, 760, 761, 817; (Anglican) 229 and note, 249; (Baptist) 254; (Congregational) 262, 265 (note), 281, 283, 722, 728; (Lutheran) 292, 293, 294, 297; (Methodist) 300, 303, 304, 306, 308, 310, 318, 320, 322; (Presbyterian) 328, 330, 331, 332 and note, 336, 353; (Roman) 374, 415,

*Only distinct authorities are mentioned in this and the next entry. Some are used more than once, but these are entered only once.

722 note, 731; (Unity) 445; (undenominational) 516, 517, 518 (note), 521, 522; *in the Antilles:* 255, 303, 342, 425=30, 482, 485, 503.
Condition of woman: 580=5.
Conferences on missions: 491, 548.
CONGREGATIONAL MISSIONS: *among freedmen*, 261, 487=91, 507, 508, 509, 727; *in Africa*, 217, 219, 222, 250=85, 376, 553, 554, 563, 565, 600=10, 643=5, 647= 54, 674=9, 687, 690, 696=700, 707, 708, 709, 711, 717, 718, 719, 728, 731, 758, 761, 763; *in the Antilles:* 489, 610; American, 219, 220, 222, 261, 262, 263= 6, 268, 376, 487=91, 507, 508, 509, 553, 563, 608=10, 687, 701, 705, 708, 709, 711, 715, 718, 727, 763; Canadian, 262; English, 217, 222, 260, 262, 266= 71, 280=5, 553, 600, 643=5, 647=54, 674= 9, 687, 690, 696, 717, 719, 728, 731, 758, 761; Norse, 262; South African, 262; Swedish, 262.
Converts: 14, 18, 20, 23, 26, 30, 99, 108, 115, 119, 132, 134, 159, 372, 472, 740=2, 744 note, 746=53, 758. *See*, also, Communicants.
Corsairs: 4. *See*, also, Berbers.
Crescentades: *See* Holy War and Islam.
Crusades: 28, 82, 90=102, 208, 414, 668; influence on civilization, 106, 140; on the intellect, 141; on missions, 144; on religion, 142; origin from Islam, 86, 90, 123, 126; participants, 83, 87, 90, 91; results, 126, 140=4; spheres, 83, 87, 91, 94, 97, 100; woman's crusade, 579=624.
Cultural statistics: 794=6.

Dahomans: 70, 167, 241.
Dama (Damara): *See* Ovambo.
DANISH MISSIONS: 179, 286, 470, 471, 517, 610. *See*, also, LUTHERAN MISSIONS.
Dawn of modern papal missions: 395=7, 401, 622.
Dawn of Protestant missions: 150, 178, 185, 203, 207=23, 228, 263, 266, 286, 300, 330 note, 336, 420, 432, 438, 462=4, 474, 478, 481, 488, 492, 493, 498, 515, 537, 538, 581, 613, 614, 647, 739.
Daza=Teda: 169.
Defects of "Moravian" missions: 452.
Development of Africa: 160=90.
Difficulties in founding missions: 103, 133, 180, 208, 245, 263, 268, 278, 281, 289, 293, 296, 310, 312, 320, 322, 325, 346, 349, 351, 385=90, 407, 409, 412, 422, 433, 437, 439, 445, 448, 516, 520, 536, 564, 566, 576, 583, 590, 591, 611, 614, 623, 626=9, 632=45, 650, 661, 667=8, 669, 713=5, 757=9.
Dikele: 544.
Dinka: 70.
Discovery: 83, 104, 126=30, 133, 137. *See*, also, Geography and missions.
Disease: 155 and diagrams.
Distinctive features of Protestant missions: 210=6, 724=5, 730, 734, 737.
Distribution of papal missions: 373, 377, 380, 383, 391=2, 393, 394, 396, 398, 400, 401, 402, 413, 731.

Dominicans: 93, 103, 106, 108, 133, 137, 144=7, 150.
Donatists: 32.
Double versions (diglots): 785.
Dream of Africa: 153.
Dualla: 256.
DUTCH MISSIONS (European Dutch): *in Africa*, 51, 178, 213, 323, 330 and note, 432, 470, 799, 801 note two; *in Surinam:* 425=6, 440 note two, 471, 806, 809, 810, 811.
Dutch Reformed Church: *See* Boer missions.

Early entrances of Protestantism: *See* Dawn of Protestant missions.
EAST AFRICAN MISSIONS: ancient, 30; *Anglican:* 217, 221, 232, 236=8, 246=50, 554, 557, 558, 594, 611, 632=43, 664, 691, 695, 718, 753; *Baptist:* 252; *Congregational:* 222, 697, 717, 811; *Lutheran:* 222, 287, 288, 289; medieval: 137; *Methodist:* 221, 321, 692; modern (*see* denominations); *Muslim:* 48, 51; *Presbyterian:* 222, 323, 334, 339=41, 693, 716, 745, 748; *Roman:* 372, 380=2, 394, 401, 402=12, 633, 664=8, 685; *undenominational:* 530, 534, 539, 548; *Unity:* 217, 448; American: 811; Boer: 222, 339; English: 217, 221, 222, 232, 235, 236=8, 246=50, 321, 410, 534, 553, 554, 556, 557=60, 692, 697, 717; French: 334, 394, 402=12, 633, 664=8; German: 222, 287, 288, 289, 294; Portuguese: 137, 380=2, 685. *See*, also, Madagascarene and Mauritian missions.
Education: Islamic: 66, 72, 99, 198, 529 note; missionary: (ancient) 14=5, 23; (medieval) 108=10, 112, 116, 125, 147, 148; (modern) 211, 216; (Anglican) 230, 231, 233, 234, 235, 238, 241, 246, 249; (Baptist) 253, 256; (Congregational) 263, 266, 268, 281, 283; (Lutheran) 288, 289, 290, 291, 292, 293, 294, 295, 296; (Methodist) 300, 301, 304, 309, 310, 314, 316, 317, 319, 320, 322; (Presbyterian) 326, 327, 329, 331, 332, 336, 337 note, 338, 340, 341, 342, 344, 349, 350, 351, 354, 357, 359; (Roman) 366, 371, 373, 375, 391, 394, 395, 397, 407; (Unity) 426, 427, 430, 431, 435, 439, 441, 445, 451, 452, 474; (freedmen) 482=6 *passim*, 490, 492, 494, 497, 498, 499, 503, 505, 511; (undenominational) 515, 516, 518, 519, 522; 524, 527, 532, 544; (industrial) 563 *sq.*; (women's work); 587, 590, 594, 597, 608, 612, 614, 615, 616, 618, 620, 621; (unclassified) 630, 640, 655, 662, 701, 705, 708, 714, 718, 719, 722 note, 724, 730, 732, 741, 743, 750, 751, 754, 758, 759, 764; (statistics) 769=77.
Efik: 343, 346, 348, 544.
Egba: 242.
Egbo: 344.
Egyptians: 5, 8, 10, 22, 46, 65, 159, 191, 230, 244, 349, 351 *sq.*, 379, 448, 515, 539, 594, 616, 761. *See*, also, Egypt and Kopts.

Emancipation: 32, 68, 131, 133, 173, 180, 185, 216, 219, 255, 282, 343, 423, 426, 427, 486, 488, 501 note, 539, 600, 670, 718.
Emba: 339.
ENGLISH MISSIONS: *among freedmen*, 491 note; *in Africa*, Anglican, 92, 217, 220, 221, 223, 227=33, 235=50, 554, 557, 558, 589-95, 610, 633=43, 690=2, 695, 701, 702, 704, 718, 723, 739, 740, 753, 761, 763; Baptist, 256=9, 553, 688= 9, 702, 704; Congregational, 266 *sq.*, 280 *sq.*, 600=7, 610, 644, 647=56, 687, 690, 697=700, 717, 719, 728, 731, 748=50, 751, 758, 761, 763; Methodist, 300=4, 319, 612, 692, 713, 761; Presbyterian, 349, 351; Roman, 383=91, 410, 735; undenominational, 515, 516, 519, 520= 1, 522, 525, 526, 535, 546, 548, 614, 615, 616; Unity, 470; *in the Antilles*, 228, 255, 299, 424, 428, 481. *See*, also, Scotch missions.
Environments of missions: xx, 14, 15, 23, 152=223, 239, 258, 271=80, 289, 325, 341, 344, 351, 422=3, 433, 442, 518, 522, 525, 626=45, 649, 668.
Episcopal missions: *See* American and Anglican missions.
Eras: of Africa, 177=87; of Islam, 45; of medieval missions, 83, 85, 104, 108, 126; of modern missions, 209, 211, 214, 216, 220, 221, 281, 361, 369, 383, 401, 419, 432, 438, 479, 552, 565, 647, 659, 662, 674, 700.
Ethics, Negro, and intellect: 167.
Ethiopians: 2, 38, 539, 703. *See*, also, Abyssinia and Abyssinians.
Ethiopic (Gheez, Gîz): 27.
Ethiopic church (Abyssinian): 173, 178, 190, 192, 460 note two. *See*, also, Kopts.
"Ethiopic Church, The" (Transvaal): 318, 764 note.
Ethnic stocks: 153, 160=77, 271, 343, 433=5, 442.
Europe in Africa: xiv, 4, 77, 83, 85, 90, 126=39, 157, 177=90, 216, 219, 221, 275=8, 382, 403=4, 409, 438, 660, 661, 664=7, 674=5, 710, 714, 754=7, 759.
Evangelical standards: 210, 214, 216, 462, 466, 469, 472=4, 518, 561, 567=9, 576, 624, 676, 679, 721, 725, 734=6, 750.
Evangelization: 22, 95, 107, 124, 298, 329, 341, 353, 472, 526, 534, 641=3, 676, 750, 762.
Evidence as to converts: 31, 47, 108, 115, 117, 134, 218, 234, 241, 242, 249, 256, 259, 268, 307, 319 (bottom), 332 (Aser), 336, 338, 343, 347, 350, 356, 359, 374, 393, 415, 424, 430, 436, 439, 444, 448, 472, 516, 526, 574=5, 599, 618, 643, 653, 714, 722 note, 740=53, 758, 761.
Ewe: 198, 331.
Expansion of missions: 216, 227, 229, 479, 512, 552, 582, 672, 700, 722, 729, 754=6, 760=5.
Exploration: (ancient) 25; (Islamic) 49; (medieval) 127=30, 132=7; (modern)
179, 186, 216, 247, 267, 268, 269, 326, 328, 348, 489, 524=5, 684=700.
Extinctions of African Christianity: 30 and note, 50 and note, 82=90, 172, 373, 374, 376, 381, 392, 394, 397, 714.
Failures of missions: 32, 34, 48, 51, 69, 76, 83, 103, 108, 126, 133, 137, 149, 180, 228, 236, 305=11, 313, 316, 373, 379, 380, 382, 393, 396, 412, 446=50, 481=2, 503, 510, 520, 526, 536, 575, 612, 650, 668, 677, 713, 733, 735, 737, 739, 741=6, 750, 758, 762, 764.
Fañ (Fang): 70, 162, 199, 326=7, 705.
Fanti: 538.
Fatimites: 65, 170.
Felashas: *See* Israel.
Fellahin: *See* Egyptians and Kopts.
Fetkana: 444.
Fields: of Islam, 45; of missions, xviii, xx, 22, 25, 30, 83=4, 156=8, 271, 424, 477.
Finances of missions: 214, 235, 294, 306, 310, 307 note, 313, 315, 341, 346, 366, 384, 430, 470, 482, 484, 491 and note, 493, 496, 497, 498, 500, 505, 517, 519, 521, 526, 529, 533, 548, 549, 557, 558, 559, 561, 566=9 *passim*, 612, 621, 626= 9, 680, 731, 733, 752, 765.
Fingu: 338, 349.
FINNIC MISSIONS: 221, 289.
Foundling asylums: 791.
Franciscans: 93, 103, 106=8, 110, 127, 133, 138, 144=7, 150, 394, 395.
Freedmen's missions: *See* American and Antillean missions and denominational missions in the West Indies.
Freemasonry: 44, 54, 61, 344 (*egbo*).
FRENCH MISSIONS: *in Africa*, 83, 88, 91, 92, 97=102, 178, 219, 222, 327, 332=5, 379, 382, 392, 394, 397=414, 523 note, 622=3, 633, 656=81, 710, 733, 735, 737=8, 759; *in the Antilles*, 503, 621.
FRIENDS' MISSIONS: *among freedmen*, 492; *in Africa*, 514=6, 614, 722; *in the Antilles*, 428, 492, 614; American, 492, 614; English, 514, 614, 722.
Fulah: 45, 49, 50 note, 52, 60=2, 72, 170, 184, 300, 713.
Funj: 50.
Future of missions: 36, 78, 150=1, 203, 250, 318, 323, 359, 418, 511, 531, 550, 624, 717, 729, 734=6, 750, 753=66.
Fyot: 521.

Ga: 517.
Gaika: 349.
Galeka: 349.
Galla (Oromo): 50 note, 51, 56, 153, 169, 171, 200, 221, 245, 287, 288, 289, 290, 292, 293, 295, 320, 341, 396, 401, 532, 754, 705.
Garamantes (Garamantians): 32, 84.
Gariepine: *See* Khoi=Khoin and San.
Geography and missions: (East Africa) 685, 690, 692, 694, 696; (North Africa) 686, 687, 690, 691; (papal exploration) 684=6; (Protestant exploration) 687=700; (South Africa) 687,

INDEX OF SUBJECTS 849

690; (value of mission=travel) 695=6, 699, 700; (West Africa) 127=30, 132=7, 688, 689, 690. *See*. also, Exploration.
GERMAN MISSIONS: *in Africa*, (Lutheran) 158, 218, 219, 222, 286, 287, 288, 292=8, 554, 587=8, 610, 701, 702, 703, 739; (Presbyterian) 220, 323, 331; (Roman) 392, 686, 733, 904; (undenominational) 218, 516=9, 553, 563, 710; (Unity) 217, 419, 432=56, 739; *in the Antilles*, 421=31.
Germans: 82, 83, 86, 89, 90, 91, 92, 105, 106, 178.
Getulian: 31.
God, idea of: in Islam, 41, 75, 194; in Malagasi religion, 279; in Negro paganism, 73, 198=202, 327, 344.
Gor: 161.
Goraan=Tubu: 170.
Grebo: 234, 544.
Grikwa: 217, 229, 266, 519, 649, 749.
Guineans: 263, 286, 433, 502.
Gwamba: 335.

Haitiens: 184, 234, 485.
Hamitic family: (Berber) 170, 333, 400, 523 and note, 765; (Fulah) 171, 184; (Galla) 171; (Kopt) 159, 172, 191.
Hausa: 164, 232, 243, 705.
Hebrews: *See* Israel.
Herero: 292.
Hindis: 56, 129, 153, 157, 233, 246, 271.
Historic events (1520=1898): 177=9, 183=5, 755=7.
Historical sketch (Madagascar, 1642=1898): 275=8, 382, 710, 719, 758.
Holy war, the: 46, 47, 48 note one, 51, 52, 56, 57, 59, 60, 62, 69 note one, 87, 92.
Hospitals: 39 note one, 149, 238, 245, 264, 292, 293, 391, 450, 516, 534, 554, 555, 556, 557, 558, 561, 586, 588, 590, 662, 730, 788.
"Hottentot": *See* Khoi=Khoin.
Hova missions: 221, 282, 283, 752, 761.
Hovas: 273 *sq*.
Huguenot missions: *See* French and Presbyterian missions.
Huma: 171.
Humanitarian statistics: 791=3.

Ibo: 343.
Idzo: 163.
Imohagh (Tuareg): 49.
Industrial mission=work: 93, 146, 179, 213, 562; (Anglican) 230, 236, 245, 248, 591, 595, 635=40; (Baptist) 252, 256, 598; (Congregational) 263, 267 note one, 281, 490=1, 563, 608, 648, 652, 709, 711; (Lutheran) 288, 295, 298, 563; (Methodist) 302, 310, 314, 563=5, 618; (Presbyterian) 332, 337, 338, 340, 348, 565=78, 620, 709, 764; (Roman) 373, 378, 380, 383, 389, 397, 417, 563, 637; (Unity) 426, 427, 435, 439, 441, 443, 445, 449, 471, 474; (undenominational) 216, 516, 519, 522, 534, 562, 563, 617, 712=3, 750, 762, 765, 773-6.

Infant=homes: 791.
Institutions as missionaries: 23, 84, 91, 93, 103=6, 110, 114, 116, 122, 125, 128, 143, 146, 147, 198, 211, 212, 213, 216, 236, 339, 459, 527=8, 548, 549, 577, 585=9, 659, 663, 736, 760 note, 761 (head).
Interdenominationalism: 212, 213, 222, 516=8, 528, 541, 549, 615, 713, 723, 724.
IRISH MISSIONS: 236, 384 note, 392 (Dominicans) 401, 733, 799, 804 note, 805, 808.
Islam: African ancestry, 37=8; ceremonies, 196; character of adherents, 61=3, 75; Christianity's opportunity, 77=9, 502; chronology, 80; conversions, 44, 46=8, 50, 51, 53, 56=61, 63, 69, 75; creed, 195; culture, 65=8, 70=2; disproof of civilizing power, 50 note, 71=2; education, 73; eras and fields, 45=6; freemasonry, 44, 54, 61; germs, 40=2; heterodoxy, 47, 58, holy wars, 46, 47, 51=3, 56, 57, 59; idea of God, 40, 46, 73, 75; importance, xix, 1, 38; influence, 82, 84, 86, 87, 89, 91, 115, 119, 126, 131, 138, 140=2, 149; lack of spirituality, 44, 58, 59, 61=3. 73, 75; *mahdi, al*, 196; methods, 57=9; missions, 43, 45=57, 59=61; Muhammad, 39=45; Negro, 62, 70=2, 74; numbers, 63; outlook, 77=9, 755; pseudo= Christianity, 38=43, 78; Quran, 193, 582; results, 38, 60, 65, 69, 75, 76, 522; Sahara, 45, 49, 55, 59, 63, 76; schism, 58; sects, 196=8; Senusiya, 45, 54=6, 63, 72; slowness, 30, 47=53, 60, 64, 76; South Africa, 50=1; Sudan (including Guinea and Nubia), 45=6, 48=50, 56, 62, 67, 69, 72; summary, 76=9; views, 38, 39, 42, 52 note, 60, 61=3, 66=8, 71, 75, 77=9, 522=3; Wahabism, 52; woman, 582=3.
Israel: Abyssinian "Jews" (Felashas) 12; Alexandrine Judaism, 14=6; dispersion, 14, 22; Egyptian experience, 9=11, 13; germ of missions, 6, 7, 112; mission=influence, 10, 13, 15, 23, 40; missions to, 18, 20, 23, 222, (Anglican) 233, 235; (Congregational) 262; (Presbyterian) 349, 355, 810; (Roman) 365; (undenominational) 89 note, 544, 558, 754, 801, 805, 808; numbers, 159.
ITALIAN MISSIONS: 83, 91, 93=6, 107, 147, 178, 393, 395, 401 (Franciscans), 733, 800, 810.

Jamaican missions: *See* Antillean missions.
Jesuits: *See* Roman missions and *Societas Jesu*.
Jewish missions, Jews and Judaism: *See* Israel.
Jihad, al: See Holy war, the.
Jolof: 53, 60, 62, 69.

Kabyles: 153, 170, 333, 399, 522.
Kafir: 229, 230, 232, 233, 262, 266, 294,

302, 336-8, 351, 438, 443=5, 534, 538, 563, 565=77 *passim*, 589, 613, 709, 711, 750, 751, 752.
"Kaiserswerth Deaconesses": *See* Women in mission work.
Kamba: 288, 690.
Ki=: 160 note.
Kindergartens: 770.
Khoi=Khoin: 118, 266, 284, 301 (Nama), 330 note, 433=5, 648, 714, 743.
Kololo: 169.
Kombe: 326.
Kongoan: 70, 160, 162, 538, 703.
Kopts: 159, 172, 191, 220, 330, 349, 351 *sq.*, 379, 489, 515, 539, 703, 762.
Korana: 217, 266.
Kru: 317.

Lamtuna: 48 note.
Language: *See* Ethnic stocks.
Lavigerie: birth and education, 657; character, 659, 679=81; contrast with Moffat, 673=9; founder of societies, 663; in Algeria, 396=401, 659=63, 686; in the Levant, 658; in Uganda, 400=10, 637, 664=8, 735; on the Tanganika, 411; opposition to slavers, 187, 413=4, 668=70; other projects, 672; responsibility for Ugandan imbroglio, 664=8; typical missioner, 646; work for Islamites, 78, 397=400, 622, 661, 676, 737.
Lepers: 449, 534, 555, 790 (statistics).
Lessons from missions: (ancient) 31=6; (medieval) 82, 97, 99, 103, 105, 108, 110, 123, 125, 133, 137, 140, 144=6, 148=50; (modern) 208=16, 227, 237, 242, 273, 281, 284, 296, 316, 372, 376, 382, 393, 410, 416=8, 425, 427, 452, 506, 514, 520 and note, 560=1, 564, 570=6, 624, 625, 646=79, 713=6, 729, 734=6, 737, 752=3, 757, 758, 761, 762.
Liberality of mission=ideals: 211=3.
LIBERIAN MISSIONS (Negro): 234 (Cust); 253, 255 (Baptist); 305, 307, 312 (Methodist); 325 (Presbyterian); 724, 761.
Lingi: 327.
Liquor=traffic: 182=3, 190, 242, 243, 254, 258, 267, 288, 348, 742, 746, 747, 756, 759, 760.
Literary statistics: 778=87.
Livingstone: 4, 27, 61, 63, 68, 127, 151, 162, 187, 216, 236, 247, 261, 267 and note, 268, 284=5, 313, 330, 334, 339, 373, 374, 381, 524, 545, 600=7, 644=5, 686, 696=700, 705, 710, 714, 748=9, 751.
Livingstone mission: *See* Baptist and undenominational missions and Belgian Kongo.
Livingstonia mission: *See* Presbyterian and Scotch Missions and Nyasaland.
Lolo: 521.
Louis IX: 87, 97=102, 145, 149.
Lovedale: *See* Industrial mission=work.
Lu= : 160 note.
Lull: bibliography, 117; birth of interest in missions, 109; entrance on life=work, 110; inner life, 118; intellectual nature, 118=20; methods, 108, 110, 111, 113=5, 119, 122=4, 141; missions, 112, 114; prospect of success, 116; rank, 109; results, 120, 125; spiritual life, 121=4, 141.
LUTHERAN MISSIONS: Afrikander, 803; American, 221, 288, 610, 764; Danish, 286, 463; Dutch, 799; Finn, 221, 289; German, 218, 219, 220, 222, 286, 287, 292=7, 463, 610, 764, 800; Norse, 220, 290, 611; Swedish, 221, 287, 289; Swiss, 292; traits, 297. *See*, also, Basel Society and Unity missions.

Ma= : 160 note.
Mackay: *See* Anglican missions and industrial work.
MADAGASCARENE MISSIONS :(Anglican)217, 221, 229, 230; (Congregational) 153, 157, 217, 260, 262, 263, 280=3, 515, 554, 610, 687, 719, 728, 758, 761; (Friends) 221, 515; (Islam) 51, 271; (Lutheran) 221, 291, 555, 611; (Presbyterian) 222, 333, 759; (Roman) 380, 382, 394, 401, 621, 728, 731, 734; (undenominational) xvi, 537=8, 539, 542, 549, 711, 752, 759; (American) 257, 515; (English) 153, 217, 221, 229, 230, 233, 260, 262, 263, 277, 280=3, 515, 538, 539, 542, 554, 610, 614, 687, 719, 728, 752, 758, 761; (French) 222, 277, 333, 382, 394, 401, 621, 728, 731, 734, 759; (Norse) 221, 291, 555, 611. *See*, also, Hova missions and statistical appendixes *passim*.
Madi: 70.
Mahdism: 45, 53, 54, 55, 57, 80, 175, 184, 188, 195=6, 489, 686, 755.
Malay: 51, 180, 272, 433.
Maltese: 246.
Mande (Mandingo): 50, 53, 60, 61, 62, 69, 161, 163, 301, 705.
Mangbattu: 71.
Mangwato: 387.
Mañanja: 340.
Maroons (Bush=Negroes): 425 note, 426, 431.
Masai: 169, 530.
Matabele (Ma=Tabele): *See* Tabili.
Mauritanian: 31.
MAURITIAN MISSIONS: xvii note, 156, 157, 217, 227, 229, 231, 246, 263, 515, 539, 615, 768, 771, 780, 795, 806, 814, 816.
Mbundu: *See* Ngolan.
Medical mission=work: (ancient) 552; (medieval) 146; (modern) 216, 448 note, 561, 724, 730, 762; (Anglican) 231, 245, 246, 552, 554, 557=60, 590, 594, 638; (Baptist) 251, 252, 256, 258, 553; (Congregational) 264, 283, 285, 552, 553, 554, 652; (Lutheran) 287, 292, 293, 298, 554, 555, 586=8; (Methodist) 305, 317, 319, 552, 557; (Presbyterian) 329, 340, 348, 349, 351, 552, 555=6, 620; (Roman) 380, 399, 557; (statistics) 776, 788=90; (Unity) 448, 449, 557; (undenominational) 516, 529, 533, 534, 536, 545=6, 554, 555, 583=4, 617,

INDEX OF SUBJECTS

MEDIEVAL MISSIONS: characteristics, 83=4; marine, 83, 126=130, 132; martial, 83, 97, 104, 105, 123 (See *Crusades*); mercantile, 126; monastic, 93, 103, 106, 122, 144, 146; multiplicity of, 103=106; philanthropic, 103=104; Portuguese, 84, 127, 133=137, 145; predictive, 150; revival of real missions, 93, 103, 109, 151; scholarship and, 109= 126, 141, 147, 150; Spanish, 83, 91, 109, 138; statesmen and, 87, 97, 128, 133, 138, 147. *See*, also, countries and men.
Memluks: 66, 99.
Mende (Mindi): 235, 240, 261, 489.
Mennonites: 537.
METHODIST MISSIONS: *among freedmen*, 493=8, 507=9, 511; *in Africa*, 218, 219, 221, 223, 299=322, 761, 763, 764, 805; *in the Antilles*, 299, 319, 320; American, 304=16, 321; British, 299=303, 319, 320; Cape Colony, 303; Negro, 318, 494, 496, 763, 764 (and note).
MINOR MISSIONS: Anglican, 230=3, 235, 246, 481; ancient, 22, 31; Baptist, 251, 485=6, 805, 807; Congregational, 261, 262, 489, 806; Friends, 492, 516, 804; Islamic, 51; Lutheran, 287=8, 292, 803; medieval, 93, 103=6, 136, 138; Methodist, 317=9, 494, 495 note, 613 (top), 806; Presbyterian, 328, 330, 334, 335, 808; Roman, 382, 394=6, 413, 503, 504, 505, 800, 806, 808; undenominational, 519 (foot), 524, 535, 536, 544=5, 546=8, 613 (top), 763 (top); Unity, 431, 448; American, 218, 220, 234 (foot), 235, 251, 252, 251 (foot), 262, 288, 318=9, 328, 483=5, 489, 492, 505, 524, 537 (top), 613 (top); Belgian, 803, 804, 806, 808; Boer, 221, 323, 330, 760 note; Canadian, 262, 495; Cape and Natalese British, 231, 233, 252, 262, 799, 800, 803; Danish, 286, 808; English, 231=3, 235, 246, 252, 262, 319=20, 349 (foot), 401, 481, 495 note, 516 (center), 519 (foot), 534 (foot), 536, 546 (top); Finnic, 221, 292; French, 103, 222, 334, 413, 809; German, 220, 288, 331, 733; Hova, 262, 282, 283; Irish, 392, 401, 808; Italian, 93, 136, 178, 392, 733, 810; Mauritian, 806; Negro, 218, 220 (head), 220 (foot), 228, 234 (Haiti), 235, 241 (Sierra Leone), 251, 252, 253, 318, 334, 485 (foot), 495 note, 613 (top); Netherlander, 323, 330, 440; Norse, 262, 291 (middle), 810; Portuguese, 138, 392; Scotch, 230 (foot), 232 (top), 336 (center), 338 (foot), 349 (bottom), 350, 524 (foot), 529, 544 (foot), 545 (bottom), 547, 808; Spanish, 392, 801; Swedish, 262, 287, 289; Swiss, 335.
Miscellaneous organizations: 795.
Mission=boats: 796.
Mission=periodicals and press: 786.
Missions: *See* churches, religions or societies; countries; individuals; nations or races; and phases of mission=work.
Modern missions; *See* preceding entries.
Moffat: character, 673=9, 682; Chwana depravity, 649; early life, 647; entrance into missions, 648; incidents, 651, 653, 687; life=work, 649; manifold activities, 266 note, 652; mastering a language, 650; representative missionary, 646; success, 653; translations, 653=4; tributes to, 655=6; views, 676; wife, 649; withdrawal, 655.
Moors: *See* Arabs.
"Moravian" missions: *See* Antillean, German, South and West African and Unity=of=Brethren missions.
Mpangwe: *See* Fañ.
MUSLIM MISSIONS: xi, xix; (medieval) 78=9, 83, 84, 91=103, 105=23, 126, 140=5, 147, 148; (modern) 170, 215, 222, 754=5, 760, 765; (Anglican) 233, 243=4, 245, 246, 529 note, 557, 559, 595, 642; (Congregational) 262; (Lutheran) 287, 292, 588; (Methodist) 301, 523 note; (Presbyterian) 51, 333, 341, 349, 354, 358, 359; (Roman) 362, 365, 369, 372, 397=401, 415, 502, 523, 622, 672, 676, 703, 738; (undenominational) 515, 522, 534, 536, 538, 539, 543, 544, 545, 546, 547, 615=7; (Unity) 448. *See*, also, Islam, missions of.
Muzarabes: 89, 117.
Mzabi: 52.

Nama: 292, 301, 648.
Native agency: (ancient) 18, 22; (Islamite) 37=80 *passim*; (modern) 160, 171, 173, 176, 184 and note, 213; Anglican: 220, 221, 229, 231, 235, 238, 241, 242, 244, 248, 249, 481, 483, 591, 641, 664; Baptist: 252, 257, 485; Congregational: 262, 264, 265, 268, 283, 555, 609, 648, 677, 728, 752; Lutheran: 286, 288, 290, 291, 293, 294, 296, 297, 298; Methodist: 300, 303, 304, 306, 310, 312, 319, 320, 322, 494, 511, 618; Presbyterian: 325, 327, 328, 329, 331, 332, 334, 335, 336, 337, 338, 339, 340, 342, 347, 352, 356, 358, 499, 568; Roman: 366, 370, 374, 376, 395, 397, 411, 414, 672, 677, 731, 734; undenominational: 516, 517, 520, 522, 527, 528, 532, 539, 540, 570, 615, 727, 729, 731, 750, 761, 765; Unity: 426, 430, 441, 443, 445, 446, 452, 613. *See*, also, Negro missions.
Natural science and missions: 707.
Nature=religion: *See* Paganism.
Negro: anthropology, 165; Bantu, 160=2; behavior in missions, 643; capacity for culture, 168; Christian character, 751; church=systems in America, 493, 507; communicants in non=Negro churches, 508; ethics, 167; general characteristics, 166; intellect, 167; location, xviii, 160, 163; missions to, 84, 128, 132=5, 137; *not* condemned by God to slavery, 7; origin of slavery and slaving, 130=2, 138=40; religion, 4, 159, 198=202, 576; rum=trade, 182; slavery and slaving, 180; specific differentiations, 166; Sudanese, 166.

NEGRO MISSIONS (those independently promoted by Negroes themselves): *among American freedmen:* (Baptist) 484, 485; (Congregational) 507; (Methodist) 494 (Presbyterian) 499; (undenominational) 491 (B. T. Washington), 507=8; *in Africa:* (Anglican) 220, 221, 228, 235, 241, 244, 249; (Baptist) 218, 219, 251, 252, 253, 256, 257, 805, 806; (Congregational) 265, 267; (Methodist) 312, 318, 319, 613 (top); (Presbyterian) 340, 810; (undenominational) 724, 799, 808; (Unity) 430; *in the Antilles:* (Baptist) 252, 486 (top), 805; (Methodist) 495 note, 810; (African) 50, 53, 56, 60, 76, 221, 235, 241, 244, 249, 253, 255, 257, 265, 267, 312, 799, 808, 813; (American) 218, 251, 252, 253, 318, 319, 484, 485, 491 (B. T. Washington), 484, 485, 499, 507, 508, 763; (Antillean) 139, 219, 220, 228, 234, 252, 430, 486 (top); (Canadian) 495 note. For missions *to* Negroes consult denominational and national names.
Ngolan: 162, 375, 376, 703, 704, 706.
Ngoni: 339, 535, 716.
Non=missionary versions: 782.
NORSE MISSIONS: (Congregational), 262, 810; (Lutheran) 220, 221, 290=1, 555, 611, 722, 728, 758.
NORTH AFRICAN MISSIONS: *ancient:* xx, 9, 12, 14, 15, 18=36; *Anglican:* 223, 230, 233, 234, 235, 244=6, 557, 594; *Congregational:* 262; *Friends:* 515; *Lutheran:* 158, 221, 222, 290, 292, 588, 703, 739; *medieval:* 82, 89, 92=130, 132, 136, 138, 148, 170, 174; *Methodist:* 523 note, 806; *Muslim:* 42=3, 45, 46=7, 49, 50, 51, 54=5, 58; *Presbyterian:* 220, 333, 349, 350, 351=9, 716, 761; *Roman:* 377=80, 395, 397=401, 413, 622, 659=63, 786, 703, 718, 737; *undenominational:* 222, 522, 536, 539, 544, 548, 555, 615, 617, 809; *Unity:* 218, 222, 448, 739; American, 218, 220, 351=9, 536, 544; Arab, Berber and Negro (*see* Muslim above); Dutch: 330; English: 91, 92, 100, 103, 128, 132 note, 148, 349, 351, 515, 522, 539, 543, 548, 555, 615=7, and Anglican references above; French, 83, 86, 87, 91, 92, 97=102, 323, 333, 380, 396, 397=401, 413=4, 523 note, 622, 659=63, 686, 718, 737, 806; German: 106, 286, 292, 448, 686; Italian: 83, 93=7, 107, 395, 396, 686; Portuguese: 83, 91, 128=30, 132, 136, 149, 174, 377=9, 685; Scotch: 349, 350, 352; Spanish: 83, 87, 91, 104, 106, 109=26, 138, 703; Swedish: 262.
Nubians: 30, 50, 84, 106, 163 note, 172, 703.
Numidians: 31, 86.
Nupe: 243.
Nursing=schools: 776.
Nyai: 330 note.
Nyam=Nyam (Zandeh): 71.

Nyanja: 342, 544.
Nyasan missions: *See* Anglican and Presbyterian missions.
Nyika: 320.
Nyoro: 70.

Orders: ("Cowley Fathers", "Kaiserswerth Deaconesses", knights, *etc.*) *See* Institutions and Index of Societies.
Organizing a mission: beginnings: 361, 383=7, 390, 629, 633, 635, 637, 641; difficulties, 642=3; education, 641; evangelism, 642; expense, 269, 310, 313, 384, 521, 529, 531, 533, 627, 629; industry, 638, 640; native behavior, 643; native money, 626; place of the secular, 637; problems, 643; qualifications, 530, 533, 625, 630, 636, 640; routine, 602, 637=42; travel, 383-7, 632=4; variety, 638.
Orphanages: 791.
Osmanli (Turks): 59 note, 63, 66, 78, 106, 177, 178, 179 note, 180, 210, 214, 352, 357, 404, 502, 542, 622.
Our Lady of Africa: *See* Lavigerie and Roman missions.
Ovambo (Dama): 221, 289, 301 note, 686.

Paganism: 8, 73=4, 159, 190, 198=202, 279, 422, 433=5, 442, 479, 495, 560, 576, 584, 637, 650, 715, 748=9, 754.
Pahuin: *See* Fan.
Papal church=provinces: 391, 401, 408, 813.
"*Pères blancs, les*"; "*sœurs blancs, les*": *See* Lavigerie and Women in mission=work.
Persians: 45, 48, 68 note.
Philology and missions: 700=7. *See*, also, Bible=versions.
Pietism: 321, 462, 463.
Pilgrims: 462, 467.
Plymouth Brethren: 536, 799. *See*, also, Arnot, Garenganze and Undenominational Missions.
Pokomo: 288.
Pondu: 230, 338.
Pongo: 220, 228.
Pongwe: 544.
Portuguese missions: *See* East African, Medieval, North African, Roman and West African missions and Abyssinia, Kongo and Mozambique.
Prefixes, Bantu: xxiii, 160 note.
Preparations for missions: (ancient) 1, 15, 36; (Islamic) 42, 78; (medieval) 33=5, 104, 116, 125, 126, 128, 136, 140=50; (modern) 177=9, 184=8, 203, 207=16, 219, 221, 227, 275=8, 321, 369=70, 401 (middle), 403=4, 420, 433, 438, 460=3, 478, 488, 492, 493 (center), 498, 515, 528, 549, 580=1, 585, 659, 664=5, 684=701, 739, 754=7, 760.
PRESBYTERIAN MISSIONS: *among freedmen*, 498, 507=9; *in Africa*, 213, 217=23 *passim*, 323=59, 555=6, 565=78, 619, 688, 690, 692, 702, 709, 716, 760, 763 and Directory, *passim; in the Antilles*, 220, 342, 343 note; American:

INDEX OF SUBJECTS 853

219, 220, 221, 223, 323, 324=9, 341 note, 555, 619, 688, 695, 709, 716, 739; Antillean: 220, 342; Boer: 221, 330, 760 and note; Canadian: 343 note; Cape Colony and Natal British: 339, 342, 760; English: 349, 351; French: 219, 221, 222, 327, 331, 759; German: 220, 323, 331, 739; Irish (?) 808; Italian: 331 note, 739; Kopt: 220, 349, 351, 754; Liberian (*See* Negro); Negro: 220, 223, 325, 334, 343, 763; Netherlands: 323, 330; Scotch: 217, 218, 220, 222, 323, 324, 336=50, 556, 565=78, 620, 690, 693, 702, 716, 730, 748; Swiss: 220, 323, 335, 556.

Propaganda, Congregatio de, Fide: *See* Roman missions.

Protestant missions: accusation of, 207; contrasts with Rome, 144, 146, 148, 150, 192, 208=9, 211, 212=6 *passim*, 361=4 *passim*, 366, 373, 376, 388=9, 395, 401 (center), 403=5, 407, 409=10, 416=7, 460=1, 464, 500, 504, 510, 514, 540=4; 587, 589, 637, 642, 646, 670, 676=7, 679, 681, 700, 710, 721, 724, 734=40, 750, 758; distinctive features, 215; evangelical ideals, 210=3; expansion, 217=23; liberality and progressiveness, 211; periods, 216; Reformation, 208=10; reply to accusation, 209; revival, 93, 103, 109, 151, 215, 760=6; revivals of religion, 214.

Puritans: 2, 32, 53, 209, 211, 212, 213, 214, 284, 460, 467, 488, 600.

Pygmies: 327. *See*, also, Sans.

"Quakers": *See* Friends missions.
Quran: 582=3. *See*, also, Islam.

Racial traits: 730, 732, 737, 740, 762 (text and note). *See*, also, Ethnic stocks.

Reflex influence: xviii, 8, 21, 33, 34, 39 note, 43, 62, 78, 87, 91, 115, 126, 140=6, 149, 182, 195, 228, 243, 256, 265, 300, 328, 332, 339, 358, 398, 430, 432, 464, 479, 511, 726, 738, 760, 763.

Refuges: 792.

Representative missionaries: (ancient) 23, 26, 29, 580; (Anglican) 229, 234, 238, 240, 241, 245, 247, 250, 481, 554, 592, 593, 690; (Baptist) 256, 257, 596, 688=90, 705 (Bentley); (Congregational) 265, 266, 267, 269, 280, 284, 488, 490, 555, 600, 608, 649, 706, 708, 709, 758; (Lutheran) 158, 245, 247, 286, 287, 290, 292, 298, 588, 610; (medieval) 87, 93, 97, 109, 128, 133, 138, 149; (Methodist) 299, 301, 304, 305, 306, 308, 311, 318, 320, 495, 612, 617, 692; (Muslim) 43=4, 46, 47, 48 note, 49, 51, 52, 54, 56, 57, 87, 92, 122; (Presbyterian) 325, 326, 328, 332, 334, 339, 343, 346, 348, 349, 358, 556, 561, 577, 619, 630, 717; (Roman) 24, 371, 377, 380, 388, 393, 396, 397, 412, 501 note two, 581, 621, 685=6; (undenominational) 491, 492, 515 and note, 522, 524, 528, 530, 534, 535, 544, 615; (Unity) 213, 420, 426, 428, 432, 446, 448, 450, 473, 613, 730.

Results of missions: (civilizing) xiv, xvii, 28, 62=72, 140=1, 245, 250, 253, 256, 259, 277, 282, 321, 324, 326, 340, 345, 347, 359, 374, 380, 431, 439, 441, 443, 445, 449, 479, 501 note one, 512, 516, 557, 571=8, 591, 597=8, 662, 670, 672, 675, 709, 712=9; (colonizing and commercial) 126, 135, 519, 563, 710=1; (ethical and spiritual) 21, 33, 75, 108, 142=3, 145=8, 239, 243, 249, 264, 281, 285, 291, 293, 294, 300, 302, 303, 316, 319, 327, 328, 336, 339, 343, 349, 358, 373, 376, 393, 415, 430, 437, 444, 453, 479, 485, 502, 516, 523, 527, 595, 599, 609, 620, 643, 653, 720=53; (*See*, also, Communicants and Statistics); (geographical) 242, 247, 269, 347, 684=700; (*See*, also, Exploration); (philological) 326, 340, 515, 520, 553, 652, 653, 700=7; (scientific) 554, 707=8; (unclassifiable) 230, 234, 237, 241, 248, 261, 270, 284, 323, 394, 397, 406, 494, 495, 506=10, 543, 561, 617, 623, 648.

ROMAN MISSIONS: *among freedmen and slaves:* 478, 501=5, 510; *in Africa:* 360=418, 556, 633, 637, 562, 563, 656=73, 677, 685, 703, 724, 732=40, 756, 764; aggressiveness, 403; beginnings, 369, 395, 401; Capuchins, 393; distribution, 391, 401; finance, 366; modern crusaders, 369, 403, 413; organization, 361, 366, 368; organizing a mission, 383=7, 390, 633; *Propaganda*, 365; results, 373, 379, 381, 391, 393, 394, 401, 405, 407, 409=10, 415=8, 557, 563, 721, 732=8, 758, 762; theory of church and state, 362; Vatican, 361=8; woman's work, 400, 505, 581, 621; youth, 361; American, 503=5, 733, 764; Belgian, 392, 417, 733, 803; English, 384 note, 410, 733, 799; French, 366, 380, 382, 392, 395, 397=414, 417, 633, 637, 656=73, 674=81 *passim*, 686, 732, 733, 735, 737=8, 802=16 *passim;* German, 392, 685=6, 803; international, 384=90, 392, 394, 802; Irish, 392, 800; Italian, 392, 396; Jesuit, 367, 369=91; Portuguese, 369, 373=9, 380=2, 392; Spanish, 369, 372 (Xavier), 392. (*See*, also, East, North, South and West African missions.)

Rutsi: xxiii, 222, 333, 524, 685.

Sakalava: 283, 291.
S'a=Leonese: 179, 218, 240, 262, 300, 320, 740.
Sans (Bushmen): 74 note, 434, 441=3.
Saracen: *See* Arabs and Islam.
Schools: 765=77, 791. *See*, also, Education.
SCOTCH MISSIONS: *in Africa*: Anglican, 230; Presbyterian (*see* Presbyterian missions); undenominational (?), 525; *in the Antilles:* 342.

Scripture=circulation: 540=5, 785.
See: 161 note.
Secular, the, and the spiritual: 472, 637, 638, 642.
Self=supporting missions: (ancient) 562; (Anglican) 241, 595; (Baptist) 307; (Congregational) 265; (Islamite) 46, 53, 54 note one, 55, 56, 72; (Lutheran) 295; (medieval) 93, 110, 144; (Methodist,) 309=16; (Presbyterian) 569, 620; (Roman) 373, 381, 384, 414, 562; (undenominational) 212, 491 (B. T. Washington), 519, 524, 526, 536, 557, 560, 564, 617, 762; (Unity) 421, 425, 426, 427, 435, 441, 468, 471, 472, 562. See, also, Native Agency.

Seminaries: See Education, Schools, Statistics.
Shemitic races: 153, 171=7, 192=8. See, also, Abyssinia, Arabic, Islam.
Shilluk: 70.
Shukulumbi: 221, 319.
Shuli: 70.
Shuna: 380.
Si = : 161 note.
Sisterhoods: 105, 391, 392, 400, 503, 505, 581, 585=9, 621=2, 659, 736, 761, 795.
Slavery and slave-trade: See America, Arab, Negro.
Societas Jesu: constitution, 370=2; Ethiopia, 377; Kongo, 373; South Africa, 382.
Somali: 47, 50, 56, 169, 170, 290, 341.
South, the: 480=511 passim.
SOUTH AFRICAN MISSIONS: Anglican: 220, 228, 230, 232, 233, 235, 589, 592, 761; Baptist: 252, 805; Congregational: 217, 219, 222, 262, 264, 265, 266, 269, 297, 553, 563, 600=9, 644, 647= 54, 687, 696, 708, 711, 718, 748=50; Friends: 516, 804; Lutheran: 218, 219, 221, 287=97, 554, 804; Methodist: 218, 221, 301=3, 314, 318, 319, 511, 563, 612, 761, 764 note; Presbyterian: 218, 221, 323, 330=8, 342, 349, 350, 351, 555, 566=78; Roman: 383=91, 396, 401; undenominational: 516, 519, 526, 529, 533, 539, 618, 694, 746, 751, 752; Unity: 217, 432, 435=51, 613, 739, 743; American: 219, 263, 264, 265, 314, 318, 511, 544, 553, 608, 618, 687, 694, 705, 708, 709, 711, 716 (top), 717=8, 763, 764 note; Boer: 51, 178, 221, 330, 433, 438, 529, 534, 618, 714, 760 and note, 761, 800, 801, 803, 807, 809, 812, 813, 816; British of Cape Colony and Natal: 231, 233, 252, 262, 302=3, 342, 529, 533, 618, 760, 761, 799= 816 passim; English: 220, 228, 231, 232, 233, 235, 262, 266, 284, 301, 319, 384 note, 515, 516, 519, 526, 539, 542, 543, 589, 592=4, 600=7, 612, 644, 647=56, 674=8 passim, 687, 696=700, 748=51, 799, 805; Finn: 289; French: 331=5; German: 288, 292, 293=8, 435=51; Irish: 802 note; Italian: 810; Negro: 332, 334, 511, 764 note; Norse: 290;

Portuguese: 380; Scotch: 323, 336=8, 349, 350, 351, 556, 566=78; Swedish: 290; Swiss: 335.
Spanish missions: See Medieval and Roman Missions.
Spelling: xxii (text and note), 1 note, 160 note, 301 note, 628 note.
State, the, and missions: (ancient) 28, 30, 36, 86; (Anglican) 244, 812 note; (Baptist) 251, 485; (Congregational) 277, 282, 675; (Islamic) 46, 53; (Lutheran) 286; (medieval) 82, 88, 98, 100, 128, 133, 137, 147, 172; (Methodist) 300, 314=5, 485; (modern) 179, 189, 202, 208=10, 212, 213; (Presbyterian) 327, 330, 333, 567; (Roman) 362, 382, 393, 396, 398, 403=4, 409=10, 416, 503, 660, 661, 668, 675, 685, 739, 758; (undenominational) 257, 501 note one, 515 note, 517, 525, 529; (Unity) 420, 423, 426, 433, 436, 445, 449, 451, 710, 757, 812.
Statistics: (Anglican) 229 and note, 230, 232, 238, 242, 246, 249, 424, 481, 482, 483, 557; (Baptist) 252, 254, 255, 484=7, 763; (Congregational) 260, 265 note, 271, 272, 281, 282, 283, 491, 554, 610, 722, 728; (cultural) 794=6; (educational) 769=77; (freedmen) 479=510 passim, 763; (Islamic) 51, 53, 63=4, 67, 115, 176, 177, 523; (literary) 778= 87; (Lutheran) 291, 293, 294, 297, 555, 587=8, 764; (medical) 788=90; (medieval) 103, 104, 143; (Methodist) 300, 303, 304, 307, 308, 311, 314, 318, 322, 494=8, 763, 764; (modern) xvi, xxv, 157=9, 162, 165, 180, 182, 438, 552, 702, 720 sq., 814=7, 742 note, 744 note, 752, 760; (philanthropic) 791=3; (Presbyterian) 328, 330, 331, 332 and note, 336, 340 note, 342, 353, 354, 499, 555=6, 566 sq., 760 note; (Roman) 370, 374, 375, 384, 391, 402, 415, 501 note, 502, 504, 505, 510, 621, 720, 721, 731=4, 764; (undenominational) 516, 517, 518 note, 521, 522, 526, 528, 533, 537, 539, 549, 615, 618; (Unity) 425=31, 437, 441, 445, 451, 461, 466=7, 470, 471, 472.
Statistics, analysis of: Africa: 720=40, 769= 96, 814=7; Antilles and freedmen: 479=510, 618, 726, 727; contrasts between Protestantism and Rome: 510, 721=2, 732, 734=8; field=forces: 723, 726, 727=30; gains: 722, 760; meaning of gains: 729; papal and Protestant statistics en masse: 720=32, 734.
Stella: 303.
Student, the, and missions: xxv, 15, 21, 23, 33, 73; 109=26, 146=8, 150, 198; 212, 213, 236, 316, 338, 339, 344, 527=9, 616, 618, 769=80 passim, 795, 809 note three, 811 note three.
Sudanese: 52, 62, 69, 175, 180, 196. See, also, Arabs, Islam, Negro and Sudan.
Suez Canal: 185.
Sunday=schools: 796.
Sunnite: 66, 195.

Susu: 240.
Sutu: xxiii, 229, 284, 294, 331, 334, 392.
Swahili: 45, 48, 51, 160, 162, 231, 237, 331.
Swazi: 229, 303.
SWEDISH MISSIONS: 221, 222, 262, 287, 289, 611.
SWISS MISSIONS: 323, 335, 517, 523 note.

Tabili: 229, 267, 380, 383, 389=91, 653, 751.
Tambuki: 443.
Temperance: 791, 810, 811.
Theological seminaries: 769.
Timni (Temne): 235, 714.
Training=schools: 769.
Translations of the Scriptures: *See* Bible= versions.
Tshi: 161 note, 181 note.
Tuareg: 49.
Tubu (Tibbu): 51, 72.
Turks: *See* Osmanli.
Typical missions: (ancient) 26, 29, 32; (Anglican) 229, 236, 248, 558, 595, 637=43, 718=740; (Baptist) 253, 257, 259, 486, 597=9; (Congregational) 264, 266, 280, 490, 649=54; (freedmen) 486, 490, 495, 497, 503; (industrial) 565=78; (Lutheran) 291, 292, 293, 294, 295, 586=8; (medical) 558=9; (medieval) 97=101, 104=6, 107, 133=6, 149; (Methodist) 299, 300, 305, 322, 495, 497; (Muslim) 46, 47, 53, 55, 60; (Presbyterian) 326, 330, 331, 337, 339, 343, 352, 565=78; (Roman) 373=82, 395, 397=409, 503, 621, 623, 661=3, 669, 738; (undenominational) 308, 313, 516=9, 520=2, 525, 530=3, 534, 538, 539, 546, 548, 564, 595, 615=6, 618; (Unity) 424= 31, 435=7, 439, 449; (women's) 595, 597=9, 615=6, 618, 622.

U=: 161 note.
Ugandan: 160, 735, 753.
Ugandan missions: *See* Anglican and Roman missions.
Undenominational mission work: (American) 524, 528, 536, 544, 546, 547, 548, 799, 807, 811; (Boer) 534, 618; (colonial British) 534, 539, 618, 801, 809, 811; (English) 515=6, 519, 520=1, 522, 535, 537, 539, 543, 545, 546, 548, 595, 615, 801, 802, 805, 806, 807, 809; (French) 809; (German) 516, 800; (international) 517, 520, 529, 549, 811; (Negro) 799, 804, 805, 808; (Norse) 810; (Scotch) 524, 529, 544, 547, 808.
United Brethren in Christ: 321, 618.
United Presbyterians (America): importance of Egypt, 357; meaning of the work, 358; methods, 353=50; opening, 351; natives, 356; results, 353, 358.
United States: *See* American, Freedmen and Negro missions.
UNITY OF BRETHREN ("Moravians"): among *freedmen*, 480 and note; *in Africa*, xxi, xxii, 150, 209, 211, 214, 215, 216, 217, 432=56, 613, 647, 714, 739, 762, 803; *in the Antilles*, 421=31;

failure, 447=8; inauguration of modern missions, 419; limitations, 451; results, 430, 445, 451=4, 456.
Unity, the, as mission=society: caliber of representatives, 466, 473; Christly spirit, 466, 469; comity, 467; constitution, 464; finance, 470; history, 460; method, 469, 472; organization, 464, 468, 803; pietism, 462; provinces, 430, 445, 465; strength, 216, 474; system, 468, 471; unworldliness, 474; worship, 466; Zinzendorf, 462.
Universities: 23, 66, 73, 114, 116, 147, 198, 212, 236, 366, 481, 490, 497, 499, 505, 568, 618, 657, 769.
Various societies: 793=6.
Veh: 163, 234.
Versions: *See* Bible=Versions.

Wa=: 161 note.
Wahabi: 52, 54.
Waldensians: 178, 331 note, 810, 816.
WEST AFRICAN MISSIONS: *Anglican*, 217, 219, 220, 223, 228, 232, 233, 234, 235, 239=44, 590, 690, 718, 740, 761; *Baptist:* 217, 218, 220, 222, 240, 251=9, 553, 596, 688, 694, 743, 745, 761; *Congregational:* 217, 220, 222, 240, 261, 262, 263, 265, 266; *Friends:* 515, 614; *Lutheran:* 221, 286, 288, 563, 610, 611; *medical:* 252, 553, 554, 556, 557; *medieval:* 133=5, 137=8; *Methodist:* 217, 218, 219, 220, 221, 223, 300, 303=23, 557, 612, 713, 718, 761; *Muslim:* 46, 48, 50, 52=3, 69, 301; *Presbyterian:* 219, 220, 222, 223, 240, 324=9, 331, 336, 342=9, 350, 555, 619, 688, 690, 695, 761; *Roman:* 373=6, 392, 394, 395, 401, 685, 686, 714; *undenominational:* 218, 222, 516, 520, 524, 535, 539, 547, 553, 554, 557, 563, 614, 618, 694, 741, 743, 746; *Unity:* 218, 240, 446, 740; American: 218, 219, 220, 221, 222, 234, 235, 251, 252=5, 259, 261, 262=4, 288, 305=19, 322, 323=9, 489, 524, 535, 553, 554, 555, 557, 596, 611, 612, 617, 618, 619, 688, 705, 706, 708, 709; Antillean: 228, 255, 343, 448, 516, 695; Belgian: 392, 417; Canadian: 262; Danish: 286=7, 518; English: 217, 218, 219, 221, 222, 228, 232, 235, 239=44, 256=9, 262, 266, 300, 304, 319, 520=1, 538, 539, 553, 554, 590, 612, 614, 688, 694, 705, 713, 718; French: 327, 333, 392, 395, 401; German: 218, 220, 257, 287, 323, 331; Irish: 808; Italian: 393; Lagos and Yariba: 242, 814; Kamerunese: 257; Liberian: 234, 253, 255, 305, 308, 325, 812, 813; Negro: 218, 219=20, 220, 221, 223, 228, 234, 235, 241, 244, 251, 253, 255, 256, 286, 306=7, 318, 325, 328, 343, 376, 446=8, 494, 516, 591, 695, 761, 763, 812=6 *passim*; Portuguese: 130, 133=5, 137, 149, 177, 369, 373=6, 392; Sa=Leonese: 241; Scotch: 240, 336, 343; Spanish: 392; Swede: 262. *See*, also, Directory of Mission= Agencies, *passim*.

856 INDEX OF SUBJECTS

"White Fathers", "White Sisters:" *See* Lavigerie; also, Index of Societies.
Wolof: *See* Jolof.
WOMEN IN MISSION=WORK: *ancient:* 9, 27, 29, 31, 580, 585, 704; *Anglican:* 232, 233, 234, 238, 241, 245, 250, 482, 483, 587, 589=95, 808, 810; *Baptist:* 252, 487, 596=600, 705; *Congregational:* 262, 263, 282, 490, 491, 554, 586, 600= 10, 647, 649, 650, 655, 727, 728, 751; *Friends:* 515, 614; *Lutheran:* 241, 245, 246, 248, 288, 298, 555, 584, 586=8, 610=2; *medieval:* 98, 139, 581, 585; *Methodist:* 301, 306, 310, 317, 318, 319, 320, 557, 565, 612, 618, 808; *modern:* 216, 561, 581=2, 585, 624, 676, 724, 729, 736, 742, 744 note, 760, 814; *Muslim:* 39, 40, 355, 582=3, 616 and note; need for women: 582; new crusade: 623; *Presbyterian:* 329, 346, 350, 355, 499, 532, 585, 619=21; providential place: 624, 760; *Roman:* 384, 386, 391, 392, 400, 503, 505, 581, 621=2, 659, 808; *undenominational:* 518 note, 521, 526, 530, 535, 536, 539, 547, 615=6, 617, 618, 792, 794, 795, 801, 803, 804, 805, 806, 807, 810, 811; *Unity:* 424, 428, 439, 447, 448, 450, 468, 473, 613, 751; American: 235, 252, 262, 263, 288, 306, 310, 317, 318, 319, 322, 329, 355, 482, 483, 487, 490, 491, 493, 503, 505, 528, 536, 557, 581, 584, 596=600, 608=9, 611, 612, 614, 617, 618, 619, 621, 727, 760, 811; Belgian: 392, 808; Boer: 533, 618; Canadian: 262; English: 233, 235, 262, 301, 319, 320, 351, 428, 450, 515, 521, 522, 526, 539, 581, 585, 589=95, 600=7, 610, 612, 614=7, 648=50, 653, 655, 728; French: 334, 400, 587, 622, 659; German: 241, 245, 246, 288, 298, 424, 518 note, 584, 585, 587=8, 610, 611; Hova: 272, 282, 554; Kopt: 355; Negro: 268, 270, 319, 327, 329, 345, 443, 447, 473, 483, 493, 503, 505, 518 note, 581, 582, 584, 591, 598, 599, 600, 608, 609, 613, 618, 621, 751; Norse: 555, 611; Scotch: 232, 339, 346, 350, 352, 593, 601=7, 620, 649, 655; Swedish: 262. *See*, also, Directory of Mission= Agencies, *passim*.

Yao: xxiii, 340.
Yariba: 198, 200.
Yolof: *See* Jolof.
Young, the, and missions: 94, 97=8, 109, 232, 236, 262, 317, 331, 344, 350, 354, 356, 397, 398, 411, 474, 519, 521, 527=9, 535, 546, 549, 609, 630=43, 647, 736, 754, 764, 794, 800, 801, 805, 811 and note three, 812 note.

Zambezians: 70.
Zanzibari: 60, 180, 181, 184, 185.
Zulu: xxiii, 72, 160, 161 note, 162, 169, 184, 185, 198, 219, 229, 233, 262, 264=5, 269, 290=1, 296, 303, 314, 338, 350, 390, 516, 526, 534, 544, 553, 575, 592, 594, 608=9, 687, 705, 707, 708, 709, 711, 715, 718, 751, 811, 812.

www.ingramcontent.com/pod-product-compliance
Lightning Source LLC
Chambersburg PA
CBHW030602300426
44111CB00009B/1074